MEMOIRS

W. A. Visser 't Hooft

W A Visser 't Hooft

MEMOIRS

SCM PRESS LTD
London

THE WESTMINSTER PRESS
Philadelphia

334 00999 5
First English edition 1973
published jointly by
SCM Press Ltd, 56 Bloomsbury Street, London
and The Westminster Press,
Witherspoon Building, Philadelphia
© W. A. Visser 't Hooft 1973
Printed in Great Britain
by W & J Mackay Limited, Chatham

Library of Congress Cataloging in Publication Data

Visser 't Hooft, Willem Adolph, 1900–
    Memoirs.

    1. Ecumenical movement.
BX9479.V5A3 1973   270.8'2 [B]   72-8924
ISBN 0-664-20965-3

Contents

List of Plates

Preface

ONE OF MY children once returned a book borrowed from my library with the remark: 'I do not like it. It is an I-book.' Have I written an I-book? I hope not. For my main interest in writing it has been to repay a part of my debt to the ecumenical movement. I said at the Uppsala Assembly that I owed much more to the ecumenical movement than I would ever be able to repay. But I can at least show my gratitude by making the movement better known than it is. So much of what has been published about it gives the impression that it is primarily concerned with conferences, solemn processions, resolutions and budgets. Of the men who have been active in the ecumenical movement for a long time only one, Pastor Marc Boegner, has left us memoirs which show that it is not just another piece of ecclesiastical machinery, but a movement in which human relations and creative ideas play the decisive role.

This book is therefore not another history of the ecumenical movement, but an account of the experiences of a man who has had the exceptional privilege of being involved in ecumenical life for fifty years. I have, however, tried to make it as accurate as possible. Since I found out soon that one's memory plays curious tricks, such as oversimplification and also juggling with dates, I have tried to check the facts by consulting the relevant documents, reports, travel diaries and the letters which Jetty, my wife, had fortunately conserved.

Even before its publication this book has been criticized as being too short. It would of course have been possible to write several volumes, to go into great detail and to include a large number of documents. But in that case the book would have become a book for specialists and insiders and probably not have reached the people whom I should like to reach – namely, those inside and out-side the churches who want to know what the ecumenical movement is all about.

I realize and I regret that the choice of a relatively condensed description of my life and work implies that I have not been able to do justice to the specific contributions of each of the many men and women, especially those who were my colleagues on the staff of the World Council of Churches, who have participated in the building up of the ecumenical movement. I hope that they will recognize that in this book 'I' means very often the writer as the representative of a group

of men and women who were never lacking in stimulating ideas and who held up
his hands when he was weary.

    It remains to thank those who have helped me in preparing this manuscript:
David Scott in New York, a friendly critic; Aat Guittart who has been my
faithful secretary for twenty-five years and knows more about me than I know
about myself; and John Taylor who has made most of the best photographs in
this book.

Geneva, July 1971

I | *Boyhood in a Quiet City*

MY EARLIEST RECOLLECTION is that in 1905 on my fifth birthday I received a quite unique present, for on that day a brother was born. I considered him of course to be my personal property. When I tried to share a piece of chocolate with him, the midwife intervened.

Most of the memories of my schoolboy-years in Haarlem have to do with the marvellous places where we spent our free time rather than with life at school. There was first of all our own rather large garden with remarkable possibilities for the construction of romantic shanties. Our heroes were the American Indians of the books of Karl May. The Apaches were good and the Sioux were bad. It was a great moment when my mother presented us with very realistic Indian costumes. An even better playing-ground was the place high up in the dunes in Overveen where my grandfather had built a week-end cottage. We would go there with his horse-carriage and play with many cousins and friends or explore the deserted dune-country. But the finest place of all was the property of our great-aunt in Dordrecht where we would go in the holidays. 'Bellevue' was right in the city, but once you were inside the gates you were in a country-place. There was the massive but friendly old house with its big rooms and surrounded on three sides by water. There was the wood with its mysterious dark places. There was the stable with the horse and different types of carriages. There was the hay-loft with its delightful smell to which you could withdraw if you had been naughty or if you wanted to be alone. And there was Aunt Marie herself, a woman of matriarchal authority who ruled the place as a benevolent despot. Had I known the phrase inscribed in the Moghul palace at Delhi: 'If paradise is anywhere, it is here', I would surely have used it for Bellevue. There were so many wonderful opportunities: taking out the boat and watching the strange life of fishes and under-water plants (I fell in the water three times but was promptly rescued), feeding the horse Nora, driving around the island and holding the reins under the supervision of the coachman, visiting relatives who lived in other country-places. I felt terrible when Aunt Marie died in 1913 and Bellevue had to make place for modern buildings. It was in order to perpetuate the memory of Aunt Marie that my father decided to add her family-name 'Visser' to our family-name, ''t Hooft'.

I was the second of three brothers. Apart from the inevitable quarrels we got on well with each other. It was an advantage that we had very different interests. My older brother turned resolutely to the world of science and became fascinated with chemistry. My main interest was in books. My youngest brother became the best sportsman of the three and turned later to medicine. My mother was the centre of family-life. She was a very dynamic personality who steered her four 'men' with great determination and total consecration. At the same time she kept our home wide open for relatives and friends who obviously enjoyed her lively conversation and her sense of humour. My father was a lawyer who did not have much professional ambition, but had many hobbies including music, stamp-collecting and especially the literature of the nineteenth century. He produced poems on all possible occasions. When my beloved dog was run over by a truck the poem he wrote for me was a real consolation.

We were a very informal family in that there was no great distance between the parents and their children and that everybody could tease everybody else. Somehow parental authority was all the stronger because it was exercised without solemnity.

My grandfather 't Hooft had been presiding judge of the district tribunal in Haarlem and lived in those years a quiet life largely devoted to his children and grandchildren. His house was a centre for family parties and his cottage in the dunes was the family playing-ground. My grandfather Lieftinck, who had celebrated his seventieth birthday in 1905, was still going strong as a member of parliament. He had become the 'Nestor', the oldest M.P., and since he spent much time in The Hague, we did not see him often.

The little world in which I now began to look around seemed to be a world of remarkable stability and security. There were of course signs of external change. A few automobiles began to appear on the road. Progressive people began to use electricity instead of gas. In 1911 Anthony Fokker, who had grown up in Haarlem, came to demonstrate to his friends that the plane he had built could really fly. Since my best friend was a neighbour of Fokker, he and I were allowed to pump air in the tyres of the plane and this made us look quite heroic to our comrades. But these innovations did not make any real difference to the style of life.

Similarly, there were many new ideas in the air concerning the transformation of society. The socialists were beginning to make their voice heard, but they had as yet so little popular support that on the Queen's birthday the marching- and dancing-song was: 'Orange on top. Long live Wilhelmina. All socialists in the Bakenessergracht'.[1] And the socialist ideals with which I flirted a few years later had more to do with utopian dreams than with practical politics. My parents and grandparents were among the pillars of this apparently imperturbable society. Two of its most typical local institutions were the gentlemen's club, 'Trou moet blijcken' (Loyalty must prove itself) and the Bach society. The first had a tradition of four centuries. For it had originally been a 'Chamber of Rhetoric' in which people of various professions with a common interest in poetry and drama came together to listen to each other's (generally very amateurish) productions. Not much of the old tradition remained. But the board-members had still the old titles: 'Emperor' for the chairman, 'Prince' for the vice-chairman. Once a year the official poet, whose title was 'Factor', had to produce a long poem which would review the events of the year in the life of the world, of the nation, of the city and of the club itself. Now grandfather Lieftinck was the 'Emperor' for twenty-eight years and my father was for many years the 'Factor'.

The Bach society organized concerts of very high quality with the orchestras of Amsterdam and The Hague and with famous soloists from many countries. The Bach evenings were at the same time the principal social occasions. All available carriages in the city were mobilized to bring those who loved good music and those who wanted to show their new evening dress to the concert hall. Father was the Treasurer of the Society and we were allowed to accompany him.

But while it was a stable world it was not stuffy. We had unrestricted access to books and magazines. And we were allowed great freedom in the use of our leisure. Tennis and dancing provided occasions to meet the girls. And though it was sometimes painful to fall in and out of love, the conversations during which my girl friends pulled my leg about my philosophizing were a necessary element in my education.

In 1912 I had gone to the classical secondary school for it was clear that I had no talent for mathematics and was more inclined to the study of languages. So far I had learned only a little French at school and I had a smattering of English because my parents had invited an English girl to stay for a few months at our home to give us a first introduction to English. The rule was that at meal time we were to speak English only. A savings-box in the form of a green pig was placed on the dining table: whoever spoke Dutch had to put in one Dutch cent for every word spoken. So the first English expression I learned to use was 'put in'. I can recommend the system.

At the classical school we learned five languages: Latin, Greek, French, German and English. In the last year I also had private lessons in Hebrew from the rabbi. It was a somewhat one-sided education, because there was little time left for other subjects. But it gave us access to many different cultures and when we reached the stage of reading the great authors in the original languages, several of the teachers succeeded in creating an abiding interest in their writings.

In 1912 and the two following years we spent part of the summer vacation in Germany. The first journey was of course an exploration of the Rhine region with its romantic castles. In July 1914 we were in the Sauerland near the Ruhr area. We had no idea that there was any danger of war. But when we heard rumours about mobilization, my parents decided to go to Düsseldorf so as to be nearer the Dutch frontier. In that city we watched the excitement when mobilization actually began and we were astounded that so many seemed to welcome the announcement and that the soldiers left in an almost festive mood. We managed to get across the frontier on foot.

In Holland the first world war remained a far-away event. We had our little difficulties – candles instead of gas-light, lack of coal for the stove, rationing of food. But this became simply a part of life. In the dunes near Haarlem you could sometimes hear the guns of the battlefield in Belgium. Though the government was strictly neutral, individual Dutchmen were either pro-Ally or pro-German and this could lead to heated debates within the family. But we were not really involved in the tragedy. Looking back I find it amazing that while next door the internecine holocaust was going on, we lived so normally and that the war did not really cast a deep shadow over those years in our boyish lives. We were unable to realize what war actually meant.

One day when part of the Dutch army held field-practice in the dunes near Haarlem my father received a telephone call asking whether the Queen could watch the manoeuvre from my grandfather's week-end cottage, which had a very wide view across the dunes. In a few hours the cottage had to be transformed into a place fit for the reception of royalty. But Queen Wilhelmina spent all her time with us on the flat roof watching the soldiers. When she said to my father that this seemed to be the highest point in the area, my father, remembering the rule about not contradicting royal persons, answered: 'Yes, your Majesty, but the place over there, is still a little higher.' I jumped around with my primitive camera to take pictures. It was typical that when the Queen wanted to cross into the dunes and the attendants began to cut up the wire railing, she stopped them and said: 'I do not want anything here to be destroyed for my sake. I can creep underneath the railing.'

I became a voracious reader. My father had a considerable library and I spent much money buying books from the secondhand booksellers who had their stalls in the weekly market. On one occasion I bought fifty-five books. There was no system in this madness. The trouble about Dutchmen is that they are tempted by books in Dutch, French, German and English, so that they get lost in an ocean of literature. I tried philosophical works which were far above my head, such as those of Spinoza and Schopenhauer. When I asked grandfather Lieftinck whether he had the works of Schleiermacher he commented bluntly, but not without reason: 'Soon ripe, soon rotten.' But that did not stop me. I tried Heinrich Heine, Oscar Wilde, Romain Rolland, Dostoyevsky and many others. Poetry became important, especially the Dutch poets of the 1880s. I began to write poems myself and made the mistake of choosing the most difficult poetic forms: the sonnet or the hexameter. Many of these poems were variations on the theme how difficult it is to express oneself, if one is not sure what this 'self' is that is to find expression. I sent some of my products to Willem Kloos, the leading Dutch poet of the time. The answer was a printed card expressing regret that my poems could not be used in his magazine. But there was the consolation a little later that the national periodical for pupils of the classical schools printed several of them.

But this was only one side of the medal. A more joyous note was struck in a musical comedy called 'Andromeda' which I wrote with a friend for a party in

Leeuwarden. The reaction of some of the spectators was that it must have been very funny, for the three of us players had laughed so much, but that it was difficult to understand laughing actors.

It is not easy to describe my religious development during these years, for my heart and mind were a battlefield of the most diverse influences. My parents belonged to the Arminian or Remonstrant Church which at that time was dominated by the modernist theology which had grown up in Holland in the second half of the nineteenth century. The local pastor, who prepared me for confirmation and who had a considerable influence on me, had worked out a philosophy of religion which was strongly Hegelian in character. This attracted me because it answered many of the intellectual questions which I had begun to ask. But its dangerous aspect was that it could easily lead to rather abstract speculations about religion in general rather than to a clear commitment to the Jesus of the New Testament. Now my indiscriminate reading of all sorts of books on religion, including those of pantheists, mystics and agnostics, made that danger very real. I was on the way to becoming a syncretist, who considered all varieties of religious experience as equally true and equally false. Many pages of the diary I kept in 1917 reveal that I lived in great inner confusion.

And there was a further complication. It was at this time that I discovered what my grandfather Lieftinck really believed. He had been a pastor in the early days of the modernist movement, but had left the ministry to go into politics. Freemasonry, in which he held the position of 'Grand Orator of the Great Orient', had taken the place of the church in his life. Now over eighty years he talked to me with all the patriarchal authority which his rich and long experience gave him and which his commanding presence underlined. He spoke of his days in the ministry and why he had left it. It was not that he had lost all faith in God. But he had come to the conclusion that God was so great and so unknowable that poor human beings had no right to talk about him. Intercessory prayer, asking God to intervene in human affairs, was wrong. All we could do was to listen to the voice of our conscience.

I had a very great respect for him, for he had lived a life of inflexible integrity and shown great courage in the defence of his convictions. So this radical calling in question of any personal meeting with God shook me considerably.

But then there was the opposite influence of the boys' camps of the Dutch Student Christian Movement. For there the personal encounter with Jesus was the centre of everything. And this message was not given by solemn preachers, but by students who were only a few years older than we were, and who used the simplest possible language. When at the end of the noisy evening meal in the great tent it suddenly became very quiet and a student whom we had come to appreciate as a sportsman or as a story-teller or simply as a friend tried to say what prayer really meant or why one should live with the Bible, we listened as we had hardly ever listened before. So far I had come to know religion in a strongly intellectualized form. Here the emphasis was not on profound ideas, but on a 'person to person' call and on commitment.

It was not easy to find a synthesis between all these influences. At the time of my confirmation I had to write down what I believed. The result was an uneasy combination of heterogeneous elements. I tried to serve at one and the same time 'the God of the philosophers' and 'the God of Abraham, Isaac, Jacob and Jesus Christ'. I spoke of Christ as an ideal and an idea rather than as God entering into human history. I recognized that faith is not merely the realization that man is part of a coherent universe, but confidence in God.

It was in 1917 that I began to wonder whether I should study theology. I wrote at that time: 'I have come to the conviction that theology would be a wonderful subject of study for me.' At that time I was only thinking of the next step, not of the more distant future. I was wholly preoccupied with the question how I could come to greater religious clarity. The study of theology seemed to offer an opportunity to get more light. The rest would take care of itself.

It was wholly my own idea. My parents were greatly surprised when I told them of my intention. They warned me that I might have to face great difficulties. But they did not oppose the plan. Talks with some of the theological students in the Student Christian Movement helped me to see what was involved in this choice. I began to see that the clarification of my own religious position was not a sufficient reason to study theology. I had to ask whether I was really called to the ministry. But what did this calling really mean? I did not have a precise conviction that God wanted me to go this way and no other way. But I did want to discover the deeper meaning of life and to help others to find that meaning. It was all very tentative and vague. I believed and hoped that 'by going in this direction I have the best chance to make something harmonious out of my life and to pass this on to other people'. That was not a very secure foundation, but it would have to serve until I could find more stable ground under my feet.

I passed my final exam of the classical school in the summer of 1918. That summer was the summer of the Spanish flu and so the boys' camp to which we had gone had to be broken up. Since we had time on our hands a group of us went off on our bikes to inspect the frontier between Holland and Germany, for the world outside our quiet neutral country exerted a mysterious attraction and we might get a glimpse of it. We were not disappointed, for we came at a late hour to an inn which happened to be the headquarters of a group of authentic smugglers. We were well received and attempts were made to recruit us for a smuggling job which would bring great profit. We declined the offer, not least of all because we had no desire to become prisoners in Germany at the very moment when our long cherished dream of becoming university students was so near to its fulfilment.

NOTES

1. A canal in Haarlem.

2 | *Student Life*

IN THE LAST months of 1918 everything changed at the same time. I left home to go to the University of Leiden and a few weeks later the world war came to an end, the doors towards the outside world opened and a new epoch began. It was frustrating to feel that tremendous things were happening and to be far away from the place of action. One evening as we were discussing the latest news in the student club we heard that in a few days King Albert of Belgium would make his glorious entry into Brussels to celebrate the liberation of his country. Four of us decided to try to get to Brussels in time. We had no passports, but we took the precaution of asking our local newspapers for press cards. Then off to the south, first by train to Breda and then on our bicycles to the frontier. We were lucky, for the German army had withdrawn from the area and the Belgian army had not yet arrived. So we reached Brussels in the night preceding the great day.

Trusting in our press credentials we approached the press stand on Place Brouckère. We were not admitted because our cards had no military stamp. At the military headquarters in the ancient Town Hall we found a remarkable confusion. But we met an officer who gave us the military consecration. Returning to the press stand we were cordially received in spite of our cycling attire. We seemed to be the only representatives of the Dutch press.

The great moment has come. Burgomaster Adolphe Max, just out of prison, gets thunderous applause. King Albert arrives on a grey horse, next to him the queen, behind them their children and the Prince of Wales. There follow detachments of all the allied armies. Bagpipes and drums. It takes time for the 20,000 soldiers to march by. But the vociferous cheering of the crowds does not stop.

Now we thought that with our press cards we could go anywhere. So we tried to get into the hall where the royal reception was to take place. Alas, we were politely informed that we were not properly dressed for the occasion. We could think of nothing better to do than to ask some passers-by where we could hire the right kind of dress. This had an unfortunate result. We were suspected of being German soldiers who were trying to disguise themselves. But the next day we were more successful. There was to be a *Te Deum* in the St Gudule Cathedral.

We found ourselves seated with the delegations of the allied armies. Cardinal Mercier, who had taken such a courageous stand during the occupation, presided at the service and gave a powerful address. He said: 'Peace and order rest upon Justice. Justice gives to each one his due. The first duty of a nation is to praise him to whom it owes everything.' When the service was over, the royal family passed right next to our places. One of my travel-companions became so enthused about the very nice-looking princess that he suddenly shouted: 'Vive la princesse Marie José.' The princess looked surprised. Some fifty years later, when I met her in Geneva, I told her of this little incident.

We continued for a few days to participate in the festivities. But now we saw also the other side of the picture. Women who had had relations with the German soldiers were treated in the most brutal manner. And there were explosions of primitive hatred against the enemy which made us realize that the end of the war did not mean the restoration of real peace.

I wrote four articles for the local paper in Haarlem and found that my first honorarium, though modest, had amply covered the cost of the expedition.

In 1919 I went with friends to Paris and to the battlefields near Reims. The trenches still looked as if the soldiers had left them the day before. The whole landscape was a picture of total destruction with the mutilated cathedral in the background. I wrote: 'If you still have any spark of militarism left in your mind, you will notice in this place that you have got rid of it.'

During the two first years in Leiden I was overwhelmed by all the opportunities which student life offered. Our freedom was practically unlimited. There was no supervision of any kind and our parents often trusted us more than we deserved. It was a life of spontaneous decisions. We might go on excursions by carriage to the sea or go off to The Hague or organize some impromptu festival. And we spent a good part of the night in the student club. I joined far too many different student societies, so that I was not much use to any of them. There were only two theological students among the hundreds of members of the student body. So I was looked upon as an unusual and somewhat abnormal character. But I made friends with people who had an attitude to life completely different from my own. And it happened often that one became involved in passionate discussions with agnostics or atheists. In any case it was a way of getting to know the world outside the Christian ghetto. It is astonishing that somehow I managed, nevertheless, to pass my exams in time. The first year I spent on theology, the second on law. For my father had agreed that I could study theology, if I also studied law. He wondered whether my choice of theology was really an expression of youthful idealism and whether I had counted the cost. And he wanted me therefore to have an alternative if the theological road proved to be an impasse. But after my first law examination I felt clearly that law was not my cup of tea and I was glad to return to theology. The only gain was that I had acquired some basic notions concerning economics.

After these two years the more superficial pleasures of student life began to lose their attraction. I felt that I was not getting on with the more important job of growing up spiritually and intellectually. So I accepted the proposal of my friend Herman Hoogendijk to go with him for a three months' term to the Quaker centre, Woodbrooke, in Selly Oak near Birmingham. Woodbrooke gave me precisely what I needed: an atmosphere in which one could concentrate on the essentials. The very attractive house and grounds had been made available by the Cadbury family in order to prepare members of the Society of Friends 'for the variety of service required in the cause of Christ today'. But very soon the place had become known internationally and there was a special link with Leiden. The first Director of Studies, Dr J. Rendel Harris, a great New Testament scholar, had been invited to join the Theological Faculty in Leiden, and had arranged that since he could not accept that invitation, some students from Leiden should come to Woodbrooke each year.

It is difficult to say what made life at Woodbrooke such a unique experience. It was not a place of outstanding intellectual production, though some of the lectures, such as those by H. G. Wood, were of fine quality. It was rather the integration of conviction and life. There was not only talk about fellowship and world brotherhood. The community lived together as people who accepted each other completely without worrying about differences in background. And there was a good balance between seriousness and humour, or again between the concern for personal spiritual development and concern for the problems of the world. So these were very rich months.

It was also an occasion to discover England. We heard G. B. Shaw produce his sarcasm and wit at a political meeting and John Maynard Keynes give one of his lectures in economics in Cambridge.

We fell in love with the atmosphere of Cambridge, but we pitied the students, many of whom had fought in the war, but who seemed to be treated as schoolboys and had to observe regulations of which we knew nothing in Holland.

The period at Woodbrooke had been a turning-point. I saw now more clearly the road ahead. And less than two years later Woodbrooke proved to be a turning point in an even more decisive manner. I went back for a reunion of 'old-Woodbrookers' and met a Dutch girl from The Hague who had spent a term at the college. The reunion provided just the right atmosphere to get to know each other. It was not quite by chance that I met her again in Oxford and in London. A few weeks later in The Hague Jetty Boddaert and I became engaged to be married. From that day until 1968, when she died, she was for me a life companion who enriched my life with a dimension of depth which I needed greatly and who challenged me with her inquiring and independent mind.

In January 1921 the Student Christian Movement of Great Britain and Ireland held its first large post-war conference in Glasgow. Thirty-eight countries were represented. The opening address was given by Lord Grey who had been the Foreign Secretary in 1914 when the war broke out and had then made the famous remark: 'The lamps are going out all over Europe; we shall not see them lit again in our lifetime.' Now he made an impressive appeal to the younger generation. He said that the effect of the European war had immensely diminished the prestige of Christian civilization and that the moral damage of the war could only be repaired by creating a world which was more Christian in spirit than the pre-war world. Otherwise civilization would destroy itself.

That was the starting point and the following speakers showed what it would mean to build a new world without violence, exploitation and hatred between nations and races. I heard several speakers who would in later years play a great role in my life. J. H. Oldham, the man who organized the Edinburgh World Missionary Conference of 1910, gave an address on 'God, the Supreme Reality' which went to the heart of the matter in a non-emotional, non-rhetorical and thereby convincing way. William Temple, at that time Bishop of Manchester, gave a series of lectures on 'The Universality of Christ'. He was a born teacher. He and several other speakers had an art of which we knew little on the European continent, the ability to tell a good story at the right moment. It was refreshing to see the frames of bishops and other dignitaries on the platform shaking with laughter. And you could remember the important theological points because of the stories. I have never forgotten William Temple's story about the young lady who asked Dr Benjamin Jowett at the dinner table what he really thought about God and who received this reply: 'That is not really important, what matters is what God thinks about me.' That was a bit of Barthianism before Barth.

When I came back to Leiden I began to give more time to the Student Christian Movement and to take my theological study more seriously. But the Student Christian Movement had a stronger influence on me than the theological faculty. The secretariat of the movement was in the hands of three outstanding men: Herman Rutgers, a Christian strategist in the tradition of John R. Mott; Maarten van Rhijn, who made bible study relevant and deeply interesting; and Nico Stufkens, the most unusual character of the three. Stufkens found the world far too fascinating to bother about formal academic studies. He had acquired an encyclopaedic knowledge of modern culture and theology and, with his penetrating critical mind, forced us to call all our easy assumptions in question. So the SCM became during these years the truly formative influence in my development.

For the first four or five months of 1922 I lived in the ancient castle of Hardenbroek which was at that time the headquarters and conference centre of the Dutch Student Christian Movement. Herman Rutgers, the General Secretary of the movement, had to attend the conference of the World's Student Christian Federation in Peking and had asked me to take his place during his absence. Life at the castle was strangely quiet after the hectic times in Leiden. Time had stood still at Hardenbroek. There was the old moat and the pont-levis, there were the portraits of the ancestors, the smoking oil-lamps and the bad heating. And there was the wide view across the meadows. But at the week-ends the castle was invaded by students and there were endless discussions on the issues of the faith in relation to the modern world.

One day I received an unexpected call from Rotterdam. Dr Georg Michaelis, the former chancellor of the German Imperial government, informed me that he was on the way to the Peking conference with his wife and Professor Karl Heim, but that the ship on which they were to travel was delayed. I proposed that the party should come to stay at Hardenbroek. But I felt I needed more support in playing host to a man of such eminence and so I invited a number of student movement leaders to join us.

We knew that Dr Michaelis had been chancellor for a few months only and that he had not been very successful in dealing with the crucial problem of domestic and foreign affairs in the critical year 1917. But since the image of a German 'Reichskanzler' had been shaped by Bismarck, we expected to meet a formidable and dominating personality with great authority. So it was a considerable surprise to meet a most un-Bismarckian elderly gentleman of small stature who looked like a professor or a civil servant, and not at all like an inspiring leader of men, one who talked with us as a friendly grandfather. He had strong pietist Christian convictions and had been chairman of the German Student Christian Movement since before the war. His great concern in going to the world conference in China was to convince the outside world that the clause in the Versailles Treaty which made Germany alone responsible for the war was a lie and an example of shameful hypocrisy. This was understandable, but he had little or nothing to say about Germany's share in war guilt and about the fundamental changes which were required in German politics for the sake of a new start in international relations. We wondered whether this very conservative man of sixty-five years of age could really represent the mind of the Christian students of post-war Germany. And that was not the only question that came to mind. I had rather naïvely taken it for granted that the statesmen who had to take the decisions on which the life and death of millions of people depended were a class apart – men with far deeper understanding of the historical situation and a much clearer vision of the future than ordinary people had. Now I saw that this was by no means necessarily true. Statesmen were often men who did not really make history, but were overwhelmed by it. That made the international world look even more fragile and insecure than it had looked before.

And what of that constantly repeated assertion that if only faithful Christians would occupy the key posts in national and international life, world peace would be assured? Here was a man who was clearly a consecrated Christian, but while his faith had certainly inspired him to give unselfish service to his country, it had not made a substantial difference with regard to his political decisions. The piety which the older generation desired to transmit to us was then largely irrelevant in the life of the world. To this extent the protest of the 'social gospel' which I had met in the World's Student Christian Federation and among the Quakers was right.

In 1921 I had become chairman of the relief committee of the Netherlands Student Organization. Our job was to raise money and to collect food and clothing for the students in Central Europe who were living in the most miserable conditions. The World's Student Christian Federation had in 1920 set up a relief agency, European Student Relief, which in the first two years of its existence had raised six million Swiss francs. In Holland we had concentrated especially on food and clothing and received a good response. Fridtjof Nansen, the polar explorer, came to tell us of the situation in Russia which was even worse than that in Central Europe. So our action had to be expanded.

The director of European Student Relief was Conrad Hoffmann, an American YMCA secretary who had directed the YMCA work for prisoners-of-war in Germany during the war years, and who was not only an able organizer but an inspiring leader. In 1922 he convened a conference in Turnov (Czechoslovakia) where some eighty students from twenty-nine countries, who had participated in one form or another in relief activities, met to discuss the future work of European Student Relief. The atmosphere was electric, for here were students of the most varied national, religious and political background, many of them deeply involved in the chaotic political conflicts of the post-war years. Hoffmann asked me to serve as secretary of the meeting. It was not difficult to reach agreement on the common practical tasks, for it was obvious that the relief work should go on. But there was a long and extremely heated discussion on the question whether the ultimate purpose of the enterprise should be described as 'world peace and brotherhood' or in some other way. The strong reaction against these terms was based on the suspicion that European Student Relief was really trying to impose a specifically American peace ideology on European students. Some objected because they saw in it an attack on their nationalism, others were afraid that to mix relief with a 'message' would mean to restrict the scope of the service. But the fact of the matter was that we had become a community with an ethos of its own. So I substituted the words 'international understanding' and 'international responsibility' for 'world peace and brotherhood'. I had to make a fighting speech to get this accepted, but finally this formulation was accepted.

At Turnov I had come to know an American student, George Pratt. He came to see me in Holland and announced that he wanted to organize a team of some six young European radicals to stir up the American students who needed to be shaken out of their complacency. We discussed the possibility that I should go, but we came to the conclusion that I was not sufficiently radical for his purpose. He chose finally a young Dutchman who described himself as an anarcho-syndicalist. I wondered how this operation was to be financed. The answer came when Pratt and I visited Herman Rutgers together. He showed us a new book about the financial dynasties in the USA. One of the families near the top of the list was the Pratt family. 'Well, those are my people,' said George. As far as I could find out later this attempt to start a student revolution in the USA did not meet with much success. The days of the Berkeley uprising were still a long way ahead.

Some months later I went with Herman Rutgers to Austria, Czechoslovakia and Germany to see how the situation was developing. Austria was in a terribly critical condition. The inflation was such that bank-notes which still had some value on one day could be thrown away on the next day as worthless paper. Vienna seemed to be a dying city. It was painful to be a foreigner with hard currency. The well-known Bristol Hotel, where we stayed and lived comfortably, had become such a scandal to the Viennese people that when we returned after a few days absence we found that it had been largely destroyed by an angry mob. When we tried to eat in the student refectories we found that we were hungry again an hour later. The galloping inflation was worst for the students and professors. In Graz we sat in the solemn senate hall with the rector and members of the senate of the university and heard one story after another of the hopelessness of the situation with regard to housing, health, textbooks and laboratories. In Prague the situation was complicated by the presence of large numbers of refugee students. So it was clear that European Student Relief needed to redouble its activities.

In 1923 another ESR conference was held in Parad in Hungary. I served this time as chairman of the programme committee. We met at a difficult moment. The French army had just occupied the Ruhr area in Germany. The German delegation opened the proceedings with a sharp declaration against the 'policy of violence' of the French government. This led to a difficult debate as to whether it was permissible to raise political questions. The chairman of the French delegation saved the situation by proposing a resolution saying that the conference took cognizance of the suffering of the world today and was united against all political violence in any land at any time, but that our conference should consider the suffering of students and not discuss politics. This proposal was unanimously accepted.

There were other explosive issues. Anti-semitism had become powerful among students in several Central European countries. It was a bad sign that the Jewish students present at the meeting were considered as a special Jewish delegation rather than as members of their respective national delegations. The question of the restriction of the number of Jewish students by a *numerus clausus* came up and led to sharp disagreement. But in the long run the spirit which the co-operation in European Student Relief had created was again victorious. The social occasions – particularly a picnic in the woods with a gypsy band, with our unsuccessful attempts to dance the 'Czardas' in the true Hungarian style, and with the chewing of hunks of meat inadequately roasted on the camp fires – did much to bring us closer together. The climax was reached when at the last session the leader of the German delegation publicly thanked the leader of the French delegation for his attitude in the conference. When the two men shook hands there was – according to the report – 'silence, then thunders of applause, then silence again'.

I put my own reaction to the conference in this way: 'The representatives of the quiet countries must be glad to have this opportunity of being at the heart of things, and of taking part in the reconstruction of a broken-down world. This is the only work that is worthwhile at present.'

On the way back from the Parad conference I made my first journey by air. The small plane had four places in a sort of box. On the way from Budapest to Vienna it had to cross the meandering Danube many times and each crossing meant a sudden drop. It was not surprising that the elderly English lady with whom I travelled became very sick. I became scared at her condition and wanted to warn the pilot. But there was no door between the cockpit and the cabin. When we arrived in Vienna the lady did not curse the inventors of air planes, but spoke the truly ladylike words: 'I am sorry I have made such a sight of myself.'

In Holland we began now to concentrate on help to German universities and a special committee was formed of representatives of various interested organizations. I was asked to take the chair and found myself to my surprise at the Red Cross headquarters presiding over a body consisting of a former minister of finance, a retired vice-admiral and several others who belonged to my parents' generation rather than to mine.

By the time of the third European Student Relief Conference at Schloss Elmau in Bavaria the material conditions of students in Europe had considerably improved. Should we then wind up European Student Relief? Most of those who had been deeply involved in the work hoped that in some way or another the organization would continue, for there was no other student body which had created such an atmosphere of constructive international co-operation. At the General Committee of the World's Student Christian Federation in England in 1924 Roswell Barnes of the USA and I spoke strongly in favour of continuation. It was decided to prolong the activity for one year. By 1926 European Student Relief was transformed into an autonomous body, 'International Student Service', which under that name and later as 'World University Service' has performed a remarkable job in the field of international exchange, in the study of university problems and in emergency relief.

In the summer of 1923 Jetty, my future wife, and I went with a large Dutch delegation to the World Conference of YMCA workers among boys in Pörschach (Austria). I hoped to pick up some new ideas that could be used in the boys' work of the Student Christian Movement. And the opportunity to go for the first time to a world meeting with people from all parts of the globe was too good to be missed. I had no idea that this conference would make plans which would have a decisive bearing on my own future.

The conference had mainly been organized by a group of Americans and British who wanted the YMCA to make a new beginning in youth work, and who were inspired by a tremendous confidence in the new possibilities which the post-war situation offered to men who would seize the opportunities for action. It was a great festival of unbroken idealism and since the Germans did not participate and there were few speakers from Continental Europe the note of post-war disillusionment was not clearly heard. But once again John R. Mott captivated me by his massive faith and the breadth of his vision. I had already met him briefly when he visited Holland. But now I could watch the great missionary statesman and evangelist operate in an international assembly. Speaking on 'Boyhood – the Greatest Asset of Any Nation' he described the 'new spirit moving on the troubled waters of the youth of the world' and defined the common element in all the many new youth movements as 'a protest against the past' and as 'a burning desire for independence and self-determination'. And he burst out: 'Thank God, we have a Gospel which can influence and guide these overflowing tides of living interest and passion. To whom else shall they go?' That was a message which our tired European Christians could not afford to ignore.

We Dutchmen made many sarcastic remarks about what seemed to us the naïveté of many speeches and proposals. And we were specially critical of the highly emotional methods by which the conference leaders sought to raise the funds for the setting up of a strong new Boys' Work Department of the World's Committee of YMCAs. It did not occur to me that one year later my salary would be paid from those very funds.

At the end of 1923 I passed my last theological examination. The time had now come to face the question of my future. I was still a member of the Arminian (Remonstrant) Church, but I no longer felt at home in it. I owed a great deal to that church. My pastor in Haarlem and the two out-standing Remonstrant professors, G. J. Heering and K. H. Roessingh, had played an important role in my education. Heering had impressed me by his radical opposition to any moral compromise, particularly with regard to war. He taught pastoral theology in a truly pastoral way and criticized our amateurish first attempts at preaching in a gentle but firm manner. Roessingh was exception-ally good at explaining the current systems of theology and philosophy from the inside. His own position was close to that of Ernst Troeltsch, the very learned German theologian-philosopher, historian and sociologist. I had to study more works by Troeltsch with their interminably long sentences than any others. Troeltsch helped me to understand the interaction between Christianity and the socio-economic forces in history. But he gave no adequate answer to the ultimate question of the criterion of truth. The point of Archimedes was lacking. Troeltsch himself came to Leiden a short time before his death and I presided over the meeting at which he spoke. He looked exactly like the image which the world had of a German professor.

But under the influence of the Student Christian Movement I had gradually moved out of the 'modernist' atmosphere which was still dominating the Arminian Church. And the discovery of the new dialectical theology hastened this process. In 1922 Nico Stufkens, a secretary of the Student Christian Move-ment, had told us about Karl Barth and made some of us sufficiently curious to buy the second edition of *The Epistle to the Romans* which had just appeared. I found it a terribly difficult book, but I did understand enough to become deeply impressed. Here was a man who lived fully in the modern world, who knew his Nietzsche and his Dostoyevsky, a man, who had struggled with the problems of historical criticism and of modern philosophy – but who had rediscovered the authority of the Word of God. This was a man who proclaimed the death of all the little, comfortable gods and spoke again of the living God of the Bible. It was as if all the different elements in my religious development could now fall into place. This was the message for which I had been waiting.

Early in 1924 I made my first attempt to pass on what I had learned from Barth in a lecture on 'Faith and Religion'. I tried to explain the radical difference between a man-centred religiosity and a God-centred faith. But since I had not yet really digested Barth's theology, I do not think that my student audience understood very well what I was trying to say.

Herman Rutgers proposed that I should set up a publishing house for the Student Christian Movement. I was to raise the necessary funds myself. I did not get on very well with my financial campaign. And then a quite unexpected event took place. A letter came from E. M. Robinson, the man who had organized the Pörschach Conference, to ask whether I would come to Geneva to talk about a possible appointment on the new Boys' Work staff of the World's Committee of YMCAs. I suppose that Conrad Hoffmann and John R. Mott had mentioned my name. I had already become so deeply interested in international work that I accepted immediately. The discussions in Geneva led to a favourable conclusion and in the summer I was appointed.

This meant also that the time had come for our wedding. It was a wedding in the old style with two weeks of dinners and receptions. Our brothers and cousins produced remarkable skits in which Woodbrooke and the YMCA had an important place. Two cousins played the roles of Ernst Troeltsch and Karl Barth arguing with each other in the most heavy and incomprehensible German phrases taken from their writings. A specially successful song, produced by my elder brother, was:

> Internationalism on the brain
> Every new flag drives me near insane.
> When I go to bed
> The map turns round my head.
> England, France and China
> Are old friends of mine,
> And the people living along the Rhine.
> But the only people that are real *OK*.
> That's the crowd that lives in dear old USA.
> My own country makes me weep,
> When I'm in Holland *I'm* asleep.
> Sure, I've internationalism on the brain.

3 | *First Years in Geneva*

WE SPENT OUR honeymoon in the romantic atmosphere of Lugano and of Venice and arrived in Geneva in October 1924 to take up our new life.

The first hours in the office of the World's Committee of the YMCAs were rather disconcerting. I went to see my new boss, E. M. Robinson, and asked him how I should tackle my new job. His answer was, that if I was the right man for the job I ought to know myself what to do. So I came back to my room and sat at my clean desk wondering how to spend the day. I knew only that I was supposed to be responsible for relations with Germany and Scandinavia and to be specially concerned with secondary school boys. I came to the conclusion that there was only one concrete thing I could do, namely to plan for an international area-conference for boys' workers. So before the morning was over I had made a first plan for such a meeting.

The new boys' work staff had a strong pioneering spirit. There seemed to be a magnificent opportunity to mobilize the new generation for the great cause of world peace and world brotherhood. The YMCA had a world-wide organization which could be used for this purpose. So our staff launched a new magazine for leaders of youth, *The World's Youth*, under the able leadership of the British author Basil Mathews. I became co-editor of the German edition. And we began to organize international camps for boys and leadership training courses.

I found myself in a somewhat paradoxical position. On the one hand I wanted to participate fully in the attempt to create a truly international outlook among boys and admired the single-minded enthusiasm with which my colleagues undertook their task. Tracy Strong, who had taken the place of E. M. Robinson as the head of our staff and who later became general secretary of the World Alliance of YMCAs, was the best possible representative of the generation of American Christians who had decided to devote their life to the cause of world peace.

On the other hand I could not share their tremendous optimism and idealism. The 'spirit of Geneva' which animated at that time a good many League of Nations officials and even more League of Nations supporters seemed to have greater affinity with Rousseau than with Calvin. And the YMCA itself seemed to be in danger of identifying itself with a social gospel theology which was far removed from the biblical message which Karl Barth was re-interpreting in such a powerful manner. So I lived in an uneasy tension between two very different worlds.

It was inevitable that the new approach made by the Boys' Work Department should lead to considerable tension within the World's Alliance of YMCAs. The very large and dynamic German branch reflected the post-war situation in German theology and in German youth. It lived in the atmosphere of an eschatological piety which looked upon the so-called activism of the Anglo-Saxon brethren as a distortion of true Christianity. I had to take part in many discussions in which the two opposing conceptions of the Kingdom of God and the two very different conceptions of the task of the YMCA were brought face to face. My own position was not yet sufficiently crystallized for me to make an original contribution to the discussion, but I tried to convince the Germans that faith in the Kingdom as God's gift should not lead to a passive attitude with regard to the great issues of social justice and world peace and I tried to convince the adherents of the social gospel that the Kingdom of God was something more and different from a world without war and exploitation.

It was also in those years that I came to know John R. Mott more intimately. I had met him briefly in 1922 in London, then at Pörschach and once in Holland. In 1924 I attended the General Committee of the World's Student Christian Federation as one of the minute secretaries, and was able to watch how he chaired and steered an international meeting. But in the following years I saw him often and served not infrequently as his interpreter. During one of his visits to Holland I presented my parents to him. My mother said to him smilingly that he was like a spider and that no one who had been caught in his web could get out of it again. There was truth in that remark. I had indeed been caught in the web which he had spun – and I never did get out of it.

We often made jokes about the standard phrases which appeared in all his addresses. Every crisis was an opportunity. And the years ahead were always the best years. But there was no doubt that he believed this with all his heart. There were occasions when we could not help laughing in his presence at one of his superlative statements; for example, when he proclaimed that we were to look for speakers who, when they opened their mouths, would produce streams of living water. But fortunately he had a sense of humour. And he continued to impress us by his total consecration to the cause of the Kingdom, by his grasp of the true priorities, by his conception of a world-wide Christian strategy.

A major task of the staff of the World's Committee of the YMCAs was now to prepare for the next World Conference of the YMCA which was to be held in Helsingfors (Helsinki) in 1926. It had been decided that the preparation would take the form of a large-scale inquiry. All young men and boys who could be reached by the YMCA would be invited to participate in discussion groups based on one identical questionnaire to be worked out in Geneva. So we had quite a time in the 'Helsingfors Inquiry Commission' when we tried to formulate the questions. The result was a document with no less than 475 questions.

At first I found it difficult to understand the rationale of this method. But soon it became clear that it was based on a new philosophy of education which had been elaborated in the USA, especially at Columbia University. The idea was that true democracy meant the full and spontaneous participation of all concerned, without any attempt to impose any particular point of view. Leaders of youth should not only refrain from providing the answers but even from formulating the problem. The process itself would produce the truth and the consensus. And according to the new conception of religious education such democracy was to be identified with the Kingdom of God. For, as Professor Harrison S. Elliott of Union Theological Seminary in New York, who played a decisive role in the preparation of the Helsingfors Conference, put it, 'God is found as individuals find themselves in the great co-operative enterprises for human progress.'

I felt again that I was in a dilemma. For there was a great deal to be said for the technique of the full participation of youth. In so far as this discussion method was simply the application of the good old Socratic idea of 'midwifery', of making youth think for themselves instead of just digesting the ideas of the older generation, it could be most useful. But the underlying theology seemed to be quite wrong. For it was clearly based on a conception of God as 'the immanent source of life'. Nothing could be farther removed from the rediscovery of the Holy God of the Bible which was taking place in European theology. So we had rather heated discussions on these subjects. The result was a compromise. The discussion method would be used, but that did not mean that we had to subscribe to the ideology of its more extreme advocates.

In 1925 I was sent to the USA to help in preparing the Helsingfors Conference and to get to know the work of the American YMCA among high school boys. Before I had been there twenty-four hours John R. Mott took me to the Yankee Stadium in New York to watch a football game between the Army and Notre Dame. Since the game itself and the tremendous enthusiasm of the huge crowd remained a mystery to me, it became a useful reminder that the USA was not to be understood in my European categories. In Washington I attended the International Convention of the YMCA which was opened by President Calvin Coolidge. His speech seemed to me a model of the complacency which characterized official America at that time. The tone was that the USA did not need any help from other countries, but that it was ready to bestow the blessings of American civilization on the rest of the world through the YMCA and similar agencies. But other speakers spoke in the more prophetic and self-critical spirit of the social gospel about the dark aspects of American life and especially about the iniquity of racial discrimination. Whatever weaknesses the 'social gospel' might have, it had at least a refreshing awareness of the gulf between the American ideal and the facts of life.

This was all the more important since the USA seemed to have arrived at a moment of transition between a stage in which all the old assumptions concerning the excellence of the American way of life were unshaken and a stage in which radical questions were being raised and in which a certain ironical critique of typically American attitudes and customs began to express itself. In the milieu in which I moved, the milieu of the YMCA, of the Rotary Clubs, of the churches, the new mood was not much in evidence. I had to keep it a dark secret that I was reading H. L. Mencken's *American Mercury* and other subversive literature. The issues of drinking and smoking and dancing were still prominent in most discussions. I got into trouble when I arrived in a midwestern city and had to answer questions from reporters about dancing in the YMCA. I said that I saw no harm in dancing if it took place in the right kind of environment. I discovered a few hours later that I had unwittingly taken sides in a great controversy which had led to considerable tension in the local YMCA.

As is so often the case when foreign visitors come to the USA, I had a heavy schedule of speeches. So far I had had little practice in public speaking, even less in giving addresses in English and none at all in the special art of speaking to an American public. In Europe the audience generally expects a thoroughly prepared address and does not take the speaker seriously unless he brings a voluminous manuscript. In America the speaker who addresses a luncheon club or a youth audience must avoid at all cost hiding himself behind sheets of paper and must give the impression of speaking extemporaneously. This was a new and difficult job. I found the speaking to hundreds and sometimes even thousands of high school boys and girls by far the hardest assignment. They resented the calling of a special assembly in a period usually their own, to listen to an unknown foreigner in whom they had no particular interest. So it was a battle every time to gain their attention. If you could get them to laugh a few times you had a good chance of winning. And you could not afford to look at your notes, for that would be an interruption of the wave length which it was essential to maintain in order to keep in touch with the audience. So I really sweated on these occasions, but I learned something about public speaking. Very solemn assemblies of a church or of a more general character have always seemed to me much less terrifying than these gatherings of schoolboys and schoolgirls. What I said in my speeches was not particularly profound. In spite of my critical attitude to the social gospel type of thought I myself spoke too easily and too superficially about world brotherhood and the new internationalism which would save the world. The influence of the Barthian theology had not yet had its full effect on my thinking. My mind was divided between the two worlds, the world as it looked from the viewpoint of post-war idealism and the world as seen from the angle of post-war disillusionment. But the American experience made me realize that I had to face the issue.

I spent a good deal of time at meetings with black YMCA leaders and at black schools and colleges. The students found it hard to believe it when I told them that I had never talked with a black man until I was twenty years old. As I learned about the conditions in which the black Americans had to live, not only in the South, but also in many cities in the North, I was surprised that there was so little bitterness and so much optimism in their midst.

John R. Mott asked me to serve as his personal assistant during the World Conference of the YMCA in Helsingfors in 1926. This meant that I was to be a general dogs-body. But it meant also that I was to be instructed in the art of running a complicated world conference by a man who had rightly been called 'a master of assemblies'. Mott took me to the big church where the main meetings would be held and went into every possible detailed question concerning seating, procedure, timing, etc. 'Now you will sit behind that pillar,' he said, 'and you must look at me. When I give you a sign, this means that I need you. It may be that I have a message for somebody or that there is a crisis' (he loved that word). The result was that I spent most of my time looking all over the place for people who were required for meetings of one sort or another, bringing reports or resolutions to the printers and acting as Mott's interpreter. I saw little of the normal life of the conference, but I saw with what sense of strategy, of priorities, of human relations and of attention to detail Mott operated.

The conference did not produce any clear ideas concerning the message of the YMCA. That could hardly be expected at a time when the spiritual climate of the German and other European delegations was so completely different from that of the very strong American delegation. At the same time the discussion method produced so many undigested ideas, that it was practically impossible to arrive at a coherent consensus. One well-known German theologian had found his own way of getting around the complications of the democratic process. When he had given his summary of the discussions someone challenged him and said: 'But the points you made were not the ones made in the groups.' He answered simply: 'I am sure these points were made, for I made them myself.' On the other hand there had been a real meeting of minds and young people had had a chance to participate fully. The problem now was how to combine the advantages of the new discussion method with a real concern for the content of the biblical message.

After the world conference I had to concentrate on the work for secondary school boys. I found that while outside Europe most of the work in this field was done by the YMCA, in Europe it was largely in the hands of the student Christian movements and of independent bodies. The first thing to do obviously was to get all concerned with the Christian approach to schoolboys to meet and since we were really dealing with the same problems to bring in the YWCA and movements concerned with schoolgirls. So in 1927 we held an international conference of Christian workers among boys and girls of secondary schools in Dassel, Germany. Fifty different national movements were represented. Since these movements were so very different from each other – ranging from the Hi-Y clubs in the USA with their 100,000 members to small struggling groups in Latin Europe, or from groups with a strongly moralistic emphasis to those wholly concerned with bible study – it was difficult to find a common language. But in the end we discovered a good deal of common ground. A German delegate commented: 'Is it not valuable that we Germans learn that we have too much theology, the French that they have too much philosophy and the Americans that they have too much activism?'

Everybody agreed that these contacts should be maintained, and so a liaison committee was set up with Miss Marianne Mills and myself as secretaries. This committee organized two other Dassel conferences in 1932 and in 1936.

But the youth scene which we surveyed in 1932 was very different from that of 1927. Already in 1928 I had asked in *The World's Youth*[1] whether we ought not to revise all our ideas about youth. In the years after the first world war we had come to think of youth as romantic, idealistic and individualistic. But was this still true? I called attention to Nicolas Berdyaev's analysis of the situation. He had said that the new generation would be anti-romantic, anti-liberal and anti-individualistic and that the trend was towards collectivism. Four years later at the second Dassel conference, in 1932, I had to confirm this. We were facing the new problem of the great social and political mass movements. And if any delegates were still unconvinced that this was the new challenge, they must have changed their mind when during the conference the groups of Hitler Youth marched past the conference hall with their swastika flags and martial songs.

NOTES

1. April 1928.

4 | *The Stockholm Conference and its Aftermath*

THERE WAS REALLY no good reason why I should participate in the Stockholm Conference of 1925. It was a conference of church delegates and the churches of course sent men of experience and maturity. The YMCA was to have one delegate, surely a man who had won his spurs. But I was very eager to go and, rather to my own surprise, I was admitted as an alternate. So at twenty-four years of age I received my initiation into the larger ecumenical movement.

On the way to the meeting we received the most generous hospitality in the country home of Prince Oscar Bernadotte, brother of the King of Sweden and President of the Swedish YMCA. It was a new experience to open one's eyes in the morning and to find at one's bedside a lady servant making a deep curtsey. Jetty and I did not agree on the proper reaction! Prince Oscar took us to visit some of the royal castles. In one of them he showed us the pictures of the famous kings of Sweden – Gustavus Adolphus, Charles XII, and so forth. Then he paused before a small picture of a very different kind of person – clearly a *petit bourgeois*. 'This,' he said, 'was my direct ancestor, a barrister who was the father of the General Bernadotte who became King of Sweden in the days of Napoleon.' Prince Oscar's simplicity was completely genuine. He was a product of the evangelical revival and kept strictly to the conviction that the Christian faith was a matter of personal conversion and should not be mixed up with social and political positions.

Then to Stockholm for the opening of the great meeting. 'The Universal Christian Conference on Life and Work' was the very first of the ecumenical assemblies of the churches. Archbishop Nathan Söderblom had won his long battle against the sceptics and the prudent. Nobody could fail to be profoundly impressed and almost overwhelmed when, for the first time in modern history, a long procession of delegates, in the most diverse ecclesiastical vestments or in morning coats with the still obligatory top hat, moved into Stockholm's cathedral church. Söderblom had done everything he could to give the conference a setting worthy of the occasion. Though he was himself a most unpretentious and informal churchman, and one could see him rushing through the streets without a hat, he had the gift of stage management. Convinced as he was that this event was nothing less than a new beginning in the history of the church, he wanted it to be memorable in every respect. And in this he succeeded, for the pictures which I have in my mind of those days have not been effaced by the impressions of the many ecumenical assemblies which I have attended since.

I think especially of the communion service in the Engelbert church, during which the vast majority of the delegates knelt together at the Lord's Table. At that time we were in the happy situation that for the great majority inter-communion had not yet become a problem. I have not forgotten the candlelight dinner in the golden hall of the Town Hall with its luminous mosaics. When the herald, after blowing his trumpet, shouted: 'Pray silence for the Patriarch and Pope of Alexandria' and the old Patriarch rose to speak in Greek, it seemed as if time had stood still and as if we were simply continuing the tradition of the ancient ecumenical councils.

In spite of Søderblom's efforts the working sessions were not so well organized. Few had any experience of the specific problems of large ecumenical meetings. Thus, at the first meeting, when Søderblom called on the interpreters to translate the first speeches, one after the other of the interpreters had to give up. After which the interpreters' bench was empty. The mistake had been to choose interpreters who were competent in the field of law or of diplomacy, but who were quite out of their depth in the sphere of ecclesiastical vocabulary and idiom. Søderblom had to ask whether any delegates could help. It was at that moment that Dr Alphons Koechlin of Switzerland took over and handled translations in English, French and German. We had to learn that even more important than purely linguistic ability was the ability fully to comprehend what a speaker was saying.

Another weakness in the programme was the lack of time for discussion. Nearly all the time was spent in listening to addresses. Few of them made a lasting impression. But I remember how Selma Lagerlöf made us sit up and listen because she told simply and movingly the story upon which her famous novel, *Jerusalem*, is based.

As a young and inexperienced participant I played only a very minor role in the meeting. Only once did I climb onto the platform for a short contribution to the discussion on youth. I spoke of the efforts being made by the Christian youth organizations to bring together young people of all nations and races, in a world-wide brotherhood based on common Christian convictions. It was not much of a maiden speech.

I did not get to know many of the conference leaders. They were far too busy. But there was one exception. One evening Jetty and I had dinner with the Countess von Rosen, whose son I had come to know in a student conference. One of the other guests was a young-looking Anglican clergyman with a most innocent look. But in conversation he proved to be extraordinarily well informed and full of forward-looking ideas. It was the Dean of Canterbury, George Bell, who would become a pioneer and builder of the World Council and with whom

I would be intimately associated for many years.

The conference was to deal with questions of 'life and work', that is with the practical problem of applying Christian principles in social and international life. The invitation had said that matters of faith and order would not be discussed. This seemed to be a perfectly natural provision, since the Faith and Order movement was already preparing for its own world conference to be held in Lausanne in 1927. The doctrinal issues which had to be solved in order to arrive at full church unity belonged to the programme of Lausanne and not to that of Stockholm. But did this mean that churchmen entering the meeting-hall in Stockholm would have to leave their theology in the cloakroom? Some statements by conference leaders seemed to recommend such theological self-denial. The slogan was coined: 'Doctrine divides, but service unites.' Søderblom himself had used more than once a phrase which he had found in a report of the Church of England, namely: 'In the region of moral and social questions we desire all Christians to begin at once to act together as if they were one body in one visible fellowship. This could be done by all alike without any injury to theological principle.'[1] The motive behind such statements was clear enough. The invitation to the conference expressed it in the words: 'The world's need is so urgent and the demand for common action on the part of all Christians so insistent at this juncture that we cannot afford to await the fulfilment of the great hope of a reunited Christendom before putting our hearts and our hands into a united effort that God's will may be done on earth as it is in heaven.' But hearts and hands cannot operate without heads. Service can only unite if you arrive at a common understanding of the nature of the service to be rendered. And the 'as if' approach does not work where there are not only divergences about the creeds or the sacraments, but also about the meaning of history and the mandate of the church in the world. So the conference which was to leave theology out of the picture became in fact dominated by a specifically theological issue. The form in which the issue arose was that of the relation of human action to the Kingdom of God. Is the Kingdom of God an ideal state of society to be realized by human achievement? Or is it the completely new world which God brings at the end of human history? The first position was most strongly advocated by American, British and French delegates of the 'social gospel' school. And the second position was defended by a number of German delegates. The debate was complicated by political factors. There had been several references to the League of Nations as a 'milestone on the road to the Kingdom of God'. There came a dramatic moment when the German Superintendent, Klingemann, attacked the League as a guarantor of a *status quo* which was intolerable for Germany and stated: 'In the present state of the League we cannot find any religious element or any relation to the Kingdom of God.'[2] One of my clearest memories of the conference is how Elie Gounelle, the leader of 'Christianisme Social' in France, sought to answer this challenge. He pleaded with passion for the League, which he called 'this noble thought, I would almost say, this prayer of President

Wilson' and stretching out his arms to the German delegation he implored them
to follow the path of love rather than that of hatred.

It cannot be said that the conference solved the deep problems with which it
was faced. But thanks to the leadership of Søderblom and thanks to the general
conviction that this first meeting of the churches was a God-given opportunity,
the conference ended on a definitely positive note. The conference message, in
the drafting of which George Bell had a considerable share, was adopted with
only very few dissenting votes. And it was decided to set up a Continuation
Committee. The 'Life and Work' movement had come into existence. Søderblom
had again won a victory. There was now at least a beginning of an ecumenical
movement of the churches.

The conference had been for me like a window through which I had come to
see the total ecumenical scene with its bewildering variety, its sharp tensions, its
heavy burden of church history and its stubborn non-theological factors, but also
with its wonderful potential dynamic. So I continued to think about all that I had
seen, heard and learned in Stockholm.

The debate about the Kingdom of God continued after the conference.
German theologians attacked American *Aktivismus* and American churchmen
criticized the otherworldly quietism of the continental theologians. In the USA
it was a current joke that the Germans had adapted the hymn, 'Rise up, O men
of God' in this way:

> Sit down, O men of God
> His Kingdom He will bring
> Whenever it may please His Will
> You cannot do a thing.

But on the European continent many said that, according to the Americans, the
definitive abolition of war and the adoption of prohibition meant that the
Kingdom of God was just around the corner.

We had of course the same problem within the World's Alliance of YMCAs
and in the World's Student Christian Federation. Almost every meeting at which
Americans and Germans were present led to a rather sharp debate between the
advocates of the eschatological, otherworldly and those of an evolutionary, this-
worldly conception of the Kingdom of God. I did not feel at home in either
camp. The German theologians used their eschatology too easily as a justification for a complete separation between Christianity and political or social life.
The American 'social gospel' enthusiasts were building castles in the air which
had little relation to the hard realities of history.

What could be done about this great misunderstanding? On the European
side the first thing to do was to find out what this 'social gospel' theology really
was. In Europe we knew next to nothing about American theology. So most of
the polemical writing about the social gospel was hopelessly superficial. My
curiosity about the new trends of thought in the USA was greatly stimulated by

my first visit to that country in 1925. For in the milieu in which I moved – the YMCA and the student movement – the social gospel was hailed as the re-discovery of the true meaning of Christianity. I had become involved in many discussions in which I had raised my 'European' critical questions and I always got a friendly hearing, but I had the impression that most people con-sidered me as a visitor from another planet. Of course there were exceptions. Pastor Lynn Harold Hough, then in Detroit and later a professor at Drew University, whom I had come to know at Stockholm as a man of truly ecumenical dimensions, told me of a brilliant young pastor who ministered to the workers of the automobile industry and who was, on the one hand, a fighter for social justice and, on the other hand, a severe critic of the social gospel theology. Would I like to meet him? Of course I would. His name was Reinhold Niebuhr. I had never heard that name before; I was astounded by his knowledge of European theology, enjoyed his sharp critical wit, and noted in my diary: 'This man would be able to do a magnificent job interpreting Europe and America to each other.'

So I chose as the subject for my doctoral thesis, 'The Background of the Social Gospel in America'.[3] I found it a fascinating subject. For it became clear to me that while we had imagined that American thought was simply an echo of European thought, 'All the time it was evolving a religious life of its own with very distinctive characteristics'. I tried to understand those characteristics by studying the historical antecedents of the social gospel in Puritanism, in the Enlightenment, in Revivalism, in modern scientific thought. All of these had left their traces, but the decisive influences were the last three. I concluded that we could learn much from the social gospel – 'its missionary zeal, its sense of responsibility for all life, its challenge to those who are satisfied with things as they are, its moral courage'. But, I contended, the movement was theologically weak, in that it did not distinguish clearly enough between church and world, in that it had a romantic conception of man, in that, in line with the attempt to make the world safe for democracy, it sought to make God safe for democracy. I could, however, note that critical voices were not absent and could, just before finishing my manuscript, insert a quotation from Reinhold Niebuhr's first major book, *Does Civilization Need Religion?*, which pointed towards a more profound theology. And I asked finally: 'May we not expect that as Americans try to dig deeper, listening to the voice of Christ and translating it into a language of their own, America will find a deeper and more genuinely Christian message?'

The outwardly solemn ceremony – carriages drawn by horses with black plumes, frock-coats, and other trappings – during which I was supposed to defend my doctoral thesis before the Rector Magnificus and the professors of the theological faculty of Leiden university turned out to be something of a farce. For none of the professors had any knowledge of the American religious scene and so their questions were remarkably irrelevant. But I was encouraged by the reaction of competent critics. André Siegfried, the author of one of the best

European studies on the United States, wrote:

> I knew, in general, about the astounding transformation which has changed
> the American Calvinist of the seventeenth century with his pessimistic con-
> ception of human nature into the astonishing optimist of the twentieth
> century. I had often asked myself how this passionate reader of the Bible
> could have read it in such a way that he came to hear it speak with the voice
> of Rousseau. I had not found a satisfying answer to that problem. You have
> answered my question.

William Paton of the International Missionary Council wrote:

> We hope that American readers will recognize in the book a tribute from a
> Continental scholar to the importance of American Christianity for the whole
> world.

Emil Brunner concluded that my book not only threw light on the history of the
social gospel, but showed the weakness of a social ethic which was rooted in the
optimism of the Enlightenment rather than in the Bible. Helen D. Hill, author
of historical and geographical studies, said in *The Saturday Review of Literature*
that the book was definitely a contribution to the history of American thought,
but that I had underrated the economic factor. This was a valid criticism. I
found many years later that Dietrich Bonhoeffer had used my dissertation for his
study of American Christianity.

The book had been published in Holland. I tried to get it published in the
USA also. But at that time no American publisher was interested in this kind of
historical approach. It was not till 1962, when the book was in many ways out of
date, that an American edition appeared.[4]

NOTES

1. I have discussed this principle more fully in *The Pressure of our Common Calling*,
pp. 16–21; see also B. Sundkler, *Nathan Söderblom*, pp. 230–32.

2. I retranslate these words from the original German; Adolf Deissmann, *Die
Stockholmer Weltkirchenkonferenz*.

3. Published in Haarlem in 1928.

4. St Louis, Missouri, Bethany Press.

5 | *Internationalism and its Decline*

WHEN I CAME to Geneva in 1924 the League of Nations was still in its early days and the focal point of an infectious idealism. At the time of the annual League Assemblies pilgrims came flocking from all over the world to this Mecca of the new internationalism. It was curious to note that so many came from the United States although the United States had not joined the League. Some of this enthusiasm took rather silly forms. I remember an international dinner organized on the principle that every couple should bring a national dish. The combination of these ten dishes was so disharmonious that the dinner served rather as propaganda against internationalism. But there was also the deep conviction that the world had made a new start. Elie Gounelle, the leader of 'Christianisme Social' in France, spoke of the League as 'a milestone on the road to the Kingdom of God'. Lord Parmoor, the Christian layman who represented Great Britain in the League Assembly of 1924, spoke of the League as a 'Christian community the members of which solve their conflicts by friendly methods'. Many believed firmly that a fundamental change had taken place in international relations. From now on there would be a true international order based on law. It was realized that the League could only function if it were backed by public opinion. As Søderblom put it: the League of Nations needed a soul. The task of the churches and the international Christian organizations appeared therefore to be to create the new spirit of brotherhood and internationalism which would enable the League to live and to develop.

For our Boys' Work Department of the World's Alliance of YMCAs this meant that we had to give boys an opportunity for a personal experience of international fellowship. So we organized a series of international boys' camps. I participated in the leadership of such camps in Switzerland, Sweden, Hungary, Great Britain and the Netherlands. The spirit of these camps was best illustrated by the closing ceremony. One boy from each of the participating nations approached the campfire, lit a torch and gave in his own language the pledge: 'We leave this fire conscious of differences, but with a new vision of Christian fellowship, a deeper faith in God our Father, and a determination to work for peace and good will among men.'

We had of course to overcome many kinds of international tension, but there were fascinating positive moments. I remember specially that during the bible study in my group we discovered that our Chinese member who had recently arrived in Europe knew nothing about Christianity, but was eager to find out about it. So I suggested that we should spend all our time in helping him to discover who Jesus was and what he meant for us. Our Chinese friend thus received his first instruction from twelve boys of seven different nations. He asked many questions and received many different answers. Whether he really became a Christian, as he said he would, I do not know, but I do know that this 'joint action for mission', long before the expression became current, helped our group to understand what the ecumenical movement was all about.

The Briand-Stresemann talks in Geneva which led to the Locarno treaty of 1925, the entering of Germany into the League of Nations in 1926 and the Kellogg-Briand pact signed in Paris in 1928 by no fewer than sixty-one governments and condemning recourse to war for the solution of international controversies seemed to justify the believers in the new international order. 'This treaty marks the end of war,' said Mr Kellogg, the American Secretary of State, arriving in Europe to sign the pact to which his name would be attached. But there were also strong reasons to doubt that the great conversion of the nations to peaceful co-existence had really taken place. The Germans reminded us on every possible occasion that their two fundamental demands remained unfulfilled: a general reduction of armaments as foreseen in the Covenant of the League and a revision of the war-guilt clause of the Versailles treaty. It was in 1931, thirteen years after the end of the first world-war, that the YMCA staff had to spend much time and energy on this discussion about war-guilt. The problem became mainly a Franco-German issue. The Germans insisted that a resolution should be adopted affirming that the clause in the Versailles treaty attributing to Germany sole responsibility for the war was unjust. The French were not ready to take this step. Just before the World Conference of the YMCAs in Cleveland in that year I spent a miserable day at Niagara Falls as interpreter at a meeting in which John R. Mott, without any success, tried to get the French and German YMCA delegates to come to agreement. The problem was fortunately solved by the World Conference.

After the great financial and economic crisis of 1929 it became more and more clear that the change which had taken place in international relations was by no means as real and as definitive as the new internationalists had thought. There were many voices which ridiculed the League and said openly that the so-called new order was nothing but a continuation of pre-war politics under a new name and with a hypocritical façade. Mussolini's fascism glorified again the imperial dream. National socialism was becoming a strong force in Germany. Internationalism was under fire. Those of us who were working for the international organizations became aware that it could only be saved by a tremendous common effort.

In 1931 all international organizations concentrated their attention on the issue of disarmament. The League of Nations had decided to hold a world conference on disarmament in Geneva in 1932. This was going to be the great test case for the international order. The governments would have to reveal their true intentions, and it would become clear whether the League of Nations was what it pretended to be or merely, as some described it, 'a bank without capital'. To stop the armaments race was important, but it was even more important to get the legal machinery of the League fully accepted as the only permissible means of settling international conflict.

It was clear that much would depend on the strength of public opinion. And this time an extraordinary attempt was made to mobilize the forces working for peace. I do not believe that at any other time, before or after, women's organizations, youth organizations, peace societies and the churches have tried so hard to get their voices heard in an international governmental assembly.

Lord Robert Cecil, one of the 'fathers' of the League who continued to be its indefatigable advocate, asked our World's Student Christian Federation to devote its energy to the cause of disarmament. In the spring of 1931 I published his letter to me[1] in which he said that nothing had encouraged him more than the sympathy with which we had received his suggestion, for disarmament had become the most topical and the most urgent of all international issues. During that year student movements in many countries organized meetings on disarmament. In Geneva the non-governmental international bodies joined together in a co-ordination committee to bring common pressure to bear upon the delegates. Archbishop William Temple was invited to Geneva to preach at the St-Pierre Cathedral at a special service for the conference. We believed that now that public opinion had so clearly expressed itself, the statesmen would not dare to go home without having arrived at some concrete result. But I had already shed many illusions. In September 1931 the invasion of Manchuria by Japan had begun. This was the first time since the creation of the League and the signing of the Kellogg-Briand Peace Pact that a major power resorted to war. I wrote on November 20th to Robert Mackie of the British Student Christian Movement: 'One gets the impression that very few people realize all that is involved in the question. It would seem that the future of the League as well as of disarmament depends largely on the outcome of that (i.e. the Sino-Japanese) conflict.'

On the eve of the conference I wrote an editorial in *The Student World* with a title borrowed from Francis Thompson, 'Wishing peace but not the means of it'. I pointed out that disarmament was only possible if we could learn to conceive of peace not as the absence of war, but as 'a dynamic process of administration of justice'. Such a process would be expensive in that all nations would have to make sacrifices. It was no good wishing peace and at the same time refusing to implement 'the means of it'.

On the day of the opening of the conference, February 2nd 1932, the international atmosphere was more unfavourable than even the strongest opponent of disarmament could have desired. For it became known on that day that Japan had attacked Shanghai. At the hour at which the solemn opening of the great conference was to take place the League Council had to hold an emergency meeting. And four of us representing the international Christian organizations were drawing up a cable to John R. Mott for transmission to the National Christian Council of Japan in which we said: 'Secretariats Christian world organizations Geneva urge you use influence convince authorities and public of growing volume moral world opinion against Japan's increasing use military action. Our love for Japan and respect for her moral standing in world affairs impels this message.'

When finally the conference was opened and President Arthur Henderson asked: 'Are we ready, each nation among us, to shape our policy with a faith that war is done with?', the answer could only be: 'Obviously not, for war is actually in progress.'

But the struggle for peace had to go on. Soon after its opening the conference held an extraordinary session to allow public opinion to express itself. It became an impressive occasion. We represented all sorts of people, all sorts of nations. The women offered a petition with eight million signatures. The students gave an ultimatum to the conference. The Christians spoke forcefully for real disarmament. Lord Robert Cecil, who had been invited to represent the United Kingdom as a delegate, but who had refused because he did not agree with the opportunistic position of his government, showed great moral courage by joining our procession and by identifying his voice with the voice of the people.

During the next few months I spent much time at the conference. One of my duties was to cover the meetings for the American Protestant journal, *The Christian Century*. So I got to know a good many of the delegates and the journalists. In July 1932 I summarized my impressions in the following way:[2]

> It would seem that the delegates at the Conference realize little that we are living in a time of crisis. One gets the impression that they believe that the world can go on indefinitely as it goes on today. These delegates do not for a moment desire the war to which they are letting the world drift. It is a sobering thought that it is this group of very human and decent people who will be responsible for the next war if it comes.

That was an outburst of an angry young man. I had not taken sufficiently seriously what Professor Max Huber, the former President of the International Court and a Swiss delegate, had tried to impress on me, namely, that the delegates were bound by the instructions of their governments and had practically no freedom of action. The real stage was not Geneva. We were always forgetting that simple fact. The real stage was there where military men were counting their guns, where reports were assembled about the plans of the actual and would-be dictators, where new wildly nationalistic movements were organizing themselves, The Geneva conference had come too late. History moved away from Geneva. The disarmament conference proved a total failure.

So from now on we lived in a different world. I wrote in September 1932:[3]

The great difference between 1927 and 1932 is that between the fool's paradise before the crisis and the crisis itself, between the atmosphere of calmness and expectation and the atmosphere of terror, between a world which was not facing reality and a world which simply *has* to face it.

The World's Student Christian Federation had to reconsider its policy in the light of this new situation. We realized that we had consciously or unconsciously been influenced by that far too superficial idealistic internationalism which expected a triumphant march forward of the democratic idea and the universal acceptance of a legal machinery for peace-keeping. The forces at work in the world did not work towards peace but towards war. Where could we find a force that would transcend the divisive trends? We believed that it could be found in the reality of the supra-national Christian community. We would have to show that there was a reconciling, peace-making dynamic in the Christian church.

There were opportunities enough for this international healing ministry. When Yugoslavia and Hungary were on the brink of war I crossed the border with a letter from the Serbian to the Hungarian Student Christian Movement. When we opened it, we found that it contained only the text of the 17th chapter of the Gospel of John – and this was just the right word in this situation.

When the Sino-Japanese conflict became increasingly acute we were able to bring Chinese and Japanese delegations together at a Pacific Area Conference in California. They talked very frankly – even bluntly – with each other, but fellowship was maintained and they began to understand that there was sin and suffering on both sides. This led to the rather bold invitation issued by the Japanese movement to Kiang Wen Han and Michael Bruce (both secretaries of the Chinese movement) to visit the Japanese universities.

In the meantime the international situation became increasingly serious.

In 1936 fascist Italy attacked Ethiopia, the League talked about sanctions against Italy, but the big powers refused to take adequate action. Emperor Haile Selassie came to Geneva as an exile. During the session in which he pleaded for the right of his ancient country to live in peace and freedom some Italian journalists suddenly shouted the crudest possible insults at him. For those who still believed in the mission of the League this was the limit. Mary Dingman of the YWCA urged that the international organizations should send a delegation to the Emperor to express their indignation about the way he and the cause he represented had been treated. I was chosen to be the spokesman.

I stood before a man of great dignity – small but straight as an arrow and with penetrating eyes. I said that we felt a deep sense of solidarity with his people. I continued: in this conflict principles were at stake, the violation of which would affect the whole world. We felt humiliated by the fact that our nations had not done more to defend the most elementary principles of international law which were the foundation of the League of Nations. We did not know what the future of Ethiopia would be, but we believed that the spiritual destiny of a nation was not at the mercy of political contingencies.

The Emperor replied that the most tragic aspect of the situation was not simply that his country had been attacked, but that this had happened after the nations had solemnly promised that they would never again resort to war. Many years later I saw in the Cathedral of Addis Ababa a fresco representing the tragic League session in Geneva. Ethiopia remembered this dark hour. I was glad that we had been able to show the nation's leader a measure of sympathy at that very moment.

It was in those days that I asked Max Huber whether in this crisis he saw any difference between Christian statesmen and others. He answered: 'Not so much in their actual positions, because they have to reflect national opinion, but in another way, namely that when most men become totally discouraged, the Christians go on struggling, because they have a mandate which is not dependent on the circumstances of the moment.'

The unreality of the Geneva atmosphere became apparent in a tragi-comic way when in 1937 the new Palace of the Nations was inaugurated. The Aga Khan had agreed to preside over the Assembly and to give a mammoth party in the new building. All Geneva and a good part of the world were there. But the music and the champagne could not make us forget that the poor old League, which had at one time been the centre of such tremendous expectations, had fallen on bad days. Jawaharlal Nehru, who made a short visit to Geneva in 1938, expressed his feelings about the League to some of us by referring to the brand new Palace of the Nations as 'that tomb'.

NOTES

1. *The Student World.*
2. In the Federation News Sheet.
3. ibid.

6 | *Nursery and Brains Trust of the Ecumenical Movement*

THE YEAR 1928 was the beginning of a period of so many changes in the life of our family and in my work that it was difficult to adjust to all of them at once. Our first child was born – a daughter named Anneke – and brought us great joy. I received the doctorate of theology in Leiden and this was celebrated with many friends and relatives in the traditional elaborate manner. But soon afterwards my mother, who had been the centre of the family, died after a long illness. Since my older brother lived in the United States and my younger brother was still at university, Jetty and I asked my father to come to live with us in Geneva. This meant giving up the old family home and so I was no longer rooted in Holland and a precious link with my youth disappeared. In Geneva we had to leave our funny little house in Petit-Saconnex in favour of a big house in Champel. Father enjoyed living in Geneva but he died in 1930. Another precious link with my youth had disappeared. In the meantime the family grew when a son was born in 1930 and another one in 1931.

It was at this time that the World's Student Christian Federation asked me to join its staff with the understanding that I would give half time to the YMCA and half time to the Federation. This invitation was quite unexpected and had considerable consequences for me. Most of us thought that Gustav Kullmann, the very able Swiss working with Russian students in France, would become General Secretary of the Federation. But Kullmann had just decided to leave his first wife and to marry again. When John R. Mott heard about this he became strongly opposed to the appointment of Kullmann. It was decided not to appoint a new General Secretary for the time being, but to entrust the leadership of the Federation to a staff-team. If Kullmann had been elected I would certainly not have been invited to join the staff, for Kullmann and I represented the same part of the world. In that case I would probably have accepted another proposal, namely that I should go to Indonesia to help in the setting up of the new theological school. I did not realize it at that time, but the acceptance of the invitation of the Federation meant in fact that I would spend the rest of my active years in the service of the ecumenical movement.

During those years of change one of the greatest steadying influences in our life was the friendship with Pierre Maury. Of the men and women with whom I worked over the years none had a deeper influence on me than Pierre Maury. He had been General Secretary of the French Student Christian Movement and had become pastor of the French Reformed Church in Ferney-Voltaire in France, just across the border from Geneva. Jetty and I were so impressed by his powerful and direct preaching that we decided to join his parish. So we crossed the border every Sunday morning to attend the service in the rather dilapidated church in Ferney-Voltaire. For us, as for so many others, Pierre Maury became the pastoral friend and the friendly pastor. He saw my weaknesses and did not spare his criticisms, but he saw more in me than I saw in myself, and so he gave me courage to do things which I would not have done without him.

Maury had an unlimited curiosity about people and ideas. He could lecture on the modern French novel, but was at the same time a theologian of great originality. I had the privilege of bringing Karl Barth and Maury together in 1925, and these two developed a friendship in which both gave and both received. Barth wrote about him: 'I have had and still have good friends. But there has been in my life only one Pierre Maury.' Jetty and I could say the same. For this man combined in a unique way the deep passion for the discovery of the great objective divine truth with an equally deep interest in persons and in all manifestations of human life.

It was of course Pierre Maury who preached at the service in 1936 at which I was ordained as a minister of the National Protestant Church of Geneva. And he remained my 'guru' until his death and, since the conversation was not really finished, even beyond.

It was in the late 'twenties that the Barthian storm swept over the theological world and that I became involved in the spreading of Barth's message. Maury had asked me in 1928 to write a short article on Barth for *Foi et Vie*. At that time no books of Barth had been translated into French and mine was one of the first articles in French about his thought. In 1930 I was invited to give a lecture on Barth in King's College, London. This was a rather formidable assignment, for Barth's theological approach was as far removed from the current British approach as could be imagined. The Dean of St Paul's was in the chair. I had the feeling that I had talked Chinese to Englishmen or English to the Chinese. The *Church Times* commented charitably: 'The lecturer, although an ardent disciple of Barth, did not altogether make his author clear: possibly through attempting to say too much at once, possibly through the nature of the theology which he set out to explain'.[1] I gave the same lecture in Toronto and it was published in Canada.[2] The French version appeared as a brochure: *Introduction à Karl Barth*. I was curious what Barth himself would say. He wrote that he admired the ability with which I had brought his thought so near to the people of that far-distant English world. Had I really done that? His next remark was more convincing. He said: 'I have always observed that I was best understood by those who saw it as their task to think through the matter themselves "at ovo" (from the beginning) rather than to repeat only what I have said'.[3]

The great objection to Barth's theology at that time was that it was a theology of despair. I tried to explain that for many of my generation it was exactly the opposite. I put it thus:

> Barth opens for us the wonderful objectivity of God's world. He delivers us from the anxious seeking for religious treasures. His is the theology of spiritual poverty. Many of us who have spent fruitless hours in building up our inner experiences and always found them wanting when we needed them most, have been saved from ourselves, from our old Adam by accepting this great truth that the only thing which matters is God's Holy Spirit and that that Spirit is with those who are hungry and thirsty, not with those who are spiritually well fed. And others who have tried to keep their ideals of human achievement and progress alive in a world where those ideals are constantly submerged by the floods of this unbearably realistic life, have been saved from both their ideals and their disillusions by accepting the truth that God's Kingdom comes at His appointed time and that God relates their efforts to it in His own way, which we do not and need not know.

I was never a Barthian in the sense that I followed him in all respects. But I remained grateful to him for giving me ground under my feet. He could be terribly intransigent and sometimes quite unfair in his criticisms of what he called 'the ecumenical circus' and I would then protest strongly. But it was really a blessing that during that formative period of the ecumenical movement there was a man who was asking us fundamental questions and calling us back to the central truths. I have therefore said more than once that without Karl Barth the movement would not have had the spiritual substance which it did receive.

In 1934 I invited Barth to an international student conference at La Chataigneraie near Geneva. The participants from many parts of the world used the opportunity to bombard Barth with critical questions. The professor was examined by the students. Somebody said that we were like pygmies throwing darts at an elephant. And I was tempted to give to the account of this discussion[4] the title: 'Karl Barth *contra mundum*' (against the world). But neither description was really correct. For Barth went far in his understanding of the questioners. When several had spoken of the centrality of 'experience' rather than of the biblical revelation, Barth answered: 'I have also a little bit of experience' and proceeded to tell how from the days of his pastorate in Switzerland to the present moment of his involvement in the church conflict in Germany he had increasingly learned to count on nothing else than the word of God. The students had not only met a great theologian, but also a human being struggling to serve God in the chaotic life of our times.

Let me before leaving Karl Barth for the moment tell two stories. In 1936 Barth came to Geneva on the occasion of the fourth centenary of the Genevese

Reformation. I had met him at the station and taken him to our home. He wanted to prepare for his speech, so I proposed that he should go into the garden. After a while my little son came running in and said in great agitation: 'The tortoises have done something on the notes which the gentleman has to sing in the church!' What on earth had happened? I found that my son had taken pity on the lonely gentleman and had brought him his two pet tortoises. But these had reacted as animals do in moments of panic. So Barth's manuscript was soiled. But he laughed and said: 'This is the revenge of natural theology.'

The second story is as much about William Temple as it is about Barth. I had told Temple in 1930 why Barth's theology had made such a deep impression on me. A few months later he sent me the sermon which he had preached at the opening of the Lambeth Conference of that year. It was a powerful sermon[5] which culminated in the assertion: 'While we deliberate, He reigns; when we decide wisely, He reigns; when we decide foolishly, He reigns; when we serve Him in humble loyalty, He reigns; when we serve Him self-assertively, He reigns.' Temple asked whether the truth which he had sought to proclaim in this sermon was not the basic theme of Karl Barth's theology. I could answer that it was indeed. Temple and Barth remained far apart in many respects, but they both knew about the Majesty of God. And it was characteristic of Temple's way of dealing with young people, that he, as an Archbishop, should ask a young man of no ecclesiastical importance to give an opinion on his sermon.

When I began to work for the Federation in 1928 I was given immediately three tasks which taken together took a good deal more than the half time which I was supposed to give to it. I was to set up a European Council of Student Christian Movements; I was to be editor of *The Student World* and I was to be secretary of the new commission on the message of the Federation.

The third of these tasks proved to be the most challenging. The initiative to begin this study of the message had been taken by Francis P. Miller, who had just succeeded John R. Mott as chairman of the Federation. Miller was a Virginian, who was very conscious of his Southern origins, but who had at the same time a wide international vision. I had come to know him in 1921 at a Federation meeting in Holland and been impressed by his passionate conviction about the urgency of bringing into being a world Christian community with a truly catholic outlook. The task of the Federation was in his view to pioneer for the church universal. Now that he had become chairman he felt that the first thing to do was to try to arrive at a deeper spiritual unity among the various parts of the Federation. He felt, as I did, that we lived in a time of spiritual and intellectual chaos. We were not helping students to find a clear sense of direction. We should become 'a pioneer battalion to lay down the lines along which the great spiritual advance of the future may be expected to take place'.[6] We agreed that the starting point would have to be a study in which all the national movements would take part and which would seek to answer the question: 'Has the Federation as a world movement of Christian students any powerful message of religious truth to deliver in the pressure of our overwhelmingly pagan civilization?'

To get this study going was no easy task. But it was in the hands of a strong group: Reinhold Niebuhr of the USA, Canon F. A. Cockin of Britain, P. C. Hsu of China, S. K. Datta of India, Pierre Maury of France and W. Zenkovsky representing the Russian orthodox who had emigrated to Western Europe. And there was a good response. I could write in 1930 that the message study had already become a strong element of unification in the Federation's life.

The study of the message of the Federation was put in a wider setting as I became involved in the post-Jerusalem crusade of J. H. Oldham. A native of Scotland, he had been closely associated with John R. Mott in the preparation of the World Missionary Conference at Edinburgh in 1910 and became secretary of the International Missionary Council. The Jerusalem conference of the International Missionary Council in 1928 had given a great deal of attention to the issue of secularism, that is the emergence of a civilization without a religious foundation or religious criteria. Oldham, who had founded the International Missionary Council together with John R. Mott, had become convinced that this was now the life and death issue for the church and the missionary movement. And when Oldham had a strong conviction he held on to it like a Scotch terrier holding on to a bone and concentrated his great energy on mobilizing individuals and organizations to get to work on the problem concerned.

I had heard Oldham speak at the Glasgow Quadrennial in 1921. But I got to know him personally when he came to Geneva in 1929 to urge the leaders of the various international Christian bodies to participate in the great task of confronting the challenge of the modern world. He brought us his paper on 'The New Christian Adventure', written for the International Missionary Council. This was a powerful appeal to stop living in a fool's paradise. He put the matter really more convincingly than the Jerusalem Conference itself. For 'Jerusalem' had suggested that the various religions could become allies in a common fight against modern materialism and 'against all evils of secularism'. And this sounded like a call to defend an old and passing world in the name of a vague concept of religion which had no biblical foundation. Oldham spoke of a new adventure. He wanted to lead Christians out of the world of illusions in which they were still living. They had to understand once and for all that the world was not becoming more and more Christian. But it was not by defence, but by facing boldly and creatively the challenge of secular civilization that the church would come to fulfil its mission. Hendrik Kraemer from Holland, who had returned from his first period of service in the Netherlands Indies, spoke at that meeting in the same way: 'We have not to make Christianity acceptable for the world, but an inescapable appeal and inevitable question to the world.' And he added a note which found a strong echo in our midst: 'We belong to the world and have in many respects fallen victim to its unChristian and deChristianized consciousness and thinking. Discussion with the modern world means primarily a searchingly critical discussion with ourselves, with Christianity as it is'.[7]

Oldham now began to carry out his strategic plan. With the tenacity of an explorer he began to look for men and women who could help in the reinterpretation of the Christian faith in the light of the unprecedented situation. As a layman himself he looked especially for laymen with creative minds. Whether they were active churchmen or not was not the most important question. The most important question was whether they could throw light on the real issues of our time.

He brought me into some of these curiously mixed groups. His role in the meetings was socratic: he would simply put questions and so stimulate the discussion. And he succeeded in getting all sorts of men – philosophers, sociologists, poets and scientists – to think about the central issue: What is the true diagnosis of the sickness of our civilization? What is the word of salvation?

This crusade by Oldham helped us greatly in our effort to rethink the task of our Federation. In the summer of 1930 Francis Miller and I called twenty-five people together at Zuylen in Holland to discover what we could say together about the message of the Federation.[8] I had to chair the meeting and found it a fascinating task, for right from the start we were dealing with the real issues. Oldham gave us again his sharp challenge. What is so deeply disconcerting about our situation, he said, is not secularism or the modern world in general, but the fact that the church, which pretends to have the word of God, has no word which comes to the modern world with real power. There was considerable agreement among us concerning the analysis of our time. But we got into deep water when we tried to draw up a common message. The differences in spiritual and cultural background between the Continent and the USA, between Britain and China, and so forth, were too great. The situations in which the students lived, to whom we had to communicate the message, were so diverse and we represented so many different theological and cultural traditions that we could not find common formulae. But we came to the conclusion that the most important thing was not to formulate agreements. It was rather to learn from the others how they understood the gospel and to let ourselves be challenged and enriched by the convictions of our partners in the dialogue. It was this intensive process of give and take which would give us the unity we sought. Thus I concluded: 'The message of the Federation is the message each of us gives after listening to the others.' And Pierre Maury gave us a final address in which he reminded us of the unshakable realities which held us together. Jesus Christ himself was the bond between us, 'richer than any of our formulas, more powerful to save than any of our theologies'.

This meeting in Holland was truly a meeting of the 'nursery' of the ecumenical movement. For seven years later eight of our number were leaders and speakers at the Oxford World Conference, and after the war twelve of us were serving as members of the staff or of committees in the World Council of Churches.[9] But it was also a meeting of a brains trust for the ecumenical movement. For many of the ideas which became part and parcel of the life of the ecumenical movement in and after 1937 can be traced back to our discussions of 1930.

At Zuylen in 1930 the topic of secularism was still a central theme and I had given an introduction on that subject. But before long I came to see that secularism was too negative a concept to explain the spiritual situation of the time. In 1931 I gave lectures on 'Nationalism as a Religion' and on 'God and the gods of the West', in which I tried to analyse the pseudo-religious character of the new movements among youth, of which fascism and national socialism were the most extreme but by no means the only examples. I was strengthened in the conviction that we were up against false religions when Karl Barth wrote at the end of 1931 his forceful article, 'Questions which Christianity Must Face' and attacked the 'Jerusalem' idea of an inter-religious front against materialism.[10] He asked whether Christians realized that Christianity was surrounded by new aggressive religions, that it had nothing to expect from these strange religions but war to the knife and that Christianity must on no account howl with the wolves? In his address to our European Student Christian Movement Conference at Bad Boll (Germany) in 1932 Oldham took up Barth's point: 'When men abandon their belief in God, they turn to false gods'.[11] He was on the way to the definition of the crucial issue which would become the theme of the Oxford Conference. Thus in the 'thirties the *leitmotiv* of my speaking and writing became the fight against the new forms of idol-worship. And the book which summed up what I had to say during those years carried therefore the title *None Other Gods*.[12]

Oldham realized that he would not be able to get very far as long as he had no organization at his disposal which could mobilize the churches. In 1934 he attended the Life and Work study conference at Paris on 'The Church and the State' at which I was also present. It was a meeting of high calibre. Max Huber, Emil Brunner and Nicolas Berdyaev were among the participants. Oldham saw that Life and Work with its study department (on the staff of which were Hanns Schönfeld of Germany and Nils Ehrenström of Sweden) could become the instrument which was needed to arrive at a thorough re-orientation of the witness of the churches. So he accepted the role of Chairman of the Study Commission of Life and Work which was to prepare for the World Conference of Life and Work in 1937. He threw himself into this task with astounding energy and expected us all to co-operate. It was said at the time that for Oldham the road to the Kingdom of God went through the dining room of the Athenaeum in London. For it was in that solemn setting that men of the most diverse background were put under the terrific pressure of Oldham's single-mindedness and almost forced to co-operate in his undertaking. Most of us, however, were grateful to be enlisted in his team and followed the leader gladly, even though on leaving the Athenaeum we realized that we had again had to promise to attend another preparatory meeting or write another memorandum. And there was this further compensation that, thanks to Oldham, one had an opportunity to meet people from all walks of life whom one would never have met otherwise.

NOTES

1. *The Church Times*, January 24th 1930.
2. *Canadian Journal of Religious Thought*, January–February 1931.
3. Letter of April 25th 1930.
4. *The Student World*, 1934, pp. 355–66.
5. See F. A. Iremonger, *William Temple*, p. 459.
6. *Introduction to Message*, Paper no. 1, 1930.
7. *The Student World*, October 1929, p. 420.
8. The only full account of this meeting which I have found is in the Dutch SCM periodical *Eltheto* (November 1930). The author is M. C. Slotemaker de Bruine.
9. The twelve were: F. P. Miller, Ambrose Reeves, Pierre Maury, Suzanne de Diétrich, Reinhold Niebuhr, J. H. Oldham, William Paton, H. P. Van Dusen, H. L. Henriod, John Mackay, W. Tindal and W. A. Visser 't Hooft.
10. I published this article in *The Student World*, 1932, p. 93.
11. *The Student World*, 1932, p. 195.
12. New York: Harper & Brothers; and London: SCM Press, 1937.

7 | *Students Find the Truth to Serve*

THIS WAS THE title which I gave to the report of the World's Student Christian Federation for the years 1931 to 1935. It meant to say that in the midst of the deep uncertainty about the future students were looking for unshakable truth demanding unreserved devotion and obedience. I quoted a student periodical which declared: 'Tired as we are of truths which are supposed to serve us, we seek the truth which demands to be served.'

There are passages in that report which sound as if they were written in 1968 or 1969 rather than in 1935. I said:

> These last few years, more than any other period of university life, have been characterized by political unrest in student circles. Student strikes, riots against minority groups (especially against the Jews), nationalistic demonstrations and anti-war campaigns, and above all the formation of student-sections of the new, generally extremist, political parties have transformed many universities from places of quiet learning into political arenas.

But there are other passages which show that the setting of those years had its own characteristics. I said:

> In East and West alike, in so-called democratic countries, in totalitarian states and in colonies, we find a tendency on the part of government and society to demand that professors and students shall study, discuss and propagate nothing except the doctrines approved and censored by the party or social group which is in power.

That is surely not as generally true today as it was then.

There was a big job to be done, but the World's Student Christian Federation seemed to be a poor instrument to do it. The great economic crisis had had a terrible effect on its income. I had become the General Secretary in 1932, but precisely at that time we had to begin to reduce the staff. There came a year (1934–5) in which the staff consisted of the General Secretary alone. But the activities were not reduced. In that year, 1935, we held a Social Studies Conference, a Theological Student Conference, a large conference on Missions

(Basle) and a meeting of the General Committee (Bulgaria). This was possible because the group of leaders of the Federation worked as a well co-ordinated team with great unity of purpose. Francis Miller of the USA, Reinold von Thadden and Hanns Lilje of Germany, Pierre Maury and Suzanne de Diétrich of France, Robert Mackie and Eric Fenn of Great Britain, Augustine Ralla Ram of India and others gave as much time and thought to the Federation and trusted each other so fully that the General Secretary was part of a team the members of which were all active in one way or another. We held our executive committee meetings in many different places, sometimes in very primitive surroundings. I remember a house in Canada where the only place to shave was the lake in front of the building. I had to ask Hanns Lilje, who was performing the same act next to me, to stand very still, for if he moved I could not see my face in the water. But I remember also a meeting in the beautiful castle Waldenburg in Saxony where we were the guests of the Fürst von Waldenburg. He was a great lover of Oriental art and so he enjoyed particularly the evenings when our colleague, T. Z. Koo, played the Chinese flute in the magnificent library. It happened that the Fürst's sister, the Princess of Wied, who had been for a short time the Queen of Albania, was staying at the castle. Francis Miller wanted to know more about that Albanian adventure and asked the Princess's old servant some questions about it. The answer revealed how totally the old-time servant identified himself with his master or mistress. He began: 'When we ascended the throne of Albania . . .'

Twenty-five years later a man came to me in a church in New York where I had preached. He asked if I recognized him. I hesitated a moment and then I remembered: 'You are Fürst von Waldenburg. But what are you doing here?' He told me that he had lost everything in the final stage of the war and the post-war period. So he had had to take a job as teacher in a small American college. Remembering his love of art my wife and I invited him to spend the afternoon among the medieval treasures of 'the Cloisters' and he responded eagerly.

From 1929 to 1939 I was also the editor of the quarterly, *The Student World*. I found this a most rewarding job. Our policy was to devote each issue to the discussion of a single problem and so to get an international and ecumenical perspective on it. Practically all issues which were debated in the student Christian movements and the university world appeared on the agenda. It was relatively easy to get the collaboration of first-rate contributors, for at that time the *Student World* was the only ecumenical magazine of a general character and could offer its contributors an international audience which they could not find elsewhere.

The list of subjects chosen reflects of course the specific religious situation of the 1930s. And most of the prophets of those years participated in the discussion: Karl Barth and Nicolas Berdyaev, Reinhold Niebuhr and Hendrik Kraemer, Emil Brunner and William Temple, Toyohiko Kagawa and J. H. Oldham, Stephan Zankov and H. P. Van Dusen. Some Roman Catholics, notably Yves

Congar and Robert Grosche, also participated. The themes included the Bible, the Church, Ecumenism, Missions, the vocation of the laity, men and women. But social and international affairs occupied an equally important place. The issues of peace and disarmament were dealt with by statesmen like Max Huber, Arthur Henderson and André Philip. And several numbers bore titles which seem today strangely familiar, for example 'The End of the Bourgeois', with contributions from Eugen Rosenstock-Huessy and Denis de Rougemont; or 'The Call to Revolution', with reports on revolutionary movements among students in many parts of the world. Student protest is not merely a modern phenomenon. And I wonder whether our protest in those days was not in some ways a more radical protest, in that it did not concentrate only on a transformation of the structures of society but also, and especially, on the basic attitude of man to society. I summarized in 1932 the articles on 'The End of the Bourgeois' in this way:

> Those communists, socialists and fascists who preach the gospel of collectivity and solidarity, but who continue to believe in the doctrine of society as an aim in itself, are no better than the individualist bourgeois with his liberalism. The end of the bourgeois is then only a new beginning, if we sacrifice our longing for securities of all kinds and subject our life and society to a God who breaks through our finiteness and makes us lead lives which point beyond themselves.

It was part of my task to visit many countries and to speak to students in many universities. That was often hard work. You had to be prepared for anything. In one university you were received as a foreign trouble-maker introducing dangerous thoughts; in the next you would be treated as a great world leader who ought to know the answer to all problems. There were badly prepared meetings with a very small attendance and there were meetings with an impressive audience. North America produced the heaviest schedules. My record was a series of 120 addresses and that meant of course that many were given between two nights in the Pulman.

The great danger of such a speaking tour is that you may get bored with your own speeches, for it is impossible to produce a new speech for each occasion. So in those unpleasant minutes when the chairman was making his generally far too elaborate introduction I had often a feeling of panic and asked myself: have I really anything worthwhile to give to these students? But once I was on my feet I felt different. All those eyes, which seemed to express a sense of expectation, forced me to produce thoughts and ideas. And even though the main themes of the speeches would remain more or less the same, each particular speech would be different. Thus every address became a new adventure in communication, and one never knew beforehand just how the address would turn out. That speaking is an adventure in communication is the reason why I have always had a profound dislike of speaking through an interpreter, for whether he was good or bad, he seemed to become a wall between me and the audience. Fortunately in many countries students could understand me directly, for I speak English, French, German and Dutch.

What did I talk about? I am afraid that in the earlier years many of my addresses did not sufficiently meet the real needs of the students. I talked about the world tasks of Christians without realizing that most of my hearers were deeply uncertain about the Christian faith. It happened in a British university that an Indian student who sat in the front row with a rather bored look on his face, opened the discussion with the simple question: 'Why bother about God?' And it happened in Djakarta that an Indonesian student asked: 'Can the speaker give an exact definition of the meaning of life?' And though few students put their questions in such an abrupt form, very many were just as much at sea as those two. I can illustrate this further by an article which appeared in the student-paper of the University of Oregon at the time of my visit. It said:

> Even the coughing had subsided. Five hundred or so students were giving their whole concentrated attention to the speaker.
>
> Dr Visser 't Hooft, with a sympathy that told of long association with young men and women, was explaining how today's youth more and more is being swallowed in the mass movements that sweep powerfully over the world.
>
> He had reached the climax of his analysis . . . 'Can this enlistment of youth in mass movements be stopped? Can youth find reintegration without those authoritarian leaders?'
>
> The speaker leaned forward. The audience almost stopped breathing.
>
> 'My answer to this question is "yes". There is a solution. I can't impose it on you or I'd be an authoritarian leader myself. I'll only lay it before you. That solution is Christianity'.
>
> Anti-climax. Again the young audience settled back to the usual foot-scraping and squirming. The speaker might just as well have said: 'the Townsend plan'.[1]
>
> It was not that they were irreligious. Almost all of them were Christians in a quiet, personal way, but the appeal of Christianity as an integrating personal and social philosophy was zero. Indeed a Christianity that is to furnish a focus in life for confused youth must be a very different Christianity from that practised today, It must be a Christianity that can find its way into the walls of everyday life, into the market places, into the courts of justice, into legislatures. Can our religious leaders give us that sort of vital social leadership? Youth will give them a chance.

That was the situation to which one had to speak. There was on the one hand the anti-Sunday school complex, the strong reaction against the traditional Christianity which they had come to know; there was on the other hand the search for certainty and reintegration. So I began to speak more and more about the substance of the faith. I wrote to Jetty, my wife:

> I try now to use everything as a pretext for evangelism. I take the line: You

do not really know what Christianity is all about. For you are confronted with a bourgeois church characterized by its sewing circles, and you are right in despising such a church. But do you really think that this means that God has disappeared? There follow many hours of discussion and real questions. There is real astonishment when they discover that there are young people who are not idiots and still are believers.

My book, *None other Gods*, which appeared in 1937 reflects the message which I tried to bring to students in those years. As the title indicates I sought to confront the Christian faith with the great heresies of the time as they found expression in politics and literature.

Various national student Christian movements felt that the time had come for a major evangelistic effort. For the movements on the European continent this was a new venture. Paris began in 1933 with a Mission to the Latin Quarter. The response surprised us all. Students flocked in considerable numbers to the Salle des Sociétés Savantes and in the discussion meetings we found students of all varieties who wanted to find out what the Christians have to say. We learned several lessons which would influence the many missions which were later organized in universities in several countries. One was that we must not present theories about God and man, but rather make 'a person to person call' and that the person who makes the call is Jesus himself. Another was that the message must be incarnate, that is, it must speak to the student as he lives in the midst of the intellectual and political crisis of the time. Pascal's 'This concerns you and the whole of you' became one of the most widely used themes. It proved also important to use Christian laymen as often as possible, for they were not suspect, as are professional Christians, and could show what the faith meant to them in their secular life. And the impact was strengthened when the group of speakers was fully ecumenical, so that there could be no question of any direct or indirect proselytism. Thus, in Paris, Nicolas Berdyaev, the Russian philosopher, Emanuel Mounier, the Roman Catholic writer and André Philip, the Protestant statesman, appeared on the same platform. And in Basle the Mission was organized by the Roman Catholic and Protestant student movements together.

I participated in twelve of these missions in Paris, Geneva, Lyons, Zürich, Basle, Montpellier, Utrecht, Lausanne and Belfast and wrote in 1935:

> We may gratefully say, without fear of overstatements, that in practically all missions of recent years we have entered in touch with large numbers of students who had no contact with the Christian fellowship. It has been a matter for constant amazement to see that in all universities where aggressive evangelistic work has recently been undertaken the response has been far greater than even the most optimistic dared to hope. And contacts have not been confined to formal addresses, for the best moments in many missions were those where there was real discussion, when questions, often difficult and critical ones, were asked or objections were raised.

It was in this give and take, in this struggle in which we were sometimes attacking or sometimes being attacked and humiliated that we have learned what evangelism means. We found that the strength of our case was not in argument or so-called apologetics, even less in the emotional fervour or oratorical eloquence with which we presented it. In so far as it went home at all, it was as a sober story about realities beyond ourselves, which needed only to be told as faithfully and clearly as possible. When we made elaborate introductions and started to beat about the bush we were just losing time and making students impatient. But when we presented Jesus Christ, we could be sure, if not of their agreement, at least of their concentrated attention. Of the many missions in which the writer of this report has been privileged to participate, none has seemed more truly to serve its purpose than the one in Paris in January 1935, which concentrated exclusively on a presentation of Jesus Christ.

An important aspect of the life of the Federation in those years was the renewed concern for bible study. This was of course part of a wider movement. Suzanne de Diétrich, a lay-woman who has done more than anyone else to 'open the Scriptures' for students and who joined the staff of the Federation in 1935, has described this movement in her *Rediscovering the Bible* and in *Le Renouveau Biblique*. After a period of a purely historical and critical approach to the Bible, theologians were again asking what the Bible was all about. Karl Barth's *Epistle to the Romans* had been a turning point and many biblical scholars were seeking to elaborate a biblical theology which took the results of higher criticism seriously, but which sought to give a coherent interpretation of the Bible as a whole.

I had to go through that process of rediscovery of the Bible. For I had left Leiden university with the impression that the Bible was really a collection of extremely heterogeneous voices. Barth had impressed me with his tremendous emphasis on the unconditional respect which the Word of God demanded. But I could not see how this authoritative Word of God could be found in a seemingly incoherent collection of writings. At this point I was greatly helped by two men. One was Sir Edwyn Hoskyns whom I had visited in Cambridge. His *Riddle of the New Testament* answered precisely the questions I was asking at that time. And soon afterwards I came into touch with Professor Julius Schniewind of Halle and studied his commentaries on the Gospels of Matthew and Mark, which I still consider the most penetrating of the many commentaries on the synoptic gospels. Hoskyns and Schniewind did not run away from the critical problems. Nor did they get bogged down in higher criticism. They showed that the historical approach leads to the conclusion that Jesus in a 'unique, isolated and creative' way 'wrought out in flesh and blood the obedience demanded by the Old Testament Scriptures and foretold by the prophets'; and that this must not be thought of as a human act, but as 'a descending act of God'. Although the

Bible was in one sense a collection of different voices, it was in another sense a book with a profound unity.

The Bible had been a bone of contention among Christians. Now it seemed to become a dynamic and creative factor in bringing Christians together again. I wrote an editorial for the *Student World* issue on the Bible in 1934 with the title: 'The Bible – a Meeting Place' and said:

> As Christians coming from different directions, we will meet here – or nowhere. The future of our unity depends on our willingness to make this pilgrimage together. It is not that we are on the verge of finding a universally acceptable formulation of the exact status of the Bible in our respective theologies, but simply that we come to the conclusion that this is the one place where we must all go to meet – no, not only each other, but God.

By the year 1937 it became possible to hold an international Federation conference which was wholly devoted to Bible study. I wrote after that meeting:

> At Bièvres not only did it become clear that the Bible is not dull, that it is not dumb and that it is indeed a meeting-place; but we found that we were being led together to such new discoveries as we had never expected to make. As we struggled together to understand the Bible 'new light broke forth from the Word' and thus Bièvres became an experience of renewal of life.
>
> How did it happen? I believe that the important point is that we did not take for granted that we knew the Bible, but worked hard for a new understanding of the Bible as a whole for our life as a whole ... The Bible becomes silent, when we try to force it to answer our questions. It speaks when we come to it as eager seekers for the truth of God. The alternative is not whether we read the Bible 'piously' or 'historically' and 'critically', but whether we read it egocentrically or theocentrically.[2]

At this point I must speak of the place which Rembrandt came to occupy in my life. For he helped me to get closer to the Bible. I had been intrigued by the fact that Rembrandt's vision of the biblical world in his mature years was so very different from that of most other great painters. His conception of Jesus was not only in sharp contrast with the Renaissance conception, but also with his contemporaries, such as Rubens, with his triumphalist Christ, or Guido Rémi with his sentimental saviour. And Rembrandt's vision was far more convincing because he seemed to have understood the secret of the coming of God in the form of a servant and in deep humiliation. Had Rembrandt really lived with the Bible? The vast literature about his life and art did not give a clear answer. The great Jacob Burckhardt had suggested that it was not because of his faith, but simply because of the popularity of biblical subjects, that Rembrandt had produced so many biblical works. I tried to get more light on this.

During the journeys in various countries of Europe and in the USA I could see most of the paintings (with the exception of the marvellous collection of the

Hermitage in Leningrad which I saw later). And I had the opportunity to visit several times the unique collection of Rembrandt etchings owned by Mr I. de Bruyn in Spiez. He was a Dutch banker who after his retirement had concentrated all his energy on gathering a complete collection of all the etchings. And he had succeeded, as no one is likely ever to succeed again, in bringing together copies of practically all of them and in a number of cases copies of the different states of the same etching. It was a rare experience to sit in that simple Swiss chalet before the self-portrait in which Rembrandt had portrayed himself as St Paul, and to pick up these treasures one after another. This was really the way to see Rembrandt. You could put side by side three different states of the 'Three Crosses' and see clearly how Rembrandt had struggled to express the full meaning of the crucifixion. Mr de Bruyn enjoyed the enjoyment of his visitors. He had acquired a remarkably thorough knowledge of Rembrandt's art. When the collection was exhibited in the Geneva museum he would himself show the visitors around. The story goes that certain visitors who thought that he was a warden, tried to give him a tip and were rather taken aback when he told them that the whole collection belonged to him.

There was also the fine collection of Pastor William Cuendet in Lausanne who had a deep insight into Rembrandt's biblical works and who gave me at the time of the invasion of the Netherlands the finest present I ever received. This was the etching of Jesus preaching, which summarizes all that Rembrandt had to say about Jesus and about the impression which his gospel made on his hearers.

I began to give lectures on Rembrandt's biblical art and found that this was a good way of confronting people with the biblical message. But there remained many questions and I found it a fascinating enterprise to endeavour to answer them. Why the great difference in interpretation of the Bible between the early and the later Rembrandt? How had he understood the humanity of Jesus? What was his relation to the baroque style of his time? What had been his attitude to the Reformed Church? In what spiritual climate had he lived? Could his art be called Protestant? I gave my answers to these questions in a number of articles which were finally collected in *Rembrandt and the Gospel*. I was pleased to find that the interest in the subject was so widespread that the book was translated into several languages, that it became the basis of television programmes in English, German and Dutch, and that it was well received by art historians. But the main gain was that the book did for many of its readers what it did for me, namely, allowed us to share in that deep encounter with the Scriptures which Rembrandt had experienced.

NOTES

1. The Townsend plan was a somewhat fantastic scheme emanating from California to solve the economic crisis by a system of old-age pensions.
2. *The Student World*, 1937, p. 352.

8 | *First Encounter with Awakening Asia*

IN 1933 I HAD a unique opportunity to meet Asian students in their own environment, for I became involved in the organizing of the first meeting of and for the Asian Student Christian Movements, held under the auspices of the World's Student Christian Federation. The idea had first been suggested by T. Z. Koo, the gifted layman from China, one of John R. Mott's 'discoveries', who with his clear, straightforward Christian message, presented in an Asian dress and often accompanied by a Chinese flute, had become a very popular speaker in the universities of many countries. The time had come to give Asian students a chance to get to know each other and to express their common mind. The meeting was to be held in Java where a new and promising Student Christian Movement had just come into existence through the patient work of Dr C. L. van Doorn and Mrs van Doorn. Thus I would have the privilege of being introduced to the younger generation in Asia in the most intensive way.

Four of us travelled together from Europe to Java: Francis P. Miller, the Chairman of the WSCF, Jean Gastambide of France, Jetty and I. We took a Dutch freighter, on which there was limited accommodation for passengers. The journey took twenty-two days and we did not touch any harbour between Port Said and Sabang (Sumatra). On such a journey the whole company on board becomes a closely knit family and on the bridge or on the deck during long evenings with the captain and the officers one is introduced to the mysteries of life on the sea.

Soon after arrival we went to an old and abandoned country home which had been chosen as the conference site. The lack of comfort was compensated by the beauty of the Javanese scenery: the winding river, wet rice fields divided in neat squares, clusters of high coconut-palms and a background of mountains in all shades of green, rising higher and higher until they became impressive volcanoes – and the whole picture dotted with the tiny figures of peasants, water buffaloes very white birds and very red flowers.

It was not difficult to get the meeting started. The students from India and China, Japan, Burma, the Philippines, Ceylon and Java were so curious about each other and had so much to talk about. Two subjects were uppermost in their minds: the issue of national independence and the question of the relation of the Christian faith to other religions. Those who came from countries under Western domination were convinced that as Christians they should participate in the struggle of their people for freedom, but they were not anti-Western. At the moment, they said, the West is in control and the East must co-operate, but the East has become so sensitive that this relation is now regarded as sinister. It must be reversed. Ours should be the initiative and control of the relationship, while we welcome the co-operation of the West. Augustine Ralla Ram of India put it in this way: We want to send all Westerners away on ships, but when they are still within a few miles of the coast we will send them a message: everybody who wants to come back in order to work under our leadership is most welcome.

Hendrik Kraemer spoke on the Christian message in relation to other religions. He was the right man for this difficult task, for he had made a deep study of Islam and of Javanese mysticism and that not only in a bookish way, but through intensive personal contact. He combined a deep respect for the faith he found in the Asian world with a profound conviction concerning the uniqueness of Jesus Christ. I had to chair the commission dealing with this theme. Up till that time the question of the centrality of Christ had been for me a formidable intellectual problem. Now I was faced with it as an everyday problem in the life of Asian students. It was encouraging to find that the very fact of meeting Asian Christians helped to answer the problem. For we saw before our eyes that Christianity was not indissolubly linked to one culture and one part of the world. Christ belonged to all men. And Jesus, as I put it in an address on 'The Significance of Jesus Christ', goes his own way. He does not accept appropriation for any partial or egotistic purposes. He does not fit into our standards of morality, or reason. He does not follow us. He asks us to follow him. And this became our common answer to the issue of uniqueness.

Sarah Chakko of India, who, nearly twenty years later, would become the first woman president of the World Council of Churches, put it very simply:

> Once the unveiled Christ is before us, we cannot say: no. We have to join with him in the creation of a new world. This naturally means an obligation to pass on the message of love and redemption, but it means no longer inflicting my ideas on another person, for what I pass on is not my gift to someone else or God's gift to me alone, but God's gift to all humanity.

During the conference the newly born Student Christian Movement in Java was admitted to membership in the World's Student Christian Federation. The chairman of the SCM of Java, Johannes Leimena, responded. He had just completed his medical studies and seemed to be destined to spend his life in the medical profession. In fact he became a minister in the first government of the Republic and later Vice-Premier of Indonesia.

Our plan had been that soon after the Java Conference the group of four should go on to Japan and China. But that plan had to be given up, for my voice went on strike. The specialist to whom I turned found a growth between the vocal chords and decided to operate immediately in his office. It was alarming that during the operation his hand holding the instrument trembled so that he did not succeed in removing the cause of trouble. He became more and more nervous. Francis Miller, who had accompanied me, could stand it no longer and said: 'Doctor, you are not in a fit state to perform an operation.' The doctor agreed meekly and asked me to come back in two or three days time, early in the morning. On that second occasion the operation was performed with the greatest precision and speed. It was only many years later that I understood what had gone wrong: I noticed an item in a newspaper that a Dutch specialist whose initials were given had been involved in a narcotics scandal. It was my surgeon. At the beginning of the day his hand was steady: later on the drug began to take its toll.

But I was told that I would have to remain silent for a period of one or two months. So Miller and Gastambide left for Japan and China and Jetty and I had to remain in Java. Where was I to go? Jetty's uncle, B. C. de Jonge, was at that time the Governor General of the Netherlands Indies. So we went to the Palace in Buitenzorg (Bogor). In this vast place with its hundreds of servants we were well received, but it proved to be rather an ordeal to sit through official dinners without being able to do more than give a nod or a smile. So the 'Great Lady' (as the wife of the Governor General was called) suggested that we should go to the mountain residence of the Governor General in Tjipanas. This was a wonderful solution. For Tjipanas is an incredibly beautiful place, and the residence had lovely tropical gardens. Those weeks were the quietest time we have ever known. Especially for Jetty, for – since the servants spoke only Sundanese and I did not speak at all – there were days when she heard no human voice. I tried to communicate by writing feverishly on pieces of paper, but that was not a very satisfactory way of keeping up the conversation.

This involuntary holiday remains a precious memory. It was not that I found silence a shortcut to sanctification. For I had not chosen to be silent. But the early mornings when Jetty and I sat looking at the mountains in that lovely tropical dawn, the long walks through the sawahs or on the slopes of the great mountain, and the remoteness from the world, provided an opportunity for reflection such as I had not had before. When the weeks of monastic life were over, the doctor declared that I could continue the journey. We decided to spend more time in Java and to visit the island of Bali about which we had heard so much.

Having received a thorough Asian baptism at the student conference at Tjiteureup I found that I was not on the same wavelength as the great majority of the Dutchmen in Java. For the Netherlands Indies was for them above all the *Netherlands* Indies. They were largely unaware of the rapid changes that were taking place among the Indonesians. The Governor General's conviction, which he expressed more than once in public, that the Dutch had been three hundred years in the country, and that it would take another three hundred years before the country would be ready for some form of independence,[1] was shared by the vast majority of the Dutch. It was certainly true that the Dutch administration had done a great deal for the Indonesian people in education, public health and economic development. But the atmosphere was one of paternalism and the one dominating preoccupation was to maintain order. Both Indonesians and Dutchmen who challenged the presuppositions of the official policy were considered and treated as disloyal citizens. H. van Mook, a government official, who was to become Governor General after the war, told me that the one Dutch periodical which stood for a policy of co-operation with the constructive forces in the nationalist movement[2] and to which he, as well as several professors of the Juridical High School in Batavia, and Hendrik Kraemer contributed, could not continue to appear, because of the fierce opposition which it aroused in government circles.

And those leaders of the national movement, like Sukarno, who made propaganda for independence, were imprisoned and (or) exiled. The government certainly had a paternal concern for the people. I found that the Governor General, in spite of his sarcasms, which gave him the reputation of being a man with little human feeling, had real sympathy for the Indonesians and that those Indonesians who accepted the principle of Dutch rule were treated with civility. It was not his fault that he had to govern in a time of financial crisis and could not do all that he would have liked to do in the realm of education and social welfare. I came to respect him as a man with a strong sense of duty and with real courage – but I had to disagree with the principles on which his policy was based.

Hendrik Kraemer helped me to see the Indonesian side of the picture. He was convinced that the only justification of Dutch rule could be to prepare the people for independence. He saw the weaknesses of the national movement very clearly: it was at that time so largely concerned with big words rather than with hard work. But he believed that it was in tune with historical development. And the Christian duty was to help to strengthen a people to arrive at real emancipation. So he gave me introductions to some of the national leaders and especially to those who were working for emancipation at a deep level. One was Dewantoro, the leader of the Taman Siswo (Pupil's Garden) educational movement. His burning conviction was that the national movement could not become strong and healthy unless the people could rediscover their cultural identity. At the moment the indigenous culture was largely unknown to the Indonesians themselves. Western education was not to be rejected, but could not replace education in the spirit of the best tradition of the East. His schools, which were now growing up in many parts of Indonesia, did not accept government subsidies, for Dewantoro felt that they should stand wholly on their own feet.

Dr Sutomo, the physician, who belonged to the first generation of national leaders, had similar convictions. What we need first of all, he said, is character. The political issues are secondary. The great obstacles put in the way of the national movement can be used as opportunities to form character. The great task is not to fight the Dutch, but to develop one's own moral and spiritual power. He agreed in many ways with Gandhi though he found him too anti-Western and too little concerned with the social structure.

I came away from these conversations with the feeling that it was an immense tragedy that there was no real dialogue between such eminently constructive national leaders and the Dutch authorities and that such builders of the future Indonesia were considered as men thinking dangerous thoughts.

On the eve of our departure from Indonesia I wrote down this question: 'If it is true that the justification of colonial policy must be to help a people to develop itself, are we not in fact undermining the *raison d'être* of our presence in Indonesia by resisting all movements which arise out of the life of the people itself?' A few months later at a Student Christian Movement conference in Holland I shared this concern with Dutch students. I spoke of the bitterness among the young Indonesians, including the Christians, and asked whether we were not failing in our historical task to lead Indonesia on the way to self-expression and self-government.

We had some time left before we had to go on to India. So we visited student centres in Java and spent an unforgettable ten days in Bali. We had heard much about it, for just at that time there was going on a passionate public debate about whether missions should be allowed to operate in the island. Some small Christian groups had been formed there and the Church of East Java had been requested by these Christians to send pastors. But then came a reaction. A number of anthropologists and artists were strongly opposed to any form of Christian work on the island. Should this precious and unique example of old Indonesian culture not be protected from Western influence? Would the astounding harmony of Balinese religious, social and artistic life not be undermined if the disturbing Christian faith were introduced? Hendrik Kraemer had taken up this challenge with his customary energy. He had shown that no culture could live any longer in complete isolation. The invasion by Western tourists was a much more disturbing element than Christianity. And missions had learned their lesson. Nobody wanted to westernize the Balinese. What the Church of East Java and he himself had in mind was to help the small church in Bali to work out its own forms of life in the light of its own cultural background.

Was Bali really that 'last paradise' which the newspapers and the tourist agency brochures described in such glowing terms? At first sight it really deserved that description. We were fortunate in arriving at a time when there were practically no tourists. On several occasions we were the only foreigners present at the village dances. And so we had the rare experience of watching a people which still expressed itself with complete spontaneity, naturalness and creativity in a common artistic life, so that beauty had become an integral part of their society. Jetty remarked that it would take a Rembrandt to do justice to such scenes. Everything seemed to conspire to produce a deep harmony: the enormous waringin trees, the gracious dancing children, the gamelan music with its haunting melodies; and even the pigs which suddenly crossed in front of the dancers, and the dogs which came to see whether they could not steal something edible from the sacrificial gifts at the temple entrance.

It was the time of the Balinese New Year. Every village was preparing its decorations. The women, straight as candles, carried on their heads the baskets of flowers and fruits to the temples. There was also the somewhat frightening monster dance, during which several boys danced in hypnotic trance and turned their daggers against themselves. When one of them came rushing up in our direction I reacted instinctively by tipping Jetty's chair over backwards so that she fell in the grass. Before long the boys were de-hypnotized as the priest rubbed their faces with the beard of the monster.

We were fortunate in having an introduction to the assistant resident for South Bali of the Netherlands Indies Government, Mr H. Jansen. He had made a deep study of Indonesian culture and could throw light on many of Bali's mysteries. Jansen had a deep affection for the Balinese, but knew too much about them to consider Bali as a paradise. It was also, he told us, 'the island of the demons'. There was much fear and much black magic. And there were many signs of disintegration of the traditional culture. He was therefore not against missions. The Balinese, Jansen said, deserved to know Christianity. But it was essential to show imagination in making the Christian approach. The Christians should not be uprooted, but should rather, as Kraemer wanted, play their full part in Balinese society.

In December 1933 we arrived in India. My first task was to give an address at the large Quadrennial Conference of the Student Christian Movement of India, Burma and Ceylon, in Allahabad. The subject was 'Christ – the Revealer of God to Man'. In my eagerness to share the insights which I had received from Karl Barth, and with the rather naïve assumption that Indian students were more or less like European students, I had prepared an address which went right over the heads of the audience, most of whom were extremely young. I thought that I had made a great mistake. But years later one young Ceylonese theologian told me that this address had opened up a new world for him. This was D. T. Niles who has since given such strong leadership to the Asian churches and who became the Asian President in the Presidium of the World Council of Churches. I do not pretend that this one example is a good excuse for neglecting the problem of communication, but I have found it a consolation to think that what seem to us to be failures may be occasions when we are used in ways we do not realize at the time.

During the days of the conference three or four of us went to call on Pandit Jawaharlal Nehru. He had been released from prison in August 1933 and was to be sent back to prison in February 1934, so we were lucky to find him at home. In the large family mansion we were received without any formality. He impressed us by his frankness and straightforwardness. There was no nonsense about him. Our questions did not receive vague or diplomatic answers, but precise and substantial ones. Thus he made it quite clear that there were considerable differences between his outlook and that of Mahatma Gandhi. For him the Mahatma remained the great leader. The masses were loyal to him. Nehru wanted to continue to co-operate closely with him. But he spoke quite openly of the two big issues on which he did not see eye to eye with Gandhi. The first was the social issue. Nehru had opted for socialism. Gandhi was not willing to commit himself at this stage to any particular social philosophy. The second issue had to do with religion. For Nehru organized religion was always on the side of the *status quo*. India stood in need of science rather than of religion. We invited Nehru to visit the Student Christian Movement Conference. He accepted and received a tremendous ovation from the students. But he did not react as a demagogue who rejoices in his popularity. His speech was extremely simple. The one thing he tried to get across was that national independence, which was now the first goal, was not an end in itself. It was a step on the way to social justice.

I was fascinated by this problem of the relation between the two national leaders and discussed the matter with every group of Indians I met. In an article on 'The Idol of Young India'[3] I described the different attitudes of the two men as follows:

> Instead of Gandhi's constant references to the age-old tenets of Hinduism Nehru relies on an astounding familiarity with doctrines of mass action and economic revolution. Instead of the never completely understood and often unexpected aphorisms of an old-world sage the matter of fact clearest statements of a twentieth century politician.

It seemed at that time that Nehru, with his strong appeal to youth, would lead India in a purely Marxist direction. But Nehru was still on the move. During the second world war he wrote *The Discovery of India* and when I met him again in 1949 it was clear that that discovery had made him a more Indian, though not less modern leader.

I was astonished to find that wherever I went in India people were ready to discuss religion. Some of the most interesting conversations were those held with fellow-passengers during the long train journeys. There was obviously a great openness for Christianity. But in the vast majority of cases Jesus was simply added as another 'avatar', another heavenly messenger, to the many others who had their place in the pantheon. The police officer who showed me his copy of the *Bhagavad Gita* with a picture of Jesus pasted inside the cover was really on the same Indian road as the monks of the Ramakrishna mission who had in their chapel a window representing Christ and another representing Ramakrishna, and who celebrated Christmas by bringing flowers to the statue of Christ and by reading the Sermon on the Mount. These monks made their position quite clear. To them when Christ says, 'I and the Father are one', he tells us to discover God in ourselves. Thus every man can find God in his own religion. And we can revere all the religious prophets and teachers. The basic principle was the old

Hindu concept of the identity of God and the soul.

It was not astonishing that in seeking to meet the challenge of this type of Hinduism a certain number of Christian intellectuals tried to work out a more Indianized form of Christianity. The leader of this group was a judge, P. Chenchiah, who had made a deep study of Hindu thought. The group called themselves 'the comrades in arms'. They were deeply critical of the methods of Western missions and considered the Indian church as a foreign institution. What was needed, they held, was a Christianity which would be wholly rooted in Indian life. The Old Testament should be replaced by the old Hindu Scriptures. Christ would be shown to be the crown of Hinduism.

I found the discussion with these men extremely illuminating. For they seemed to be so very right in their criticisms of Western missions. All during our Asian journey I had been shocked by the self-evident manner in which Western traditions in music, in architecture, in liturgy, in doctrine, had been transplanted in Asia. Were we not ourselves to blame for the great outcry in Asia that Christianity was no more than an aspect of Western civilization and that missions were just an expression of Western imperialism? But I saw at the same time that a simple adaptation of the gospel to Asian culture would lead to a distortion of its central affirmations. To put Christ in the setting of the Hindu scriptures rather than of the Old Testament was to make him another Christ, a Christ who would not face men with a clear choice, but confirm them in their natural tendency to a vague syncretism.

I left India with a strong desire to return, for I had come to have a deep affection for its people and to take a deep interest in its struggles for new nationhood and new answers to its spiritual problems.

At the end of 1938 Jetty and I visited India again in order to attend the World Conference of the International Missionary Council at Tambaram (Madras). The IMC had invited the World's Student Christian Federation to bring some twenty students to the meeting. Two of these travelled with us: a German student, Gerhard Brennecke, who was already deeply interested in missions, and a Swiss student, Jacques Rossel, who had so far not been in contact with the missionary world. The best proof of the wisdom of inviting young people to ecumenical gatherings is that Brennecke became director of the Berlin Missionary Society and Rossel of the Basle Missionary Society.

'Tambaram' was the first ecumenical meeting in which one half of the delegates were from the churches in Asia, Africa, Latin America and the Pacific islands. So it provided an ideal opportunity to get an overall view of the Christian situation in the world. That view was in some ways encouraging. For here one could see that in nearly all parts of the world the church had taken root and had produced its own national leadership. And the quality of that leadership was high. To take just a few examples: Toyohiko Kagawa, who was at the same time a great evangelist and a social prophet in Japan; V. Azariah, the pioneer of church unity in India; Albert Luthuli, best known as leader of the Bantu National Congress in South Africa, but at the same time a convinced Christian; C. Y. Cheng, the grand old man of Chinese Christianity. And my old friends of the Student Christian Movement were there: D. T. Niles who gave one of the most substantial addresses, Leimena of Indonesia, Ralla Ram of India and so many others.

But we could not forget that we were meeting in an hour of peril. John R. Mott, who presided, said in his emphatic manner, 'We have assembled at one of the most fateful moments in the life of mankind. Not in our life-time, if at any time, have Christians come together when men were bearing such impossible burdens, or undergoing such persecution and suffering.' The hour in which the universality of the church became clearer than ever before was also the hour when the divisive and oppressive forces were stronger than ever.

Within the fellowship of the meeting the very real tensions among the conference members – between Chinese and Japanese, British and Indian, South African whites and South African blacks, Germans and other continental Europeans – were transcended by the one common purpose. The conference was less successful in dealing with the basic theological conflict for which Hendrik Kraemer's book, written for the conference, on *The Christian Message in the Non-Christian World*, provided the focus. The issue was once again in what sense the Christian message was unique and whether there is divine revelation in the non-Christian religions. In fact that conflict was not resolved in Tambaram, but Kraemer had at least forced the whole missionary movement to reconsider its basic assumptions.

The real significance of the conference was that from now on it would be impossible to think of the missionary and indeed of the total ecumenical task without taking the voice of the churches of Asia, Africa and Latin America seriously. It was a great gift that this happened just at the time when the World Council of Churches started its process of formation. For it was clear that before long these churches would help to make the ecumenical movement truly world-wide.

NOTES

1. See *Herinneringen van Jhr. Mr B. C. de Jonge*, 1968, p. 351.
2. *De Stuw*.
3. *The Student World*, XXVII, no. 2, 1934, p. 260; and *The Christian Century*, May 23rd 1934.

9 | *Discovery of the Eastern Orthodox World*

DURING MY YEARS at the University of Leiden I had learned next to nothing about Eastern Orthodox Christianity. The great authorities of those days such as Adolf von Harnack and Ernst Troeltsch considered Eastern Orthodoxy to be a petrified form of medievalism. We were given the impression that nothing had happened in the East for the last thousand years.

The first inkling that Orthodoxy had a vital word to say came to me from Dostoyevsky. I devoured the great novels. Raskolnikov and Prince Mychkine and the Karamazovs were real human beings who knew the deeper dimensions of life. They were far more real than the pale figures of the so-called realistic Western literature. They were fighting with God and with the devil. So I wondered whether the Christianity of the East had not been misunderstood and might not bring to us in the West a much needed challenge to face the ultimate questions of life and death.

At the first ecumenical conferences which I attended I heard a number of Eastern speakers. The venerable Patriarch Photios of Alexandria and Metropolitan Germanos of Thyateira were prominent figures at the Stockholm Conference. And at the Helsingfors World Conference of the YMCAs a very tall and impressive Greek bishop, Athenagoras of Corfu, led one of the worship services. But I was just a greenhorn and did not approach them. There was no way of my knowing or imagining the role this Greek bishop would play in my life at the time when he would become the Ecumenical Patriarch of Constantinople.

The first strong personal impression of the significance of Eastern Orthodoxy for the ecumenical movement came to me in 1926 at the meeting of the General Committee of the World's Student Christian Federation in Nyborgstrand (Denmark). The evening during which we heard the story of the Russian Student Christian Movement formed in emigration opened our eyes to a new world, a world of suffering, but also a world of victorious faith. Gustav Kullmann, a Swiss who had identified himself totally with the Russian refugees, and Nicolas Zernov succeeded in making us feel that the experience of the Russian Christians was part of the history of the whole Christian family. Did not the fact that, suddenly, hundreds of thousands of Russians, including outstanding Christian thinkers, had been forced to come to the West mean that we had at last an opportunity to come to know the treasures of Orthodox spirituality, and that we could enter into a true sharing between the East and the West? In the hour of crisis the young Russians had rediscovered the true meaning of their worship and the relevance of the Orthodox conception of the church. Did the rationalistic and individualistic West not need this contribution?

My curiosity had been awakened. I was therefore glad that soon afterwards I had an opportunity to become involved in the creating of closer contacts between the West and the East. The youth commission of 'Life and Work', of which I was at that time the secretary, had decided to organize a meeting on religious education in Orthodox countries. In order to prepare that meeting I had to visit the main Orthodox centres in south east Europe. Jetty and my brother Hans accompanied me. The journey proved to be full of adventure, for those winter months of January and February 1929 were exceptionally cold and stormy. On the primitive boat which took us from Brindisi to Corfu Jetty and I had the 'Cabine de Luxe', but the 'luxury' consisted in visits of rats to inspect our luggage. So it was a relief to arrive in Corfu.

Our host was Metropolitan Athenagoras, a keen supporter of the YMCA and of the ecumenical movement. I wrote about him:[1]

> The Metropolitan is certainly the most widely loved man among the Corfiotes. If you take a walk with him through the narrow picturesque streets where the money changers at their small tables remind you of Biblical narratives, you will only proceed slowly. Small boys will run up and kiss his hand, while they chatter merrily about their many daily interests with him. He takes time for them and will not let them go without throwing a ray of friendly interest in their hearts.

The Metropolitan was already deeply concerned about Christian unity. He had the convictions which would later make him a Patriarch of Constantinople who deserved the title Ecumenical Patriarch, not only because of ancient tradition, but also because he was a leader in the cause of Christian unity. I noted especially his questions: 'Is unity not the desire of Christ? And is not Christ strong enough to realize it even if we go on sleeping? Does not the whole peace of the world depend finally on this condition of unity among the followers of Christ?'

It was fortunate that the first Eastern Orthodox church leader whom I came to know personally was a man of such spiritual calibre and of such deep conviction about the common destiny of all Christians. He made me believe that it was not an illusion that East and West could meet again.

After Corfu, Athens. It was a bit of a shock that when we approached the Acropolis we were received by a barrage of snowballs. Professor Hamilcar Alivisatos, who had been one of the very first Orthodox theologians to participate in ecumenical meetings, gave me a thorough introduction to the theological and ecclesiastical complexities of the Orthodox world. In the field of Christian work among youth I found far more activity than I had dared to hope. Next came Istanbul and my first visit to the Ecumenical Patriarchate of Constantinople. The aged Patriarch Basilios was friendly, but it was clear that he had little freedom of action because of the political tension between Greece and Turkey.

The Orient Express was to take us to Sofia. But before it had reached the Bulgarian border the train found itself confronted with such masses of snow that it was quite impossible to continue. The only available snow-ploughs were on the Asian side of the Bosporus. So there we stood, three days and three nights. When bread became scarce, an attempt was made to dispatch some peasants with camels to the next village, but the camels refused their perilous mission. So the men walked for twenty-four hours through the snow to get us bread. I asked what they would be paid. The answer was that they were just commandeered. I organized a collection in the train and found the peasants delighted with this unexpected gift.

In Sofia I was warmly received by Professor Stephan Zankov, a prophet of ecumenism in the Orthodox world. He was extremely interested in the plan for the conference. And in Yugoslavia Bishop Ireneus of Novi Sad, friend of many Western church leaders, gave great encouragement. It was now clear that I could go ahead with the proposed conference.

In 1930 I made two visits to Greece. The first was to attend a consultation of Orthodox church leaders called by John R. Mott, to discuss the policy of the YMCA in Orthodox countries. It was a most representative gathering and included many of the ecclesiastics and theologians whom I had come to know during my first journey to the East. Dr Mott presided over the meetings with such authority and solemnity that no Eastern patriarch could have done better. I was again his adjutant. The only trouble was that Dr Mott's private remarks to me could be easily overheard. I had a shock when he said in quite audible voice, 'Is that man who wants to speak a gasbag?'

One of the most impressive figures at the meeting was Bishop Nicolai Velemirovitch, at that time bishop of the ancient but small diocese of Ochrida in Macedonia. I asked him how many church members he had in his diocese. He said, 'Many millions'. He saw my amazement and added,'I count all the faithful who have lived there since the beginnings of Christianity.' This was for me a lesson in Orthodox thought about the nature of the church.

On the way back I travelled on the boat with Metropolitan Evlogii, Russian Metropolitan in Western Europe. He told me that he was going to Bari in Southern Italy to visit the shrine of St Nicholas, for this saint had a very great place in the life of Russian Orthodoxy. He asked me whether I would like to accompany him. To a Dutchman, for whom St Nicholas is the saint to whom we owe the most important family festival of the year, this invitation was irresistible. In the Cathedral in Bari we had some difficulty in making ourselves understood. The Metropolitan spoke in Russian to his interpreter, the interpreter in English to me and I in a mixture of Latin and Italian to the local priests. We were brought to the crypt; after prayers a small door was opened in the altar, through which only the upper part of the body could enter. When my turn came to put my head into the altar and to pay respect to the relic of the Saint I was still reflecting on the ecumenical problem how the saint had acquired a significance in the West which was so completely different from that in the East.

The conference on religious education, for the preparation of which I had been responsible, met later in the same year in Salonica. It was a small meeting, but of high quality. Father Nissiotis of Athens told the remarkable story of his Association of Orthodox Youth and its attempts to bring Orthodoxy to youth and youth to Orthodoxy. The representatives of the Russian emigration, Professor Zenkovsky and Professor Leo Zander, gave a moving account of the Orthodox renaissance among the Russians of the emigration. A report was worked out and this was submitted to all Orthodox churches.

The main impressions I had so far gathered from these contacts with the Orthodox world, and which I reported in various articles, were the following: (It was certainly not true that the Orthodox churches were fossilized. Instead there were signs of spiritual vitality.) I wrote:

One has, however, to remember that the Orthodox Church has its own standards of evaluation. Its future development will not necessarily follow the lines which Protestants or Catholics want to follow in their own churches. A true Orthodox will, for instance, never agree with certain liberal Protestants that progress must lead the church away from the doctrinal tradition of the ecumenical councils. Neither will he measure the vitality of his church by a purely pragmatic standard of its social effect on civilization.

But it was true (and it had been strongly emphasized by the Orthodox speakers at our various meetings) that a critical situation had arisen with regard to the younger generation. I further wrote:

The Orthodox nations are passing through a process of rapid secularization. What took place in Western Europe since the days of the Renaissance seems to happen in Eastern countries in the course of a few decades. The struggle is, as the Bishop of Ochrida put it, between various kinds of intellectualism and the revelation in Christ; the battle on the Areopagus between the Athenians and St Paul is to be fought once more.[2]

I found that there was a great lack of communication between the Orthodox churches themselves. In fact most of the relationships which existed were not due to initiatives taken by the churches, but rather to initiatives taken by the ecumenical organizations. The time had come to strengthen these contacts.

As to the relationships between Eastern and Western Christianity, the question was whether Western churches were willing to enter into true fellow-ship with Orthodoxy – based on mutual respect and understanding – and to help the Orthodox world to express its own God-given mission in a fuller way.

I felt therefore that in addition to the discussion between European and American theologies a real dialogue between Eastern and Western Christianity was urgently required for the health of the ecumenical movement. I wrote therefore a small book in French on Non-Roman Catholicism[3], in which I tried to show that there was a 'catholic' tradition which was quite different from Roman Catholicism, and which was now becoming one of the main components of the ecumenical movement. I called attention to the great spiritual contribution which this catholicism could make to the other churches, and I noted what questions Protestantism would want to address to non-Roman catholicism. I concluded: 'Non-Roman Catholics and Protestants need each other in order to be challenged, warned and humiliated. A genuine discussion between them will lead to less cocksureness, less pride and a deeper understanding of God's Will for each confession.'

In the following years my conviction that much light would come to us Western Christians from the East was strengthened as I came to know Nicolas Berdyaev, the Russian Christian philosopher who had been exiled because of his courageous stand for spiritual freedom. I published a number of his articles in *The Student World* and brought him to our student conferences. To visit him in his study in Clamart (Paris) was almost like visiting the Doctor Faust of the famous Rembrandt etching. With his velvet biretta on his disorderly shock of hair, surrounded by books, which even filled the bathtub in the next room, he seemed the incarnation of the search after truth. He has said in his autobiography: 'I brought with me the consciousness of the crisis of historical Christianity.' He understood, as few others, what the rise of communism meant for both West and East. So he could help us to understand our own crisis. And his message was not that of a mere return to tradition, but that of the actualizing of all the deep potential forces of the Christian faith. He was, so to say, not a pre-communist; he was a post-communist and pointed the way to a Christianity which would combine true freedom with a deep sense of community. I have a feeling that his message will still play a decisive role in the future of his own beloved Russia.

NOTES

1. *The World's Youth*, April 1929.
2. *The World's Youth*, April 1930.
3. The title of the English translation is *Anglo-Catholicism and Orthodoxy, A Protestant View*, London, 1933.

| *First Contacts with Roman Catholics*

In the milieu in which I lived in Holland Roman Catholicism was considered as a strange survival of an unenlightened age. My grandfather, on mother's side, a leader and spokesman of Free Masonry, had been engaged in many battles with the Roman Catholics. I still have his annotated copy of the Encyclical *Pascendi Dominici Gregis* of 1907 in which Pius X condemned modernism. The annotations reveal my grandfather's indignation about the obscurantism of the encyclical.

During the years at the University of Leiden we heard a good deal about the history of the Roman Catholic Church. But it did not occur to anybody to take Roman Catholicism seriously as a partner in the theological dialogue, and among the many books we were supposed to study there were none by Roman Catholic theologians.

I met a good many Roman Catholic student-leaders in the relief work for Central European students, but this did not lead to any deeper contacts. And in the years when I began to participate in the ecumenical movement the general Roman Catholic attitude to the new attempts to bring the churches together was so negative and even hostile that I felt little inclination to give much time and energy to the study of Roman Catholicism. Soon after the Stockholm Conference of 1925 the Swiss theologian Charles Journet (later Cardinal Journet) had written a violent attack against 'Life and Work'.[1] Journet described the undeniable theological weakness of the Stockholm Conference not in terms of an extraordinarily difficult new beginning but in terms of the general failure of Protestantism. In his view the early ecumenical movement was a movement towards theological indifferentism and towards a woolly liberalism. This seemed to me to be of the nature of caricature rather than of valid criticism.

In 1928 the Encyclical *Mortalium Animos* made this view of the ecumenical movement the official view of the Roman Catholic Church. It was a disconcerting document. The authors had obviously not even taken the trouble to make a real study of the available ecumenical documents. That the Roman Catholic Church, given its conception of the church, felt obliged not to participate in ecumenical meetings was one thing, but that it should misinterpret the motives of the ecumenical leaders in such an irresponsible manner was another thing. A few months after the publication of the Encyclical I attended the Life and Work meeting in Prague and heard Archbishop Nathan Söderblom, Archbishop Germanos of Thyateira, Professor Wilfred Monod and others express their sorrow about the stand which the Vatican had taken. The one consolation was that the encyclical seemed to prove that the ecumenical movement had begun to make a deep impression among Roman Catholics in a number of countries. For Rome would surely not have felt the need for such a sharp warning, if the attempt to bring the churches together had not made a considerable stir among Roman Catholic theologians and laymen.

These were indeed black years in the relations between the ecumenical movement and the Roman Catholic Church. In 1932 I had occasion to visit Rome. Because of my interest in Eastern Orthodoxy I went to see the head of the Oriental Institute, Monsignor Michel d'Herbigny. He was at that time the number one specialist of the Vatican on relations with the Eastern churches and the chairman of a special committee concerning Vatican policy with regard to Russia. I found him most ready to express his opinions. He did not believe that a renaissance was taking place in the Orthodox churches. The Russian professors in Paris were not following the true Orthodox tradition. Their teaching was innovation leading to deformation. He gave me a brochure in which he had expressed his anxiety about the Protestant influence on Orthodoxy which would make the Orthodox indifferent Christians or even unbelievers. This conversation threw a good deal of light on the general attitude of the Vatican at that time. The policy was obviously to use every opportunity for converting individual Orthodox Christians to Rome. Monsignor d'Herbigny's special interest was to prepare Roman Catholic missionaries for the conversion of Russia. I heard many years later that he had secretly ordained a number of priests and sent them to Russia as laymen. But the plan proved a complete failure. The priests were arrested one by one. What could be the reason? It was found that Mgr d'Herbigny's organization was infiltrated by communist agents. The monsignor was later sent back to a monastery.[2]

Fortunately this conversation was not the only one I had in Rome with prominent church leaders. I visited the Benedictines at San Anselmo and was much impressed by the classical simplicity and beauty of their liturgical life. When we walked in the garden I pointed to the Vatican on the other side of the city and asked whether San Anselmo had close relations with the Vatican. My Benedictine companion answered, 'That is another world'. I began to realize that Roman Catholicism was not as monolithic as we imagined it to be.

It was in that same year 1932 that I had at last opportunity to participate in a serious ecumenical dialogue with Roman Catholics. The World's Student Christian Federation, true to its pioneering tradition, did not accept *Mortalium Animos* as an insuperable obstacle to ecumenical contacts with Roman Catholics. Its ecumenical commission, on which Henri-Louis Henriod and Suzanne de

Diétrich were especially active, decided to hold an ecumenical retreat with Orthodox, Protestant and Roman Catholic participation. This had to be done very quietly and without any publicity so as to avoid ecclesiastical difficulties. So we met in a remote place in the Alsace, in a house which belonged to the family de Diétrich. This was a new experience. Here were together such Orthodox spokesmen as Nicolas Berdyaev of the Russian emigration and Stephan Zankov of Bulgaria, two men who had helped us to understand the meaning of the Orthodox tradition; such Roman Catholics as Father Brillais, superior of the 'Oratoire' and Father Hildebrandt of Austria; such Anglicans as Father Gabriel Hebert of the Society of the Sacred Mission and Professor Enkichi Kan of Japan; and such Protestants as Pastors Marc Boegner and Pierre Maury of France and Pastor Augustine Ralla Ram of India.

We had no other purpose than to come to know each other as Christians. We concentrated on the meaning of the Incarnation and found how much we had in common and how much we could learn from each other. On the Sunday we held our separate services – four of them – but there were also times of common reading of the Scriptures and common prayer. Both our unity and our division became very real.

From those days onwards Roman Catholics were to me no longer spiritual foreigners. In spite of the existing barriers Protestants and Catholics could have that same precious experience together which we had already among Christian churches participating in the ecumenical movement.

In the following years I had frequent contacts with Roman Catholics, particularly in France. In the 'Semaines universitaires', in the Latin Quarter of Paris, in which we made an attempt to state the Christian message in relation to the concerns of students, we had the participation of the Roman Catholic layman, Emanuel Mounier, the inspiring leader of the movement which published the magazine *Esprit*. And the Federation held three other ecumenical retreats in the neighbourhood of Paris.

Both Roman Catholics and Protestants had to learn how to arrive at a true ecumenical dialogue. We realized that we had to overcome the bad habit of judging each other without having really listened to each other. But we saw equally clearly that we had to face the deep divergences which existed between us. The new thing was that we said to each other: the existence of *your* church is a challenge and a question addressed to *my* church, and the meaning of our dialogue is that in seeking to respond we are both led to deeper understanding.

I wrote in 1935:[3]

It is one of the impressive facts of our time that it has again become possible for Roman Catholics to take Protestants seriously (as illustrated by the widespread Roman Catholic interest in Karl Barth) and for Protestants to feel that Roman Catholicism constitutes a most pressing theological (and not merely church-political) challenge to their own theology.

It was not by chance that I mentioned Karl Barth in this connection. Roman Catholics, who had thought that Protestantism was 'shipwrecked' and in 'agony' (as an Italian Roman Catholic author put it) suddenly discovered a Protestant theology of extraordinary vitality and creative power, which could not be dismissed as a weak modernism and which asked the great decisive question of all churches: Are you still faithful to the source of your being? This lifted the whole discussion to a new plane. In 1934 Karl Barth came to lecture in Paris. I was all the more interested in his confrontation with the French theologians since I had introduced him to French readers in my *Introduction to Karl Barth* which had appeared in 1931. Before the meetings Pierre Maury and I helped Barth to discover the city of Paris. Barth reacted with youthful spontaneity and curiosity. We spent a long time inspecting the old books displayed on the banks of the Seine.

The lectures proved to be a major theological and ecumenical event. Barth had occasion to meet the leading Roman Catholic theologians and philosophers: Jacques Maritain, Gabriel Marcel, Etienne Gilson. Gilson wrote later: 'The greatness of the work of Barth – and this is valid for every Christian confession – is to have affirmed and maintained unconditional respect for the Word of God.'[4]

It was also in 1934 that I first met Father Yves Congar, at that time a young-looking Dominican. He had already made a thorough study of Protestant theology and surprised us by his deep, though by no means uncritical, appreciation of the Reformers. He had that rare combination of qualities which characterize the true ecumenist: spiritual curiosity and openness on the one hand, strong conviction on the other. And at a time when a Roman Catholic ecumenist seemed, in the eyes of the hierarchy, a dangerous type of *franc-tireur*, he showed both remarkable courage and admirable patience. Congar soon became the chief Roman Catholic partner in the ecumenical dialogue. I published[5] in 1937 his penetrating critical analysis of the real issues in the debate between Protestantism and Catholicism, together with a comment by Pierre Maury. Congar's thesis was that while liberal Protestantism became wholly man-centred and Protestantism in its Barthian form was wholly God-centred, Roman Catholicism maintained a true balance and dialectic between the divine and the human. Pierre Maury's main point was that Catholicism's great danger was to transform the biblical theology of the Cross into a theology of glory.

A strong contribution to our conversations was also made by Father Robert Grosche of Germany who had taken the initiative in publishing a quarterly, *Catholica*, which was almost wholly devoted to a permanent dialogue with the new dialectical (Barthian) theology.

Just before the Oxford Conference on Life and Work in 1937 Congar's *magnum opus – Chrétiens Désunis –* was published.[6] It was the first attempt to elaborate a conception of ecumenism from a Roman Catholic standpoint and exerted a wide influence. In a long review I expressed my gratitude for the remarkable achievement. This book could inaugurate a new era in the discussion between Roman Catholics and Christians of other confessions. Congar stated clearly that for him the Roman Catholic Church was, purely and simply, *the* Church, but he added that, none the less, Catholics have to learn from their separated brethren. What was genuinely Christian in Protestant, Orthodox or Anglican piety was needed by Roman Catholicism, not for its substance but for its expression. I raised the question whether Congar had taken the Protestant challenge sufficiently seriously. Was it enough to speak of spiritual values in other confessions? Was not the real issue one of faithfulness to the original gospel? I also noted that Congar's description of the theology of Life and Work was really outdated, in that he had not taken into consideration the very profound change which had taken place in the Life and Work movement since about 1934 when J. H. Oldham had taken the lead.[7]

All our contacts had been quite unofficial and our meetings strictly confidential. We had no idea whether this pioneering would, in the long run, have any effect on the official position of the Vatican. In 1937 the outlook was by no means bright. We had hoped to have Father Congar with us at the Oxford Conference, but the Vatican Secretariat of State refused the necessary permission.

During a holiday in Italy in that same year I visited Ernesto Buonaiuti, one of the last survivors of the Roman Catholic 'modernists', who had been excommunicated and whose works had been placed on the Index. I was impressed by his attitude: no bitterness and unquenchable hope that a day would come when the Roman Catholic Church would allow greater freedom to its thinkers. But he could only give a discouraging account of the actual situation in the Curia. If one could only then have told him that in about twenty years his school comrade Roncalli would become Pope John XXIII . . .

In 1939 our group of leaders of the World's Student Christian Federation met again with our Roman Catholic friends in Bièvres near Paris for an ecumenical retreat. In my opening speech I said that we would surely all have liked to continue the specifically theological discussion of such subjects as biblical exegesis and liturgy. But we were meeting at an hour of terrible crisis. The shadow of total war was falling over Europe. The churches in Germany were engaged in a life and death battle with the national socialist state. So this time we would discuss the Christian attitude to the State. Jacques Maritain introduced the subject. André Philip, the socialist leader, and Gabriel Marcel, the philosopher, were active participants. In the discussion we found that our divergences did not follow confessional lines. But we found above all that we had a common cause to defend. That insight was to grow during the war years and it would help powerfully in creating a new climate between Protestants and Catholics.

From 1939 to 1945 there were no ecumenical retreats, but in the camps of prisoners-of-war and of refugees, and in the meetings of the resistance movement, strong personal contacts were established. The quiet discussions of the

1930s and the common battle fought against totalitarianism in the 1940s prepared the way for the *aggiornamento* of ecumenical relations between the churches in the 1960s.

NOTES

1. *L'Union des Eglises*, Paris, 1927.
2. See the biography of Dom Lambert Beauduin by Louis Bouyer, 1964.
3. *The Student World*, 1935, p. 138.
4. *Hommage et Reconnaissance à Karl Barth*, Neuchâtel – Paris, 1946, p. 41.
5. In *The Student World*, 1937, No. 2. These were the papers discussed at the 1937 Retreat.
6. In English, *Divided Christendom*. The English translation is in many ways unreliable.
7. Congar wrote in 1964 (*Informations Catholiques Internationales*, June 1) that in his conception of Life and Work he had been too much influenced by *L'Union des Eglises* by Charles Journet.

11 | *The World Conferences of 1937*

THE TWO WORLD conferences of 1937, Life and Work in Oxford and Faith and Order in Edinburgh, were the first world conferences of the churches at which I belonged to the headquarters staff and could watch (and to some extent participate in) the process of steering the meetings. In Oxford Mott, as Chairman of the Business Committee, and Oldham, as the *auctor intellectualis* of the whole enterprise, wanted me to get as much practical ecumenical experience as possible; and so I found myself, somewhat to my surprise, among the small group responsible for the running of the meeting. In Edinburgh I took part in the leadership of the conference as a member of the Executive Committee of Faith and Order.

The quality of a world meeting depends generally on two conditions: whether it has been adequately prepared and whether it brings together the right people. In the case of the Oxford Conference these two conditions were wonderfully fulfilled. With a small group of collaborators Oldham had done an astounding job. He had succeeded in getting the most creative people in many churches to give time and energy to the preparations, and he had given the whole process a clear focus by concentrating on the issue of the new situation in which the churches found themselves in relation to their environment and particularly to the state. I had become deeply involved in these preparations and collaborated with him in writing the first volume of the Oxford series, *The Church and Its Function in Society*. This gave me an opportunity to express my hopes for the ecumenical movement. My main point was:

> Over against false conceptions of state and community, the Church needs to affirm the existence of a God-given community which transcends all human divisions, and that as a reality and not merely as an ideal; and that therefore the Conference should not only speak about the Church, but manifest the living actuality of the Church and its relevance to the world.[1]

As to its composition the Oxford Conference was stronger than any previous meeting of the churches. The Asian and African churches were not yet sufficiently represented, and there were only some twenty-five Eastern Orthodox delegates. But there was an exceptionally strong group of laymen from many different walks of life. And many of them like Max Huber, President of the Permanent Court of International Justice, Sir Walter Moberly of the University Grants Committee, and John Maud, at that time professor in Oxford, were leaders of sections. It was also on this occasion that John Foster Dulles participated for the first time in an ecumenical world meeting and became deeply interested in the ecumenical movement. The new generation of theologians was also present: Reinhold Niebuhr, John Bennett, John Mackay and Paul Tillich from the USA, Hendrik Kraemer and Emil Brunner from the Continent, John Baillie from Scotland. Karl Barth was still somewhat suspicious of the ecumenical movement and had not come, but some of his close friends such as Eduard Thurneysen and Pierre Maury were present.

This time youth was also taken more seriously. A hundred youth delegates had been invited. I had to give them an introductory talk. I told them that the significance of our meeting was that it took place at the end of one era, the Constantinean era when Christianity was in a dominating position, but at the beginning of another era when the church was again obliged to confront powerful ideologies. This was a chance for the renewal of the church. And this was the special mission of our generation. Much of what this Oxford Conference stood for had grown out of the youth movements. We were now privileged to become part of a wider ecumenical community.

One of my tasks was to chair the sub-section on 'The Christian Attitude to War'. This was a rather formidable assignment. The subject was, of course, highly controversial, and I found that I had to keep the peace among a group of very experienced elder statesmen and churchmen most of whom belonged to the generation of my parents. I wrote to my wife: 'I had to warn them from time to time that we could not afford to play the parliamentary game.'

It happened that the main protagonists of the various positions were three Englishmen. Canon Charles Raven took the consistently pacifist position. War is always ultimately destructive and corrupts even the noblest purpose for which it is waged. The church must renounce **war** absolutely. Archbishop William Temple spoke of the sinful situation in which all Christians are caught. In that situation they face a conflict of duties, and each must choose that which is relatively best. But to do what appears as relatively best is an absolute duty before God.

Lord Robert Cecil approached the whole subject from the point of view of the League of Nations, which he had helped to bring into being and for which he had fought for the last twenty years. He gave me a paper in which he expressed his sorrow that one of the conference documents had called the League 'a ghostly shadow of what it was hoped it might become'. He argued that 'in spite of recent events the level of international morality is higher than it was'. The churches ought surely to advocate the use of the League.

It was of course impossible to reach a full consensus. But our statement, incorporated in the section report on 'The Universal Church and the World of Nations', succeeded in clarifying the situation. We described the various basic positions, but we said together that the churches must pronounce a condemnation of war, unqualified and unrestricted, and that the churches must hold together in one spiritual fellowship those of its members who take different views concerning their duty in time of war. And we agreed strongly that 'if war breaks out, then pre-eminently the Church must manifestly be the Church, still united as the one Body of Christ, though the nations wherein it is planted fight each other, consciously offering the same prayer that God's Name may be hallowed, His Kingdom come and His Will be done in both, or all of the warring nations'. This sentence which Temple composed and which was inserted in the Conference Message was to become a charter for the ecumenical movement in the second world war.

During the second half of the conference one of my main jobs was to act as assistant to Temple in the production of the conference message. The group responsible for the elaboration of this message had wisely decided that a statement written by one person would surely be more effective than a composite piece of work. And it was well known that Temple had the quite exceptional ability of formulating a consensus in clear and straightforward language. So Temple withdrew from the meetings. I went back and forth between the section-meetings and his room to bring him the results of the discussions as they became available. It was a joy to find how quickly he grasped the essential points of the oral or written reports which I brought. It was tempting to stay in his room for further discussion, but I knew I must leave him alone so that he could do his writing. The result was a draft which was adopted with very few alterations. He had hit the nail on the head.

In view of the active concern which Life and Work had shown for the fate of the church in Germany and in view of its theme – 'Church, Community and State' – the Conference had of course to express its mind about the German church conflict. There were those who wondered whether a public declaration would not create new danger for the church in Germany. But Bishop George Bell was strongly convinced that the Christians who were giving clear and courageous witness in Germany expected a word of encouragement and solidarity from the ecumenical family. I had just come from Germany where I had attended a lively student conference in Würzburg and had conferred with Pastor Otto Fricke, one of the members of the Provisional Leadership (*Vorlaüfige Leitung*) of the Confessing Church. So I could confirm Bishop Bell's conviction. The imprisonment of Martin Niemöller and the refusal to allow any German Evangelicals to attend the Oxford Conference had strengthened rather than weakened the determination of the confessing Christians to take a clear stand, and they looked to the ecumenical movement for support. Even if that support would have adverse political effect, it would be a great spiritual help to them in their struggle.

I participated in the discussions of the small group which was to draw up the message to the Christians in Germany. The other members were Bishop Bell (chairman), Dr Samuel McCrea Cavert (USA), Professor Anders Nygren (Sweden), Pastor Marc Boegner (France) and Dr Alphons Koechlin (Switzerland). The most effective message would have been to put the weight of the ecumenical movement behind the specific witness of the Confessing Church against the 'German Christian' heresy with its two sources of revelation: the gospel and national socialism. But there were too many in the ecumenical movement who did not understand or did not share the convictions expressed in the Barmen Declaration, the basic statement of the Confessing Church. They saw the church conflict wholly in terms of religious freedom, not in terms of a fundamental choice between the biblical witness and a modern form of syncretism.

So the message which we adopted did not say all that men like Dietrich Bonhoeffer or Karl Barth or some of us in the group drawing up the message wanted to have said. But it did speak of our solidarity with those 'who have stood firm from the first in the Confessing Church for the sovereignty of Christ and for the freedom of the Church of Christ to speak His Gospel'. And it expressed gratitude by saying: 'We are moved to a more living trust ourselves by your steadfast witness to Christ and we pray that we may be given grace in all our Churches to bear the same clear witness to our Lord.'

In the first draft of the message there was a strong phrase concerning national socialism as 'a view of life which rejects Jesus Christ as King of Kings and Lord of Lords and blinds their minds lest the light of the glorious Gospel of Christ, who is the image of God, should shine unto them (II Cor. 4.4)'. But it was finally decided to leave this out in order to avoid the impression that the message was motivated by a political rather than a religious concern.

Bishop George Bell presented the proposed message to the conference and Pastor Marc Boegner seconded the motion. The proposal was accepted *nemine contradicente*, and it was decided that a delegation would be sent to the German Evangelical Church to deliver the message.

On one of the last days, when we were all very tired, relaxation was provided by a meeting of former members of the World's Student Christian Federation. The rule was established that every speaker was allowed two and a half minutes for memorable stories about his experiences in the Federation and two and a half minutes for a more serious contribution. As chairman of the conference John R. Mott had rung the bell so authoritatively for many others that we decided to give him special treatment. Before he had finished a very loud bell was rung. He rather enjoyed the joke and made a grand exit: 'I will now have to confer with one of the Eastern Patriarchs.'

I left Oxford with the feeling that the ecumenical movement was on the right road and that it would be thoroughly worthwhile to work for its further development. It was no small achievement that a very substantial consensus had been worked out concerning such burning issues as the Christian attitude to the State, to race, or to international and social relations. Now we had a real basis for common action in the years ahead.

After Life and Work in Oxford came Faith and Order in Edinburgh. This was a less exciting meeting because it did not break much new ground. At the same time it was very largely composed of theologians and church administrators. One missed the layman with his sensitiveness to the realities of the modern world.

At the same time I did not feel happy about the tendency to produce verbal agreements before the real differences had been thoroughly faced. It was of course true that we ought to get on as quickly as possible with the task of giving substantial expression to our unity. Temple was surely right when he said in his opening sermon: 'We could not seek unity if we did not possess unity.' But had we really reached the point where we could formulate our consensus? I wrote in *The Student World*:

> We have not yet arrived at a sufficiently deep understanding of each other's positions to be able to agree substantially. We must first find out what our real differences are, so that we can stop our quixotic fights against the caricature impressions which we still have of each other, and only then can we come to substantial agreements.[2]

Was it really wise to deal with these deep and difficult questions of the faith in a large world conference where we had little time for discussion and had to spend most of our energy in producing reports? Should we not first spend time together in smaller meetings without having any obligation to produce documents?

I enjoyed, however, the work in the section on 'The Church and the Word of God', for in that section we tried to define the most important differences and I learned a great deal about the theology of various churches.

There was a shocking moment during the conference when a German Methodist and a German Old Catholic produced a statement saying that they did not believe that the totalitarian state in its actual existence was necessarily opposed to the Gospel and when this statement was received without any reaction from the conference leadership. I protested in a letter to Temple and it was finally agreed to send a special message to the German Evangelical Church. But the very guarded and vague wording of that message showed that the Edinburgh Conference had not really understood what was at stake in the conflict between the Church and the State in Germany.

NOTES

1. *The Church and Its Function in Society*, pp. 97, 99.
2. *The Student World*, 1937, p. 351.

IN THE EARLY 'thirties the ecumenical movement went through a period of uncertainty and confusion. Søderblom and Brent had died and the new leaders had not yet taken hold of the situation. The financial crash meant that there was little money available for the various secretariats. But there were also deeper reasons. One was that the movement was not clearly rooted in the churches. For the churches had been asked to participate in the main conferences, but not to accept responsibility for an ongoing movement which would be controlled by the churches themselves.

Another reason was the multiplicity of ecumenical organizations. All of them desired to interest students in their work. So as General Secretary of the World's Student Christian Federation I had to deal with four different bodies, each of which expected us to attend its main conferences. It was really quite impossible to meet all requests. I served from 1928 to 1930 as secretary of the Youth Commission of Life and Work and became later a member of its Study Commission. In 1930 I became a member of the Continuation Committee of Faith and Order, and in 1934 I found myself a member of its Executive Committee, a lonely representative of the younger generation among highly respected church leaders and theologians. And our Federation had, through John R. Mott and later through William Paton, close connections with the International Missionary Council.

It seemed obvious that some form of integration of the ecumenical movement had to take place. I was especially interested in bringing Faith and Order, which dealt with the doctrinal differences between the churches, and Life and Work, which dealt with practical co-operation, more closely together. One of the so-called 'theses' which I had presented as an appendix to my doctor's dissertation in 1928 was: 'The unity of the Christian churches and confessions cannot be promoted in a substantial manner, unless a synthesis is found between the rapprochement in the practical and ethical realm (Stockholm) and the rapprochement in the realm of church doctrine and church order (Lausanne).' And in 1934 when I had to speak for the youth delegates at a meeting of Faith and Order in Hertenstein (Switzerland) I said:

They (the students) feel rather confused about the relations between the various ecumenical movements, and wonder whether sooner or later there may not come into being a World Council for ecumenical Christianity with different sections.

But this was easier said than done. For the four movements – International Missionary Council, Life and Work, Faith and Order and the World Alliance for Friendship through the Churches – had each worked out their own specific ethos and objectives, and they had also their own *idées fixes* and their diehards. There had been misunderstandings. When Life and Work had used the slogan, 'Doctrine divides, service unites', this could easily be taken as a negative judgment on the Faith and Order approach. On the other hand the opposition of a number of delegates at the Lausanne Conference of 1927 to Söderblom's report on 'The Unity of Christendom and the relation thereto of the Churches' seemed to imply an unfriendly attitude to Life and Work.

Could anything be done to prepare the way for an ecumenical movement which would be a manifestation of unity rather than of disunity? There was one very positive factor, namely that most of the responsible leaders of the movements were not partisans, but men of a comprehensive ecumenical outlook. This was largely due to the fact that nearly all of them had been formed by the Student Christian Movement and that they had come to trust each other.

In 1933 Professor William Adams Brown of the USA, while spending a year in Europe, had the good sense to suggest to Archbishop Temple that this group of responsible leaders of the various movements should meet together to see what could be done to bring some order into the ecumenical disorder. Ten of us met at Temple's home, at Bishopthorpe, York. Oldham and Paton represented the International Missionary Council, Temple and Dean H. N. Bate, Faith and Order, William Adams Brown and Samuel McCrea Cavert, Life and Work, Bishop Valdemar Ammundsen and H. L. Henriod, the World Alliance for Friendship through the Churches, Charles Guillon, the YMCA and the World's Student Christian Federation. The completely informal, non-prelatical atmosphere which the Archbishop and Mrs Temple created, the good stories that were told, always accompanied by that unique high-pitched laughter of Temple himself, led to the result that, without as yet committing ourselves to any specific plan, we became a group of people united by the common purpose of giving the ecumenical movement a more truly ecumenical shape. Two years later our informal group was given official standing and received instructions to submit to the 1937 conferences at Oxford and Edinburgh proposals concerning the future organization of the ecumenical movement.

But this job could not be done by such a small body. It was therefore decided to call together a group of thirty-five church leaders and officers of the various ecumenical bodies. These thirty-five met in July 1937 at Westfield College, London, just before the world conferences in Oxford and Edinburgh. Archbishop Temple was again in the chair.

The meeting began in an atmosphere of uncertainty. Could the basic problem of ecumenical structure which had plagued us for many years really be solved in a meeting of two days? We knew that several of the most influential leaders (particularly William Adams Brown of the USA, Temple and Oldham of Great Britain and Brilioth of Sweden) were eager to arrive at a clarification of the ecumenical situation. But none of them had as yet produced a specific and concrete proposal. Everybody seemed to be waiting to find out how far the others were willing to go. I discovered however that Oldham had something up his sleeve, for he came to me at the very beginning to ask whether I would be willing to become the executive officer of a new ecumenical body if such a body were to be created. To such a very vague question I could only give a very vague answer.

We were so little aware of the fact that this meeting would become a turning point in ecumenical history that we did not even make arrangements for the keeping of minutes of the discussion.[1]

Things began to happen when Archbishop Temple expressed his conviction that the divisions in the ecumenical movement obscured the very witness which it was endeavouring to bring to the world. The time had come to bring Faith and Order and Life and Work together in one ecumenical council. The other movements could not be brought in at this time, since they had a different constitutional structure.

Yngve Brilioth of Sweden (later Archbishop of Uppsala) supported this proposal with strong arguments. He had been the closest collaborator of his father-in-law, Archbishop Nathan Söderblom, and had in mind what Söderblom had already proposed in 1919: one ecumenical council representing Christendom. He felt that doctrinal and ethical problems could not be separated from each other. A definite step towards unification of Life and Work and Faith and Order should be taken this summer. Brilioth's statements marked the beginning of a process of crystallization. The question was no longer whether a new, more comprehensive body should be created, but what shape it should take. Boegner and Oldham emphasized strongly that any new council should be rooted in the life of the churches. Oldham put it this way: 'We want the national churches to think of their problems as part of an ecumenical body.' But he added that the task of Life and Work could not possibly be performed without the full participation of the laity.

But should this body only embrace Faith and Order and Life and Work, or also the International Missionary Council and the World Alliance for Friendship through the Churches? Mott took the line that the International Missionary Council could be related to the new body for certain functions and that its task in this connection was to bring the gifts of the younger churches into the whole ecumenical movement. Professor Stephan Zankov of Bulgaria felt that the World Alliance of Friendship through the Churches should be included in the new ecumenical organization, but most others present felt that the World

Alliance in most parts of the world did not consider it desirable to be officially dependent upon the churches.

I raised the question of the theological basis. Should the new Council not make it clear what its fundamental Christian position was? But Oldham felt that it was not wise to bring this question of the basis before the Oxford Conference.

So the time had come to produce a precise draft of the new plan. As I have said earlier, Temple had a unique gift for drafting and was undoubtedly the principal architect of the plan. But it is easy to detect in it also the hand of Oldham. Thus the emphasis on the indispensability of 'a first class intelligence staff' reflects his concern for more serious study of the problems facing the church in the modern world. And the paragraph which says that in certain spheres the predominant voice in bringing the church's witness to the world must be that of 'lay people holding posts of responsibility and influence in the secular world' is a formulation of the policy which Oldham had adopted in preparing the Life and Work conference in Oxford.[2]

When the proposal was brought to the whole group it met with general approval. There was little discussion concerning the general structure of the new body. The idea of a 'General Assembly' of about two-hundred members and a 'Central Council' of sixty members was accepted. In fact the only point which led to a long discussion was the provision that one-third of the membership of the Assembly and the Central Council should be lay men or women. Churchmen from countries which would have only one person on the Council or small delegations in the Assembly objected that this provision would create grave difficulties. But Oldham's principle was nevertheless adopted.

The new council had so far no name. It was Dr Cavert (USA) who suggested that the name be 'World Council of Churches'.

Finally, the report as a whole was unanimously adopted. There was general astonishment that it had really been possible to arrive at this substantial result in such a short time. A brief impressive service of thanksgiving and dedication of our work closed the second day.

On the next morning I was asked to leave the room since there would be a discussion about the question of staff and my name would come up. After a while Archbishop Temple informed me that 'the 35' had unanimously expressed the conviction that I should be invited to be the principal staff member of the new Council. He said that by gifts and experience I was clearly the man to take this place. I was not so sure about the gifts, but I could not deny that I had had a unique opportunity to get an all-round ecumenical education.

I was thus put in a strange position. For all that Westfield could do was to produce a plan. The architects seemed to have worked out a good blueprint, but they could hardly extend a firm invitation to live in the house. That could only be done by the prospective owners (in this case the churches) and it would take a good deal of time before we would know whether these owners would approve the plan.

I was by no means certain about the answer I should give. The proposal seemed rather frightening. I was thirty-six years old and felt very much at home in the World's Student Christian Federation. Was it really my duty to move on into a world where relationships would certainly not be so free and easy and in which church politics and diplomacy would inevitably play a considerable role? Jetty, my wife, and my most trusted friends felt that I should give a positive answer. The Executive Committee of the World's Student Christian Federation, meeting in that same summer at Farnham Castle in England, spent a long time discussing whether they should bring pressure on me to stay with the Federation, but finally decided in the best tradition of that movement to leave me free to make my own choice. If I should accept the new position, they would propose to the Central Committee of the Federation that Robert Mackie should become General Secretary and that I should become Chairman. So I would, in any case, not have to cut the strong ties with the Federation altogether.

At the Oxford Conference on Life and Work the new plan was well received. But at the Edinburgh conference on Faith and Order there was a certain amount of opposition. The leader of that opposition was Bishop Headlam (of Gloucester), the chairman of the Council on Foreign Relations of the Church of England. His main argument against any association with Life and Work was that it was largely concerned with political matters. It was not easy to understand Headlam's definition of politics. He seemed to believe sincerely that when Bishop Bell wrote a letter to *The Times* protesting on behalf of Life and Work against national socialist interference in the life of the church in Germany this was a highly political act, but that when he wrote to the same paper that the national socialists were quite right in taking measures against these turbulent men of the Confessing Church this had nothing to do with politics. However, William Temple, seconded by John R. Mott and Marc Boegner, succeeded in convincing the vast majority of the Edinburgh delegates that the World Council plan would strengthen and not weaken the work for church unity which was the concern of Faith and Order. But the conference decided to formulate a number of requirements to which the constitution of the new council would have to conform if Faith and Order was to enter into it. Oldham felt that Edinburgh was really saying: 'Let us get married and yet remain single.' And I was inclined to agree with him. But Temple was in this case the better strategist, for these requirements which caused some trouble at the time, did not have any adverse effect on the long-range development.

The time had now come for me to consider seriously whether the new job would be one that I could and would want to perform. In my correspondence and discussion with Oldham and to a lesser extent with Temple and Mott, I raised a series of questions. One had to do with the basis. I wrote to Oldham (letter of August 7th 1937): 'I would find it very difficult to accept a full-time relationship to the Council unless it would have a simple but definite basis which would make it quite clear that it is indeed a Council of the Churches of Christ and not merely a federation of religious associations.' I made the further point that it would be essential to set up a department for interchurch aid, for there could not be ecumenical fellowship without practical solidarity. And I said that I would not find it worthwhile to undertake this job unless it would give opportunity to relate Life and Work and Faith and Order more closely to each other, and that not merely in an external manner, but also in their policies and their study work.

But the Committee of Fourteen which had received the mandate from the Oxford and Edinburgh conferences to carry the World Council plan forward could not answer such questions by itself. They decided to call a more representative meeting of church leaders in order to draw up a constitution for the World Council and to make provisional arrangements for the continuation of the ecumenical activities until the time of inauguration of the Council.

This conference was to be held in Utrecht (Holland) in May 1938. Until that time I continued to live in an atmosphere of suspense. I went to Utrecht, not as a candidate for the General Secretaryship, but as a representative of the World's Student Christian Federation. The conference was more representative than the Westfield meeting had been. The constitution which was worked out was largely along the lines of the Westfield proposal. By far the most intensive and the longest discussion was concerned with the question of the Basis. The great majority were convinced that the Council should have a clear orientation and since most of the churches which were expected to join had already accepted the Faith and Order invitation addressed to churches 'which accept our Lord Jesus Christ as God and Saviour' there was everything to be said for adopting that formula for the Council as a whole.

As to the immediate future it was hoped that the World Council could have its inaugural Assembly in 1940 or 1941. In the meantime the members of the committee of fourteen together with a number of other representatives of Life and Work and of Faith and Order would form the Provisional Committee of the World Council of Churches in Process of Formation. This horrible name was chosen so as to make it abundantly clear that the World Council would come into existence in a definite way only when the official representatives of the churches would meet in the first assembly.

Were the fathers of Utrecht over-cautious? I do not think so. They realized that in many churches a hard battle would have to be fought to convince the membership that this new and unprecedented body which they were invited to join would really be an instrument and servant of the churches themselves and not some sort of super-church.

The Provisional Committee elected Archbishop Temple as chairman and Dr Boegner, Archbishop Germanos, representative of the Ecumenical Patriarchate of Constantinople, and Dr Mott as vice-chairmen. When Dr Mott was approached he answered in the real Mott style: 'I shrink from it, but I will take it.' I could have said the same when at last the Provisional Committee invited me definitely to become its General Secretary. It was only many years later that I

heard that serious questions had been raised about my age. Was I not too young
for the responsible post of General Secretary? According to William Temple's
biographer[3] it was Temple who insisted that this was not an insuperable obstacle.

The last battle about the council plan was fought at the Faith and Order
meeting in Clarens, Switzerland, in August 1938. It was fortunate that William
Temple was in the chair. For many hours he had to face a barrage of questions
and objections from some four or five of his fellow Anglicans, again led by the
Bishop of Gloucester, who remained deeply suspicious of the whole plan.
Temple remained wonderfully patient, and Boegner supported him. When one
of the suspicious diehards spoke of the danger that Faith and Order would be
absorbed by Life and Work Temple remarked very appropriately: 'Here we are
concerned with Faith and Order, but I am told Life and Work is in panic lest it
be swallowed by Faith and Order.' The outcome was that only two members
voted against the final motion of acceptance of the scheme.[4] So we could at last
send to the churches the invitation to participate in creating the World Council
of Churches, the proposed constitution of which was enclosed. It was now the
turn of the churches to speak and act.

For the future of the council it was essential that it should develop a close
relationship to the younger churches. And this could be done only through close
co-operation with the International Missionary Council. At the end of 1938 I
was able to discuss this problem with the leaders of the IMC and of the churches
of Asia, Africa and Latin America at the World Conference of the IMC at
Tambaram, Madras. I found that the younger churches were eager to come into
a body in which they would be on a footing of full equality with the older
churches. And I was glad to find that John R. Mott accepted the responsibility
of heading up a joint committee of the IMC and the WCC which would in the
first place seek to bring the younger churches into the WCC. And there was
more. It was agreed that William Paton, one of the secretaries of the IMC,
should give part time to the WCC as one of its Associate General Secretaries.
With Paton in London, Henry S. Leiper in New York, and me in Geneva, we
had a strong set-up, for we trusted each other and saw eye to eye about the
nature and purpose of the ecumenical movement.

NOTES

1. My account of the meeting is based on personal notes made by Miss C. M. van
Asch van Wijck, on letters to my wife and on my own recollections.

2. The Report of the Committee of Thirty-Five can be found in *The Churches
Survey their Task*, the report of the Oxford Conference on Church, Community and
State, p. 276.

3. F. A. Iremonger, *William Temple. His Life and Letters*, 1948, p. 411.

4. One of these was of course Bishop Headlam (Gloucester). Thirty years later I read in Armin Boyens' *Kirchenkampf und Oekumene* that Headlam wrote to Heckel in Germany after the Clarens meeting: 'We have not been successful in preventing the World Council . . . The people who have engineered it have been much too clever for us.'

WHEN THE NATIONAL socialists took over in Germany in 1933, I was on a lecture tour in the American universities. There was a strong reaction in the American press and in public opinion; I reacted to that reaction and took the line: 'Do not get excited, these Nazis will have to put a lot of water in their wine when they have to bear responsibility.' But a few weeks later I had to change my mind radically.

In June 1933 I attended the national conference of the German Student Christian movement in Neu-Saarow (Northern Bavaria). It was a chaotic meeting. Most Germans were still baffled by the national socialist doctrine and uncertain how to behave in this new world. Thus at the beginning of a meeting a man standing next to me who had not yet learned the correct way of making the 'Heil Hitler' gesture, succeeded, inadvertently, in putting his fist in my eye. This was not the only reason for my growing apprehension. The first battle of the church struggle had begun. The 'German Christian' party which advocated a synthesis between Christianity and the national socialist ideology sought by all means to get rid of the newly elected Friedrich von Bodelschwingh as presiding Bishop of the Evangelical Church of Germany, in order to replace him by Hitler's friend, Ludwig Müller. At our conference there were heated debates on this issue. Student Christian Movement leaders like Reinold von Thadden and Hanns Lilje were strongly on the side of Bodelschwingh, but among the students the opinions were divided. Many still thought that national socialism was basically a Christian movement. Few saw at that time that it was fundamentally pagan.

One evening as we were marching in a torch procession towards a castle where there would be a commemoration of national heroes, I asked von Thadden what he really thought of Hitler. He answered in a loud voice: 'Hitler is a charlatan.' Noting that we were surrounded by S.A. men in their brown uniforms I whispered: 'For heaven's sake, not so loud.'

When I came home I wrote in *The Student World* (Third Quarter 1933):

The real issue is whether the Church is to regard itself as supra-national, as utterly dependent on God and therefore independent of the state, or rather whether it should accept a *Gleichschaltung*, an identification of its life with a totalitarian state and thus give up its inner independence. If the 'German Christians' demand a 'racial expression' of Christianity, if they reject the ecumenical task of the Church, if they absolutize the nation as 'the highest value to be found in creation', they introduce in reality a sort of bi-theism, a worship of two absolutes at the same time.

A few weeks later I had an unexpected opportunity of getting a firsthand impression of the new regime. International Student Service, an organization which had grown out of the relief work of the World's Student Christian Federation, held its annual conference in Ettal (Bavaria). As we were coming to the conference hall for the opening meeting we saw a number of big cars arriving, out of which stepped an impressive number of men in brown and black uniforms. We were told that these were men from the 'Brown House', the national socialist headquarters, that they had heard that an international conference was taking place and desired to welcome us. The only name which we recognized was that of the chief of staff of the S.A., the famous Ernst Röhm, one of the founders of the Nazi Party who had the appearance and the manner of a regular fire-eater. It was also Röhm who gave us an address of welcome. His theory was wonderfully simple. He said: 'We have become strong nationalists. Now if all of your peoples also become nationalistic we will be able to understand each other.'

After the meeting the old abbot of the Benedictine monastery at Ettal invited the conference leaders to dine with the national socialist dignitaries. Each of us foreigners sat between uniformed men. In the ancient refectory we were served, and very well served, by the monks. At the end of the dinner I approached Röhm, but just at that moment we were asked to proceed to the hotel nearby, where the mayor of Ettal offered an evening of Bavarian folk dances and singing. So I went out with Röhm and found myself walking beside him in the village street between two solid rows of excited tourists from Ober-Ammergau and other places who had come to acclaim the new leaders with much raising of arms and interminable shouts of 'Heil Hitler'. The bustle gave me no chance to engage him in serious conversation.

In the hotel I sat down at a table with several men in black uniforms. The man next to me said his name was Heinrich Himmler, a name that meant nothing to me. I asked about the meaning of his black uniform. He explained that this represented a new national socialist formation called the S.S. and that he was its *Reichsführer*. I tackled him about the speech of Röhm and raised the question whether the national socialists really respected the national traditions of other countries. Owing to such national figures as William the Silent, the Dutch national tradition had become a tradition of tolerance. But the national socialists in the Netherlands were preaching anti-semitism. He answered that

if we did not get rid of the Jews in the Netherlands we would lose the Netherlands East Indies, but failed to make clear the logic of his argument. When I told
him that I would be leaving in a few days for Asia, he asked me to bring his
greetings to an Indian professor in Benares who had participated in the street-
fighting during the nazi uprising in Munich in 1923. He gave me his card and
wrote a message on it. During my journey in India I tried to find this professor,
but could not locate him. So the card is still in my possession.

In the following years when Himmler's name came to signify cold-blooded
terrorism and genocide on a scale never known before I have often asked myself
whether I had on that evening had any premonition that this man would become
one of the greatest evildoers in history. But I had to admit that I had had no such
awareness. In fact he had not made a lasting impression on me. With his pince-nez,
his insignificant face and his crude ideas he had seemed to me just a narrow-
minded *petit bourgeois*. But that was perhaps the secret of his life: that he had so
little humanity and imagination that he could become the machine-like execu-
tioner of millions.

Some time later I told Karl Barth about this meeting. He suggested that I
should exploit my acquaintance with Himmler. So I wrote to Himmler about the
case of one of Barth's pupils who had been sent to a concentration camp.
Himmler answered that an enquiry would be made. I thought that I would hear
no more about it. But before long a letter came to say that this pastor had been
liberated. So I tried again and wrote about another prisoner whose name Barth
had also supplied. But this time I received no answer. Later on when the church
conflict became very acute I tried once in Berlin to see Himmler to urge him to
stop intervening in the life of the churches, but I did not succeed in reaching
him. I was received by one of his adjutants who promised to pass on my concerns,
but there were no noticeable results.

Within one year of the strange evening in Ettal Ernst Röhm was murdered.
The official reason given was his immorality and his insubordination. The real
reason was of course that the nazi leaders were engaged in a struggle for power.
But on that same day, June 30th 1934, many other people were assassinated for
no other reason than their refusal to accept the Nazi ideology. Among them was
the Roman Catholic student leader, Fritz Beck, who had been the genial and
much appreciated organizer of our Ettal Conference. And there could be no
doubt that this was primarily the work of Himmler and his associates.

During those first years of the church conflict I tried hard to ensure that the
true facts should be known in influential circles outside Germany. In a report
sent in October 1934 to a number of newspaper editors in various countries
I said:

> On various occasions during the last year it has become clear that the voice of
> public opinion in other countries has influenced the attitude of the (German)
> government and tended to act as a brake on the ('German Christian') church

Father and three sons, 1928.

Karl Barth (*centre*) with Pierre Maury and Visser 't Hooft during the student conference in La Châtaigneraie (Switzerland) in 1934.

One of the first private meetings between Protestants, Roman Catholics and Eastern Orthodox in Bièvres (near Paris) in 1939. The philosopher Jacques Maritain is between Maury and Visser 't Hooft. Père Yves Congar is standing on the second step in a white habit, with the French philosopher Gabriel Marcel beside him.

A meeting in the Archbishop's palace at Bishopthorpe (England), in preparation for the Oxford Conference. William Temple is in the centre with J. H. Oldham on his right. On his left are Visser 't Hooft and Reinhold Niebuhr. On the second step, between Temple and the author, is Michael Ramsey, later Archbishop of Canterbury.

government. Whatever can be done to show that quite apart from political considerations the world's conscience rejects the regime of force and compulsion which rules today in the religious life in Germany, should be done . . . What is needed today is that through the secular and the religious press the whole world should say to the German government: the cost of further interference with the conscientious convictions of Christians in Germany is a further and very serious loss of confidence on the part of other nations in the present leadership of the German *Reich*.

Almost every other issue of *The Student World* (which I then edited) contained an analysis of the developments in the German church, written by men who were in close touch with the German situation such as Karl Barth, Pierre Maury, Francis House and I. We knew that this was the front-line battle, fought for the whole Christian church. It was good to know that the Student Christian Movement leaders in Germany were among the most courageous fighters.

Thus Reinold von Thadden was one of the ten signatories of the prophetic document issued by the Confessing Church, that is the memorandum sent to Hitler on June 4th 1936, which in the name of the gospel challenged the very basis of the national socialist ideology and practice and which attracted worldwide attention. The headline on the front page of the *Herald Tribune* said: 'Reich Clergy Warn Hitler He Does Not Outrank God.' That was a good description of the main point of the document, but it was incorrect because von Thadden was a layman. As such he was in even greater danger than the clergy who had the protection of their ecclesiastical status.

The most effective help which the Student Christian Movement gave in the church conflict was by sponsoring conferences called *Evangelische Wochen*, three or four-day meetings at which leaders of the Confessing Church (that is the movement in the Evangelical Church of Germany which resisted the penetration of the nazi ideology into church life) spoke to the church people who were badly in need of encouragement and guidance. In most cases the addresses had to be given twice because there was no church building large enough to hold all the participants. These were truly assemblies of the Church Militant. During these assemblies smaller groups of leaders were given full information on the dramatic developments in the church conflict. I remember Martin Niemöller's *Lagebericht* (report on the state of the Church) at the *Evangelische Woche* in 1935 in Hanover which he closed with the words: 'We must remember that the Church can stand so much more than we are inclined to think.'

At that same meeting I began my address with this greeting:

When in these days a man from another nation and another church comes to speak in a meeting of confessing Christians in Germany, his first word must be a word of deep gratitude for the message and the example which come to Christians all over the world from the life of the churches in Germany. I happen to visit many countries and I can render witness to the fact that innumerable Christians have been strengthened in their faith, or have understood anew the meaning of a living church as they came to take a deep personal interest in the struggle of the Confessing Church in Germany. It is of course true that the sympathy for the Confessing Church is not always based on pure motives, but even if we see that clearly, it remains true that the church conflict in Germany has a purely churchly ecumenical influence for which every believing Christian ought to be thankful. It is gradually better understood, especially among younger people, that the confrontation in Germany is the prelude to a world-wide confrontation in which the very existence of the Church is at stake. The fact that to the German Church, as in the time of Martin Luther, has been given the pioneering role in this struggle, should give you some consolation and help you to bear the burden of the battle.

Two years later, in the spring of 1937, I went to Darmstadt to speak at another *Evangelische Woche*. I was met at the station by Hanns Lilje, who told me that the Minister for Church Affairs had forbidden the holding of this *Evangelische Woche*. I asked whether I should return to Geneva. 'No,' he said, 'we are going to hold it anyway and want you to stay.' I gave my first address and participated in a meeting of some thirty pastors and other leaders who drew up a common declaration addressed to the local police authorities saying that the prohibition was an interference with the missionary work of the church, that this work was entrusted to the church by its Lord and that no power on earth could invalidate this mandate. The signatories declared, therefore, that they had asked the organizers and speakers to continue to give their witness and were in full solidarity with them. The police made one concession. The local speakers and the two speakers, who had come from outside Germany, would be allowed to speak, but the speakers who had come from other places in Germany would not be allowed to speak and had to leave the city. The organizers of the meeting rejected this and decided to carry out the full programme.

At the end of the afternoon on April 1st it was announced that because the speaker that evening was to be Pastor Busch from Essen and because the police had forbidden him to speak, it was preferable that as many participants as possible should remain in the church, for it was by no means certain that those who would leave would be able to re-enter the church later on. I could not believe that the police would really go so far as to stop people from coming to a church meeting. I went out. But I had been mistaken. When I came back for the evening meeting I found the church surrounded by a solid cordon of policemen holding back hundreds of delegates and local people who wanted to get in. I tried to think of a way to outwit the police. So I began to walk around the church. I noticed that it was still possible to get into the parsonage and that, with luck, one might reach the church through a gallery behind the backs of the policemen. So I entered the parsonage and found a man standing there who said: 'I am Pastor Busch from Essen and I am to speak tonight. How can I get into the church?' I showed him the way. We ran through the gallery. The policemen were looking at the crowd and not at us.

When Pastor Busch suddenly turned up in the pulpit, there was a loud gasp from the people in the church who could not understand how Pastor Busch had succeeded in passing through the police cordon. He began his address by saying that if we were to let ourselves be preoccupied with the sensational aspects of the evening the devil would have won. We were just to listen to the Word of God. He then gave an incisive and moving address on 'Jesus Christ the Lord'. The audience became very quiet. During the address I saw a man come in who looked very much like a secret policeman. When Pastor Busch was finished and tried to escape by the same door through which he had entered, this policeman rushed out behind him. He was for a time held up by a rather formidable deaconess who would not let him pass. But nevertheless Pastor Busch was caught. Since he had refused to obey the prohibition to speak he was arrested.

In the meantime the people who had waited outside the church and those who had been inside formed a large crowd. When Pastor Busch was taken forcibly by two policemen to the police-van which was to take him to the prison the crowd began to sing: 'A safe stronghold our God is still.'

The lines:

> And were this world all devils o'er,
> And watching to devour us
> We lay it not to heart so sore,
> Not they can overpower us

seemed to have been written for this hour. On the next day we continued the programme 'as if nothing had happened'. The title of my address seemed singularly appropriate: 'Tumult about God in the world of nations'.

A few days later I spoke at the *Evangelische Woche* in Kassel to some 5,000 people. This time there was no interference.

I wrote in the Editor's Travel Diary of *The Student World* (Third Quarter, 1937):

> There is no need to pity the German Church. Its external and internal condition is impossibly difficult, and in some ways hopeless. But we would be wrong to believe that the church conflict is a matter of church administration, of church committees, synods and bishops. The real story of the conflict is a story of revival and of a new understanding of the implications of the Christian faith. The important and wonderful thing about the condition of the Church in Germany today is that its message is eagerly listened to by many who formerly would not listen to it.

It was really a miracle that the German Student Christian Movement could continue to operate and that in July 1937 it could still hold a national conference in Würzburg with more than three hundred students. Although all contacts with the ecumenical movement were at that time very suspect in the eyes of the authorities, the SCM leaders again demonstrated their attachment to the World's Student Christian Federation by inviting Suzanne de Diétrich and me to be among the speakers.

But in January 1938 the situation of the movement became critical. I received information from its leaders that the government was obviously planning to dissolve it. I wrote to the Ministry of Education in Berlin, calling attention to the international repercussions which such action would have. I tried at the same time to exert pressure through diplomatic channels. In a telegram to Dr John R. Mott in New York I informed him of the danger and asked him to approach the German Ambassador in Washington. Mott rose to the occasion. He wrote in true Mott style: 'I changed my programme at once and went to the German Embassy and presented our case as strongly as I know how. I took Professor William Adams Brown with me and he was in a position to support my appeal.' I asked Archbishop Lang in London to take similar action and he wrote to Ambassador von Ribbentrop. It was probably due to this international action that the German Student Christian Movement survived another eight months. It was finally banned in August 1938.

One of the most acute problems of the Confessing Church was how to maintain their own centres of theological education. In September 1937 Himmler had decreed that all such schools were forbidden. What could be done? Professor Heinrich Schlier from the theological school in Barmen-Elberfeld came to me with an adventurous plan. There was in Southern Bavaria a small Austrian enclave. Could we not set up a theological school under ecumenical auspices in that place to which German students could come, but where the German Gestapo had no jurisdiction? I agreed to organize an international committee for this purpose. But by the time the committee had been formed and we were ready to go into action Hitler annexed Austria and our plan had to be abandoned.

In 1938 I happened to be in Germany on that terrible night of November 9th which became known as the 'Crystal Night', when nearly two hundred synagogues were burned and thousands of Jewish shops were looted. I saw synagogues in Tübingen and Stuttgart go up in flames and on the next day I walked through the streets of Nuremberg and saw the sickening signs of destruction. National socialism had thrown off its mask. It was an explosion of inhuman, anti-human and demonic forces. I asked my German friends when and how they were going to protest against these beastly atrocities. Most of them were deeply disturbed, but they explained that the Confessing Church was going through one of the most perilous moments in its turbulent history. Its leaders were under violent attack because of an incident which had happened a few weeks earlier in the days before the meeting, on September 29th at Munich, of Hitler, Mussolini, Chamberlain and Daladier. At the height of the crisis concerning Czechoslovakia the Confessing Church had issued a form of service, including a very concrete confession of sins of the German people. The nazi authorities considered this an excellent opportunity to destroy the Confessing Church. In the press its leaders were described as 'Christian traitors', and most of them were dismissed from their offices on November 11th. In those circumstances, common action against the persecution of the Jews was practically impossible. But there were a few courageous pastors who protested on their own. And the office for the emigration of Jewish Christians which had been set up by the Confessing Church under the leadership of Pastor Heinrich Grüber redoubled its efforts to help Jewish Christians to leave Germany.

It was obvious that the ecumenical movement had to take immediate action. On November 16th H. L. Henriod, representing the World Alliance of Friendship through the Churches, Adolf Keller, representing the Office for Inter-Church Aid and I, representing the World Council of Churches, sent a letter to the churches in which we said:

> At the moment when the terrible persecution of the Jewish population in Germany and in other Central European countries has come to a violent climax, it is our duty to remind ourselves of the stand which we have taken as an ecumenical movement against anti-semitism in all its forms.

The letter mentioned the various relevant resolutions adopted at ecumenical meetings and asked the churches to approach their governments requesting that they should immediately allow a larger percentage of non-Aryan refugees to enter provisionally or definitely into the country concerned and to work for the acceptance of a plan to secure a permanent settlement of non-Aryan refugees.[1]

Many churches joined in the protest. And in a number of countries Christian committees to assist non-Aryan refugees, working together with the courageous and energetic Pastor Grüber in Berlin, made a great effort to get more refugees admitted. The finest example was given by Bishop Bell who guaranteed personally to support twenty non-Aryan pastors and their families. It was also Bishop Bell who convinced the Provisional Committee of the World Council at its first full session in January 1939 of the need to create the special secretariat for the co-ordination of the refugee work of the churches, of which Pastor Adolf Freudenberg of Germany became the executive officer. But these various efforts were not sufficiently backed up by the church people. Public opinion remained lukewarm and the governments did not develop a general and truly adequate plan to save the millions of Jews in Germany whose situation was steadily getting worse.

My task with regard to the German church in those days has been described by Martin Fischer.[2] He says rightly that I knew myself to be in one boat with the struggling brothers of the Confessing Church and that I sought 'to raise the eyes of the Confessing Church beyond its own battle-field'. That is a good description. It became increasingly difficult for Christians in Germany to understand that their government was destroying the fabric of international order. 'Munich' had seemed to them and to very many in the West a victory of the forces of peace. I knew that it was not. For soon after Munich I had visited Prague and found my Czechoslovak friends in despair. I remember that the worthy Dean of the Theological Hus-Faculty, Professor Francis Zilka, wept as he told me what this treason by the West meant for Czechoslovakia. It was clear that Munich had settled nothing, that to give in to national socialism meant only to increase its voracious appetite and that things would become very much worse before they could become better.

NOTES

1. See Johan M. Snoek, *The Grey Book*, p. 100; and International Christian Press and Information Service, 1938, no. 49.
2. 'The Confessing Church and the Ecumenical Movement' in *The Sufficiency of God*, London, p. 137ff.

The WCC and the German Church Conflict in 1939

WHEN AT THE beginning of 1939 I took up my new task as General Secretary of the World Council, now entering into its 'process of formation', I found that the most difficult immediate problem was the one of relations with the German Evangelical Church. There had been no official representation of the German Evangelical Church at the Utrecht meeting, in 1938, at which the constitution of the WCC was worked out. And the first meetings of the Provisional Committee in Utrecht and St Germain were also held in the absence of German delegates. But it seemed clear that in some way or another new relationships would have to be established. The difficulty was of course that the church situation in Germany had become exceedingly complicated. There was the 'official' church leadership, which was largely dominated by the 'German Christian' heresy and basically against ecumenical work. There was the 'Foreign Office' of the German Evangelical Church which had still a legal existence, but which in view of its compromising attitude had lost the confidence of the Confessing Church and of the friends of the Confessing Church in other countries. There were the Lutheran bishops who took an intermediate position. And there was the Provisional Church Government of the Confessing Church which had set up its own ecumenical office.[1]

The 'Foreign Office' under Bishop Heckel was making a renewed attempt to become the spokesman and sole channel of representation of the German Evangelical Church in the ecumenical organizations. They found an ardent advocate in my German colleague, Dr Hanns Schönfeld, from 1929 the director of the Study Department of Life and Work, which had in 1938 become the Study Department of the World Council. Schönfeld had a strong position in the ecumenical movement. For his department had been at the centre of the remarkably thorough process of preparation for the Oxford Conference of 1937, of which J. H. Oldham had been the master mind. And, according to the plans which had been made for the creation of the World Council, study and research were to be the foremost task of the new organization. Schönfeld's dominating concern was to ensure that the process of study and exchange would continue. He believed that in the case of Germany this could be achieved only by collaborating closely with the Foreign Office of Bishop Heckel. For that office could provide the necessary facilities, including permits for journeys, finance, etc. So he pursued a policy of close collaboration with Heckel's office. Schönfeld argued that the men of the Foreign Office, and especially his close friend Dr Eugen Gerstenmaier[2] in it, were engaged in a battle against the policy of the nazi regime with regard to the churches and against the 'German Christian' party and that they deserved all the help they could get. I took a different line. I had not yet met Bishop Heckel, but I knew a great deal about his record. In his relations with the ecumenical movement he had systematically denied or minimized the interventions of the nazi regime in the life of the churches and opposed the attempts of the Confessing Church to maintain direct contacts with the ecumenical movement. So I had no intention of allowing Heckel to obtain exclusive control of the relationships between the churches of Germany and ourselves. My own contacts in Germany had so far been almost wholly with the men of the Confessing Church. I had come to know them through the Student Christian Movement. I trusted them as genuine and courageous Christians. I had shared in their battles. With them I felt at home and from them I received the inspiration which comes from working with single-minded men who felt that they were under divine orders. So I had to tell Schönfeld that I would oppose any moves which would lead to the isolating of the Confessing Church or the weakening of its links with the World Council. But Schönfeld was a strong individualist and I remained uncertain as to whether he was carrying out the policy of the World Council or rather his own.

Heckel obviously considered me a dangerous person. When, in 1939, the proposal was made that I should become also secretary of the European Continental Section, he wrote to Marc Boegner, on February 24th, protesting against my nomination, because I had had no relations with the German Evangelical Church and was not sufficiently informed about the European churches. On the first point he was right, if by the German Evangelical Church Heckel meant the official leadership which had sought to adapt the Church to the Nazi regime.[3]

I visited Germany in March and April in order to speak at a student conference on missions in Halle. I used the occasion to make a formal call on Bishop Heckel, but spent most of my time with my friends of the Confessing Church – Reinold von Thadden, Hanns Lilje, Martin Fischer, Julius Schniewind and Hans Böhm. I remember especially that in order to find a safe place for frank conversation on religious and political affairs which could not be overheard, von Thadden, Roland Elliott (World Student Christian Federation leader from the USA) and I spent a long afternoon in the Berlin Zoo. It seemed unlikely that spies were hidden in the cages of lions or elephants.

With regard to the representation of the German church I found that the leaders of the Confessing Church were opposed to having Bishop Heckel on the Provisional Committee of the WCC, unless the Confessing Church was also given a seat. I wrote therefore, on April 7th, to Bishop Bell and Dr Boegner suggesting that we wait until Bishop Heckel demanded a place on the committee and then consult Bishop Mahrarens of the Lutheran Church of Hannover and Dr Hans Böhm of the Confessing Church, before entering into negotiation with Bishop Heckel. Bishop Bell replied on April 13th: 'I am entirely in agreement with your proposed policy.'

In the meantime a new crisis developed. For, on April 6th, eleven German church leaders, headed by Friedrich Werner, the most powerful man of the 'official' church government, published a declaration which was based on the Godesberg statement of the 'German Christian' party and contained scandalous affirmations concerning the ecumenical movement and the relations between the churches and Judaism. Two of the key sentences were: 'All supra-national or international churchliness of a Roman Catholic or World-Protestantism type is a political degeneration of Christianity'; and 'The Christian faith is the unbridgable opposite to Judaism'.

Immediate reactions came from Karl Barth and from Bishop Bell. Both asked whether the time had not come for a clear protest on behalf of the ecumenical movement against these obviously unchristian affirmations. Bell suggested that such a protest should be signed by Archbishop Temple, Dr Boegner, William Paton and me. The proposal was accepted by all concerned. So we went to work. I received, simultaneously, drafts from Temple and Barth. They made the same fundamental point, but were completely different in style and terminology. My task of harmonizing them was far from easy. Temple wrote that he had some difficulty in swallowing the phrasing of the combined text, but that he was ready to associate himself with expressions that he would never dream of using on his own account because, unless we were all prepared to do this, there was no hope of full co-operation between British and Continental Christians. Somewhat to my surprise Barth wrote that my harmonized draft was better than his original. Boegner and Paton also expressed their readiness to sign.

Our declaration, published in our International Christian Press and Information Service (No. 19, 1939) and in the London *Times* (May 10th), took the following form:

> In relation to the recent declaration of eleven German Church leaders, we feel obliged to ask the Christian Churches of all countries to consider seriously the following declaration of Christian truth:
>
> 1. We believe in the One, Holy, Catholic and Apostolic Church. The national organization of the Christian Church is not an essential element of its life. It has its blessings, but it has also its dangers. But the recognition of the spiritual unity of all those who are in Christ, irrespective of race, nation, or sex (Gal. 3.28; Col. 3.11) belongs to the essence of the Church. The Church is called to give clear and visible expression to this unity.
>
> 2. The Christian Faith is the practice of obedience to Jesus Christ, who is the Messiah of Israel. 'Salvation is of the Jews' (John 4.22). The Gospel of Jesus

Christ is the fulfilment of the Jewish hope. The Christian Church owes it, therefore, to the Jewish people to proclaim to it the fulfilment of the promises which had been made to it. And it rejoices in maintaining fellowship with those of the Jewish race who have accepted that Gospel.

3. The Church of Christ owes its allegiance to Jesus Christ alone and the right distinction and relationship between politics and ideology on the one hand and the Christian faith on the other hand is, therefore, one which serves to make clear that to Jesus Christ is given, not merely some, but all authority in Heaven and Earth, and that the Church is bound to proclaim His Lordship over all areas of life, including politics and ideology.

4. The only form of order and tolerance which can be accepted by the Christian Church must be based on the acknowledgment of the unique revelation offered to the world in Jesus Christ and the full freedom to proclaim His Gospel.

> William Ebor.
> *Chairman of the Provisional Committee of the*
> *World Council of Churches* (in Process of Formation)
>
> Marc Boegner
> *Chairman of the Administrative Committee*
>
> W. A. Visser 't Hooft
> *General Secretary*
>
> William Paton
> *General Secretary*

The Foreign Office of the German Evangelical Church reacted sharply. They wired me in Geneva:

> Expect immediate withdrawal declaration to the churches which greatly exceeds competence, is based on wrong understanding of factual general church situation in Germany and represents an intolerable intervention in domestic German affairs.

A long letter followed. It laid strong emphasis on the lack of competence of the World Council during its process of formation to make any such statements. The declaration of the eleven German church leaders did not have the significance which World Council leaders had attached to it. In any case it was a domestic affair and Christians outside Germany had no right to interfere.[4]

Gerstenmaier sent a further message emphasizing that the eleven church leaders were quite unrepresentative of the German church and that we had made a great mistake in taking them seriously.

I answered that we had been obliged to speak because the affirmations of the eleven church leaders had to do with truths which are absolutely vital to all ecumenical work. They could not be allowed to go unchallenged.

In the following weeks it became clear that we had not been barking up the wrong tree. Minister Hanns Kerrl who carried the portfolio of church affairs in the German government, tried to force the leaders of the regional churches to make a clear statement concerning the attitude of the Church to the State and to national socialism. He saw that the Godesberg declaration in the form in which it had been adopted by the eleven church leaders, would not get wide acceptance. So he presented a modified and a less crude edition of the declaration and then brought the greatest pressure to bear on the leaders of all the regional churches (*Landeskirchen*) to sign it. Bishop Mahrarens finally signed, though reluctantly, and with a commentary which did not get much publicity. Other bishops proposed a modification of Kerrl's modification, but the watered-down document finally issued was everything except a clear statement of the mission of the church in relation to a pagan ideology.[5] In any case it had now been clearly shown that the World Council's word had come at the right time and had dealt with the crucial issues of the moment.

Bishop Heckel asked me to come to Berlin to discuss future relations with the World Council. I went to see him on June 15th and we had a session of four hours. The discussion took place in an atmosphere of cold diplomatic negotiation. Heckel had the domineering attitude of a self-conscious prelate and adopted the arrogant tone which was typical of German diplomacy in those days, but to which we were not accustomed in the ecumenical movement. He complained about the isolation of German Protestantism. This was largely due, he said, to the political tendencies dominating the World Council. The time had come for better representation of the German Evangelical Church in the responsible organs of the WCC. He demanded that there should be two more places for Germany on the Provisional Committee and these places should be offered to a representative of his office; also that a person in his office should be recognized as an Associate Secretary of the WCC in the same way as Dr Henry Smith Leiper in New York. Unless these conditions were fulfilled, he would find it impossible to collaborate further with the Provisional Committee and would even work against it.

That was a real ultimatum and a serious one, for Bishop Heckel was still in a sufficiently strong position to make all ecumenical contacts with Germany impossible. But his plan to recognize his office as an official secretariat of the WCC was, of course, absolutely unacceptable. So I answered that I could of course not give a definite answer before I consulted the officers of the Council. It seemed to me, however, I continued, that the action proposed would not solve the problem of our relationships. What would happen if the Provisional Committee were to make statements unacceptable to the German government? Moreover, the World Council would not accept any arrangement which would cut us off from other sections of the German Evangelical Church. Bishop Heckel said that Bishop Mahrarens, who was a member of the Provisional Committee, represented an important section of the church and that the Provisional Church

Government of the Confessing Church had become insignificant.

It was a relief to sit down afterwards in the same city with Dr Böhm of the Provisional Church Government with whom I could speak as a trusted friend and without diplomatic reserve. He felt that Bishop Heckel, in protesting against our declaration concerning the statement of the eleven church leaders, had shown himself to be a political propagandist rather than a spokesman of a Christian church. If the ecumenical movement were to work solely with Bishop Heckel, Dr Böhm continued, it would no longer be able to express its mind about the real issues raised by the German church conflict, and would not be able to give such real help to the cause of Christ as we had recently given by our declaration. The Confessing Church would, however, not object to the appointment of Bishop Heckel on the Provisional Committee, if another place on the committee could be given to a German churchman in whom they had real confidence.

I felt strongly that we should support these proposals of the Confessing Church. Strong help came from Bell. The bishop wrote (July 13th):

> I find myself quite convinced that it would be undesirable, and in my opinion wrong, to allow the German Evangelical Church to be represented in any way, whether officially or unofficially, by Bishop Heckel or members of his office, if that was to be the only way in which the German Evangelical Church could be represented. I would, in fact, prefer that there should be no Germans attending. In all the circumstances the best arrangement, in my opinion, would be that a representative each of: (1) the Lutheran Council, or the Churches of Hanover, Bavaria and Wurtemberg; (2) the Confessing Church, Dahlem,[6] and (3) Bishop Heckel's office should be present. That is three Germans in all, representing each of the three sections.

At the end of July, at the meetings of the Administrative Committee in Zeist (Netherlands), the matter was again fully discussed. Schönfeld made a strong plea for meeting Heckel's desires, but the committee decided that of the two additional places which would be offered one would have to be given to a person who had the full confidence of the Confessing Church. The great question remained now whether we could get Heckel to accept this plan. Bishop Yngve Brilioth of Växjö (Sweden) and I were to go to Berlin to work out such a solution. But before we could go, the war broke out. For the next six years the relations between the World Council and the German Evangelical Church would remain undefined. This had at least the advantage that we were free to maintain personal contacts with all who were true friends of the ecumenical movement.

NOTES

1. It should be explained that the Confessing Church (*Bekennende Kirche*) was the movement within the German Evangelical churches which carried on the struggle against the attempts of the nazi regime and the 'German Christians' party to introduce into the churches ideas and practices reflecting national socialist rather than biblical teachings. In a wider sense the term Confessing Church includes all churches or groups in the churches which took their stand on the Barmen Declaration of 1934. In a narrower sense the term is used to describe the movement embracing those sections of the German Evangelical churches which had broken off the relationships with a church government unacceptable to them and who, in 1936, had formed the Provisional Church Government of the Confessing Church.

2. He became President of the Bundestag of the Federal Republic of Germany in 1954.

3. The European Continental Section had been organized in the early days of Life and Work to facilitate the co-operation of the European churches within the Life and Work movement. Another example of the negative attitude of Heckel's office to my nomination is mentioned by Armin Boyens in *Kirchenkampf und Oekumene 1933–1939*, Munich, 1969, p. 251.

4. I did not learn until thirty years later, when I read Armin Boyens' *Kirchenkampf und Oekumene*, that Schönfeld had written to Gerstenmaier to express his disagreement with the declaration of the World Council officers. See his letter in *Kirchenkampf und Oekumene*, p. 380. This illustrates the fact that at that time Schönfeld and I were, to put it mildly, not on the same wavelength. Our relations improved in the following years when Schönfeld identified himself more clearly with the resistance against the Nazi regime.

5. See Eberhard Klügel, *Die Lutherische Landeskirche Hannovers und ihr Bischof*, 1964, pp. 363ff.; and Armin Boyens, *Kirchenkampf und Oekumene 1933–39*, pp. 271ff. Mahrarens explained that one of the reasons why he had signed the declaration was that he desired to protest against the speech of Archbishop Lang (Canterbury) in the House of Lords on March 20th 1939.

6. Berlin – Dahlem was the seat of the Provisional Church Government.

15 | *Youth Meets on the Eve of War*

IN THE MIDST of the depressing days when the lights were once again going out over Europe the World Conference of Christian Youth at Amsterdam was a moment of invigoration. The conference was a common undertaking of the World Alliance of YMCAs, the World's YWCA, the World's Student Christian Federation, the Ecumenical Youth Commission of the World Council of Churches and the World Alliance for Friendship through the Churches. It had been prepared very thoroughly. In the last year of his life Walter Gethman, the former General Secretary of the World Alliance of YMCAs, had, with the collaboration of Denzil Patrick of Scotland, produced a remarkable study guide which had been used by youth groups all over the world.

The conference was to begin on July 24th, 1939. In the last weeks before that date I was increasingly uncertain whether it would really be possible to hold the meeting. On the basis of what Dietrich Bonhoeffer had told me in March and what I heard from other German friends, I considered the international situation so serious that I told Edwin Espy, the young American who was the organizing secretary, that we would probably have to cancel the meeting. But I was wrong by one month.

As the political atmosphere grew more foreboding, the Netherlands government became nervous about possible political repercussions of the conference. Would some of the speakers make strong attacks against national socialism and would this lead to further tension with the German government? Early in July we received word that Professor Reinhold Niebuhr, the eminent American theologian, would not be allowed to speak at the conference. The argument given was that he had communist sympathies. This strange accusation showed that the Dutch security organization was not particularly competent in theological questions, for in his Gifford lectures in May of the same year Niebuhr had rejected the communist ideology in no uncertain terms. Dr Jo Eykman, who was the secretary of the local committee in Amsterdam, and I went to see the Minister of foreign affairs in The Hague. I explained that Niebuhr was active in the socialist party in the United States and that this party was comparable to the Labour party in Great Britain. I was rather taken aback when the minister answered that socialism was almost the same as communism.[1] The minister agreed, however, to reconsider the matter. Professor William Adams Brown of Union Theological Seminary (New York) was asked to put in writing that his colleague Niebuhr was not a disguised communist. It was finally agreed that the manuscript of Niebuhr's speech would be submitted to the Dutch authorities. This was done, but it did not mean very much, for Niebuhr was not the kind of speaker who reads a prepared text, but the inspired orator for whom his own text is only the point of departure for a spontaneous outburst of ideas.

Finally the government received the conference generously. Professor J. R. Slotemaker de Bruine, who had been deeply involved in the ecumenical movement and who was now the Minister of Education, was our host at a reception in the Rijksmuseum where thousands of candles threw their soft light on the Rembrandt paintings. Prince Bernhard brought a message from Queen Wilhelmina saying: 'In my conviction the call of the Gospel, *ut omnes unum sint*, is a call that comes as a special vocation to young people in this time.' Prince Bernhard returned several times in order to meet different groups of delegates and took part in the main communion service.

There were no official delegates from Germany. By this time the German government considered the ecumenical organizations to be far too dangerous to allow them to influence German youth. But a score of young Germans had succeeded in finding their way to Amsterdam. They were so eager to join their fellow-Christians from other countries that they were willing to take the risk of getting into trouble with their own government. D. T. Niles asked one of them, a girl, why they had taken that risk. The girl replied: 'We could not allow the church in Germany to go unrepresented. We belong with you all.' I interviewed them one by one to find out whether they were reliable and if the result was positive I gave them their admission ticket. But I kept the list with their names in my pocket so as to protect them as much as possible.

A meeting of 1,500 young people with the purpose of mobilizing the Christian community for its world-wide task could at that particular time have easily become a very unreal affair – a sort of anachronism similar to some of the demonstrations of simple-minded idealistic internationalists of which I had seen a good deal in Geneva. But the conference became something quite different. There was a profound realization that the old international order was going to pieces. No one felt that we should therefore stop building the Christian community. On the contrary. Now we saw how much we needed a true sense of the reality and mission of the people of God. Thus the weight of the coming catastrophe did not make the conference superfluous, but rather supremely meaningful. The Conference Message said: 'The nations and peoples of the world are drifting apart. The Churches are coming together ... In war, conflict and persecution we must strengthen one another and preserve our Christian unity unbroken.' Amsterdam 1939 was the time to receive our marching orders for the trials ahead.

The conference confronted a new generation with the convictions and insights which had grown up in the life of the movements not directly dependent on the churches. John R. Mott, who had been the key figure in those movements and who was now our deeply respected patriarch, spoke of the personal commitment to the cause of the Kingdom which had been the secret of the pioneering period of the ecumenical movement. William Temple spoke as the undisputed leader of the ecumenical movement in and of the churches. Thus the two streams of a more spontaneous form of ecumenical life and of a church-rooted ecumenicity became one stream.

But Amsterdam 1939 also made its own specific contributions to the ecumenical development. For one thing it gave a greater central place in the conference programme to Bible study than any previous world conference had done. Delegates were divided in some forty-odd groups in which central biblical passages were introduced and then discussed. This was rather a risky undertaking in a meeting with such tremendous variety in background. But the result was, as the Message said: 'Many of us have discovered the Bible afresh, and in so far as we have allowed God to speak to us, He has become a living God, declaring a living message for our own lives and our generation.'

The conference became a new adventure in ecumenical worship. In the preparatory meetings the question had been raised by Leo Zander (of the Russian Orthodox Church in Paris) and others whether the kind of worship which we had had so far at ecumenical world conferences was really adequate. Did it sufficiently help the participants to get a deep understanding of the spiritual life of other communions? Could we not find a way to provide opportunity for all participants to share in the fullest expression of the worshipping life of the main Christian traditions? It had not been easy to arrive at a common mind on this point, for the acceptance of this approach to worship would mean that there would be several services of communion, at none of which all delegates would receive the sacrament together, and that our disunity would thus be emphasized. But the committee had come to the conviction that at the present stage of the ecumenical movement this was the right thing to do, for in this way the young delegates would be brought face to face with the real ecumenical problem: that we had so much in common but that we had not yet overcome our divisions.

Before the different communion services were held there was a service of preparation for the Holy Communion during which Robert Mackie and Benjamin Mays reminded us that we should ask forgiveness for our disunity, but also seize the opportunity to learn more about Christ through the services of other churches.

The great majority of the delegates attended the Reformed, Lutheran, Anglican and Orthodox communion services. For most of them this was the first time that they were present at the celebration of the Orthodox liturgy.

Had this adventure in worship succeeded? As the conference statement said, most delegates had been puzzled and distressed about the fact that we were unable to receive the sacrament all together, but they had arrived at a deeper understanding of the spiritual gifts embodied in other traditions and they had become more determined to work for full church unity.

The Amsterdam experiment had a considerable influence on the development of ecumenical worship in subsequent years. Worship at the first Assembly of the World Council of Churches in 1948 was to a large extent shaped according to the pattern elaborated by the World Christian Youth Conference of 1939.

My task was to be convener of the group of six daily chairmen of the joint sessions and to give the opening and closing addresses. We quickly became a very united group. Three of these chairmen: D. T. Niles of Ceylon, Madeleine Barot of France and Jean Fraser of Scotland were later to become my colleagues in the service of the World Council.

In the closing address I spoke of the world around us, the world in which there was war, rumours of war, fear, suffering and cruel injustice and which would oppose in one way or another all that we had dreamt of and hoped for during our meeting. But Jesus Christ had overcome the world. He had also overcome our man-made divisions. Our unity in him was a fact of faith – a fact so powerful that the worst facts of this world could not do away with it and a fact which demonstrated in a world of conflict that men can be brothers and create order out of the chaos of human relationships.

None of us knew with certainty that war was around the corner. But all of us knew that a time of severe testing was ahead.

I have never heard *À Toi la Gloire* sung as it was sung at the closing meeting in the Concertgebouw. It was a cry: *Kyrie Eleison*, but also a clear commitment to the faith that had brought us together and would hold us together.

Less than one month after the conference ended the second world war began. Had it all been in vain? Certainly not. All during the war young men and women in armies, in prisoner-of-war camps, in resistance movements, remembered that they belonged to the family gathered by *Christus Victor*. They were aware of the great truth: 'The Church *exists today* as a world-wide society which continues to work and pray for the healing of the nations'.[2]

I do not believe that any large ecumenical conference has been so completely timely and relevant or has had such direct influence on the life of the delegates. Twenty years after the conference, when I came to Japan in 1959, I found that the Amsterdam delegates were still holding an annual meeting together to reflect on their Amsterdam memories. During the Uppsala Assembly in 1968 the men and women who had been at Amsterdam in 1939 met to tell each other what had happened to them and other delegates in the years immediately following the conference. The story which summarized the experience of many was that of a girl from Lithuania. Soon after her return she had become a refugee. She had had to make her way through Spain and South America to the United States.

The two most precious and helpful things she had carried with her were the Bible and the list of addresses of the delegates of the Amsterdam Youth Conference.

NOTES

1. It was ironical that a few weeks later two socialist leaders became ministers of the Dutch government.

2. See the preface of the *Report of the World Conference of Christian Youth, Amsterdam 1939*, which appeared after the beginning of the second world war.

16 | *Is War Inevitable?*

IN THOSE LAST six months before the second world war broke out the ecumenical movement was in a paradoxical position. Church leaders in many countries were making feverish efforts to save the peace. But the mountain seemed to produce only mice, so that there was a general impression that the church was inactive and silent.

The main reason for this ineffectiveness was, as William Temple wrote, 'the multitude of counsels'. By April 1939 I was involved in discussions concerning some eight different initiatives or proposals from responsible persons and church bodies. And this at a time when the World Council of Churches was really more a plan proposed to the churches than a representative body, and when there was a general feeling that the Provisional Committee would endanger the formation of the World Council if it acted as if the World Council had in fact already been created.

The Archbishop of Canterbury, in a speech in the House of Lords in March, made an appeal to the heads of all Christian confessions and especially to the Pope to declare together that the new exaltation of the state at the expense of the human personality and the new exaltation of force as a means of solving international problems was contrary to Christian principles. But when I visited Germany I found that this appeal had been very badly received and that not only among the official church leaders. I wrote to Paton (April 7th): 'Even those in Germany who agree on the whole that the democratic countries should take a strong stand regret that this speech was such a mixture of religion and politics and would therefore be unable to take part in any action initiated by him (i.e. the Archbishop of Canterbury).' And Bishop Berggrav (of Oslo) wrote (with considerable exaggeration) that 'not only in Germany, but also in Holland, Switzerland and Scandinavia this speech was regarded as a combination of church and imperialism' (Berggrav to Bell, May 25th).

In the light of Berggrav's judgment it was surprising that the Swedish Ecumenical Council proposed in April (after Germany had occupied Czechoslovakia), that the World Council together with the World Alliance for International Friendship through the Churches should pronounce – if possible together with the Pope – their firm disapproval of acts of violence against small nations, since such acts imperilled the peace of the world. They wanted to add that the growing brutality in the relations between states had its origin in the injustice of the Treaty of Versailles. In the light of recent developments I advised against issuing such a statement. We had just made our protest concerning the declaration of the eleven German church leaders and that was clearly within our competence, but the Provisional Committee did not have sufficient authority to make a specifically political statement. I added that such a statement would almost certainly lead to a breaking off of all relations with the German church leaders. Ironically enough I would find myself less than a year later in the position of defending against the same Scandinavian church leaders the right and duty of the Provisional Committee to speak out concretely on the issues of international relations.

We considered the possibility of another kind of statement of a less political nature. Paton made a specific suggestion along this line. Bell wondered whether we could not propose a new conference or a procedure of arbitration. But the dilemma was that we would give the impression either of working for another Munich agreement or of repeating the language of the Western democracies. If we were only able to get signatures of church leaders in democratic countries, the impression would be given that the churches of these countries were forming a front against the other churches. Berggrav's remark (Berggrav to Bell, May 25th) was typical of the dominant ecumenical mood: 'We must not build a Maginot line of churches.' We were strongly, indeed too strongly, influenced by desire to avoid the situation created in the first world war when the churches had 'presented arms' and identified themselves almost completely with their national interests.

The difficulty of arriving at any agreement was shown again when the Archbishop of Canterbury took the initiative of getting as many church leaders as possible to sign an appeal for prayer at Whitsuntide. He approached the Pope, but received – after long delay – the answer that the Pope had already made an appeal for prayer for peace. Dr Boegner refused to sign because the statement included a reference to the earlier appeal of the Pope and he had to consider the reaction in France caused by the fact that the Pope had said nothing concerning Italy's aggression against Albania (Boegner to Canterbury, May 16th). So the Whitsun appeal came out with only five signatures, those of the Archbishop of Canterbury, of the Moderator of the Church of Scotland, of Archbishop Germanos of the Greek Orthodox Church, of Archbishop Eidem of the Church of Sweden and of the Moderator of the Council of Free Churches in Great Britain.

In the meantime Bishop Bell was working on a more ambitious scheme. He consulted a number of church leaders in different countries about a plan to hold, in Rome, a meeting of theologians to discuss the fundamental Christian principles involved in a true international order and in the establishment of social justice. Berggrav approved and suggested that three or four ecumenical leaders should personally go to Rome to find out what possibilities for common action existed and that one of the three or four should be a German (Berggrav to Bell, May 24th). Berggrav seemed to imply that he was willing to go. Bell proposed that Berggrav, Boegner, the Bishop of Novi Sad, Yugoslavia, and he himself might go together with a German, if the right man could be found (Bell to Novi Sad, May 25th). Later on he suggested that I should join this group. On June 12th Bell sent an official letter to the Apostolic Delegate in London, describing his proposal in great detail. Bell also discussed the matter with Dietrich Bonhoeffer. Bonhoeffer urged 'extreme care in not telling people who are in the least likely to leak to the press' (Bell to me, June 14th).[1] I told Chichester that it seemed to me most unlikely that any German church leader would be found ready to go to Rome on this kind of mission and that if the group going to Rome were not to be fully representative of all viewpoints held in the ecumenical movement, it was undesirable that I should directly participate in this plan.

On July 12th Bell received the reply that since the Pope had made the teaching of the church on the questions concerned perfectly clear, it was not easy to see the practical utility of the proposed meeting. Bell was deeply disappointed. I did not share his disappointment because I had not really expected a positive reply. It would take another twenty-five years before that kind of ecumenical discussion with the Roman Catholic authorities would become possible.

In March the German army had entered the already mutilated Czechoslovakia. This meant the definitive end of the illusions created by the Munich agreement. I was worried about my Czech friends and particularly about Professor Josef Hromadka, the Czech theologian, who had taken a strong stand against national socialism and was therefore in great danger. What could be done? I tried the simplest method of all, that was to send him a formal invitation to give lectures on Calvinism in Geneva. The method was more successful than I had dared to hope. The Gestapo had probably not had time to organize itself in Prague. In any case my invitation made such an impression on the visa-granting authorities that he received an exit permit and appeared in Geneva with his wife and daughters. It was difficult to determine whether he or I felt the greater surprise. American friends quickly arranged for him to spend the years of the war in the USA.

It was also in March that I met Dietrich Bonhoeffer for the first time. It was strange that we had not met before. As early as 1931 he had used my book on the Social Gospel for his own studies on American Christianity. We had been invited to the same conferences and even been members of the same ecumenical youth commission, but we had not attended the same meetings. I had read a number of Bonhoeffer's writings. His challenging and hard-hitting article of 1935 on 'The Confessing Church and the Ecumenical Movement'[2] had made a deep impression on me. Here was a man who dared to ask the really important questions about the *raison d'être* of the ecumenical movement. In 1936 when

Oldham asked me to join him in writing the preparatory volume for the Oxford Conference of 1937[3] and I had to answer the question whether the churches could really act and speak together, I had made full use of Bonhoeffer's ideas.

When I came to London in the last week of March 1939 I received a message from Bishop Bell that Bonhoeffer was in London and wanted to see me. Since I had to take the train to Aberdeen we made an appointment to meet at Paddington station. We talked together as we walked up and down the station platform. I had expected that he would want to discuss the relations between the Confessing Church and the World Council. So I was surprised that he began immediately to tell me about the grave choice concerning his future which he had to make. He said substantially what he had already written to Bishop Bell in a letter which I had not seen. I quote:[4]

I am thinking of leaving Germany sometime. The main reason is the compulsory military service to which the men of my age (1906) will be called up this year. It seems to me conscientiously impossible to join in a war under the present circumstances. On the other hand, the Confessing Church as such has not taken any definite attitude in this respect and probably cannot take it as things are. So I should cause a tremendous damage to my brethren if I would make a stand on this point which would be regarded by the regime as typical of the hostility of our church towards the state. Perhaps the worst thing of all is the military oath which I should have to swear. So I am rather puzzled in this situation, and perhaps even more because I feel it is really only on Christian grounds that I find it difficult to do military service under the present conditions, and yet there are only very few friends who would approve of my attitude. In spite of much reading and thinking concerning this matter I have not yet made up my mind what I would do under different circumstances. But actually as things are I should have to do violence to my Christian conviction, if I would take up arms 'here and now'. I have been thinking of going to the Mission Field, not as an escape out of the situation, but because I wish to serve somewhere where service is really wanted. But here also the German foreign exchange situation makes it impossible to send workers abroad. With respect to British Missionary Societies I have no idea of the possibilities there. On the other hand, I still have the great desire to serve the Confessing Church as long as I possibly could.

My Lord Bishop, I am very sorry to add trouble to your trouble. But I thought, I might speak freely to you and might ask your advice. You know the Confessing Church and you know me a bit. So I thought you could help me best. It was with regard to this matter that I wanted to see Visser 't Hooft, too.

An important point which he had not mentioned in his letter but which he made during our conversation, was that his problem was particularly acute since Hitler would surely attack Poland in the summer or autumn and that this would lead to war on a large scale. He did not tell me what special information he had,[5] but I had the strong impression that he knew what he was talking about and I took his prediction very seriously.

I was strangely moved that he had not only chosen his friends, Bishop Bell and Reinhold Niebuhr,[6] but also me as confidant and adviser, though we had never met before. I remember his urgent questions better than my answers. It was not simply the old issue of pacifism. The issue was whether a Christian could participate in a war started by a ruthless regime which would bring untold misery to many nations. On the other hand, what would happen to the Confessing Church if he were to become a conscientious objector and others follow his example? The best help I could give was perhaps simply to show a real understanding of the awful dilemma which he was facing. But, as I wrote soon after his death in 1945, 'in the hazy world between "Munich" and "Warsaw", in which hardly anyone dared to formulate the real problems clearly, this questioning voice had a liberating effect on me'.[7] This theologian wanted his life to be in full accord with his affirmations.

Karl Barth made a proposal concerning the same dilemma which Christians in Germany had to face. He urged in a letter of April 13th that when war should break out a message on behalf of the churches should be addressed to the German people. The idea had arisen in conversations Barth had had with Hermann Rauschning, the former President of the Senate in Danzig and author of *The Revolution of Nihilism*. The message should make clear that Christians in the other countries did not consider this war as a war against the German people, but against the dangerous usurpers who were ruling Germany and that Christians in Germany should face the question whether it was not their duty to do everything they could to end this war and to prevent a victory by the usurpers.

I discussed the question first with Pierre Maury. He felt that Barth's proposal went too far. We could say what our own attitude was going to be. But we should let the Christians in Germany draw their own conclusion. I also wondered whether we had the right to urge Christians in Germany to take a course which would certainly lead to martyrdom, and have the gravest consequences for the church. I proposed therefore to Archbishop Temple and Paton that the churches outside Germany should say clearly to the Christians in Germany that there was no choice left for most Christians but to resist a regime which sought to dominate other nations and spread its anti-Christian conceptions. But I did not propose that we should tell the Christians in Germany what their own decision should be. Temple wrote (April 21st) that he was doubtful about such a statement. He added: 'It is so supremely difficult to avoid making that sort of appeal appear other than hypocritical in the eyes of those to whom it is addressed.' Paton submitted the proposal to the Director of the BBC, Mr F. W. Ogilvie. In his reply Mr Ogilvie said that this suggestion deserved the fullest consideration. Much would depend on the specific circumstances at the critical moment. And care should be taken to avoid anything which might adversely affect the position of Christian communities in other countries. 'We do not want inadvertently to encourage throwing Christians to the lions' (Ogilvie to Paton, May 2nd).

Barth returned to the attack and felt that to leave out the word concerning the duty of Christians in Germany to oppose Hitler actively was to leave out the decisive part of the message. When a few months later he put the matter to leaders of the German Confessing Church he also failed to convince them.[8] They also felt that such a message would put the Confessing Church in an impossible position. We were obviously not ready for such radical action. We had not thought and prayed enough about our attitude to war and had not formed a sufficiently strong ecumenical fellowship to speak with authority on this question of life and death.

In the meantime the World Council itself was working on two lines. The first was to arrive at an understanding among the churches concerning their attitude in war-time. During the first world war Christians had failed miserably to 'be the Church, still united as the one Body of Christ'. Since that time the ecumenical movement of the churches had been formed. The attitude of the churches in war-time would show whether the ecumenical movement was a reality or not. So I drafted a document, largely based on convictions expressed by the Oxford Conference, on 'The Church as an Ecumenical Society in Time of War'. Paton and Temple revised it and Temple wrote a very fine 'Form of Prayer for use by Christian people in all countries during times of war and rumours of wars'. With regard to prayer and preaching we said: 'If Christians in warring nations pray according to the pattern of prayer given by their Lord, they will not be "praying against" one another.' The church should never present the war as a holy crusade. We urged that even during the war brotherly relations should be kept between the churches and that church leaders in neutral countries should be asked to keep in touch with the churches on either side and keep the lines of communication open. We spoke of the duty to prepare for a just peace and added: 'Constant efforts should be made in time of war, as well as immediately after the war, to ascertain from brother Christians in the opposing camp what terms of peace may create a lasting peace.' These documents were sent to the members of the Provisional Committee with the suggestion that they should pass them on to the churches in their respective countries and thus our recommendations received wide circulation. These convictions remained the basis for the work of the officers and staff of the Provisional Committee of the Council and for the attitude of many churches during the following six years.

The second plan based on a suggestion made by the Federal Council of Churches of Christ in the USA to the World Council's Provisional Committee was to call a small international conference 'to consider what action is open to churches and to individual Christians with a view to checking the drift towards war and to leading us nearer to the establishment of an effective international order'. Our purpose was to bring together about fifteen laymen with thorough knowledge of international affairs with fifteen theologians and church leaders.

We were fortunate in getting such able men as Max Huber (Switzerland), John Foster Dulles (USA), Alfred Zimmern (Great Britain), Charles Rist (France), F. M. van Asbeck (Netherlands). There were two Germans: O. H. von der Gablentz and Wilhelm Menn. We met in July, in Geneva. Our task was of course impossible, for by that time war was approaching like an uncontrolled bulldozer and a discussion on Christian foundations for international order seemed to be completely irrelevant. There were difficult moments. Dulles and Zimmern who had both been at the Versailles Peace Conference after the first world war, disagreed strongly about the attitude which the Western governments should adopt to nazi Germany. Dulles was ready to make considerable concessions. Zimmern felt that far too many concessions had been made already. One of the American delegates, Dr Albert W. Palmer, made a passionate plea that Christians should all together demand the calling of a meeting of all governments to study again the issues of world order and to reorganize the League of Nations. The plan was extremely vague and unrealistic. Professor van Asbeck reacted sharply and said that to sit down again in conference with the present German government after what it had done in the last two years would be considered by many Christians as a betrayal of Christianity. He mentioned specifically the persecution of the Jews and the violation of human rights. This statement led to a serious incident. The German delegates felt hurt and announced that they would no longer participate in the meeting. Roswell Barnes intervened and arranged a private conversation between the German delegates and van Asbeck. I heard later that that conversation had not been easy. The Germans had counter-attacked by criticizing the discrimination which according to them the Dutch practised in the Netherlands Indies. But in the end they decided to return to the meeting. It is likely that they were in such a delicate situation with regard to their own government that they had to make some sort of protest. But Dr Palmer's plan was not accepted by the conference.

But while the meeting could do little about the immediate situation it proved to be useful in a long range perspective. We drew up a report on 'The Churches and the International Crisis' and sent it to the churches. This report served as a basis for the ecumenical discussion on peace aims and international order in the following years.

The report gave a balanced account of the causes of the disorder, but the most important section was that on the application of Christian principles. Max Huber's point on the necessity of an international ethos as a basis for international law was developed, and Dulles's conviction that 'the collective will of the community shall be used to secure the necessary changes in the interests of justice to the same extent that it is used to secure the protection of nations against violence' was included. And it is remarkable that already, at that time, an ecumenical conference spoke of 'the responsibility of the whole of mankind for the whole earth'. For 'all peoples have an interest in the wise use of the resources of individual countries and in the planning ahead for future generations'.

With regard to the task of the churches the conference confirmed what we had already said in 'The Church as an Ecumenical Society in Time of War'.

The July conference had not been able to check the drift towards war, but it had made a contribution to the development of a common mind about the church's role with regard to international order. It set in motion a process which led to the formation of the Peace Aims Group in Great Britain, and to the creation by the Federal Council of Churches in the United States of the Commission on a Just and Durable Peace. And it was through the work of these two bodies, together with the World Council's Study Department, that the foundations were laid for the Commission of the Churches on International Affairs, created in 1947.

NOTES

1. But Bell made his plan public in his Penguin Special on *Christianity and World Order*, pp. 152–3, published later in 1940.

2. Dietrich Bonhoeffer, *Gesammelte Schriften*, Band I, pp. 240–61 (London, *No Rusty Swords*, pp. 326–344).

3. *The Church and its Function in Society*, London, 1937, pp. 88–100.

4. The letter appears in Bonhoeffer's *Gesammelte Schriften* I, pp. 281–2 (London, *The Way to Freedom*, pp. 205–6).

5. Eberhard Bethge's biography of Bonhoeffer shows that through his brother-in-law, Hans von Dohnanyi, he had indeed much inside information.

6. See Eberhard Bethge, *Dietrich Bonhoeffer*, German edition, pp. 715ff.

7. *Das Zeugnis eines Boten*, Geneva, 1945, p. 6.

8. See Helmut Gollwitzer, *Forderungen der Freiheit*, pp. 337–8.

17 | *Is This Really War?*

THE MEETING OF the Continuation Committee of Faith and Order in Clarens began on August 21st, 1939. Dr Boegner, who was in the chair, opened the meeting by saying that we were praying on a volcano. I found it hard to listen to learned addresses on ecclesiology. So I appointed myself as information officer and tried to listen to broadcasts from various countries and then to inform the committee about the development of the international crisis. On August 23rd I burst into the session to report on the conclusion of the pact between Germany and Russia. It seemed that war was now inevitable. So the meeting broke up.

I went to Evolène in the mountains of the Valais where my family was vacationing. Swiss mobilization in that beautiful setting seemed an almost idyllic affair. The men inspecting their uniforms and guns with which they would defend their own beloved valley; the women in their colourful traditional dress in a great circle around them; and the astounding beauty of God's world on a glorious summer day.

War had come and was terribly real in Poland. But in Western Europe we entered into that strange period in which it was neither peace nor war. I wondered what possibilities for ecumenical action would remain. Would the still provisional and fragile structure created at Utrecht a year ago be able to survive in wartime? This was the first large-scale war since the ecumenical movement had come into being as an organized body. Had it struck sufficiently deep roots in the life of the churches to overcome the divisive forces that would now gain tremendous momentum? It was clear that many plans would have to be postponed. It would not be possible to hold the first Assembly in 1941 as we had hoped. But there would be new responsibilities. As I wrote to the members of the Provisional Committee, the main tasks seemed to be: to prepare for the actual formation of the World Council, to maintain contacts between the churches, to continue the study and discussion of the issues of international order, to set up a ministry for refugees and a ministry to prisoners-of-war.

With regard to the follow-up of the July conference on international affairs, great progress was made when William Paton succeeded in organizing the Peace Aims Group in England with such eminent people as Arnold Toynbee, Sir

Alfred Zimmern and A. D. Lindsay (the Master of Balliol); and when Roswell
Barnes, acting by authorization of the Federal Council, set up a similar group in
the United States. From that moment onwards it became possible to have a continuing exchange of thoughts on international problems between New York,
London and Geneva. We in Geneva were responsible for representing the views of
ecumenically-minded Christians on the Continent, including those in Germany.

In October I visited France, Great Britain and Holland. The impressions
I received during this trip made me wonder whether the line which we had
taken in the ecumenical movement was the right one. Had we perhaps been too
successful in our stand against attempts to present the war against Nazi Germany as a crusade? And had we stressed so much that the church should not
identify itself with any political cause or ideology that the church was in danger
of living in the clouds?

I wrote a report on 'The Attitudes of Christians to This War' and sent it
around to church leaders in several countries. I had found a curious moral
relativism. One friend in England summed up the attitude of younger Christians
as follows: 'We must fight this war, but it is dirty business. And if any bishop
tells us that this is a Christian thing, then let's at least string up the bishop.'
There was such a fear of national self-righteousness and such a sense of the
failure of all nations that very many refused to make up their minds about the
basic issues of this war. Reinhold Niebuhr had hit the nail on its head when he
wrote at that time: 'We are actually in the paradoxical situation that the revulsion
against moral over-simplifications in the last war now tempts people to abstain
from moral discriminations which are justified and essential in the present situation.'

Clearly now we were to some extent ourselves responsible for this situation.
We had placed such an emphasis on the duty for the church to remain the truly
ecumenical church that there was a danger that the church would be looked upon
as a haven of refuge above the world and not give guidance to its members for
their decisions in this world. I came therefore to the following conclusion: 'The
ecumenical movement dare not be silent at a time when various forms of
nihilism tend to submerge large parts of Europe, and when the validity of such
basic norms of human relationships as justice and freedom for the life of our
whole civilization is at stake.'[1]

I found myself in an uncomfortable position. On the one hand I became
more and more convinced that the World Council should not only speak of the
maintenance of ecumenical fellowship, but should also render witness to the basic
issues. But this was abhorrent to many church leaders whose one and only
concern was not to increase the existing tensions. On the other hand I could not
go along with Karl Barth who reiterated (and this time publicly)[2] his demand
that the World Council should ask Christians in Germany to refuse to participate
in the war.

I hoped that at the first war-time meeting of the Administrative Committee it would be possible to arrive at a common word which would be concrete and relevant but which would not throw the Christians in Germany 'to the lions', and also would not break up the ecumenical movement.

But things turned out differently.

NOTES

1. *Notes on the Attitudes of Christians to This War*, November 1940, p. 10.
2. In his letter to France of December 1939, which appeared (heavily censored) in *Foi et Vie* and which was reprinted in its original form in *Eine Schweizer Stimme*, 1945, pp. 108ff.

18 | *Is This Really the Way to Peace?*

THE BISHOP OF CHICHESTER (George Bell) proposed on November 23rd, 1939, that the Provisional Committee should be called together as soon as possible. He felt that 'the Church has got something very creative and positive to say at the present time'. William Temple agreed strongly. Since, however, it seemed quite impossible to get a quorum of the rather large Provisional Committee it was decided to call a meeting of the much smaller Administrative Committee, together with some members of the Provisional Committee who would be able to attend. The meeting was to be in Amsterdam.

Soon after this had been decided a new situation arose. Scandinavia moved onto the centre of the stage in the person of Bishop Berggrav of Oslo.

Bishop Eivind Berggrav had become Chairman of the Executive Committee of the World Alliance for Promoting Friendship through the Churches. He had been an admirer and friend of Nathan Söderblom, an earlier Scandinavian ecumenical leader, and it was very generally thought that the mantle of Söderblom had fallen on his shoulders and that he was therefore the right man to do, in the second world war, what Söderblom had tried to do in the first world war. Berggrav felt deeply that the Scandinavians had a special mission to perform during the war and he responded strongly to the proclamation of the Scandinavian chiefs of state that the task of Scandinavia was to work for reconciliation. Various approaches were made to him, one of them by the German churchmen, Gerstenmaier and Schönfeld, to suggest that he should take the lead in an action for peace. But he needed little urging. A *pro memoria*, emanating from persons in close touch with Weizsäcker of the German Foreign Office, was given to him as a basis for his action.[1] Paton, who had met him in Copenhagen in October 1939, invited him, after consultation with the Archbishops of Canterbury and York, to visit Great Britain. Berggrav arrived in London on December 8th, 1939. He came first of all to find out whether there was a real possibility for peace negotiations. Paton arranged that he should see 'the top people in Church and State'. Halifax, the Foreign Secretary, listened carefully to Berggrav's exposition, but made it clear that the British Government did not trust Hitler's word. Berggrav answered that he did not do so either, but that a risk should be taken and that total war would work in favour of dictatorship. Berggrav hinted that forces were at work seeking to overthrow Hitler, and that these forces might be strengthened if there was a real possibility of an acceptable peace.[2]

The second purpose of Berggrav's visit was to arrange for a meeting of British and French church leaders with Scandinavian church leaders. Afterwards a similar meeting with German church leaders would be held. Berggrav spoke so convincingly that the two Archbishops, the Bishop of Chichester and William Paton all agreed to the idea of a meeting. It was decided to propose that this meeting should be held just before or after the meeting of the Administrative Committee.

Berggrav rather forced my hand with regard to the place of meeting. As a supporter of the Oxford Group he was in touch with a Dutch businessman in Rotterdam who was very eager for the cessation of the war and considered Hitler to be a lesser evil than communism. He offered to make all the necessary arrangements and so the meeting was held in a quiet country hotel near Apeldoorn. Our host was present at the meals and did not hide his convictions, which again led to strong reactions from those who thought, as I did, that peace with Hitler would mean the end of Europe. I felt this all the more strongly since on the way to Holland I had had a long conversation in Paris with Hermann Rauschning, who, through his books, had opened the eyes of many concerning the true nature of national socialism and had made it as clear as possible that concessions to Hitler would lead to more and not to less violence and bloodshed.

On January 6th the meeting proposed and prepared by Berggrav began. Although it was conceived as a meeting between the Scandinavian, British and French church leaders, Koechlin (of Switzerland), Berkelbach van der Sprenkel (of Holland) and I were asked to be present. Schönfeld was the only German.

Berggrav opened the discussion. He said that the Church had its greatest opportunity in time of war. He explained the origin of the meeting. He gave an account of his conversations in Britain and made reference to his meeting with people in authority. (Most of us knew he was referring to Halifax.) He had found in Britain a remarkable open-mindedness. The British wanted, however, to teach Hitler a lesson. Thus from the British standpoint this was a 'pedagogical war'. But if one would be consistently pedagogical, one should avoid the intensification of the evil which one sought to avoid. The most urgent task was to prevent total war which would make the situation worse for all concerned. The governments should be urged to clarify their peace-aims and the conditions under which negotiations would become possible. Poland and Czechoslovakia should certainly be independent. He added that Finnish friends had told him that the only way to save Finland was to establish peace in Western Europe.

If my memory is correct, Berggrav did not at this time make any reference to the desirability and possibility of a change of regime in Germany. So his proposals could only be taken as proposals concerning a peace to be concluded between the Western governments and Hitler.

That explains why I wrote in between my notes on Berggrav's speech on that morning: 'All this sounds as if we were in the nineteenth century. Is there no understanding of the demoniacal element in national socialism?'

William Temple and Marc Boegner spoke next, but confined their remarks for the time being to the spiritual attitude which Christians should maintain in time of war.

The main discussion took place in the afternoon. The question was: Should the churches demand that peace negotiations should take place immediately and, if so, under what conditions? Boegner warned strongly against a second 'Munich' which would in fact be an immense success for Hitler and would be followed by another war. The Bishop of Chichester and the Archbishop of Uppsala supported Berggrav, but Koechlin and I supported Boegner.

In the next meeting only the Scandinavian, the British and the French participated, for now the question was whether the British and the French could draw up a common statement concerning peace aims and peace negotiations which Berggrav could bring to his German contacts. I heard later that Boegner had consistently refused to sign the statement which William Temple had prepared.[3] This statement was therefore only signed by the four British church-men: William Temple, George Bell, William Paton and Henry Carter. The key sentences were:

> They (the signatories) believe that it would be right to enter into negotiations if the following points were secured:
> (a) that the Czech, the Slovak and the Polish peoples be recognized as independent and sovereign – and that practical guarantees for this be forth-coming; the nature of such guarantees cannot be defined in advance, because they may greatly depend on the conditions existing at the time.
> (b) that the definitive peace be negotiated in a congress including at least the European nations, the Czechs, Slovaks and Poles being full partners in the Congress.

This statement was not intended for publication. Berggrav was to take it to Berlin. He did so later in January when he met Weizsäcker at the Ministry of Foreign Affairs and had a conversation with Goering. But before long rumours began to circulate about a secret meeting of churchmen in Holland. It was said in the press that the reports about our meeting had been a factor in President Roosevelt's decision to send Mr Sumner Welles to Europe for a sounding out of the opinions of the European statesmen. William Temple commented: 'I have no reason to suppose that the conference had any effect on Mr Welles' visit or any reason to suppose that it did not. It might have been one of several straws.' In these circumstances it was thought best to publish the 'Zilven document' and it appeared in the London *Times* (February 8th, 1940). In his introduction to the statement William Temple said: 'We also made it clear that the whole British people, though free from anything like war-fever, is united in determination to

A talk in a work camp in Switzerland for men going to England, who had reached Switzerland and had to wait until they could travel further.

The family, about 1944.

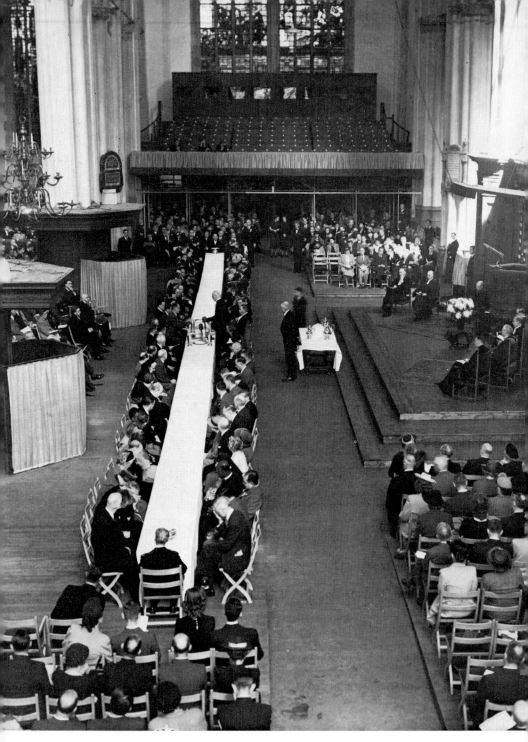

Eucharist in the Nieuwe Kerk in Amsterdam during the first Assembly of the World Council of Churches, 1948. (*Photograph : studio Heno*)

pursue the war until the objects for which our nation entered it are secured.'

The document had no effect. Those who had taken part in the discussion in de Zilven did not know that a few weeks before their meeting Hitler had told the generals of his definitive decision to begin soon the great offensive and to attack Belgium and Holland as well as France.[4]

The only hope was really for a military coup in Germany. A declaration of peace aims by the Allied governments might have been meaningful if it could have been used to encourage the leadership of the army to get rid of Hitler. And this was indeed the purpose of other peace negotiations such as those of Ambassador von Hassell in Switzerland[5] and Dr Joseph Müller[6] in Rome during the same period. The weakness of the action taken by the Scandinavians and British at de Zilven was that it did not make it clear that peace could not be achieved *without* a change of regime in Germany.

The World Council as such was not involved in this action for peace. It could not because the chairman of the Administrative Committee (Boegner) and the General Secretary were against it. And the Scandinavians did not want the World Council to have anything to do with it. In their eyes the World Council was not 'neutral' because the German churches had not joined it and its leadership was in the hands of British, American and French churchmen.

But the meeting of the Administrative Committee which took place on January 7th and 8th was of course quite different from the meeting that I had hoped for. The action taken on January 6th during the discussions on the possibility of peace negotiations acted as a brake on any initiative that might be taken to speak a clear word about the international situation. The Scandinavians were so afraid of being linked up with a body in which the Germans were not represented, that they decided not to participate officially in the meeting, though some of them came to a few sessions. I had prepared a draft for a statement which the Administrative Committee might issue. What I proposed was certainly not very radical. I maintained that while the church could not take sides, it could not remain indifferent when such basic issues were at stake and when the very bases of the common life of men were threatened. The church should therefore protest against the gross injustice committed both in the international and national realm. It should lift up its voice against the violation of whole nations, against the attacks by big nations on small nations, against the suppression of national and individual freedoms.

Boegner and Koechlin backed me up, but nearly all others took the line that a statement of this kind would interfere with the peace action which was now the primary concern. The important thing was to prevent total war, and so nothing should be said that would make the gulf between the nations any greater. Moreover what would be the value of a statement which would be made against the clearly expressed wish of the Scandinavian church leaders and in the absence of the Germans?

William Temple proposed a statement which would only speak of basic moral principles. But Boegner and Koechlin felt that at this critical moment a 'timeless' statement would be worse than no statement at all. So we only adopted one paragraph of the Temple statement about the maintenance of relations between the churches. It was a poor result and nobody felt happy about it.

The meeting was quite useful in respect of the organization of the work of the Council in war-time. But the fact remained that at a critical moment the ecumenical movement had been unable to speak out on the grave issues at stake.

The religious periodicals in several countries rightly complained about the 'silence of the ecumenical movement'. I was in the unpleasant position of not being able to tell the story of what had really happened at the meetings in the Netherlands. All I could do was to make another attempt to break through our silence. This I did a few weeks later.

NOTES

1. Printed in Berggrav's own account of his peace action, *Forgjeves for Fred*, Oslo, 1960, p. 173.
2. These remarks of Berggrav, which he had reported in a letter to a Norwegian friend, became the basis of a violent attack on Berggrav by the Reichscommissioner Terboven in 1942.
3. See Marc Boegner, *The long road to Unity*, pp. 140–3.
4. H. A. Jacobsen, *Der zweite Weltkrieg*, p. 70.
5. Ulrich von Hassel, *Vom anderen Deutschland*, pp. 114, 131.
6. ibid., p. 124.

19 | *War Becomes Very Real*

IN THE FIRST months of 1940 I became increasingly worried about the astounding insensitiveness of Western Europe and the United States to the menace of national socialism. Visiting Oxford I found that the combined influence of communism and pacifism made it practically impossible for the students to face the realities. And in Holland the attitude was 'It cannot happen here', and the clear warnings from anti-nazi Germans were not taken seriously.

In order to arrive at a better understanding of the situation we had to face I wrote for circulation by the World Council's Study Department a paper on 'Germany and the West'.[1] After describing the different trends of political thought in German history I said:

> It is by no means accidental that National Socialism has grown up in Germany. It is not so much a completely new creation as the *reductio ad absurdum* of one of the main traditions in German political thought which have dominated German life for several decades. While outward circumstances, particularly the faults of the Western powers, have given it its great opportunity, it is rooted in certain aspects of German thought which have been widely held in Germany for generations.
>
> On the other hand, it is equally clear that the thesis that National Socialism is the typical expression of the German soul cannot be substantiated. The Germany of a century ago would surely not recognize its ideals in the present German regime. And the large groups in German life which have remained attached or found their way back to the traditions of the old style conservatism, to the original notions of liberalism, to socialism, or to one of the two main Christian confessions, are all in one way or another and in greater or lesser degree in inner conflict with National Socialism, even if they do not oppose it openly.

My conclusion was that 'the West' had a positive role to fulfil with regard to Germany: to facilitate the task of those Germans who were trying to counteract the demonic tendencies of the state by building up the spiritual life of the nation.

I participated also in the discussions of the International Consultation Group in Geneva which consisted of staff members of the League of Nations and other governmental or non-governmental international organizations and which sought at that time to analyse the reasons for the breakdown of the international order. After we had completed papers on 'Political Factors in the Peace Failure' and 'Economics of the Peace Failure', I had to draft the document on 'Spiritual Factors in the Peace Failure'.[2] About the League of Nations I said:

> The tragedy of the League (and indeed of the whole post-war settlement) was that it became the plaything of utopians who made impossible claims for it and surrounded it with a mystic glamour, and of hardheaded 'realists' who sabotaged its efficacy. Thus public opinion swung between moods of optimism and cynicism, and the League was constantly diverted from its true task of making slow but real progress towards the ordering of international life.

I emphasized the responsibility of the Western democracies for the present crisis. The democratic tradition which once was dynamic had become static and sterile. The peace failure was not only due to the present impotence of the democracies. The task ahead was not merely to conserve the European tradition and to defend it against the Western ideologies but primarily to renovate that tradition so that it could become the basis of a new spiritual integration.

But my chief concern was that in spite of the impasse reached at the January meeting the ecumenical movement should still speak a clear word of guidance. So I wrote a rather long document on 'The Ecumenical Church and the International Situation' and sent this to a number of friends and colleagues in April. My main point was that we were really faced with two wars. There was the war which was a great conflict of national interests, having its roots in the power politics of past decades. Behind that war there was another war, one which was fundamentally a spiritual conflict concerning the nature of the state and its right to impose an anti-Christian ideology. In that second war the church was deeply involved. The church could not of course defend its own life by force. But it had to be concerned for the state, and it had the duty to remind the state that it was a 'minister unto God' for the good of man, and could not let itself become the prey of forces which would turn it into a counter-church. War could of course only fulfil a negative function – namely, to hold back a force which threatened to achieve even more costly destruction than war itself would achieve. So the ecumenical movement should not keep silent in a period when life and death decisions for the church and civilization had to be taken. Its word could not be a blessing of certain nations over against other nations, and even less a blessing of war itself, but it could be a recognition that the anti-Christian forces had to be resisted, and that those who did so without ulterior motives, without hatred and with the humility of men who knew themselves to be sinners, would be fulfilling a terrible but none the less real duty to God and man. We should speak not only on behalf of the churches who were still free to express themselves, but also on behalf of the other churches which could not speak out. We should therefore make it clear that we were not defending a Western ideology, for we realized that in a less tangible way anti-Christian forces were also operating in the democratic countries.

I received a few positive reactions. Thus John Bennett wrote from the USA: 'This memorandum states provocatively and perhaps in slightly exaggerated form the real situation as I am coming to see it.' But the most important answer was negative. Archbishop William Temple, the Chairman of the Provisional Committee, wrote in a letter of May 20th:

> I am much impressed by your plea for the ecumenical movement to speak . . . My difficulty is twofold: (1) Does the ecumenical movement actually exist in such manner as to be capable of speech ? If we get our Assembly to meet, it will do so. I am really anxious lest we spoil our greater opportunities later by speaking beyond our authorization now. But of course much depends on what might be said. If we can really say a purely spiritual word which carries a judgment upon all nations and churches, I think the difficulty would be overcome. But can we ? (2) It is impossible to consult with the Germans; it is also impossible to forecast their outlook when the war is over. If we are silent because we have no authority to speak, the Faith and Order Section at least can come together at once on its own ground after the war and begin to build up Christian fellowship again. If we speak corporately, we may find that we have erected fresh barriers to the reconstitution of that fellowship. Christians from one country can meet Christians from a country with which they have been fighting in an organization which has not corporately taken sides; it will be difficult, almost impossible, to do this in an organization which has officially condemned, directly or by implication, their own country or so far contributed to its defeat. For of course this kind of difficulty will be felt only on the defeated side. The national feeling on the victorious side will not care in the least who or what has condemned it.
>
> I want us all to prophesy individually, and to do this in contact with one another through your office, so the same message will be given ecumenically though with a variety of emphasis. But I remain doubtful about an utterance by the ecumenical movement at this stage acting quasi-corporately.

If only one could have talked this out with Temple! He seemed to be thinking in terms of the first world war. But was not this war completely different? I wrote (June 6th) saying that we could of course not speak out unless we could meet together to arrive at a common mind. But should we not call Christians to spiritual resistance against the evil spirits? Was not the lack of a deeply rooted spiritual resistance the deepest cause of the catastrophe? It turned out that no ecumenical meeting of a truly representative character could be held for many years and I did not see William Temple for two years. So this was, at least for the time being, the end of the struggle for a common word about the deeper issues of the war.

The invasion of Holland was of course a tremendous shock. We Dutchmen had become so accustomed to sit in the spectators' gallery. Now we were right in the midst of the tragedy. But that tragedy took on cosmic proportions. Was the whole of Europe, including before long Britain also, to become the prey of a wild totalitarianism? Was everything that we loved, all that we had worked for, going to be destroyed?

Under the deep emotion of those hours I sent on May 14th a telegram to Professor William Adams Brown in New York:

Desire state personal conviction to American colleagues stop admitting common responsibility all countries for this catastrophe now all Christians particularly in America must face question will we let all possibility Christian public ministry and action go under in large part world stop will we let ecumenical movement be destroyed stop For God's sake let churches face consequences of Hitler victory. Pray God may lead you in immediate decisions.

That was certainly not a very carefully worded message but that day was not a day for quiet reflection. Professor Brown replied three days later as follows:

Presented your cable Executive Committee Federal Council today, which officially sends you following message: 'We members Executive Committee Federal Council Churches Christ in America, meeting at a time when great numbers of our fellow-Christians in Europe are victims of ruthless invasion, send this message of sympathy and brotherly affection through Provisional Committee of World Council of Churches. We express our horror and indignation at unprovoked violation of neutrality of Holland, Belgium and Luxembourg – states which have scrupulously maintained their neutral position and for whose invasion there was no shadow of excuse. We are concerned at this outrage, not simply because it is one more violation – following upon others as real if less flagrant – of those principles of international law upon which any stable society must rest, but also because it brings Christian brethren, with whom we have been co-operating for years in the ecumenical movement, under domination of a state that in its own domain has limited in many ways freedom of churches whose fellowship in the ecumenical movement we greatly prize. We are calling upon our fellow Christians in American churches to lend all help and support in their power to our brethren in all churches of Europe suffering from war. To Dr Visser 't Hooft especially, General Secretary of Provisional Committee of World Council Churches, we would express our sympathy and assure him of our support in added responsibility laid upon him. In co-operation with those who represent American churches on Provisional Committee of World Council we pledge ourselves to take such steps as may be necessary to make this support effective. Calling special meeting Joint Executive Committee Life and Work, Faith and Order to assure added American support of Provisional Committee.

I had asked Karl Barth to support my appeal to our American colleagues. He answered (June 8th) that he hoped of course that the Americans would take action before it was too late but that as a functionary of the canton of Basle and of neutral Switzerland he could not sign an appeal concerning such a political and military decision. He felt also that since the World Council had not taken that clear attitude to the war for which he had asked and which I had at last proposed in the memorandum on 'The Ecumenical Church and the International Situation', we did not have the right and authority to make such an appeal. So it would be best to turn to the very urgent tasks which had been entrusted to the Provisional Committee and which were especially urgent in time of war.

It was a new situation for me to be reminded by Karl Barth of all people that none of us were free agents and all of us had to remember our responsibilities to the bodies which we were serving, for I had had to make this point so often to him. But this time he was surely right.

As the German armies advanced farther into France I had to ask whether I should stay in Geneva. Would Switzerland not be invaded soon? And even if that did not happen would we in Geneva not be cut off from the rest of the world? But there were other considerations. What these were I explained in a letter (June 14th) to my colleagues, William Paton in London and Henry Leiper in New York. The main points of this letter were as follows:

> ... It seems now that the moment has come for me to decide whether I should get out of Geneva, and indeed out of the European Continent, or whether I should stay here. It may be that for a certain time to come there will remain possibilities for a Dutchman to leave Geneva for the USA, but it may also be that within a few days all routes leading out of Geneva will be cut off, and so this seems the moment for me to make up my mind as to whether I should get out or stay here. The intermediate solution about which I had written before, namely that one might go to Bordeaux and await further developments there, is now practically out of the question in view of the chaotic refugee situation in France.
>
> I have now come to the conclusion that it is my duty to stay here. The main arguments are the following: It seems now likely that the European Continent will be for a certain time to come practically cut off from the rest of the world. At the same time there is some reason to hope that for a certain time to come a good many ecumenical activities can be carried on as from Switzerland. Even if Switzerland were occupied by the German Army, this would not necessarily mean the end of our work with the various European countries. It would only be in case Switzerland would be directly incorporated in the Reich and in case the Gestapo would become all powerful here that our kind of work might become completely impossible. But this last possibility seems as yet to be pretty far away. If one considers how many of the churches which have been keenly participating in our work are in this part of

the world one feels little inclined to let oneself be completely cut off from them. This argument is reinforced by the present distribution of our staff. It does not seem that I am really needed in America where Henry (Leiper), can carry on not only the national work, but if necessary a good deal of the contacts which can best be maintained from America. Bill (Paton) will remain in touch with a good many countries as long as Great Britain is not directly attacked. On the other hand, one would not like at this moment to have Schönfeld as a German alone responsible for the work in Europe. To have a German plus a Dutchman may at this time mean a strong combination, while a German alone would give our European work a flavour which would not be helpful in many countries.

To put it quite shortly, I do not feel that at this moment I can serve the ecumenical cause very specially by working as from New York, and I do see that a very definite and difficult task remains to be done on the European Continent to save whatever can be saved of our work . . .

I hope that you agree with these proposals. It is extremely hard to visualize just what the future holds in store. After a period of hesitation I feel now pretty certain that I ought not to desert my present post and that my staying is in the best interest of our common work. It might be that the reality and vitality of the Ecumenical Movement will depend on the spiritual resistance against the evil forces which it can manifest in those many countries which are being submerged. To leave at such a time would seem too much like desertion and an escape from the carrying out of the decisions which one has constantly advocated . . .

It is a curious fact that precisely at this critical moment we have so much to encourage us in our own work. I refer especially to the three very important churches which have decided to join the World Council during the last few weeks: The Methodist Church of the USA; the Swiss Protestant Church Federation and the Church of England. It was a consolation to receive a telegram about the joining of the Anglicans on the morning after British bombs fell in the garden next door and had broken all our windows. Is this not perhaps a symbol? While the bombs drop in increasing numbers, the Christian fellowship increases. It is this certainty that we can even keep our Movement going at a time of little or no communication which makes it possible to continue with confidence to work . . .

I was not a little astonished when twenty-seven years later the President of the Geneva government quoted parts of this letter when he bestowed upon me the *bourgeoisie d'honneur* of Geneva.

In those first weeks and months after the total victory of the Germans in Western Europe everybody had to readjust himself to the new situation. The world had become unrecognizable. There were many voices which counselled acceptance of the *fait accompli*. They said that Europe was going to be dominated by national socialism and fascism for a long time to come, and that it was advisable to make the best of it and to arrive at some form of compromise with the dominant powers. Such voices were also heard in ecclesiastical circles. And this was all the more dangerous since attempts were made as from Berlin to bring the ecumenical movement in line with the new political situation. In those circumstances it was a blessing that the one member of the Provisional Committee whom I could still consult was Dr Alphons Koechlin, President of the Swiss Federation of Churches. For he proved to be a man of clear insight and of strong character.

Even before we had received full information about these plans Dr Koechlin formulated the principles which should guide us in the period immediately ahead. In a letter of July 11th 1940, he referred to the great changes which were taking place in Europe and continued: 'For there is in these circumstances only one possible course, that is to stick inexorably to our line and in no case to accept the establishing of an ecclesiastical *fait accompli* . . . In our church life we must not commit treason, not sell anything and so keep at least in this realm our full independence.' A few days later I wrote to Koechlin that, through my Swedish colleague, Nils Ehrenström, I had now received a detailed report showing that he (Koechlin) had understood exactly what we were up against. I wrote that there were three groups in Germany, one represented by the ideological specialist of national socialism, Alfred Rosenberg, who wanted to destroy the ecumenical movement, one represented by Heckel who wanted to exploit the new powerful situation of Germany by making Berlin the centre of the ecumenical movement in Europe and one represented by the Confessing Church who were the true friends of the ecumenical movement.

About Heckel I wrote:

He desires to strengthen his own position and seems to feel that the best way to counteract Rosenberg is to create an ecumenical movement controlled by himself. For that reason he seems to feel that there should be formed some kind of European ecumenical organization which would cut off its contacts with the extra-European and particularly the Anglo-Saxon world. He has, of course, a special grudge against the World Council. The curious thing is that Heckel's most important collaborator, Gerstenmaier, belongs, according to the common testimony of Schönfeld and Ehrenström, very definitely to the third group and is in constant opposition to Heckel. It seems that Gerstenmaier is convinced that a Berlin-centred ecumenical set-up in Europe would remain an organization on paper, but would in no way gain the confidence or active support of the European churches. In fact, he and those who work rather closely with him (e.g. Hanns Lilje) seem to use the very powerful and true argument that that kind of ecumenical movement would lead to an even greater isolation of the German church. He seems therefore to aim in the direction of some temporary relationship of an informal character between the

European churches without, however, breaking off existing contacts with the outside world.

I informed Koechlin that I would go to a meeting in Yugoslavia which would also be attended by Gerstenmaier, that in my conversations with him I would represent the views which he had so clearly stated in his letter and that I would report to Boegner and himself.

In the conversations in Belgrade I received the impression that Gerstenmaier was really concerned about the maintenance of the ecumenical movement as a worldwide Christian fellowship. He volunteered the opinion that Heckel did not have a clear policy and that he would not take any important initiative because he was really afraid that through deeper involvement in ecumenical affairs he would get into trouble with the nazi authorities. So we agreed on a rather vague plan to have five secretaries for the ecumenical work in Europe, namely Ehrenström, Schönfeld, Keller, Zankov and myself. But this plan was never carried out. At the meeting in Geneva, in January 1941, at which Boegner and Koechlin were present, it was once again emphasized that the relationships existing between the European churches and the other churches in the ecumenical movement should in no way be jeopardized and that there was no need to take formal steps to create a new form of organization between the European churches. We did not need to fear any longer that the new political constellation would lead to the disintegration of the ecumenical movement.

NOTES

1. Bishop Bell reprinted considerable portions of this paper in his Penguin Special, *Christianity and World Order*, pp. 92–5.

2. Printed in *International Conciliation* (Carnegie Foundation), October 1940, no. 363.

Holding the Ecumenical Movement Together

FOR THE ECUMENICAL movement the war had come at the worst possible moment. The World Council was only 'in process of formation' and had as yet no legal existence and no fixed membership. Would such a shaky body be able to stand the strain? The Provisional Committee was not able to meet between January 1939 and January 1946. After 1940 the only meetings that could be held were meetings of the staff with a few members of the Committee, in particular, Dr Boegner of France and Dr Koechlin of Switzerland. It was fortunate that William Paton held the fort in London and Henry Leiper in New York, but would we be able to keep in touch with each other? Of our small staff only Schönfeld who was German and Ehrenström who was of Swedish nationality could visit the territories under German control. Would we be able to do what we were supposed to do – namely, hold the ecumenical movement together?

And most important of all, would the churches under the tremendous pressure of the situation have any energy left for ecumenical tasks? Would they not consider the ecumenical movement as a peace-time luxury?

The period of uncertainty did not last very long. Soon new tasks and opportunities presented themselves. And there were signs that in a number of countries church people were coming to the conclusion that the organized ecumenical movement was a war-time necessity. My semi-annual reports of the war years were all dominated by a grateful astonishment that the task of holding the churches together was made easy by the fact that the churches were so eager to give and receive tangible evidence that the *Una Sancta* was still, or rather more than ever, a reality. There was no need to make propaganda for the ecumenical cause. All that was necessary was to respond to the demand for ecumenical information, contact or encouragement.

We were in a good situation to maintain contacts between the churches in different situations. From neutral Switzerland it was possible to keep in touch not only with most of the countries under national socialist and fascist domination and with unoccupied France but also with Great Britain, the USA and Sweden. And Geneva became before long a magnetic pole, attracting all sorts of people, including those engaged in relief activities, in resistance movements, in spying. So information was plentiful. The International Christian Press and Information service (later called the Ecumenical Press Service), of which Alexandre de Weymarn of the World Council staff was the director, became an indispensable channel of communication between the European churches involved in the confrontation with national socialism and between these churches and their sister-churches in other parts of the world.

Between the summer of 1940 and the summer of 1942 I could make only a trip to Yugoslavia and pay a number of visits to the unoccupied zone of France, but my German colleague, Schönfeld and my Swedish colleague, Ehrenström made many journeys to different parts of Europe and came back with a harvest of news and documents.

Schönfeld developed his own system of communication. He had good relations with the men around State-secretary Weizsäcker in the German Foreign Office. And he exploited to the full the very fortunate circumstance that the German consulate in Geneva happened to be staffed by diplomats who had no sympathy for national socialism. So he could use the diplomatic bag between Berlin and Geneva and in that way bring documents which could not be allowed to fall into the hands of the Gestapo. In this way and through other channels provided by resistance movements, we received a considerable amount of information which we distributed in various ways to church leaders, to underground periodicals and, of course, to our colleagues in Britain and the USA. The Gestapo seems to have received tips that curious things were going on in the World Council office, for they sent an inquiry to the German consulate asking whether it would not be desirable to station a Gestapo man in Geneva to keep an eye on ecumenical activities.[1] The German Consulate replied that Lausanne rather than Geneva was the place to be watched. I have always wondered whether a man was actually sent to Lausanne and how he spent his time.

Schönfeld showed great courage during his dangerous missions. He had to 'cover' himself by giving the impression that he was useful for the so-called 'cultural policy' of the German government, but he was in fact concerned about the maintenance of ecumenical relationships. And he had a passionate desire to convince his fellow Christians in other countries that Christians in Germany were resisting national socialism. This desire led him often to give an exaggerated picture of the extent and effectiveness of German resistance. It was not easy to learn to distinguish between reality and wishful thinking in the reports he gave me. I appreciated what he did to help church people in occupied countries, but I was sometimes irritated when he came to tell me ever so often that the overthrowing of the Hitler regime was just a matter of days, but nothing happened.

Our relationships were not of the easiest. For it was part of the rules of the game that we did not tell each other all we knew or all we did. For reasons of security no one should know more than he had to know in order to perform his particular mission. And we did not always agree about the right methods. We could only collaborate as men who trusted each other's motives and left each other free to act according to his own insight.

I had my own direct contacts – with Holland through the courier service of the 'Swiss road'; with France through a number of visits; and with other European countries through the many visitors who came to Geneva.

In unoccupied France the churches were at first inclined to co-operate with the 'national revolution' propagated and led by the Pétain government. But before long it became clear that that national revolution was in fact introducing totalitarian conceptions into the country. Among the first to take a stand against totalitarianism were the former members of the Student Christian Movement. I met with them in Pomeyrol in September 1941 and gave them a full report on the stand which the other European churches had already taken with regard to national socialism. We worked out together the 'theses of Pomeyrol' which included the following affirmations: 'The church protests solemnly against any legislation which rejects the Jews from the communities in which men live'; and 'While accepting the material consequences of the defeat, the church considers that resistance against every totalitarian and idolatrous influence is a spiritual necessity.' These theses were circulated over the signature of twelve pastors and laymen including Madeleine Barot, René Courtin, Suzanne de Diétrich and Roland de Pury. I noted in a report of February 1942: 'There is some theological opposition from those who consider that the church has no right to speak on political issues, but there is also a surprising amount of agreement with the uncompromising attitude expressed in these theses.'

I was also in contact with the remarkable group of Roman Catholic priests who were issuing the excellent French underground paper, *Le Témoignage Chrétien*. I could provide them with material on the churches in other countries and it was through us that they received a number of statements in which Roman Catholic church leaders in Germany or German-occupied countries protested against the national socialist ideology or particular national socialist policies.

I can best summarize my contact-work at that time by using a paragraph from an article written in 1941:[2]

> My present work can be described as the maintaining of contact between the churches, and that in such a way that the fighting and suffering churches may be encouraged by a sense of the presence of the whole Christian community, and that the other churches may share in the very real blessings which come to a Christian church in time of trial.
>
> And I may gratefully say that in spite of the tremendous barriers, it has proved possible not only to maintain these contacts, but even to intensify them.

There were also new tasks.

One of these was the work for refugees. It was fortunate that Adolf Freudenberg, who had been appointed World Council secretary for refugee work just before the war, was in Switzerland in 1939, and could take this work in hand. The refugees who were our most immediate responsibility were those non-Aryans who had been sent to southern France and who lived in the most primitive conditions in internment camps. The Cimade, a relief organization created by the French Protestant youth movements, did a noble work among them. I visited Madeleine Barot and her colleagues in one of the camps and found that the only place where they could sleep without being attacked by vermin was on the wooden dining tables. It was our privilege to give them all the assistance we could manage. I wrote in the autumn of 1941: 'One wonders whether anywhere in the world men and women are more conscious of their relationship to the ecumenical church than in these camps where non-Aryan Christians speak of the "ecumenical meals", the "ecumenical shoes", the "ecumenical literature" which they receive through the Refugee Commission.'

Before long we had also to begin saving refugees from deportation to Poland. Madeleine Barot made several 'illegal' journeys for this purpose and appeared in my office covered with mud from the banks of the stream which she had crossed on the French-Swiss border. Her purpose in coming to Switzerland was to make sure that the Jewish refugees whom her colleagues of the Cimade brought at great personal risk across the mountain passes to Switzerland, would not be turned back at the frontiers. With the help of Swiss church leaders an agreement was reached according to which the refugees who were in danger of being deported and whose names would be communicated beforehand to the Swiss authorities would be accepted.[3] The method worked, but owing to the immense difficulties of getting the refugees safely across the mountains without being caught on the French side of the frontier, it was not a large number that escaped in this way the extermination in Auschwitz or other camps.

Refugees were 'orphans' cut off from their churches and therefore they had a special claim to be helped by an ecumenical body. But the same was true of prisoners of war. Our particular role was to ensure that in the prison camps 'congregations in captivity' should be established and that these congregations should receive all the help they needed. In this matter the churches of all the countries concerned participated very actively through the World Council's Ecumenical Commission for the Chaplaincy Service to Prisoners of War. The Commission was first chaired by Dr Koechlin and later by Professor Jaques Courvoisier of the Geneva Theological Faculty. There was none of that indifference to the needs of prisoners of war that had been so scandalously evident in many churches during the first world war. We worked together with the Red Cross and the YMCA. The work grew so rapidly that we had to appoint new staff members for it and expand our office space. Oliver Béguin from Switzerland became its executive director. Jaques Courvoisier visited camps in several countries on our behalf and brought encouragement to many. We sent books and especially bibles. The American Bible Society gave the strongest possible support. Special Easter and Christmas brochures were written for the prisoners of war. We began by publishing a few thousand of each and finished up by printing several hundred thousand.

I wrote in my semi-annual report in July 1943:

> The prisoners' work is not only a service rendered by the churches to the prisoners, but also a service rendered by the prisoners to the churches. The churches help their imprisoned members to feel that they are surrounded by the wide fellowship of the *Una Sancta*. But the prisoners help the churches by demonstrating that precisely when men feel lonely and uprooted the Gospel is there to give them hope and to create a new deep communion between them. A number of liberated prisoners of war, especially laymen, are already bringing back the story how they discovered in the prison camps the true meaning of the Christian faith and the true significance of Christian fellowship.

Since May 1940 the officers and staff members of the World Council on the European Continent had had no direct personal contact with their colleagues in Britain and the USA. So it was a great event for me that I could visit London in April and May 1942, and meet with William Temple, William Paton, George Bell, J. H. Oldham and even with Henry Leiper and William Adams Brown, who had come from the USA for the enthronement of Temple as Archbishop of Canterbury. We were able to bring each other up-to-date on developments in various parts of the world and to make plans for the future. When I went to say goodbye to William Temple I found him in one of the few habitable rooms of his battered Lambeth Palace residence in London and still under the impression of the bombardment of Canterbury which he had witnessed the night before. But he had not changed. He was still the same man of large vision and generous mind.

It proved to be our last meeting.

Thus the war years had the paradoxical result that, on the one hand, the process of formation of the World Council was arrested; but, on the other, that the process was intensified. Many who had not been much concerned about ecumenical affairs discovered that the movement was spiritually indispensable for churches in time of need. It also became clear that there were urgent practical tasks which could be performed only by an ecumenical body.

But there was one decisively important task which the movement was not fulfilling – namely, to give public expression to common Christian convictions concerning the concrete decisions which the churches and their members had to take in this war which confronted all with new and acute spiritual and moral problems. It is true that we encouraged individual churches to speak out, we collected for that purpose all statements and protests which the churches of different countries were issuing and we published them in our press service.[4] It was also true that I participated – through addresses and memoranda and in other ways – in defining the right attitude of the churches to the issues of the war. And as soon as some members of the Provisional Committee could meet we sent messages of encouragement to the churches. Thus in September 1942, when Dr Boegner, Dr Koechlin and Dr Cavert were in Geneva, we put our individual signatures to a statement saying to the struggling churches:

> The good confession of the struggling churches is a call to all churches to renewal of faith and life. They show us what it means to be the church of Christ as they stake their all on the Word of God, as they rebuild their parish life on the biblical pattern of fellowship and solidarity, and as they seek to fulfil the prophetic mission of the church to the nations by their protests and warnings against anti-Christian ideologies and practices.

But the World Council as a corporate body did not take a stand on the grave political issues of the war years. This was not only because it was still 'in process of formation' and that it had as yet no clear membership and no definite structure. It was also because we had not solved the problem with which we had struggled in 1939 and 1940 – namely, that some desired the Council to be as neutral as possible in order to remain available for the task of reconciliation, and that others believed that in spite of all difficulties the Council should render a clear, concrete witness.

Karl Barth was convinced that 'Geneva' should speak for the whole ecumenical community and speak with authority. In letters, conversations and articles he put strong pressure on me to speak out, not only as a person, but as the mouthpiece of the World Council. He made his point most sharply in his 'Letter to an American Churchman' of October 1942.[5] He asked what use an ecumenical movement was which talked about the message of the church to the world, but which did not actually proclaim that message in a concrete and relevant way. He added that if 'Geneva' did not have the authority to do this the churches should immediately endow it with such authority.

I did not take that challenge lightly. It was all the greater since Barth himself issued during those years a series of letters which I helped to distribute and which gave pastoral guidance to Christians in several countries concerning the stand which the churches should take.

I agreed with Barth that the ecumenical movement should have been able to fulfil this 'watchman's office'. I had tried in 1939 and 1940 to get the World Council to speak out in spite of its provisional character. But even at that time, when we were still able to get together, we had failed to find a common word. Now that we could not meet it was quite impossible to speak as a World Council on the most controversial issues. For a World Council word could never be the word of one man by himself. It could only be a word hammered out through the confrontation of different minds. Moreover, as a servant of the World Council, I could not disregard the conviction of our most responsible leaders (especially William Temple) that as long as the World Council was not definitely established it could not act as a spokesman for the churches.

Such arguments did not impress Karl Barth. He thought only in terms of the prophetic mission of the church and dismissed all other considerations as irrelevant. For a time it seemed impossible to find any common ground between us. I continued in lectures, articles and books to express my own personal convictions about the spiritual and political issues of the war.[6] But I did not claim that in these matters I was speaking officially on behalf of the World Council or its member churches. The fear of some church leaders of carrying responsibility for any ecumenical statements which might identify them with a political position became clear again in 1942. Dr Koechlin and I submitted the draft of a Christmas message to a number of members of the Provisional Committee; the plan was that we would sign it together but as individual persons. The message spoke in general terms of the victory of Christ over injustice and violence. But Archbishop Eidem of Sweden wrote[7] that he could not sign it, for he did not want to give the impression that he had taken sides with Anglo-Saxon Christianity and believed that Christians of neutral countries should not endanger their chances of making a contribution to the forging of peace. So Dr Koechlin and I signed the message alone.

NOTES

1. As early as 1937 the Gestapo planned to send an agent to the ecumenical bodies in Geneva, since the ecumenical movement was 'marxist, pacifist and Jewish' (Schmid, *Apokalyptisches Wetterleuchten*, p. 208).

2. *The Student World*, Fourth quarter, 1941, p. 281.

3. The story is told in *Les Clandestins de Dieu*, Paris, 1968 (American translation: *God's Underground*, St Louis, 1970); and in *Rettet sie doch*, edited by Adolf Freudenberg, Zürich, 1969.

4. See also *The Church Speaks to the World*, published in three languages in 1942.

5. Karl Barth, *Eine Schweizer Stimme*, 1945, p. 299 (The American churchman was Dr Samuel McCrea Cavert).

6. See *The Wretchedness and Greatness of the Church*, London, 1944, first published in French in 1943 and *The Struggle of the Dutch Church*, London, 1944; New York, 1945, first published in French and German in 1944.

7. Letter of December 15th 1942.

21 | *The Swiss Road*

THERE WAS ANOTHER aspect of my life during the war years. I was obliged to enter into an unknown territory and accept responsibilities for which I had not been prepared. No one was more surprised than I when I found myself in charge of a secret network of relationships between the resistance movement in the Netherlands and the legal government of the Netherlands which had established itself in London.

It began in a most innocent way. When Hitler occupied the Netherlands in May 1940 Dutchmen in London, in the Netherlands Indies and in other lands were cut off from their own country. But they were desperately anxious to know what was happening in their homeland. In neutral Geneva it was still possible to gather a good deal of information, and so I began to circulate *Voices from the Netherlands*, a digest of articles and letters about the ways in which the Dutch were responding to the hour of crisis in their nation. I collected articles from the religious and the secular press and when censorship became more severe I began to reproduce documents and brochures which were produced illegally in the Netherlands and which found their way to Geneva in various ways. These materials reflected the deep searching of hearts over the new, completely new, situation which the country had to face: the onslaught of the national socialist ideology, the anti-semitic measures. And they spoke of a renewal of the Christian faith and an awakening of the churches. The documents were forwarded to Queen Wilhelmina, to members of the Netherlands government in London and to a number of other contacts.

When it became known that I was concerned about the maintenance of contacts between Dutchmen in the Netherlands and their countrymen elsewhere I began to receive a good deal of correspondence and many personal visits of those who were still able to travel. The burden of the messages I received was that the Netherlands government in London did not seem to understand what was really happening in their country. Radio Oranje, broadcasting from London, was not speaking to the condition of the people. London did not seem to realize that what was needed above all was not just propaganda against the nazis, but the building up of the morale of the nation. Effective and prolonged resistance to the tremendous pressure of the national socialist ideology could only be offered by those who had strong positive convictions. London, I was advised, should help the Dutch to see how their struggle was part of a world-wide battle for the defence of the most precious values of our civilization.

I also reported to London on the various groups which were preparing for the hour of liberation, for even at that early stage of the war the general expectation was that victory was not far off.

Another subject of discussion was that of peace aims. My Dutch correspondents, while rejecting any form of compromise with national socialism, and while insisting on a complete restitution of all countries occupied by Germany, believed that we should work for a new Europe in which a reborn Germany would find its place on a footing of equality.

I reported fully on these points to the Netherlands Government in London. Professor Gerbrandy, who presided over the Council of Ministers, replied. He reacted most strongly against the views of my Dutch contacts concerning the peace. According to him this was no time to have pity on the German people. He wondered whether this 'poor darling theory' was not a result of clever German propaganda. Justice demanded sterner measures.

It became clear that the different points of view could not be brought together through the exchange of letters. So Professor Gerbrandy wired, in February 1942, that I should come to London as soon as possible. He wanted me to help in clearing up the misunderstandings which were arising between his government and important sections of the Dutch people.

I had little hesitation in accepting this invitation. I might be able to help London obtain a clearer impression of the situation in the Netherlands. And after talks in London I might be able to explain the London situation to the Dutch. And it was also an excellent opportunity to renew contact with William Temple, William Paton, George Bell, J. H. Oldham and other leaders of the ecumenical movement.

But how would I get to London and back again? The only possibility was to travel through the unoccupied part of France to Spain, then to Portugal and from there to Britain. I was given a diplomatic passport and collected the necessary visas. The most difficult moment came just after leaving Geneva when I was thoroughly searched by French *douaniers* who were supervised by civilians who had that typical Gestapo-look. But all important papers, including those given to me by the German resistance men, were, fortunately, in the diplomatic bag. I stopped at Nîmes to see Pastor Marc Boegner. He gave me a full account of his battles with the Vichy government about the anti-semitic measures, about the refugees and about religious liberty. He was happy that he could take advantage of my journey to send a message to Archbishop Temple about the measures that ought to be taken at the end of the war to complete, as soon as possible, the process of formation of the World Council of Churches.

From Nîmes to Montpellier, where Philippe Maury brought me in contact with Professor René Courtin, a leader in the French resistance movement. Late at night, as we were discussing what messages I should pass on from the French resistance to General de Gaulle's headquarters in London, there was a knock on the door which startled us. We looked at each other with some consternation. But happily it was not the police; it was a most striking woman whom I recognized from an earlier meeting in Annecy. Madame Bertie Albrecht was one of the most courageous and able resistance leaders. She was surprised and glad to meet a man who could reach London within a few days. The messages I was asked to pass on were in many ways similar to those I had from the Dutch: they had to do with the measures to be taken to maintain order at the time of liberation. I was not to see Madame Albrecht again. This energetic and beautiful woman was arrested by the Gestapo in May 1943 and executed at Lyons.

Madrid and Lisbon, the next steps, had the unreal atmosphere of countries trying to live normally while the whole world was abnormal.

To fly by the Dutch KLM from Portugal to Britain was like coming home. At Lisbon airport the Dutch pilots and passengers sat at one table and the German Lufthansa pilots at the next table. If one asked why the Germans allowed these flights, which they could so easily have intercepted, the answer was given that the German Foreign Office and intelligence services found it essential to receive the London *Times*.

London had become a quite different place. It was no longer the easy-going, somewhat sleepy city which I had known in the pre-war days. London had woken up. And it was now springtime in more senses than one. The signs of the Blitz were everywhere, but nobody doubted that the tide had turned. And there was an exhilarating sense of common purpose between people of all classes and of the many nationalities who had their governments-in-exile in the city. On the other hand this London, with its mind on the tremendous military task to be accomplished, had little time or energy left to be concerned about the everyday problems which the European peoples under nazi domination were facing. The English channel was wider than ever.

I stayed in the old-fashioned and dignified Brown's Hotel. Professor Gerbrandy lived there, so it was easy for me to spend many hours with him. 'Cherry Brandy', as the British called him, was a remarkable character. He had grown up in the Frisian country in a strongly Calvinist environment and his later life in the academic world and in politics had not weakened the convictions which he owed to that background. For him the world was essentially a study in black and white. There were Christian nations like the Dutch and the English, and there were other nations, like the Germans, in the grip of paganism. He came as near as anybody to seeing the war as a true crusade. This single-mindedness made him an effective leader of government in time of war, but it did not give him an adequate perspective on the complicated post-war problems.

On some evenings, especially when his secretary, Dr Peter Kasteel, joined us, it seemed as if I had arrived in the study of a professor of theology rather than that of a statesman. The unadulterated Calvinist Gerbrandy, the convinced Roman Catholic Kasteel and I, with my ecumenical outlook, would enter into a triangular debate about the mysteries of theology.

Gerbrandy saw clearly that an all-out attempt should be made to overcome the growing estrangement between the government-in-exile and the Dutch people. He asked me to work out a plan with Dr A. H. J. Lovink, who had just arrived from the Netherlands Indies and who had been appointed secretary of the department of general warfare. Lovink had considerable experience in the field of intelligence, and he and I found it easy to understand each other. We worked out an agreement, the main points of which were the following:

1. There is a lack of contact between the Netherlands Government in London and the Dutch people. This is not due to political differences, but to the difference in atmosphere between London and the Netherlands. It is therefore extremely important to ensure that the contacts between the two partners be intensified.

2. At the same time it is important that the real leaders of the Dutch people be informed about the intentions and plans of the government.

3. Contacts can be maintained through Switzerland. A centre will therefore be established in that country, which, in co-operation with the Netherlands Embassy, will ensure the gathering of information concerning the trends of thought in the Netherlands, the spiritual resistance against national socialism, the conflict taking place concerning the churches and the educational system, the discussion concerning the main lines of political and social development after the war and the fundamental attitude to Germany. The centre will pass on relevant books and periodicals appearing in the Netherlands, and give to Dutch leaders back home information concerning the policies of the exiled government.

4. The centre will work under the directives and responsibility of the department of general warfare.

This agreement was approved by the government. A budget would be provided. I made it clear, however, that I would not accept any remuneration since I was and remained the servant of the World Council and could not become a civil servant of any government.

The visit to Queen Wilhelmina was an intense and moving experience. I was not told where I would be going for her address had to be kept secret. As I entered the room where she received me, it was immediately clear that this was not to be a formal audience but a working session. She began by saying that she had used the documentation I had sent and found it most valuable. The conversation which followed resembled an examination. The Queen sat at a little table with pen and paper, asked questions and wrote down my answers. Some-

times she would read aloud what she had noted and ask: Did I get it right? The
intensity of her desire to find out what was happening in her country was deeply
impressive. She did not have that divided mind which so many refugees seemed
to have. Her mind was wholly concentrated on the sufferings and hopes of her
people. After I had given my report she asked many questions. What did the
people say about her radio speeches? I could only say that these were very
deeply appreciated. But she insisted: 'Don't they criticize me?' I said that while
many voices from London were criticized, she seemed to have found the right
tone. She commented: 'It is so very hard to know what is going on in the hearts
and minds of our people.'

She spoke of her great desire for a renewal of society. After the war politics,
she said, should no longer divide us and new social structures should be
elaborated.

I tried hard to convince her that new life had come to the churches – but
without much success. She spoke almost bitterly about the division of the
churches. This was against the will of Christ. She called herself a 'world
Christian', and by that I think she meant that she sought to be a Christian
outside the denominational ecclesiastical structures. But she made it very clear
that she wanted to render a positive witness to Christ. 'Right now,' she said, 'I
am trying to think out what are the very simple things which I should say in my
broadcast at Whitsuntide.'

Soon after this meeting with the Queen I wrote to friends in Holland: 'It is
impressive to find that she, more than anyone else in her environment, feels
instinctively what lives in the heart of her people. Her energy is astounding
and she dominates, now more than ever, the total situation. No one in the
government can touch her.'

I talked with many people in the Netherlands government, but met also a
good many representatives of the other allied governments. Some quite prominent Frenchmen told me that General de Gaulle was a great military leader, but a
dilettante in politics and therefore obviously not the future leader of France! My
general impression was that, while there was total agreement among all allied
governments on the immediate task, there was, not only between the various
governments but within each of them, a complete lack of clarity concerning war
aims and the future shape of the international order.

On the way back to Geneva I stopped again in France in order to bring to my
contacts in the French resistance the messages which I had received for them at
the London headquarters of the Free French.

The problem was now whether I would be able to deliver the goods according
to the promises made in London. The information which came to me in Geneva
by the way of the few Dutchmen who were still allowed to travel to Switzerland,
or through the refugees, was clearly insufficient. What was needed was to get a
responsible group in Holland to gather systematically the reports and documents
which could give the Dutch leaders in London a full picture of the situation and

of the trends of thought in the nation. But it would not be easy to organize such a group from Geneva and to find means of regular communication with the Netherlands.

Then came the first windfall. A few weeks after my return from London, on a summer afternoon when I was working in the garden, a short, but exceedingly determined young lady entered the gate. She introduced herself as Hebe Kohlbrugge and told me, as if it were the most natural thing in the world, that she had sneaked across the Belgian, French and Swiss frontiers without being caught. She was closely associated with some of my friends in Holland and had become convinced that the time had come to establish closer contacts between the Dutch resistance and the government-in-exile and that the best place to serve as a liaison centre was Switzerland. I could not believe my ears, for her plans and mine were practically identical. So I told her that she had turned up like an angel from heaven.

We agreed on the names of people who should be asked to collect the necessary material in Holland: Nico Stufkens, a man with a truly comprehensive knowledge of the spiritual, social and political life in the country, and Gerard Slotemaker de Bruine, who had been engaged in the battle against national socialism for a long time.

After having visited Karl Barth, who gave her a pastoral and prophetic letter to his friends in Holland, Hebe Kohlbrugge returned in the same adventurous way as she had come. So the foundation was laid for a regular information service.

There were more windfalls. I found an energetic medical student, Joop Bartels, who was ready to give full time to the setting up of our centre. And he brought me in touch with an engineer, E. Eisma, who had made a special study of the mysteries of photography and knew of a process by which the microfilms could be made so thin that it became possible to hide – in a fountain pen, in a hollow tooth brush or similar objects – no fewer than three hundred films representing three hundred pages of letters or documents. J. G. van Niftrik, who had had to flee Holland when his role in the resistance had been discovered, and who assisted the Dutch military attaché in Berne in collecting military intelligence, helped us in the technical work of producing the various objects in which the films could be hidden. He proved also to be an expert in forging identity-cards.

So we were ready to start. At first the traffic along our so-called 'Swiss road' was quite irregular. Bartels and a young Dutch sculptor, Jan van Borssen Buisman, made risky journeys to Holland carrying messages and bringing back a good many microfilms. Some material arrived in the covers of books. During the first year some hundred documents came through from Holland and were sent on to London. But it was not until the summer of 1943 that we succeeded in organizing a quite regular courier service and thus in greatly increasing the amount of information carried to and from Holland. At that time I had the good fortune to find Jean Weidner ready to accept responsibility for the service between Geneva and Brussels. Jean was a Dutch business man who lived in France.[1] He had become deeply concerned about the fate of the Dutch – mostly non-Aryan – refugees in the unoccupied part of France, and started a one-man campaign to help them. When he could no longer finance it he came to me. Fortunately I was able to raise the necessary funds for his relief work. Before long Jean became deeply involved also in helping people who for various reasons wanted to get out of the occupied territories. But these activities became known to the police, so that he had to give up his fixed address and remain constantly on the move with false identity papers. This was exactly the man needed to organize a regular courier-service. He was a convinced Seventh Day Adventist, and when one asked him whether he was worried about his next assignment he would look astonished and say: 'But am I not in the hands of God?'

So Jean became responsible for the Geneva–Brussels part of the Swiss road and my Dutch colleagues set up the Amsterdam–Brussels service. By the autumn of 1943 the line functioned with remarkable regularity. Every two weeks the 'mail' would come in and leave again a few days later. The couriers travelled by train to a small station just behind the Salève (the mountain just across the French frontier near Geneva), then climbed the Salève from where they could watch the patrols below and could also see my house, and finally crossed the frontier when the situation seemed to be safe.

One of the important stations for the couriers was Louvain. Now my good German friend, Reinold von Thadden, was the 'field commander' in Louvain. What would he have done if he had caught one of our couriers and found out that the man was working for me? Fortunately the problem did not arise, but we could tease each other about it after the war.

The volume of material became rather overwhelming. Eisma, the technical leader of our bureau, calculated after the war that we had used well over a mile of film, representing thousands of pages. The method of dispatching the material to London was exceedingly simple. The films were hidden in specially bound books and these were sent by ordinary mail to cover-addresses in Portugal and Sweden where the films were taken out and sent on by airmail to London. We owe it largely to the good organization of the German postal system that not a single book got lost or fell in to the wrong hands!

I was much amused when Elisabeth Wiskemann, the political intelligence-officer of the British Embassy in Berne, came to ask me whether I knew of a way to get documents to London. She had material which she was eager to send to her government. I asked of course whether the famous British secret service could not take care of this. She answered that that service was so secret that she had no contact with it. 'All right,' I said, 'your documents will be in London in about ten days'.

The Swiss road was becoming very crowded. This was partly due to the fact that my partners in Holland had improved their organization and were now in touch with a number of different groups of the resistance. But there was another reason which did not become apparent until the war was over. In 1942 the German counter-espionage had succeeded in capturing some of the Dutchmen who had secretly been dropped into Holland by the British Special Operations Executive. This led to the operation 'North Pole', also called *Englandspiel*. The Germans began to control and dictate messages to these agents in their transmissions to London. Incredibly enough, during at least a year and a half, this strategem worked.[2] It is easy to imagine what confusion this created with regard to the radio communications between the Dutch resistance and London. We received constantly messages of inquiry, of warning, of protest without fully realizing what was going on. One of the results of this situation was that those who had become suspicious about all radio contacts with London used our road which seemed much safer. That is not to say that we were alone in the field, but that through the circumstances of those years we had a rather unique opportunity.

What did we receive from the Netherlands? First of all the underground press. Once the organization was running smoothly we could pass on a most varied and substantial collection of illegal papers, giving a clear impression of the different types of resistance movements; secondly, a large number of descriptive reports concerning developments in the fields of economy, of medicine, of school and university, of the churches. With regard to such documents our centre was merely a sort of post-office. But there were other matters which required closer attention. Our Dutch contacts in Amsterdam had formed a 'political committee of the Swiss Road', consisting of persons who were in close contact with the underground paper, *Vrij Nederland*. This committee made it its business to collect material from different groups about such urgent issues as the co-ordination of the resistance, the relations between the resistance and the government in exile, the arrangements to be made for the transition from occupation to liberation and the future organization of political life. Now some of this type of information had to be transmitted very quickly. So I had to draw up telegrams to London and give those to the Netherlands Embassy in Berne to be sent to London in code. And with regard to these matters I did not merely act as a postman. Everything sent from Holland for transmission to London was of course passed on. But I often added a commentary giving my own opinion formed on the basis of the documents, of my own private correspondence with Dutch contacts, or on the conversations I had with couriers or other people who were still arriving in Switzerland.

And what did we send to Holland? Every bit of information about the activities and plans of the government-in-exile that we could get hold of. In the first year, when Lovink was my London contact, we received a good deal. When Lovink had become ambassador in China, and when through the occupation of southern France contacts became far more difficult, almost the only source of information in this field were the short telegrams from London to Berne. So the original intention to arrive at a real two-way traffic was never fully carried out.

The government-in-exile could have done far more to keep responsible leaders in Holland informed about its work and policies. In the nature of the case the broadcasting from London had a different, more propagandist and popular character. There was at this point a failure of imagination. The people living in the free world were wholly concentrated on winning the war as they saw it, the war of bombardments, convoys and invasions. But they did not see the full importance of the less obvious battle for the minds of men which had to be fought in the occupied countries and for which resistance leaders needed all the help that could be given.

We in Geneva tried to fill the gap by sending as much material about political, economic, military and religious developments in the world as we could collect. Much of this information found its way into the underground press. By January 1944 we were able to send such a quantity of material that the editors of *Vrij Nederland* could start an additional paper, *International Information Papers*, which reproduced articles from such magazines as *The Economist*, from daily papers such as the *Neue Zürcher Zeitung* and even printed summaries of important British and American books about international affairs.

During these two years, from the summer of 1942 to the summer of 1944, I was therefore in the strange position of having a substantial spare-time activity about which my colleagues in the office of the World Council knew nothing and should know nothing.

There were moments when I found the responsibility for this work terribly heavy. At one time I sent a young Dutchman who had been strongly recommended to me to Holland. Soon afterwards a message came asking whether I realized that I had put my Dutch partners in a most dangerous situation, for the man had been a member of the Dutch national socialist party. It was added that it might become necessary to take his life so as to save many other lives. Fortunately the man came back soon. His explanation was that he had indeed been a national socialist, but had broken with the party at the time when the persecution of the Jews began. He had wanted to show that he was a good patriot and therefore agreed to work for our organization. And he had not told me the truth about his past because he knew well that if he had done so I would not have accepted him. I appreciated his motives, but had to explain that we could not possibly use him and that for his own sake as well as ours.

Another very bad moment came when the Dutch resistance asked us to transmit to London an urgent request to destroy the printing works of the firm Enschedé in Haarlem. The message said that the new identity cards for the Dutch population were being printed there. When these new identity-cards were distributed it would be easy for the occupation force to arrest the hundreds of thousands of people who had false or stolen identity-cards. I transmitted the message immediately. But a few days later there came another urgent message saying that it was not in Haarlem, but in The Hague that the new identity-cards were being prepared. Not realizing at the time that it would take the airforce several weeks to get ready for a pinpoint bombardment I wondered whether I would share responsibility for the destruction of the inner city of my home town through a meaningless bombardment. But my second message arrived in London in good time; in April 1944 the bombardment of the Kleikamp building in The Hague was carried out and, though it cost a number of lives, the result was that many more lives were saved.

One day Hanns Schönfeld told me that he had heard a strange rumour – namely, that I had a secret courier-service with Holland. It was of course far too dangerous to let him know the truth, for he made frequent visits to Germany and ought to be able to say with conviction that he knew nothing about this kind of thing. So all I could say was: 'Is it not astounding what wild stories people tell in wartime?' He told me after the war that he had not felt quite convinced by that answer.

It was of course impossible to carry on this kind of work without some understanding with the Swiss authorities, for the Swiss security system was extremely effective. On the basis of personal contacts and of the informal agreement that we should pass on information which would be of value to the Swiss, such understanding was readily established.

In spite of all the contacts through microfilm and telegrams, there remained many points of misunderstanding between the partners in the conversation. The North Sea was never wider. I tried to act as an impartial go-between. But I must confess I gave priority to the point of view of the people in Holland for, like the Sabbath, the government was made for man and man was the Dutchman under foreign occupation.

The big issues which dominated the laborious dialogue were the co-ordination of the resistance, the preparation of the change-over at the time of liberation and especially the underlying problem of the tension between those groups which had a military outlook and those others whose orientation was civilian. As one looks back from the perspective of later developments the great nervousness of the military-minded about the plans of the politicians and of the civilians about the intentions of the military, seems exaggerated. But at that time this issue appeared to be decisive. For it had a direct bearing on the future of our institutions. The civilians suspected that the military did not want the country to resume its parliamentary democratic tradition. The military believed that the civilians were just playing party politics. And since for reasons of secrecy there could be little contact there was no real dialogue. At one time the conflict led to the almost ludicrous result that one of the resistance groups organized a systematic espionage to find out what our Swiss road was really up to.

The situation was complicated by the fact that at the end of 1942 – that is *after* my visit to London – our government in London had set up a new intelligence unit under the leadership of military men and given to that unit the comprehensive task of handling all forms of intelligence. But I was not informed of this. When I began to hear rumours about this new development I asked London whether I should continue to report to the Minister-President directly, and the answer was affirmative. But it is obvious that the officers in charge of intelligence in London were not very happy about the existence of a quite independent service which had direct access to the Minister-President!

In Switzerland there was no real problem. For there was excellent collaboration between the Dutch military attaché, General van Tricht, and me. If any military information came our way, it was immediately passed on to him. But in time it became clear that in certain circles in Holland and in London our work was being sharply criticized. Was not this pastor in Geneva trying to impose his views on the government, and was he not attempting to get his friends placed in positions of influence? It was certainly true that my reports reflected the concern of the civilian groups in Holland. But these groups were not just one among many. Taken together they were the people who were seriously trying to maintain the cohesion of the country by bringing together leading men of different political persuasions. They had formed the 'National Committee', later called the 'Fatherland Committee', of which Dr Willem Drees, the socialist leader who was respected by all parties and who was later to become Prime Minister, was the chairman. I had transmitted many messages from that committee to the government-in-exile and vice versa and the result had been that 'London' had recognized that committee as the central advisory and co-ordinating body with which it would maintain contact.

When a number of leading Dutch resistance-groups had agreed to send G. J. van Heuven Goedhart[3] to London as their common representative, when our organization had enabled him to make the risky journey to London; when he was made a member of the government-in-exile; and when I sent him a telegram expressing our deep sense of satisfaction about this appointment – this was interpreted in some military circles as a clear proof that I was plotting to get my friends promoted to the key positions. But the truth was that I had never met van Heuven Goedhart, and that I was of course delighted to find that a trusted resistance leader had now joined the government, for my concern was to bridge the gulf between the government and the resistance.

I had similar reactions when I supported the proposal that Mr L. H. N. Bosch Ridder van Rosenthal be authorized by the government to co-ordinate the resistance movement. I had never met him, but I knew of his courage, his energy and his statesmanlike qualities. So I was glad that he was not only asked to perform this delicate operation, but later on became the chairman of the group of 'guardians' appointed by the government to take the necessary decisions at the moment of liberation.

The liberation of France in the summer of 1944 meant that our work was coming to an end. Switzerland was no longer important. I wanted, of course, to get to Holland as soon as possible. So, in the first days of October, I joined a friend who was going to try to reach Holland by car. France was in a chaotic state. Bridges had been blown up. There were innumerable controls by the *maquisards*. The biggest problem was to get petrol. But my friend had foreseen this and when we drew up at one of the army depots he would produce a bottle of brandy. This led inevitably to the filling of our tank.

It was a joy to be back in Paris with Pierre Maury, whom I had not seen for four years, and of course with Pastor Marc Boegner, who helped me to work out plans for the first post-war meeting of the World Council. Then on to Belgium. Before long we found ourselves in the uninterrupted stream of slow moving army traffic, including all the equipment that would be needed to cross the Rhine. Brussels was so full up that we had no chance of finding a room. So on to Louvain, a bad idea, because Louvain had been so largely destroyed. After midnight we turned to the police station which was temporarily housed in the old Pope Hadrian College. The policemen suggested that we might try to get a room in the college. As I knocked a worthy cleric appeared. I gave my name. He said: 'I have read several of your writings. We must have a talk about theology. Come right in.' This was Professor J. Coppens. More than twenty years later, when I received an honorary doctorate from Louvain University, I stood again before him when he gave the official address.

Then Eindhoven and the little bit of Holland which had been liberated. It was not, as I had hoped, the first stop on a journey to other parts of the country, for the frontline was only a few miles beyond Eindhoven. But it was good to be back among my countrymen. The relatives with whom I stayed were exactly the kind of people I had hoped to find. They had taken a Jewish child into the family, they had distributed the illegal press, they had their secret hiding-place and they had a great faith in a spiritual renewal of the nation. I had an opportunity to broadcast to the still occupied territory and said that, though it might seem that we who had lived during the war years in Switzerland had been very lucky, I felt that in many ways the people in Holland had lived through a much deeper and richer experience of new found solidarity and a deepening of spiritual life.

It was time to go to London to make my final report to the government. I found the Dutch community there in a highly nervous condition. Now that the expectation of a quick and full liberation of the Netherlands had not been realized there was a sense of frustration and deep concern about the coming winter, which would surely bring near famine and terrible oppression. At the same time the Dutch community in London was torn by all sorts of conflicts.

Gerbrandy and van Heuven Goedhart received me with open arms. They explained that there was very strong tension between two points of view and two mentalities. There were those who wanted to make a completely new beginning in the Netherlands, which would mean ignoring the old political parties and their leadership and setting up a more authoritarian form of government. And there were those who put their confidence in those political leaders who had proved their worth in the resistance and who believed in the democratic institutions, though these would need to be adjusted to the new day. Now the work of the Swiss road had in this context become a bone of contention. I was being accused of having created a political pressure group. Members of the Dutch Intelligence Service had violently attacked van Heuven Goedhart and had lodged a formal complaint against me. The main accusation was that I had withheld information and documentation which had been sent to me for transmission to the Netherlands government.

It was not difficult to convince Gerbrandy and other ministers that these accusations were quite pointless. He gave me a letter in which he expressed the government's gratitude for the very useful work which we had done, and added: 'Your information work has been of special importance for London, and it is owing to this channel, together with others, that the Netherlands government has been kept so well informed about the situation in our country.'

I asked whether I should report to Queen Wilhelmina. Gerbrandy tried to arrange this but failed. For the Queen, who was more than ever the dominating figure in the situation, had heard the accusations against the work of the Swiss Road and was inclined to believe that we had indeed defended a policy which she did not approve of. Her mind was at that time completely concentrated on the idea of the radical renewal of the whole life of the nation. Now the fact that I had been the liaison man and sometimes the spokesman for Dutch leaders who were not completely new men, but men who had already played a role in the political life of the country, made me appear in her eyes as a man who was against renewal. There was the further fact that I had allowed a book of documents on the spiritual resistance of the Dutch churches, which I had written in French, to be published in Zürich in German. She found it quite inadmissible that a book on resistance should appear in the language of the enemy. The fact that in German Switzerland there was very strong sympathy with the Dutch did not make any difference to her.

Gerbrandy tried to explain to the Queen that the misunderstandings concerning my role had been cleared up. But I was not received. The Queen did not easily change her mind. That was the other side of her strong character. For me this was a deep disappointment. But it did not change my appreciation of the moral leadership which she had given during the war years. It was to take a good many years before she invited me to visit her again.

The main accusations against the Swiss road were finally withdrawn in writing. It was nevertheless most helpful that the Inquiry Commission set up by the Dutch parliament after the war to make a comprehensive inquiry concerning the policies and activities of the Netherlands government in London, gave the most thorough attention to all the problems which had arisen in connection with the Swiss road. Its very substantial report, together with the reports of innumerable hearings,[4] proved fascinating reading, for I learned from it many things I had not known before. Its conclusion was that the government had not sufficiently taken care to ensure an adequate co-ordination between the various information services which would have helped to avoid friction. The committee did not agree with the opinion that I had gone beyond the limits of my competence. For I had in fact simply carried out the instructions of the government. The way in which I and my collaborators in Switzerland and the Netherlands had done this deserved, according to the judgment of the commission, the highest praise.[5]

After the war, as I looked back on the adventure which had taken me into regions which I had never expected to enter, I had much reason to feel that it had been truly worthwhile. I had had an opportunity to do something for my country and to become involved in its life, and so to avoid the uprootedness which was the danger of an international life. I had learned a great deal about the realities of politics and government. I had worked with men and women whose single-minded courage was a constant source of inspiration. And was it not astounding that, after all the risks they had taken, all our couriers had survived the war? There was another side. Some of those who had opened their homes to our couriers had been caught. Thus Jean Weidner had lost his beloved sister who lived in Paris and who had helped him and others so much. And the old lady of the haberdashery shop in Annecy, which had been an important link in the chain, also died in a concentration camp. So many others whose messages we had transmitted had disappeared. So often we had not been able to help where help was urgently needed. Thus it was difficult to know whether these years had been the worst or the best years of our lives.

This chapter may give the impression that during those years of war my Dutch activities were mostly political rather than pastoral. But that was not really the case. For there was a very great influx of Dutch refugees, and for a long time I was the only Dutch pastor available. So I had to take responsibility for church services, weddings, baptisms and funerals. And I visited regularly the work camps where the younger refugees were assembled. These men, many of whom had left Holland in order to join the allied armies, were of course terribly impatient. They had not taken such great risks just to work for the Swiss! But it was a slow business to get them through France and Spain to allied territory. And in the meantime their morale had to be kept up. I have seldom had such an intense audience as in those days. The issues of life and death were so tangible and the need of a faith to hold on to was so evident.

NOTES

1. The story of his wartime activities is told in *Flee the Captor* by Herbert Ford (Nashville, Tenn.: Southern Publishing Association, 1966).
2. See *Great True Spy Stories* by Allan Dulles, pp. 364ff.
3. Later United Nations High Commissioner for Refugees.
4. The volumes on the relations between London and the occupied territory appeared in 1950.
5. Report, p. 249.

22 | *Relations with the German Resistance and Peace-feelers*

MY CONTACTS WITH resistance groups in Germany and our common attempts to achieve peace must be described together, because they were so intimately related. For the main reason why the internal opponents of Hitler came to me was to ask my support in approaching responsible persons in Britain and the USA. And nearly every visit of one of these Germans to me in Geneva led to the transmission, in one way or another, to colleagues of mine in the Allied countries, of documents or letters concerning the road from war to peace.

In the German resistance the finest minds maintained that the one sufficient motive for the attempt to overthrow the nazi regime would be that that regime was an incarnation of evil. It was not that only by revolt could a tolerable peace be secured for their country. And this was a point which I made myself in many conversations with German visitors. The outside world could not be expected to consider, as a true change of heart, an attempt to salvage as much as possible of the national interest. But here arose a dilemma which made the story of the German resistance truly tragic: responsible men must give thought to the consequences of their actions. The men of the resistance had to ask themselves what would happen to their country – and indeed to Europe – if they succeeded in overturning the regime. So they had to attempt to find out how the Allied nations would react to the ousting of Hitler. Even if their basic motive was a moral one, they were obliged to find out as much as they could about the probable results of their action.

What the resistance men really wanted to find out was whether the Allied nations still considered the war to be a war against the nazis. Could the anti-nazis count on the support of the Allied governments? Or was the war now considered, in Britain and America, to be a war against the German people as a whole? On the one hand resistance leaders heard the voice of Bishop George Bell who emphasized strongly the distinction between the national socialists and the German people. On the other hand they heard Lord Vansittart who propagated the notion that that distinction was a mere illusion. Which of these voices was to be taken as representative?

And there was this further important consideration: the only chance for success was to convince a sufficient number of army leaders to join. And among them there were few who put moral principle before every other consideration. In order to win a sufficient number of them to the side of the opposition it was important to get assurances from the enemy that the overthrow of Hitler would lead to a peace which would not mean the annihilation of Germany. Thus even Dietrich Bonhoeffer, whose motivation was certainly not opportunistic, made it quite clear in 1941[1] that the attitude of resistance groups in Germany would depend on the answer given to feelers concerning possible conditions of peace. It is well known that no such answer was given, and that this had a discouraging effect on the opposition inside Germany. Nevertheless, the men of July 20th 1944, proceeded to act anyway, thus proving beyond doubt that they were not motivated by opportunism.

From Hitler's assumption to power, I had been in touch with many groups and individuals in Germany who opposed national socialism. But it was not until early in 1940 that I heard of specific plans for a *coup d'état*. From that moment onward there came to us in Geneva a constant stream of information and especially of rumours. I do not know how often I was told that the moment of action was approaching. And when one asked, more and more insistently, why in spite of these predictions nothing happened the answer was always the same: 'At the last moment the generals on whom we counted got cold feet.'

My German colleague, Hanns Schönfeld, who visited Germany regularly, sought to convince me of the increasing strength of the opposition, but I could not help feeling that he often took his wishes for realities. The two men, both deeply involved, who made me believe in the seriousness of the resistance were Dietrich Bonhoeffer and Adam von Trott zu Solz.

Bonhoeffer came to Geneva in March 1941. During the two years since our first meeting he had become more deeply informed of the conspiratorial activities of the opposition to Hitler. But he did not give the impression of a man torn apart by the tensions of his dangerous life. With his round, almost boyish, face, his cheerful expression, his eager enjoyment of a good story or a good meal he seemed to have a more affirmative attitude to life than many of us who lived in the comparative quiet of neutral Switzerland.

This time we had opportunity to have long discussions. I was glad to find that with regard to the theological as well as the political issues we were on the same wavelength and could speak together with complete frankness. I wrote to our common friend, George Bell:

> Bonhoeffer was a week with us and spent most of his time extracting ecumenical information from persons and documents. . . . We learned a lot from him. The pressure is greater than ever. But fortunately he could also tell us of many signs that their (the Confessing Church) fundamental position has not changed at all and that they are as eager as ever for fellowship. Many of them have the same reaction to all that has happened and is happening as you have or I have. And this is remarkable after such a long period of isolation.

I sent on March 12th a document concerning the post-war settlement to William Temple and to John Foster Dulles, at that time chairman of the Commission on a Just and Durable Peace of the Federal Council of Churches in the USA. In my covering letter I explained that the document was the outcome of discussions among four persons of four different countries. It is most probable – though I cannot say it with absolute certainty – that these four were: Bonhoeffer, Ehrenström (my colleague from Sweden), Denzil Patrick (Scotland) and I. The main points of the document were that Europe was rapidly becoming a political vacuum, that after the war no regimes should be allowed to exist which were totalitarian in character, that several countries might have to be under authoritarian rule for a period, but that this should be phased out in due order, together with the introduction of freedom of speech and the right of opposition, and that Europe should be organized as a Federation with a certain limitation of national sovereignty. Mr Dulles replied that in his opinion this line of thought while idealistic was also realistic and would prove a help to the thinking of his commission.

In my letter to Temple I asked – surely on the basis of the discussions with Bonhoeffer – 'What are the minimum conditions on which peace would be possible?' I added:

Would their country (i.e. Germany) have a chance of being offered acceptable terms if it changed its regime? Or would such a change of regime be used to crush their country altogether? This is a problem which is much discussed, and it is clear that an answer on this point may be of considerable importance for the decisions which this group (i.e. the resistance in Germany) may take. At present their fear is that it is too late for an action of this kind. If, however, they could be convinced that this is not the case, they might get busy again.

The Archbishop answered in a letter of April 29th:

I was immensely interested in your letter and especially in what you said about the discussion of prospects of people of varied types. It is very hard to say what would be the minimum conditions of peace put forward in this country, but I think that the main body of opinion would support the start of negotiations if the following conditions were fulfilled: (1) the disappearance of the Nazi regime; (2) the evacuation of all the occupied countries; (3) the cessation of that type of tyranny which is represented by the Gestapo.

The Archbishop added that Czechoslovakia and Poland were of course included in the occupied countries. This was a relatively encouraging reaction.

Several months later, in September 1941, Bonhoeffer was again in Geneva. In those early weeks of the German invasion of Russia the general impression was still that the German army had met little effective resistance and that Hitler might succeed in the East as he had succeeded in the West. So I was taken aback when he opened the conversation by saying: 'So this is the beginning of the end.'

He saw my startled expression and added: 'The old man will never get out of this.' He felt sure that Hitler was making the same mistake which Napoleon had made.

Bonhoeffer was eager to meet other theologians so as to get their reactions to the line of thought he was developing. So we got a group of Genevese friends to join us for a long discussion in the garden of a restaurant on the shores of the lake. Bonhoeffer told us of the approach he was taking in his *Ethics*. He wanted to overcome the dualism which had characterized Christian ethics for so long. The sacred and the secular, the church and the world, had been kept separate. But in Christ we receive the invitation to participate at the same time in the reality of God and in the reality of the world. Bonhoeffer quoted often the first chapter of the Epistle to the Colossians and especially verse 16 which says that the world is created 'unto Christ'. In this way Christians could get rid of that dangerous pietism or otherworldliness which really left the world to the forces of darkness. And they had a strong starting point for their task in the world.

We also spent an evening with Swiss friends in the apartment of Adolf Freudenberg. One of us asked Bonhoeffer: 'What do you pray for in the present situation?' He answered without hesitation: 'Since you ask me, I must say that I pray for the defeat of my country, for I believe that this is the only way in which it can pay for the suffering which it has caused in the world.' That crystal clear answer characterized the man. Truth was to be served without reservation whatever the cost. I knew him well enough now to realize that this hard saying was not a denial, but rather an affirmation of his love for his country.

This time Bonhoeffer and I wanted to send a more substantial contribution to our friends in Britain and the United States. Our purpose was, as we said in the introduction to our common statement, to present reflections on the post-war order in Europe representing the thinking of two Continental Christians who were on opposite sides in the war. We took William Paton's useful book, *The Church and the New Order*, as our starting point. Bonhoeffer wrote a first draft in German[2] and I used that draft to produce a document in English which would express our common convictions.

The final document[3] on which we agreed begins with theological considerations in which one recognizes the Bonhoeffer of the *Ethics* with his christocentric conception of the world. We tried to show why the discussion concerning peace aims had now become of crucial importance. In Germany the attitude of considerable groups who were against the regime, but were at the same time good patriots, depended on the answer to the question: how will Germany be treated if it loses the war? The statement underlined that recent events (i.e. the German attack on Russia) had created a psychological situation in which the resistance groups had an opportunity such as they had not had since 1933. Concerning the form of government we reiterated what we had said already in March of the same year, namely that our common rejection of state-absolutism did not necessarily mean the acceptance of an individualist form of democracy. I added to

Bonhoeffer's draft the point that democracy still had real roots in the smaller countries of Europe, but that this was not the case in some of the larger countries. The important thing, we said (and this should be guaranteed on an *international* basis) was that the state should be limited by law in its relations to its own citizens and to other states. We spoke further of the next steps to be taken. The Allied nations spoke about safeguards against a return of national socialism, about occupation, about disarmament. But what was their positive policy? Was it not possible to offer such terms of peace to Germany that a new government of non-nazi German leaders, who would be ready for international collaboration, would not be discredited in the eyes of their own people? If such a government were formed and were to make a genuine peace offer (evacuation of *all* occupied territories, ousting of all nazi leaders, willingness to disarm) and if such an offer were rejected it would become impossible for any government worthy of that name to survive. We expressed our conviction that the answering of these questions was an urgent matter, since the attitude of the opposition groups in Germany would depend upon the answer given.

Bonhoeffer had written in his draft that such an anti-nazi government might be formed suddenly. But I omitted that phrase and he did not object. I had found that to announce again and again that Hitler might be overthrown at any moment made it more, not less, difficult to take the warnings of the resistance seriously. For you could not say at the same time: 'The attitude of the opposition groups in Germany will depend on the answer which they will get from the Allied governments' and: 'The opposition is ready to act in any case.'

This commentary on Paton's book was in fact an SOS, an attempt to elicit sufficient help from the Allied nations to enable the rather small group of determined resistance men to convince the large group of the hesitant, including the generals who could not make up their minds. I added therefore in my covering letter to Hugh Martin (of the Ministry of Information in London):

> You must accept my word for it that all that we say about the next steps and the urgency of the situation is not based upon wishful thinking on our part, but on actual developments in discussion with responsible people in the country concerned. This is also why I hope that some of these considerations will be brought before responsible people in Britain.

The document reached indeed a number of responsible people in Great Britain and the USA. Henry Van Dusen (a Professor of Union Theological Seminary, New York) wrote that this was one of the most valuable documents on issues of the peace which had reached him and that he had circulated it to a few selected people, including John Foster Dulles. Paton reported that he had shared it with 'very important people'. But the urgent question we had asked remained unanswered. Reinhold Niebuhr and John Bennett expressed the opinion that it was futile at that moment to speak of a peace that would be regarded as 'honourable' by the German army. Paton said that he and his friends had no doubt as to the reality of a German resistance, but doubted 'whether there really can be a sufficiently strong party on the lines described to be able really to affect the situation'. He added, however, that it was widely agreed that any action which had the effect of making life impossible for Germans would be bad for Europe.

This was a meagre result. It is all the more remarkable that Bonhoeffer did not give up.

In the meantime I had also had close contact with another very active representative of the German resistance: Adam von Trott zu Solz. In 1928 when he was nineteen years old Adam spent a holiday in Geneva and visited us several times. I felt strongly attracted to this very bright student who was so keenly aware of the perilous and tragic situation of the younger generation in Germany in the spiritual confusion after the first world war. His good looks, his tall figure, his high forehead gave him the appearance of the perfect aristocrat. But in his conversation he showed the humility of a young man desperately anxious to find some stable foundation for his life. He told me at that time that in his family he had received an overdose of religious nourishment and had now reached the point that he could no longer read the Bible, but got his religious inspiration from the novels of Dostoyevsky. Soon afterwards he had attended a conference of the Student Christian Movement in Great Britain and become deeply impressed by the straightforward and practical form of Christian life of British students. He had found there something which seemed to be lacking in his own country. German students, he wrote, are passing through a valley overhung with a gloomy and all-penetrating mist – while English students are standing on a headland.[4] He had already come to believe that the future belonged to socialism. But he believed also in the need for maintaining historical continuity. In England he found a socialism which was not a violent break in the English tradition, but 'a crusade against inhumanity and injustice'.

So he had eagerly seized the opportunity of spending two years at Oxford as a Rhodes scholar. During that period he had developed close friendships with men who played already or were to play a very prominent role in British life: Sir Stafford Cripps, A. D. Lindsay, David Astor, R. H. S. Crossman and others. He had come to believe that his special task was to interpret Germany to Britain and Britain to Germany. In the period just before the outbreak of the second world war he had made desperate attempts to use his contacts to avoid war, but his approaches to Lord Halifax and other British statesmen had been unsuccessful. After the outbreak of the war he had visited the United States where he had also met a good many leading politicians.

In the nervous atmosphere of those years it was inevitable that questions should be raised about the international activities of this young man who did not seem to have any credentials. Whom did he represent? What was his game? Some thought that he was a secret agent of the Hitler government and since

Adam could only carry on his activities by giving the German authorities the impression that he was working in their interest, they found enough 'evidence' to prove that their suspicions were well-founded. But those who knew him well were aware that he was an ardent anti-nazi and that, while he certainly loved his country, he was really concerned with salvaging the common European civilization.

He had joined the Foreign Office in Berlin in 1940 and was therefore allowed to travel to neutral countries. In September 1940, during the 'Battle of Britain', he came to see me in Geneva and gave me an analysis of the situation in Germany. He asked me to transmit a summary of his points to David Astor and other friends of his in England. The picture which he gave was gloomy. The nazi regime had been apparently successful and nothing succeeds like success. The various opposition groups had been weakened. In these circumstances it was absolutely necessary to resist Hitler by force. For that was the only hope of changing the present regime. In other words at that time Adam did not seem to believe in the possibility of a revolt by the German army or at least a part of the army. He added, however, that all concerned should begin to think about peace. Such a peace should give Germany, as far as possible, her ethnographical frontiers. For if the peace were based on the attempt to annihilate Germany the whole nation would rally behind Hitler.

Adam closed with a confession of his deepest faith. The struggle was in the last analysis a spiritual one. Christians had fundamental spiritual ideals in common; they believed in the spiritual mission of Europe and they would serve as links to draw the nations together after the war.

Adam felt strongly that all those who held the same fundamental Christian convictions about the social and international order were on the same side in this war, even if their governments were on opposite sides. I shared this conviction and this gave our friendship a strong basis.

During 1941 and 1942 he came several times to Geneva. His visit in April 1942 was specially important. He had heard about my plan to visit Britain and this seemed to him an excellent opportunity to get in touch with his friends in Great Britain. Sir Stafford Cripps was now an influential member of the British government and so Adam gave me a memorandum to be handed to Sir Stafford.

The memorandum[5] was of course unsigned, but its contents show clearly that it is not merely a personal document. Whether the actual formulation was left to Adam alone or whether it was approved by a group of his friends, the memorandum expressed the thinking of a large part of the opposition in Germany. For by this time Adam had made contact with a considerable number of men who were actively organizing a movement of resistance and preparing for the overthrow of Hitler. He was now far more hopeful about the success of a *coup d'état* than he had been in 1940. But much would depend on the attitude of the Allied governments. The memorandum was therefore an appeal to the sense of solidarity and fairness of British leaders and a strong request to take seriously those forces in

Germany which had consistently fought nihilism and its national socialist manifestations. It stated that the most urgent and immediate task was to overthrow
the Hitler regime as soon as possible. The opposition had support from substantial parts of the working class, from influential circles in the army and the
civil service and from militant groups in the churches. Their common purpose
was to rescue the substance of personal human integrity which was equally
threatened by nazism and anarchic Bolshevism. The opposition stood for
federalism in Germany and a federal organization of Europe. All nations should
have the right of self-determination within such a federal framework.

The document enumerated several obstacles which the opposition in Ger-
many had to overcome. One was the necessity of national defence against the
Soviet Union. Another was the complete uncertainty concerning the British and
American attitude towards a change of government in Germany.

Soon after I arrived in London, in May 1942, I handed the document to Sir
Stafford Cripps. When I told him that it came from Adam von Trott he showed
genuine interest and promised to show it to the Prime Minister. It was agreed
that I should come back a week later to hear the result. During the second visit
he told me that Mr Churchill had studied the document carefully and had
written underneath it: 'very encouraging'. But the British government maintained the position that Germany would have to be defeated. I asked whether this
was the only answer I could bring back. Sir Stafford said that this was indeed the
case. It was necessary to demonstrate that what the nazi regime had done could
not be tolerated. There would therefore have to be a definite surrender. But the
peace would not be a peace of revenge. The Allies would follow a positive policy
and seek to establish a new order in Germany. In the meantime the Germans
should dissociate themselves from the present regime. He added that he did not
believe that the Russians desired to exterminate Germany.

I was of course very dissatisfied with this answer which was no answer. Sir
Stafford said a few weeks later to Bishop Bell that he had said to me that I 'might
encourage von Trott on the basis, however, of Germany being defeated'.[6] That
short formula was indeed a summary of what he had said, but it showed very
clearly that the British government took away with one hand what it was giving
with the other. For the refusal to consider any other possibility than total
military defeat was in fact a most discouraging reply.

The British government had obviously developed a conception of the war in
which there was no place for anything like negotiations with the German
resistance. This was confirmed by many other conversations in which I spoke in
more general terms about the German opposition. In Oxford the men of the
Peace Aims Group (A. D. Lindsay, Arnold Toynbee, Sir Alfred Zimmern) said
that it was 'useless' and 'indecent' to talk about linking up with any German
government to defend the West against Russia; the British public would not
accept an anti-Russian policy. German militarism had to be destroyed. But since
one could not keep a great people down, the argument went, the Germans had

to discover that they could play a great role in other fields, particularly in the economic field. A. D. Lindsay said, however, that if there should be a change of regime in Germany this would be such a miracle that a wholly new psychological situation might be created. In later conversations William Temple and R. H. S. Crossman made the same point. One of the few who showed a more positive interest in the message of the German resistance was the Bishop of Chichester whom I met just before he undertook his journey to Stockholm. He did not know at that time that he would meet there Bonhoeffer and Schönfeld and receive from them the same SOS which I had heard from von Trott.

Adam came to see me soon after my return to Geneva. When I told him about the British reaction to his memorandum he was so deeply disappointed that he was near despair. What I could tell him about the good intentions of the British was no consolation. He felt that the men whom he considered as comrades-in-arms in the battle against Hitler had let him down. The supra-national solidarity of men defending the same fundamental values on which he had counted so strongly had been denied. That was a terribly hard thing to accept. And there would now be much less chance of creating a really effective opposition in Germany. Adam felt obviously that he had failed in the very mission with which he had been entrusted. It was no wonder that there was bitterness in his words. We sat for a long time in my garden on that warm summer-night. I tried to find words to encourage him, but all I could do was to show that I understood what this blow meant to him.

A short time later I had to transmit a similar message. In the last days of May 1942 Bishop Bell had met Dietrich Bonhoeffer and Hanns Schönfeld in Sweden. The two Germans had not only given the bishop the same information about the plans and desires of the German opposition that was contained in Adam's memorandum, but also revealed the names of the most prominent leaders of the opposition.[7] It had been agreed that Bishop Bell should give a report on these conversations to the British government and send to me in Geneva a telegram indicating the result of his approach to the government. In July I received the following telegram: 'Interest undoubted but deeply regret no reply possible.' Chichester's regret was certainly most real.[8] For he had done and continued to do all he could to advocate what he called a policy of 'discrimination', that is of distinguishing between the Hitler regime and those in Germany who were its victims or its adversaries.

When Adam came again to see me in January 1943 I found that the disappointment of his hopes concerning an understanding with the Allies had had a deep effect on his thinking. There was now a strongly emotional element in his analysis of the situation. He said that there was no point in continuing the conversations with the Western powers. British and American propaganda, in his view, took a very high-handed attitude towards the opposition in Germany. It was not understood that Germans, as well as Frenchmen or Dutchmen, lived in an occupied country and that the opposition in Germany had to take tremendous

risks in continuing their activity. This pharisaic attitude and the unwillingness
to think and act in more radical terms, Adam went on, made many in Germany
wonder whether they should not turn rather to the East. The Russian and
German peoples had both suffered deeply and both were in the process of
returning to the spiritual foundations of their tradition. The real issues were not
the military, but the social ones. The new experience of the fraternity between
the oppressed common people would be the basis on which a completely new
Europe would be built.

I knew that Adam had always had a strong social concern. But I had known
him as a man who understood and deeply appreciated the abiding values in the
Western democratic tradition. What worried me was not so much his interest in
the East as his bitterness about the West. And we had received in those days
other evidence of a growing anti-Western mood in the ranks of the German
opposition. I reported fully on this conversation to Mr Allan Dulles, hoping in
this way to reach responsible American leaders.[9] In a covering letter[10] I commented:

> I am afraid that Anglo-Saxon propaganda is indeed too 'high-handed'
> towards these groups and has failed to encourage them. In one respect it has
> even definitely discouraged them, namely when it says that in any case and
> quite irrespective of the creation of a new regime Germany must be defeated
> on the battlefield. Now the opposition in Germany should not depend for its
> dynamism on promises from abroad, but it is clear that the response within
> the country varies according to the measure of encouragement which is given
> to it. Thus the question to be faced in political warfare seems to be: Are the
> United Nations willing to say to the opposition: 'If you succeed in over-
> throwing Hitler and if you then prove by your acts (punishment of nazi
> leaders and nazi criminals, liberation of occupied territory, restoration of
> stolen goods, installation of a regime which respects the rights of men,
> participation in economic and social reconstruction) that you have wholly
> broken with national socialism and militarism, we will be ready to discuss
> peace terms with you?' As long as that is not clearly and definitely said, the
> process of development of an anti-Western, anti-liberal complex is likely to
> go on. And, as long as that is not said, large groups in Germany, who are
> psychologically prepared to join the opposition, will remain hesitant and
> wonder whether, after all, Hitler is not a lesser evil than total military
> defeat.

But two weeks after that letter was sent we received the clearest possible
negative answer. For at the Casablanca conference President Roosevelt and
Prime Minister Churchill decided rather suddenly to define 'the objective of
this war in terms of an unconditional surrender by Germany, Italy and Japan'.
It is true that in his press conference President Roosevelt added that this did not
mean the annihilation of the peoples concerned. But it was the term 'un-

conditional surrender' rather than the explanation which became widely known. And it seemed to say that defeat would practically mean the end of any national existence for the Axis powers. Thus the task of the German opposition had again become vastly more difficult. The Allied nations had publicly closed the door to all possibilities of negotiation.

In spite of these deep disappointments the resistance in Germany continued. Other men came to tell me about the plans. Hans Bernd Gisevius[11] turned up several times. Our relations were based on our common concern about Martin Niemöller. Through his connections with the German police and with the German Foreign Office Gisevius was extraordinarily well-informed. But he was critical of the leftist line which men of the Kreisau circle like Adam von Trott were taking. I had occasion to introduce him to another Kreisau man, Eugen Gerstenmaier,[12] with whom my relations in the years before the war had not been of the best because of his connection with Bishop Heckel, but who was now wholly identified with the opposition. I sat back as these two men entered into a heated discussion concerning the question whether several hundreds or several thousands of nazi leaders should be eliminated at the critical moment.

Gerstenmaier's visit proved the efficiency of the Swiss security system. Three or four of us had dined with him in a reserved room in the Schweizerhof in Berne to hear all that he could tell us about preparations for the overthrowing of the nazi regime. The next morning an officer appeared in my office to ask just what we had been discussing together. Knowing the discretion of the Swiss Intelligence I gave him the information he wanted.

In the meantime the opposition continued to prepare for the *coup d'état*. In January 1944 I received a top-secret message via the 'Swiss Road' concerning an approach made to two Dutch resistance leaders[13] by a representative of the German opposition. A German *Oberst*[14] had informed the two Dutchmen that the Hitler regime would soon be overthrown and the Dutch resistance movement should make arrangements for the transition period in Holland. The Dutchmen had answered that they could not co-operate until they had a definite approval from the Netherlands government in London, but that they were willing to discuss in the meantime the measures that might have to be taken. In the conversations with the German officer the Dutch representatives had become convinced of the good faith of the German resistance. They now wanted to know whether the government allowed them to go on with the discussions.

I was especially impressed by the urgency of the message, for it was clearly stated that the *coup* would take place in January. So the essential points of the memorandum were telegraphed to London. The reply was completely negative. The Dutch government did not want to have anything to do with this action. The British government was of the opinion that such German approaches, if not actually inspired by the German secret service, could only take place with the knowledge of that service.

So once again 'London' refused to take the German opposition seriously[15] and the discussion between the German resistance and the Allies remained till the end a *dialogue de sourds*.

In one important respect the 1944 situation was even less favourable than the situation in 1942. For in the meantime the policy of 'unconditional surrender' had become solidly established. And it had, at least in the minds of the people who determined the official policy, the implication that a German resistance or opposition could not be recognized as an effective political force. Even when a few months later, on July 20th 1944, the resistance men acted in an unmistakable manner and nearly succeeded in overthrowing Hitler, the allied governments and press continued to speak of the attempted *coup* as just a quarrel between different types of nationalistic militarists.

I tried to get the story of the German resistance across. A few months after the *coup* of July 20th 1944, I gave a full report to the Peace Aims Group in London which met under the chairmanship of Bishop Bell. I said:

In this country there has been a tendency to present those happenings as eminently a military *coup d'état*, the main motive behind which was that a certain number of generals wanted to save something from the ruins and perhaps save it in order to get ready for a third world war. I am not going to say that there was nothing of that in it. But I am personally quite convinced that that was not the main stream of it. What kind of people were they? They were made up of three groups which overlapped at some points: (1) a group of civil servants, to a large extent in the ministeries, perhaps the most important in the Ministry of Foreign Affairs; (2) Trade Union leaders; (3) lay leaders and some ordained men from the church, both Roman Catholic and Protestant. The very fact of this combination shows that something really new has happened in Germany – a drawing together of the socialists and convinced Christians. We know – through all sorts of study groups which have been working in these last years, preparing for the renewal of the social order in Germany – that they have been striving to find for the first time in modern German history a meeting of minds between Christians and men who are quite definitely on the Left in political affairs.

One of the reasons why this civil resistance group has not been able to act earlier is that it has been unable to get assurance from the United Nations, and in particular from Great Britain, the country from which they asked the assurance in the first place, that they would be taken seriously in any sense if they acted . . . Certain advances have been made to this country and have been wholly turned down. I will not go into the merits of the whole situation because I have always had a divided mind about it myself. In one way one regrets tremendously that the group has been weakened by the lack of backing from the outside. But one can to a certain extent understand the attitude that your Foreign Secretary has expressed quite openly. He said: 'If there are people who want to overthrow Hitler and his regime, let them act and we will talk with them after they have acted.' It is very difficult for a government to deal with a group in an enemy country which says it is a resistance group, when one does not know at all what they really represent in the way of political or military power. But I think that a little more political imagination brought to bear on the problem might have solved it. The group has had great discouragement and I think we can only say that it is to their credit that, in spite of the fact that they had nothing to go on from other countries, they have nevertheless acted.

As Louis P. Lochman has stated: 'Stories of the existence of a resistance did not fit into the concept of unconditional surrender'.[16] I discovered this again when in 1944 I had occasion to tell my part of the story to Robert Murphy, political adviser to General Eisenhower, at General Eisenhower's headquarters in Versailles and to Richard Law, a member of the British cabinet, in London. When friends arranged for me to hold a press conference on the subject in June 1945 in New York, practically nothing appeared in the New York papers, though several major newspapers and journals were represented.

The question whether the British and American governments were right in ignoring the approaches made by the German resistance is still an open question. After the appearance of Christopher Sykes' biography of Adam von Trott,[17] David Astor has reopened the debate.[18] My own view remains that the arguments used to justify the refusal to encourage the German opposition were not convincing.

There was the argument that the Allies could not be sure that these peace feelers were not inspired by the nazis. But by 1942 there were so many trustworthy people in Switzerland, in Sweden and in the occupied countries who were informed about the German resistance (including Mr Allan Dulles in Berne) that it ought to have been possible for the Allied secret service to discover the truth.

The second argument was that it was essential that Germany should be defeated on the battlefield. Was that really a sound pedagogical principle? Would it not have been better for everybody concerned if Germans had solved their own problem?

The third argument was stronger. The German resistance seemed to think in terms of a separate peace with the Western governments and these governments could not break faith with the Russians. But would it not have been possible to discuss this matter with the German opposition so as to arrive at an understanding which would include the Russians?

It is impossible to reconstruct history, but one cannot help thinking of the millions of lives which might have escaped violent death on the battlefield, in gas chambers, in bombed cities, if the resistance in Germany had been encouraged to act quickly and decisively.

The Western world did not understand that men like Adam von Trott and Dietrich Bonhoeffer were not German nationalists who were trying to avoid the defeat of their country, but pathfinders of a new and better social and international order. I quote what I wrote about Adam in 1969:

> If Adam was so often critical of British and American policies this was not so much due to a national reaction as to his conviction that the Western nations did not understand the depth of the crisis of our whole civilization and tried to apply outworn methods to unprecedented situations. He really belonged to that wider European resistance movement which was dreaming of a great renewal of Europe through radical social reform and new federal structures.

Adam was executed soon after the revolt of July 20th 1944. Since Dietrich Bonhoeffer had already been arrested before the coup, we hoped that his life would be spared. But he was murdered in the very last month of the war. We would miss these men greatly. Both died as young men who had not yet given all that they had to give. Or should we rather think that through their death they rendered a more telling witness than they could possibly have rendered by their words or actions in a longer life?

NOTES

1. See his memorandum in *Gesammelte Schriften* I, 370 (in English).
2. See Bonhoeffer, *Gesammelte Schriften* I, pp. 356–60.
3. See Bonhoeffer's *Gesammelte Schriften* I, pp. 361 and 371 (in English).
4. *The World's Youth*, November 1929.
5. The memorandum has been published in the *Vierteljahrshefte für Seitgeschichte 1967*, p. 302 and in van Roon, *Neuordnung im Widerstand*, München, 1967, p. 572.
6. George Bell, 'The Church and the Resistance Movement in Germany', in Bonhoeffer, *Gesammelte Schriften* I, p. 410.
7. Ronald C. D. Jasper, *George Bell, Bishop of Chichester*, London, 1967, pp. 267–73.
8. The correspondence with Eden concerning Bell's discussions with Bonhoeffer and Schönfeld is published in Bonhoeffer, *Gesamelte Schriften*, pp. 372–88. Chichester told me in November 1944 that the two arguments which Eden had advanced in conversation were: (1) It is possible that the peace feelers come from men who are really nazis; (2) in relation to Russia all our actions must be 'above board'.
9. I did not realize at that time that Adam had another channel to reach Mr Dulles. See van Roon, op. cit., p. 311.
10. Letter of January 11th 1943.
11. Author of two books on the German resistance: *Bis zum bitteren Ende* and *Wo ist Nebe?*.
12. After the war President of the *Bundestag*.
13. I heard later that these were Dr G. J. van Heuven Goedhart (who became the UN High Commissioner for Refugees) and Dr J. Cramer (who became Commissioner of the Queen in Drente).
14. I heard later that this was Oberst Stähle who was in close contact with von

Trott. The full story is in *Vierteljahrshefte für Zeitgeschichte*, 1966. Vol. 2, by G. van Roon.

15. The later Dutch Prime Minister Willem Drees, one of the few Dutchmen who was informed about these contacts with the German opposition, expresses in his memoirs the opinion that in this matter the Dutch government in exile made a mistake.

16. *Always the Unexpected*, pp. 294–5.

17. *Troubled Loyalty*, London, 1968.

18. *Encounter*, June 1969. See also the following issues.

19. *Encounter*, September 1969, p. 94.

In OCTOBER 1941 WE received, in various ways, extremely alarming reports about the mass deportation of Jews from Germany and the occupied countries to German occupied Poland and about the miserable conditions in the concentration camps there. We sent a strong appeal to President Max Huber of the International Committee of the Red Cross and Dr Karl Burckhardt of the 'Mixed Commission' of the national Red Cross societies in Geneva, asking them to send a special representative to Poland to investigate the situation. At that time we did not believe that the situation could become any worse. But in August and September 1942 we began to hear, first through the World Jewish Congress and then through reports which we received ourselves, that thousands of Jews were being killed. The first stories came in the form of rather mysterious messages using Hebrew words so as to conceal their meaning from the censors and their interpretation was difficult. But, before long, there was enough information from different sources to show that large-scale extermination was indeed taking place. I wrote on December 3rd, 1942, to the Red Cross: 'In one single place in Poland 6,000 Jews – men, women and children – are being shot every day, and this has gone on for several weeks.'

What could we do with this knowledge? Would anyone believe this story? Could we really believe it ourselves? For this was a dimension of man's inhumanity to man which did not fit in with any previous experience. We had knowledge of incidental explosions of human cruelty, but this was different. This was the deliberate annihilation, organized in cold blood, of vast numbers of people – old and young, sick and healthy – for no other reason than that they were born as Jews.

I must confess that it took several months before the information received entered fully into my consciousness. That moment occurred when I heard a young Swiss businessman tell what he had seen with his own eyes during a business trip to Russia. He had been invited by German officers to be present at one of the mass killings of Jews. He told us in the most straightforward and realistic way how group after group of Jewish men, women and children were forced to lie down in the mass graves and were then machine-gunned to death. The picture he drew has remained in my mind ever since. From that moment onward I had no longer any excuse for shutting my mind to information which could find no place in my view of the world and humanity. And this meant that I had to do something about it.

Hitler's strength was that he did the unimaginable. When people heard about the wholesale massacre they could still not realize what it really meant and therefore they would not react in time. That was the strange situation in the years 1942 and 1943. A considerable number of people in Germany, in occupied countries, in the allied and neutral countries, heard stories about mass killings. But the information was ineffective because it seemed too improbable. Everyone who heard it for the first time asked whether this was not a typical piece of wildly exaggerated war-time propaganda. The neutral press did not dare to publish these stories. Even the underground press in occupied countries did not report the facts until very late. And in the Allied countries the press spoke only in vague terms about the great Jewish catastrophe.

It has been said that the outside world remained indifferent because the victims were Jews – in other words that the lack of reaction was due to a latent anti-semitism. I do not underestimate the reality of such anti-semitism, but I have found little evidence that this played the main role in this situation. It was rather that people could find no place in their consciousness for such an un-imaginable horror and that they did not have the imagination, together with the courage to face it. It is possible to live in a twilight between knowing and not knowing. It is possible to refuse full realization of facts because one feels unable to face the implications of these facts. It must be added that the perfidious trick of forcing deportees to send postcards giving a completely false picture of their real circumstances succeeded in creating doubt as to whether the fate of the deportees was really as terrible as rumour would have it. Even at the end of 1943 I received reports from the Dutch resistance according to which the Dutch Jews deported to Poland were taken to work-camps, except older ones who were sent to the ghettos. Even at that date these resistance men, who were constantly in touch with Jews in Holland, did not realize that deportation to Auschwitz meant death.[1]

During the last months of 1942 the facts were made available to many governments through several different channels. Through reports of the World Jewish Congress, of the Polish resistance, of the S.S. officer, Kurt Gerstein, to Swedish and Swiss diplomats and to the Papal Nuncio in Berlin, and of our World Council to colleagues in London and New York, the horrible news reached many responsible people. But the reaction on the part of the govern-ments remained hesitant and ambiguous. It is true that a statement made by the Allied governments on December 17th 1941, did speak of the determination of the nazi government to exterminate the Jewish population of Europe, but it gave the impression that this extermination took place as a result of hard work in the camps and through killing the disabled. So this statement did not convey the simple and terrible truth.

At the same time the Allied governments weakened the impact of their statement by relativizing the suffering of the Jews. Answering an *aide-mémoire* from the British government of January 20th 1943, the American Secretary of State, Cordell Hull, wrote that 'the refugee problem should not be considered as being confined to persons of any particular race or faith' – a dangerous half-truth which could only serve to distract attention from the fact that no other race was faced with the situation of having every one of its members, in lands under nazi domination, threatened by death in the gas chambers.

It was encouraging that some Christian voices in the free world spoke out clearly. Thus, the Assembly of the Federal Council of Churches in the USA adopted a resolution on December 11th 1942, stating that:

> It is impossible to avoid the conclusion that something like a policy of deliberate extermination of the Jews in Europe is being carried out. The violence and inhumanity which nazi leaders have publicly avowed towards all Jews are apparently now coming to a climax in a virtual massacre. We are resolved to do our full part in establishing conditions in which such treatment of the Jews shall end.

In Great Britain the newly formed Council of Christians and Jews, one of the Presidents of which was Archbishop William Temple, sent a delegation, under the leadership of the Archbishop, to the British government, on December 16th 1942. The delegation urged that assurances should be given to neutral governments concerning financial assistance and food supplies needed for Jewish refugees who could reach these countries, and that pledges should be given to these governments concerning the ultimate resettlement of these refugees after the war. A memorable debate took place in the House of Lords on March 23rd 1943. Archbishop William Temple moved a resolution asking again for immediate measures for providing help and temporary asylum for Jews and others in enemy and enemy-occupied countries in danger of massacre.

Temple made one of the greatest speeches of his life. He had received full information through the World Jewish Congress, and I had sent him a telegram strongly urging that European neutral nations should be asked to grant temporary asylum to Jews with the understanding that the Allied countries would guarantee re-emigration and provide in the meantime food and financial resources. In his speech the Archbishop described the situation in its full seriousness. He said that we must, of course, remember all victims of persecution, but that there had been a concentration of fury against the Jews. All that could be done should be done. The statement of the Allied governments of December 17th had led only to meagre action. It was grotesquely irrelevant to speak of relief already given to refugees when what you were confronted with was wholesale massacre. The Allies should offer help to European neutrals to encourage them to admit new refugees and promise to relieve them of a proportion of refugees after the war. Quick action should be taken. The Jews were being massacred, and all that was being proposed was a preliminary exploration by an inter-governmental conference. Temple's closing sentence was: 'We stand at the bar of history, of humanity and of God.'

The answer of the government given by Lord Cranborne was disappointing. He reiterated the misleading statement that this should not be regarded as a Jewish problem. He reported that Mr Hull and Mr Eden had agreed on an agenda for urgent and immediate action, but he failed to give any specific undertakings.

During these same days of March, my colleague, Adolf Freudenberg, and I were in constant touch, in Geneva, with Gerhart Riegner, Secretary General of the World Jewish Congress, who was himself a refugee from Germany. He was remarkably well-informed, but had also great difficulty in convincing responsible persons in the USA, Britain and neutral countries that immediate action should be taken. So we joined forces and drew up a memorandum to the High Commissioner for Refugees of the League of Nations, with copies for the American and British governments. The proposals contained in it were based on plans which were already being discussed between the leaders of the London branch of the World Jewish Congress and the governments concerned. We hoped that the inter-governmental meeting which had been announced would take action on these proposals. Before sending the document I discussed the matter with Allan Dulles, who was known as the personal representative of President Roosevelt in Switzerland. He said that we should try to get confirmation of the information we had received. As to our proposals concerning guarantees for re-emigration, he felt that the main difficulty would be that the American Congress could not bind its successors. This was not a very helpful reaction. For what confirmation would be considered sufficient? Were the many concordant messages we had received not clear enough? And had not the American Congress often made treaties which did in fact bind its successors?

In order to facilitate immediate telegraphic transmission the British Minister in Berne asked us to provide a summary of our memorandum. This summary was as follows:

AIDE-MEMOIRE

by the Secretariat of the World Council of Churches and the World Jewish Congress.

The Secretariats welcome the warm determination of the Allied governments to bring help to the victims of nazi persecution of all nationalities, races and religions, and wish to emphasize that the situation of the Jewish communities under direct or indirect control of the nazis is the most urgently acute problem and requires immediate action as the campaign of deliberate extermination of the Jews in nearly all European countries is now at its climax. It is therefore essential that measures of immediate rescue should have priority over the study of post-war arrangements.

Steps should be taken to enable neutral states to grant temporary asylum to Jews who succeed in reaching their frontiers. A scheme to enable refugees to be re-emigrated or repatriated as soon as possible after the war should be drawn up by Great Britain and the United States, and possibly other Allied nations, particularly the Dominions.

In view of the special characteristics of Jewish problems and the political neutrality during hostilities of neutral states, the latter would not consider sufficient assurances of repatriation by exiled governments alone.

Neutral states should also be granted facilities concerning the supply of food and funds.

In view of the fact that the number of Axis nationals in Allied countries greatly exceeds the number of Allied nationals in Axis countries, a scheme for the exchange of Jews in German-controlled countries for German civilians in North and South America and Palestine should be pressed forward by all possible means.

Jews should be admitted to the exchange scheme *en bloc* as it is impossible in present circumstances to carry out individual investigations. War-time security measures might also be included in the scheme. The submission of concrete proposals to the governments representing Allied interests should be made immediately, and eventually to the International Red Cross.[2]

What happened to this memorandum? Sir Herbert Emerson, the High Commissioner for Refugees of the League of Nations, received it through the British Embassy in Berne and the Foreign Office. He sent copies to William Paton who made it available to several church leaders. Sir Herbert Emerson and Dr Paton discussed the matter on April 20th 1943. The account of this conversation did not become known to me until many years later.

Sir Herbert felt strongly that we had made a great mistake in emphasizing only the plight of the Jews. As to the main point concerning guarantees to neutral states, it was being met. For he had proposed to the United Nations that they should tell the neutral countries into which refugees had come that they would regard the dealing with the refugees after the war as a part of the total problem of rehabilitation. This point was also part of the proposals which were being laid before the Bermuda inter-governmental conference on refugees.

In this way the teeth were taken out of our proposals. Once again the theoretical concern for all refugees drew attention away from the immediate danger of wholesale extermination of the European Jews. And instead of a specific guarantee to neutral states there remained only a vague promise.

Bishop Bell with his great concern for refugees understood the urgency of the matter. He wrote to Paton (May 21st 1943): 'I am much interested in this memorandum. The attitude of the government is peculiarly lukewarm and unhelpful . . .' But some British church leaders were equally unhelpful. One of them told the High Commissioner that in identifying the World Council with the proposals of the World Jewish Congress I had gone much too far and had become the victim of Jewish propaganda. So there was little hope of developing a strong common conviction in the churches which could put pressure on the governments.

It is well-known that the inter-governmental Bermuda Conference on the refugee situation, held in April 1943, did not produce any tangible results. The *News Chronicle* described the conference under the headline 'How not to hold a Conference on Refugees'. The *Observer* remarked that the conference was a declaration of bankruptcy on the part of the two most powerful nations on earth.[3]

Once again Bishop Bell spoke up as a true defender of persecuted fellow-men. He said in the House of Lords (July 28th 1943) that there had been a deterioration in the determination to grapple with the problem. At Bermuda not a word had been said about 'temporary asylum'. Priority, Bell stated, should be given to the persecuted Jews: 'With the appeal of the stricken people in our ears, we should be false to our tradition if we failed to do everything we can'.[4] The reply to Bell's speech given by the government was once again evasive.

In Geneva I co-operated closely with the Dutch 'Jewish Co-ordination Committee' organized by M. H. Gans, himself a Jewish refugee from Amsterdam. This committee did admirable practical relief work by sending food parcels to the internment camps, by seeking openings for emigration for Jews who had reached neutral territory, and by giving financial support to Jews who were in hiding in the occupied countries. It received substantial help from the American Joint Distribution Committee. I agreed to act as liaison between this committee and the Netherlands government in London, for I appreciated the energy and inventiveness with which M. H. Gans fought for the Dutch Jews in the hour of their great catastrophe.

The committee had to use unorthodox ways to save as many Jews as could possibly be saved. Thus it bought up passports from certain countries in Latin America and sent those to Jews in Dutch internment camps. Surprisingly enough this method was at least partially successful. It was therefore a blow when in January 1944 M. H. Gans received word that several governments refused to recognize these passports as valid. This could only mean that these Jews would be deported to the places of extermination. M. H. Gans had been informed in the middle of the night of this new danger. Very early on the next morning he came to see me with the old Dr Lewenstein, chief rabbi of Zürich. It was decided that Dr Lewenstein and I should together send a telegram to Queen Wilhelmina. This time there was a very quick reaction. Diplomatic interventions by Dutch diplomats resulted in a confirmation of the validity of the passports concerned, and this action meant the saving of hundreds of Jewish lives.

The spring of 1944 brought a further crisis. News was received that hundreds of thousands of Hungarian Jews were being deported to the extermination centres. This time we decided not only to alert our friends in the USA and Britain but also to make a public protest. We issued a communiqué, signed by the World Council's Ecumenical Committee for Refugees, calling attention to the deportation of 400,000 Jews to Auschwitz, where already hundreds of thousands of Jews had been deliberately murdered and asked Christians to raise their voice against this crime.[5]

During this entire period of extreme danger for the Jews and especially from 1942 to 1945 we sought also to get as many Jewish refugees admitted to Switzerland as possible. This was done especially in collaboration with CIMADE, an organization set up by the French Protestant youth movements. The official policy of the Swiss government in those years was not to admit those who were seeking refuge on racial grounds alone,[6] and this meant that even after it was known that the Jews in German-occupied territories were being exterminated, many Jews were refused entry into Switzerland. It even happened that Jewish refugees who had already succeeded in reaching Switzerland were sent back to the German-occupied territories. I cannot forget the family of Polish Jews from Antwerp who came to my home, whom I brought myself to the police with a strong recommendation that they should be allowed to stay, and whose arrival I reported to the Polish consulate. I telephoned several times to ask whether they had been given permission to stay, and after a few days I was told that they had been sent back. There could be little doubt about their ultimate fate. The Swiss churches sought to put pressure on the government to open the doors more widely. After long discussions with the Swiss government in which Pastor Boegner and Dr Koechlin played a prominent role, it became possible to get those Jews admitted whose names appeared on lists transmitted by CIMADE. Thus several hundreds of Jews were 'smuggled' across the mountains by the courageous and inventive young Cimade workers.

As I look back on these attempts to help the Jews during the war years I feel far from proud. In some post-war publications my role has been presented as an example of active assistance to the Jews in their hour of crisis. But does this not amount to the truth that in the land of the blind the one-eyed man is king? For there was indeed an astonishing blindness in nearly all quarters with regard to the dimensions and the meaning of the wholesale murder of European Jews. Here, if anywhere, the churches should have cried out, not only because fellow-men were persecuted to death, but also because an attempt was made to get rid once for all of the people through whom and from whom salvation had come to the world. But only a few Christians spoke out, and only a few went out of their way and stretched out a helping hand. I know now that I should have done a great deal more, that I should have tried more persistently to break through the wall of apathy and indifference. In face of a crime and a tragedy of such a magnitude the weight of the things one has not done is vastly greater than the weight of those which one has done. I can only add that in those years I learned to have deep appreciation for the Jews with whom I was in constant touch. So I could say with conviction in a Jewish meeting at the end of the war that during the war the Jewish people had won in me a friend.

NOTES

1. The leaders of the Jewish community in Holland did not take the reports concerning general extermination seriously at that time. See Presser, *Ondergang*, vol. II, p. 121.

2. See the full text of the 'Aide-Mémoire' in *The Grey Book*, Johannes Snoek, Assen, 1969, pp. 275-7.

3. See Presser, *Ondergang*, 1963, Vol. II, p. 136.

4. Ronald C. D. Jasper, *George Bell, Bishop of Chichester*, p. 156.

5. Ecumenical Press Service, 1944, no. 26.

6. See the report to the Conseil Fédéral by Prof. Carl Ludwig, Berne, 1958.

As THE WAR continued, the international discussion concerning peace aims and the post-war settlement became more intensive. Our role in Geneva was first of all to pass on to churchmen in Germany and the occupied countries all the books and documents on this subject which we could get hold of. Most of the material came from the Peace Aims Group in Britain, organized by William Paton and under the chairmanship of William Temple, and from the Commission on a Just and Durable Peace of the Federal Council of Churches in the United States, organized by Roswell Barnes and under the chairmanship of John Foster Dulles. Books like Paton's *The Church and the New Order*, documents like the reports of the Malvern Conference in Britain and the Delaware Conference in the USA were duplicated by us in Geneva and circulated to many groups in Europe.

But our task was also to ensure that the voice of European Christians should be heard in the international discussion. So we commented critically on the proposals from Britain and the USA and produced our own documents, based on the work of discussion groups done in various parts of Europe, including Germany.

My own line in these discussions was to urge that the Allies should make a positive statement about their conception of the post-war world. I found that, among the people resisting national socialism in Germany and in the occupied countries, there was a great disappointment about the lack of guidance from the 'free' world. What was needed was something much more substantial than the Atlantic Charter. Thus I stated in a memorandum to John Foster Dulles, in autumn, 1941, that the Atlantic Charter had nothing to say on many of the urgent issues which had already become acute before the war and which had been made far more acute by the war. The European peoples wanted to know whether a reborn Germany could have a place in Europe and the world. I returned to the attack in 1943, in an article published in the USA and in Britain,[1] saying:

It is perhaps the only effective weapon of nazi propaganda that it can pretend with some justification that the 'plutocracies' have no concrete proposals concerning a just peace and a new social order. Allied propaganda is far too busy convincing the oppressed people that national socialism is a bad thing, which is no news to them and that the United Nations are going to win the war, which they do not doubt for a moment . . . Europe needs a clear lead concerning the reconstruction of its political and social life . . . Even more than bread and peace the European nations need hope. This can only be given to them by showing that a serious attempt is being made to create a world of freedom and security in which they will not be mere pariahs in a struggle for power, nor tools in a system of production . . . There must be concrete and positive political and social proposals.

In order to give a focus to the ecumenical discussion I produced in 1943 an 'Analysis of agreements and disagreements concerning the message of the church about the creation of a just and durable peace'. It was based on the many documents and letters which had been received from the churches, from groups and from individuals. I said in the introduction:

> We are now in a situation in which equal attention must be given to our agreements and our disagreements. With gratitude to God we may state that – owing to the confrontation of the churches in the ecumenical movement, and particularly owing to the hard lessons which the churches have had to learn during this war – an ecumenical consensus is emerging concerning the function and message of the church in relation to international life. The importance of this fact must not be minimized. It means nothing less than that – for the first time since centuries – these churches are enabled to take a common attitude and to render a common witness to the true foundation of peace.
>
> But our gratitude for this fact should not make us blind to the equally certain fact that the present consensus is as yet lacking both in theological substance and in concrete content . . . We must not accept the present ecumenical position, but struggle on towards a more substantial consensus.

The analysis covered the main international issues about which the churches had to make up their mind such as the problems of national sovereignty and international law, of concentration of power in the hands of a few nations or decentralization of power, of the inclusion in the peace settlement of an element of punishment or of reconciliation without sanctions and of the sharing of the resources of the earth between all nations.

This analysis was used in many countries to stimulate further discussion. The value of this conversation in the midst of war was not only that Christians in countries separated by war and occupation remained in spiritual and intellectual contact with each other, but also that a foundation was laid for the task which the World Council would have to perform in this field after the war. Several of those who had participated in the war-time discussion became active leaders or participants of the Commission of the Churches on International Affairs established in 1946.[2]

We had at the same time to prepare for the task of post-war reconstruction. In 1942 the Federal Council sent Samuel McCrea Cavert to Europe to find out what could and should be done in this field. He came just in time, for a few days after his visit southern France was occupied. We worked out together a plan for a 'Reconstruction Department' of the World Council of Churches and this was accepted in a meeting attended by Dr Boegner of France and Dr Koechlin of Switzerland. The main idea was to set up a truly ecumenical service agency in which all churches which could help would help all churches which needed help, which would constantly survey the total situation and seek to co-ordinate the interchurch aid activities of the churches. This undertaking would become the great test of the reality of the ecumenical movement. If it proved possible to act in a truly brotherly fashion in this realm, the ecumenical movement would be seen as a living organism. The plan was to set up national agencies to facilitate co-operation and co-ordination in giving countries and in receiving countries. We underlined that the purpose was not merely to replace that which had been destroyed, but to enable the churches to fulfil their new tasks. For the churches of many countries had through those years of conflict developed a much stronger sense of their responsibility for the life of their nations and had come to occupy a more central place in society. They had therefore greater opportunities with regard to spiritual, social and political reconstruction than they had had before. But they would need outside help to perform these tasks adequately.

This plan was well received by the churches which were in a position to provide help. Strong national inter-church agencies were set up in the United States, Great Britain, Sweden and Switzerland and went into action in 1944 when it became possible to give aid to the churches of France, Belgium and the liberated provinces of the Netherlands. During the first months of its activities I had to carry through the work of our new Department of Reconstruction and Inter-Church Aid, but in March 1945 Dr J. Hutchison Cockburn, a former moderator of the Church of Scotland, arrived in Geneva and became the first director of the department. Under his leadership the inter-church aid activities became a vast operation which not only helped needy churches and brought relief to the suffering, but which also created a strong sense of fellowship and solidarity between Christians of many countries.

There was also the wider question of the whole task of the World Council after the war. I wrote in 1943 a rather long memorandum which in the language of today might be called 'futurological' and which became the basis for discussions in America, Britain, Sweden and Switzerland about the shape and responsibilities of the Council in the years ahead. I said of the post-war period that it was 'likely to be a period in which both chaotic mass forces and spiritual forces will be at work, a world characterized by a sometimes hidden, sometimes open conflict between a more naked practical paganism and a more determined aggressive Christianity than we have known in recent history . . . In any case it is to be expected that the church will be less in the position of the spectator, and that church history in the coming years will not be an appendix, but a central element in world history.' I discussed the difficult task of reconciliation which we would face, spoke of the urgency of evangelism and of the help which the Council should give to the churches in this realm. I expressed the hope that the International Missionary Council and the World Council would be merged. With regard to education I spoke of the need of 'an Ecumenical Staff College' which would be a centre for ecumenical study and help towards the crystallization of an ecumenical mind on the great issues of the day. I discussed the relations with the Roman Catholic Church and the new opportunities for contact which had arisen during the war and said: 'The World Council should make it perfectly clear that it is willing to collaborate with the Vatican in any form which does not involve the sacrifice of its own principles or the principles of its member churches.'

Coming to organization, I spoke rather apologetically of the need of a staff of about twenty-five secretaries. As a matter of fact we would reach that figure already at the first post-war meeting of the Provisional Committee. My least accurate prophecy was that the Reconstruction Department would need five secretaries during the emergency period and only three later on. By the time of the First Assembly this department alone had twenty-three secretaries. As to the budget I asked for $100,000 stating that this might seem a considerable figure. By the time of the first Assembly the budget came in fact to $363,000. In those days, it should be recalled in my defence, futurology had to be carried on without the help of computers.

NOTES

1. In *Christianity and Crisis* and in the *Christian News Letter*.
2. Thus the CCIA officers, van Asbeck (Netherlands), Grubb (Britain), Dulles and Nolde (United States) had all been involved in the wartime discussions.

25 | *European Resistance Movements Meet 'Somewhere in Europe'*

IN THE SPRING of 1944 the Swiss press reported that leaders of the resistance movements in the various European countries had just held their first international meeting 'somewhere in occupied Europe', and that they had decided to remain in close contact, in order to co-operate in their common struggle and in the organization of the peace.

This information was neither wholly true nor wholly false. A meeting of representatives of resistance movements had indeed taken place, but the reference to 'occupied Europe' was simply a bit of war-time obfuscation. We had actually met three or four times in my home in Geneva, but we did not intend to facilitate the work of nazi spies and we had to respect Swiss neutrality as much as possible.

It was also an exaggeration to speak of 'the leaders' of the resistance movements. Geneva had in that last stage of the war become a place where men and women of the resistance movements congregated to make contacts with each other, to find out what was being thought and planned in the free world, or simply to seek refuge. Some of these people could be described as leaders, others were less than that. But this was clearly an opportunity, such as existed nowhere else, to make the deeply felt solidarity of the resistance movements visible and to find out whether in the light of their common experience they could not arrive at a common stand concerning the future of Europe.

In the latter half of the war several of the resistance movements had become interested in the idea of European federalism. It was remarkable that although these movements, up to 1944, had had very little contact with each other, they had come to the same conclusion that some form of union or federation of the European nations was indispensable if Europe was to live in peace and to accomplish its task in the world. Hitler's conception of the unification of Europe was unanimously rejected but it was also seen as a challenge. The French underground paper *Résistance* wrote in February 1943 that it would be regrettable if 'the odious exploitation of a true conception and its caricature in the propaganda of Goebbels, would lead to a rejection of the necessity and urgency of a great federation of the European nations'. In the Dutch underground papers, *Het Parool* and *Vrij Nederland*, H. J. van Heuven Goedhart and H. M. van Randwijk advocated the closer union of European states. The Italian resistance had even a special illegal periodical, *L'Unita Europea*, which became in August 1943 the organ of the European Federalist Movement in Italy. I have already mentioned that the men of the *Kreisau* circle in Germany had made the idea of a federated Europe the cornerstone of their foreign policy. Helmuth von Moltke had written the basic document on the subject. Adam von Trott had given it an important place in the memorandum which I had transmitted in 1942 to the British government.[1]

So far there had been no opportunity for the various resistance movements to discuss their ideas. The initiative for an international consultation came from the Italians. Ernesto Rossi and Altiero Spinelli, who had elaborated their plan for a European federation in 1941 when they were prisoners of the fascist regime, had come to Switzerland to make contact with the resistance movements of other countries. In November 1943 they sent an invitation to all resistance movements to participate in an international conference to consider plans for the future of Europe. A Frenchman, Jean-Marie Soutou, who was associated with the underground paper *Témoignage Chrétien* and who was himself a keen European federalist, brought me in touch with these Italians. They had no difficulty in getting me to co-operate with them, for what they proposed was in line with the thinking and planning we had done in the ecumenical movement. In the still delicate situation in Switzerland we had to avoid publicity. So I proposed that they should meet in my home. We succeeded in finding men from Czechoslovakia, Poland and Yugoslavia who were active in resistance movements of their countries and we invited a Norwegian and a Dane who were residents of Geneva but could help in making contact with their national resistance movements. The whole group was finally composed of some fifteen people. We were certainly not sufficiently representative to speak for the resistance movements, but were sufficiently in touch with these movements to make proposals which would be considered seriously by their leaders.

At the very first meeting the question arose whether a representative from Germany should be invited. This became the theme of a somewhat heated discussion in which I spoke in favour of a positive decision. The majority felt that in a discussion about the future of Europe German resisters should be included. A young lady who represented the socialist movement in Germany entered rather shyly into the room. It was a good augury that while we were still in the midst of the war these resistance-men were willing to work with Germans who had proved their determination to oppose national socialism.

In our first meeting it became clear that we had more in common than the desire to resist national socialism and fascism. We agreed that resistance meant not merely the rejection of a false ideology, but also the affirmation of positive values. So we had little difficulty in drawing up a first declaration for submission to the movements we represented. It said:

We declare that the heroic struggle of the resistance movements against the enemy on all fronts is not only a clear testimony of patriotism and of faith in the resurrection of their countries, but that all the sacrifice and suffering accepted for the same cause have created ties of brotherhood among them and have given birth to a new conscience of European solidarity of the free peoples, the maintenance of which will be one of the essential guarantees of peace.

But in our later meetings we had to define just what we meant by a European federation. And the discussion turned again to the German problem. It was agreed that our goal should be a federation in which Germany should have full membership. The attitude which these men and women took to Germany can best be described by quoting a report I made later in the same year to the Peace Aims Group in London. I said:

While all these resistance movements are fighting against the German military and political machine, none of them says that they will boycott the German nation and treat them as the nazis have treated the Jews. Not one of them takes the attitude that there is no distinction between nazis and Germans. It is precisely because they have had so much to do with Germans in the resistance that they feel this way. If you asked them: 'Does that mean that the Gestapo contains all the bad Germany and the rest is the good Germany?', they would say that was not so . . . They have no illusions on this score. Nevertheless, we know that there are Germans with whom we can work and with whom we want to work, they say.

    In their plans for Europe they say: 'We do not want a soft peace. We want the war criminals to be definitely punished.' But they always add: 'We want a peace that is not so intolerable for the German people that it will drive them into despair.' They want the Germans to have some kind of hope for the future. They think in terms of a federal solution, though not immediately after the military breakdown. They want Germany to go through a period of testing, of recrystallization, in which the good elements can come to the top. In the light of what happens in Germany they want to decide just when Germany can be admitted into some kind of European federation.

Among the participants in the Geneva meetings it was also agreed that Europe should accept responsibility for its own destiny, not be organized from without, but from within, and should demonstrate its readiness for solidarity and unity. But there was considerable disagreement on two points. The first was the extent to which national sovereignty should be limited in order to create a truly effective and strong federation.[2] The French and the Italians desired to go very far in this direction. The other participants were by no means sure that the time had arrived for a fully-fledged federal union, in which national sovereignty would be greatly restricted,

The second difficult problem was that of the relation of the USSR to a European federation. The Czechoslovak and Yugoslav participants wanted to keep the door wide open for active Russian involvement, but the others were hesitant for they wanted the federation to take a definite stand for human rights and for the normal functioning of democratic institutions and doubted whether the USSR would accept and implement such common principles.

After a good deal of discussion and several meetings a rather considerable document was accepted.[3] It represented of course a compromise. But it contained, nevertheless, a substantial plan for a new order in Europe. It gave strong reasons for the creation of a European federation. It did not say specifically which countries should be included, but declared that it should be comprehensive and that participation should be offered to all states whose territory lies wholly or in part within Europe. The federation should be based on a declaration of human rights. The plan provided for autonomy for each country with regard to its specific interior problems, but specified that matters of defence, relations with powers outside the federation, international economic relations and transportation should belong to the competence of the federation as a whole. The federal government should not be responsible to the national governments, but to the peoples themselves.

The two declarations on the solidarity of the resistance movements and on European federalism were completed at a meeting on May 20th 1944, and sent out immediately afterwards to the various resistance movements of the countries represented in our group. We asked for quick reactions, so that the standing committee which we had set up would be able to publish the declarations in the name of a considerable part of the European resistance. But a few days later the Allied armies landed in Normandy, and the resistance movements had to concentrate on the immediate tasks of liberation and of setting up new structures of government. Most members of our Geneva group hastened back to their countries where they had to undertake new responsibilities. At the same time the Allied armies were now in control and they carried out a policy in which there was no place for the idea of a European federation. At the Teheran Conference in 1943 Roosevelt and Stalin had already rejected the idea of European union. And in this one matter de Gaulle agreed with them.

But we received, nevertheless, some interesting reactions. Letters received from different resistance movements in Holland expressed warm appreciation of the fact that the European resistance representatives were getting together and approved in principal the idea of European federation. But the letters stated at the same time that the resistance did not want to commit itself to such a far-reaching blueprint of European unity before having consulted the Dutch government (in London). And strong doubts were expressed with regard to the possibility and desirability of limiting national sovereignty in such a radical way as the Geneva plan proposed.

Much more positive reactions came from Italy and France. Under the leadership of Spinelli who had returned to Italy the federalist movement made active propaganda for the Geneva proposals. In France resistance men from various movements had formed a '*Comité français de la Fédération européenne*'[4] and this committee issued a declaration which followed the lines of our Geneva document.[5] And when these main French resistance bodies formed together the inclusive '*Mouvement de Libération Nationale*' and announced their programme by large posters in the main cities of France, the international part of that platform was based almost exactly on the proposals which our group had worked out in Geneva.

In Great Britain Sir Walter Layton, former editor of the *Economist* and former chairman of the Joint War Production Staff, expressed his agreement with the Geneva declaration in an address to the Royal Geographical Society.[6]

Although the proposals made in the Geneva meetings had no immediate effect on the decisions concerning the post-war settlement taken by the Allied governments, they had served to show that in an important part of the resistance movement there was a strong desire for European unity. And many men and women who had seen this vision continued to fight for its realization. In the ranks of the movement for European unity, which became such a strong force in European life from 1948 onwards, there were many who had learned in the resistance movement that (as an underground paper had said): 'The terrible equality which has arisen in the common disaster must transform itself in solidarity for the sake of peace.'

NOTES

1. In his *Europa-Föderationspläne der Widerstandsbewegungen 1940–1945* (Munich, 1968), Walter Lipgens has collected the relevant articles and documents which show the impressive convergence of thought in the resistance movements concerning European unity. For the German resistance see also Ger van Roon, *Neuordnung im Widerstand* (Munich, 1967).

2. The French participants were probably not yet fully aware of the fact that their leader, de Gaulle, was taking a quite different line.

3. Printed in H. A. Jacobsen, *Der zweite Weltkrieg*, Fischer, 1965, p. 302; and in Lipgens, op. cit., p. 393.

4. One of the members was Albert Camus.

5. Jacobsen, op. cit., p. 306; and Lipgens, op. cit., p. 244.

6. Lipgens, op. cit., p. 401.

26 | *The End of the Tunnel*

THE TWO LAST years of the war brought even more human suffering than the previous years. But it was also the time when we began to see the light at the end of the tunnel.

It was now becoming crucial to arrive at a common mind and common decisions about the post-war tasks of the ecumenical movement. The different parts of the world – the 'free' nations, the occupied countries, the neutrals, the Axis countries – had lived through completely different experiences. It was especially necessary to help the churches in Great Britain and the USA, as well as their governments, to understand the situation in Europe. Before long they would have to take far-reaching decisions about the policies of occupation and reconstruction.

So we made a rather desperate attempt to arrange for an ecumenical meeting in war-time. The plan was that American, British, Scandinavian and Swiss church leaders would meet in Sweden together with those members of our staff who could reach Sweden. I would not be able to participate since I could not travel through Germany or countries occupied by the Germans. The agenda would include both the problems of reconstruction of church life and the task of the churches with regard to the restoration of international relations. For a time it looked as if a representative group, including Reinhold Niebuhr, John Foster Dulles, William Paton, Alphons Koechlin and the leaders of the Scandinavian churches could be brought together, but the whole plan failed because the Allied authorities did not grant the necessary visas. I suspect that they did not want the churches to interfere in the delicate discussions concerning peace aims. In the meantime the American churches had chosen their first representative to be sent to Europe as a World Council staff member concerned with the preparation of the post-war tasks. This promising young Congregational pastor, Ted Hume, whose arrival meant that at last our little staff was growing again, was to begin his work in Sweden. I was deeply distressed to learn that, on the way between London and Stockholm, the plane in which he was travelling had been shot down by the Germans.

From the autumn of 1942, that is, after the occupation of southern France, till the summer of 1944, travel between the European continent, on the one hand, and Britain and the USA, on the other, was practically impossible. So I wrote a series of memoranda and reports for our colleagues on the other side. A number of these had to do with government policies and were submitted to the Federal Council of Churches in the USA, to the Archbishop of Canterbury and to Mr Allan Dulles. My main point was to urge that the churches should be taken seriously in the planning for the immediate post-war period. They had been one of the strongest factors in the resistance against national socialism. They had learned a great deal in the last years. They realized in a new way their responsibility in and for the national life. They should be allowed to make their specific contribution.

I raised at the same time the question whether it was realized in Britain and America that the mass bombardments of German cities created the impression that Britain and America were no less totalitarian in warfare than the national socialists. I wrote to Archbishop Temple on December 15th 1943:

> Many Germans (including some, but not all of our most trusted friends) tend to take an attitude of naïve astonishment at such brutality in warfare and seem to forget suddenly all or most of what their nation has done to others. There is often a mood of injured innocence and self-pity in their utterances. This is also shown in the fact that some ask the ecumenical movement for the first time to intervene. On the other hand, in the occupied nations there is too much unholy joy that at last the tables are turned and that 'they get what they deserve'. Still there remains a real issue . . . The United Nations have been put in the strategically favourable, but morally unfavourable position of doing what the nazis wanted to do, but could not really carry out. Thus the impression is created that the United Nations are at least equally, if not more, totalitarian in their warfare than the nazis . . . How can the assurances that the bombardments have a purely military purpose be taken seriously when in fact they blot out whole cities? Is it not playing with words to use the expression 'military purpose' to cover the total disorganization of life, including all centres of population?

On February 9th 1944, the Bishop of Chichester made his memorable speech in the House of Lords on this subject of bombing. This courageous utterance – in which he raised the question: 'Why is there this inability to reckon with the moral and spiritual facts?' – made him very unpopular with many politicians and military men. But I could write to him on February 29th:

> I must tell you that your speech concerning the bad weather (code-talk for the bombing) has had a great echo over here and has been discussed very widely. I need not tell you that the reactions have been of different kinds. But I think that all family members (i.e. church people) are most grateful that you have broken the silence on this point, which for many had become an intolerable

silence. Quite apart from the question what the final answer is to this tragic problem, it is essential that men everywhere should know that it is for us a problem, and more than a problem.

But I did not want any Christian protest to be exploited for the purposes of nazi warfare. So when Professor Max Huber of the Red Cross asked me to receive Professor Fritz Berber, who had come from Berlin to urge the inter-national organizations to help in achieving a change in the policy of mass bombardments, I refused to see him. I had known him in Student Christian Movement days as an ardent pacifist, but he had in the meantime become chief of the High School for Politics in Berlin and had taken his part in propagating the nazi conception of international affairs. Years later I read in the diary of Ambassador von Hassell[1] that Berber had come to Geneva as an emissary of Ribbentrop.

The spring and summer of 1944 brought good and bad news in quick succession. The liberation of Europe had actually begun and the ecumenical movement could again begin to function on a world scale. But on July 20th, the long-expected attempt to liberate Germany through the efforts of the Germans themselves failed, and the courageous men who tried to overthrow Hitler, and whom I considered as comrades in a common struggle, were imprisoned and in most cases executed. I felt especially strongly about the death of Adam von Trott zu Solz, with whom I had often had heated discussions, but whom I had come to respect as a man of deep integrity and great moral courage.

I had not been able to get out of Switzerland for nearly two years, a long time for a man to whom travel had become second nature. In September 1944, I could at last begin to travel again. I have already mentioned the journey I made at that time to France, Belgium and Holland. Then London. After a call to his office I gave a big surprise to Robert Mackie, the General Secretary of the World's Student Christian Federation, and other friends, by walking into the restaurant where they were just discussing how to get into touch with the chairman, that is, with me in Geneva. Archbishop Temple was ill, but he gave me nevertheless an appointment to see him. But on the day before my appoint-ment there was suddenly the shattering news that he had died. I felt this as a very great blow. The three men in Great Britain who had been foundation pillars of the World Council were Archbishop William Temple, Dr William Paton and Bishop George Bell. Paton had died in 1943. Now Temple had left us. Where would we find men of such ability, of such loyalty? Moreover, Temple had a wonderful capacity for friendship, which I felt to a high degree. There were men in all churches and in many countries who looked to him as their own archbishop. The funeral service in Canterbury Cathedral was a reunion of men and women each of whom felt that his passing was a personal loss. Jetty realized how I felt about the death of this leader on whose help I had relied, and this friend who had always encouraged me and sent me just the right word from

Geneva, saying: 'Very sorry, Keep faith great work.'

Pastor Boegner had also come to London and so we were able to have a well-attended meeting of British members of the Provisional Committee, along with the two of us. At last we could begin to make specific plans for the post-war period. It was, however, not easy to harmonize all the various ideas that were represented in the meeting. Everybody agreed that a representative group of church leaders should meet as soon as possible. Beyond that, there were different conceptions about the nature of the meeting. The Bishop of Chichester felt that since the German churches had not joined the World Council, and their presence was indispensable, there ought, first of all, to be a meeting of church leaders under 'neutral' auspices. Archbishop Eidem of Sweden had agreed to invite some twenty or thirty leaders to meet in Sweden. In Bishop Bell's mind the purpose of this meeting would be especially 'before any treaty negotiations are commenced to make a declaration of Christian unity'.[2] Others were eager to ensure that the World Council would as soon as possible complete its process of formation, and did not feel that there would be great difficulty in meeting the German churches under World Council auspices.

It was decided to plan along both lines: meetings of the available members of the Provisional Committee in the spring of 1945 in Britain and in the United States, and the informal meeting in Sweden or Switzerland as soon after the cessation of hostilities as possible.

The letter sent by this meeting to the member churches spoke of the new common tasks: the task of church renewal, of reconstruction of church life, of re-creating international order.

Back in Geneva I was glad to receive Dr A. L. Warnshuis, who came as an emissary of the American churches to discuss the plans for reconstruction. He could tell us that the American churches were getting ready for action on a large scale. His report to the churches of the USA with the significant title, 'The Church's Battle for Europe's Soul', helped greatly to prepare the way for the extremely generous response of American Christians to the post-war needs of Europe.

In April 1945 I was back in London, where we held another meeting of available members of the Provisional Committee. The attendance was again becoming truly international: in addition to the British members, Archbishop Germanos and Professor Alivisatos from the Greek Orthodox Church, Bishop Fjellbu from Norway, Dr Boegner from France and Dr Koechlin from Switzerland. We had much to tell each other but were surprised to find that fundamentally our experiences during the period of isolation had been so similar.

We discussed the relations with the German church and decided that as soon as possible contact should be made with the leaders of the Confessing Church. But there were very diverse opinions about the desirability and possible content of a message to the German church. How deeply should such a message enter into the question of guilt? Should it speak also of the sins of other nations? It was finally decided not to send any message to the German churches before the meeting which World Council representatives were to have with German church leaders.

As to contacts with the Russian church, the Greek Orthodox Archbishop Germanos reported a conversation with Patriarch Alexis of Moscow, in which the Patriarch had asked him whether the Russian church should participate in the ecumenical movement. It was therefore decided to send the Patriarch a short report on the history and work of the World Council.

It was also agreed that the vacancy left on the Provisional Committee by the death of Archbishop Temple should be offered to his successor, Archbishop Geoffrey Fisher. When Dr Boegner, Dr Koechlin and I went to see the Arch-bishop to ask him to accept this appointment, he answered simply that he knew little about the World Council, but that he wanted to follow in the steps of the two Williams (Temple and Paton) and that he was therefore ready to accept. The unreserved support which he gave from that time onwards to the World Council was a great help in the decisive period until the second Assembly. The rest of the time in London was filled with preparations for the visit of our small ecumenical delegation to the USA. Bishop Bell, Dr Boegner, Mrs Boegner and I were to make the journey together. The only way by which civilians could fly to the United States at that time was by the Clipper route, that is, via Africa and South America. Just before leaving Geneva I had been involved in a traffic accident, with the result that I had a broken foot and was limping around with a plaster cast. I had not realized how useful that cast would become. For during the few days in London I had to see many people and acquire visas for six countries and several inoculations. But this could only be done by finding taxis at the right moment. I felt rather a fraud when the many people waiting for taxis made way for what seemed to them the poor wounded soldier straight home from the battle-front.

The journey by clipper took four days. We came down in eight harbours in seven countries. In Lisbon we heard that Hitler was dead. The Third Reich had only lasted twelve years, but because of all the suffering they had brought, these years had seemed interminable. When we arrived in New York the first news-paper headline I saw said: 'Holland liberated.' So one of my first appointments was a special service held at the Netherlands Embassy in Washington. The psalmist's verse: 'They that sow in tears shall reap in joy' was at the centre of my thoughts. There followed a whole series of meetings with American church leaders. These men were deeply interested in Europe but they lived in a com-pletely different world from mine. The government, the army and also the church had made many plans for Europe, but these plans, I felt, took so little account of the changes that had taken place in Europe during the war years. The role of the three of us from Europe was therefore to explain as best we could the spiritual and political realities of the European situation.

Our small delegation had two meetings in New York with the North American members of the Provisional Committee. I could and did thank the American church leaders for their unfailing support which had kept us going during the war. The time had now come to decide what steps should be taken to complete the process of formation of the World Council. It was agreed that the first step should be a full meeting of the Committee to be held in Switzerland as early as possible after October 1st. In the discussion on the desirability of a statement from the New York meeting, John R. Mott and others warned us that any statement with specific reference to the issues of the war would endanger the World Council. These men were obviously thinking of the war-guilt problem, which had created such acute tensions after the first world war. They did not realize that now the leaders of the Confessing Church in Germany strongly desired to have a fraternal conversation about the responsibility of their nation for the war. Bishop Bell and I spoke strongly in favour of a message, and at the second meeting in New York one was finally adopted. It was signed individually by the members and officers of the Provisional Committee present at the meeting. It was not a strong document, but at least it made the points that there were great differences of national guilt, that these differences had to be faced, that the deep wounds which the war had made could be healed if we realized that forgiveness was costly, and that because of the Cross reconciliation with one another was possible.

In that spring of 1945 a memorable and highly useful evening was the one which we spent at the home of Mr and Mrs Thomas Lamont. Among the guests were Mr and Mrs John D. Rockefeller Jr. I glanced many times at the original 'Blue Boy' of Gainsborough on the wall facing my chair at the table. When coffee was served the hostess asked each of us three Europeans to tell the story of our experiences during the war years. So we spoke of all that had happened in the life of the churches in various parts of Europe.

The next morning Mr Rockefeller sent a message to me that he wanted to see me. Later that day, as I entered his room near the top of the Rockefeller Centre, I saw that he had before him an article I had written about post-war reconstruction. He asked me about the plans of the World Council. I had to do some quick thinking, for we had many plans, and the great question was which would be of greatest interest to Mr Rockefeller. But it soon became quite clear that he was especially interested in the plan to create an ecumenical institute which would confront young people who had to rebuild their lives after the years in the armies or in the resistance movements with the challenge of renewal in the life of the churches and the nations. Mr Rockefeller asked me to give him a memorandum on the subject.

I did this soon afterwards but, because I had become accustomed to living on a shoe-string, I mentioned a rather modest figure. Mr Rockefeller answered that I should have asked for more! He finally made a gift of a million dollars with the suggestion that one half should be used for the Ecumenical Institute and one half for the work of reconstruction of church life in Europe.

It was interesting that Mr Rockefeller made it very clear that he did not expect us to report to him on the use of the money, for he had full confidence that we would use it in the right way. When I saw him a year later and tried to express my thanks he interrupted me with the remark: 'I should thank you for making such good use of this money.' This is the only time in my life that I received thanks for using a million dollars.

It was also during these days in New York that the leaders of the World Student Christian Federation could meet again after long years of separation. It happened that Dr John R. Mott was just reaching his eightieth birthday. So we organized a party. The only condition that we agreed to observe was that we were not to mention the figure '80', for Dr Mott was still so concerned with the future that he did not like to be reminded that he was no longer in the prime of life. When the time came for him to rise he told us his memories of the founding of the World's Student Christian Federation in 1895. It was good to find how human and humorous the great world-strategist could still be in his twilight years. He told of his first unhappy experience with the formidable eiderdowns used in Germany, of seasickness during that first astounding journey around the world, when he produced Student Christian movements in all parts of the world. And he spoke of the abiding task of helping students to respond to the call of Christ. We all loved it.

During the summer months of 1945 the Geneva staff began to grow considerably. The new Department of Reconstruction and Inter-Church Aid began its operations with ten staff members. We were at last able to tackle the practical tasks in an adequate way. My job as General Secretary received new content. We were no longer trying to weather the storm; we were getting ready for a new stage of the journey. The new beginning was symbolized by our moving out of the old villa in the Champel area of Geneva to what seemed at that time the spacious chalet at Route de Malagnou. Before long we had to put up several wooden barracks to make more space.

In October, with Bishop Berggrav and Dr Samuel Cavert, I represented the World Council at the solemn meeting in the New Church at Amsterdam in which the Netherlands Reformed Church reconstituted itself after the spiritual upheaval of the years of the war. I felt moved to say that the Netherlands Reformed Church had been used in war time to give a witness to the world which had met with a strong echo and had encouraged many other churches. In this way the Church had done what it had not done for centuries – namely, fulfil its true ecumenical task.

NOTES

1. Ulrich von Hassell, *Vom Anderen Deutschland*, p. 317.
2. Ronald C. D. Jasper, *George Bell*, p. 317.

THE WAR WAS over. But before we could undertake the new tasks one essential condition had to be fulfilled – namely, to arrive at a true reconciliation between the churches whose nations had been fighting each other. For only by being reconciled as Christians would we be able to work for the wider reconciliation of the peoples. We wanted to avoid a repetition of that long, sterile debate about war guilt which had cast a shadow over ecumenical relations after the first world war. Yet this time the war-crimes and the suffering had been vastly greater. The estrangement between the nations could not be overcome by simply turning the page or by a vague and general admission that all had been involved in a great tragedy and that all had shared in the sinful situation. A more specific and costly expression of repentance was required. It would have to come from the churches for they represented the gospel of renewal through repentance. And the first word would have to come from the church of the country which had produced national socialism.

I had some reason to hope that such a word would be spoken. In 1942 I had received a long and impressive letter from Pastor Hans Asmussen, a man who had stood in the front rank of the Confessing Church. He had raised the question how the nations were to bear the burden of the terrifying guilt resulting from the war. His answer was that the question of guilt should not be dealt with as a political problem but as a spiritual problem. Christians were called to stand together before God and make their confession of sins to him and to each other.

Dietrich Bonhoeffer had spoken even more concretely. In his talks with Bishop Bell in Stockholm and with me in Geneva he had expressed the conviction that the only road open to the Christians of Germany was the road of repentance. Soon after his death in April 1945 I had received the poems which he had written during his imprisonment. In one of these called *Nächtliche Stimmen* ('Voices in the Night') he had stated, in words reminiscent of the penitential psalms, what the Christians of Germany should say as they confessed their sins before God. I was deeply impressed by the voice coming from a man who had given a faithful witness in his life and by his death and hoped that the church in Germany would speak as he had done. So I wrote to Bishop Dibelius in Berlin on July 25th 1945:

> I can assure you that on our side we will do all we can to restore the fellowship among us. Do I need to say that considerable obstacles have to be overcome, especially in the churches which have suffered much under the German occupation? A fraternal conversation will be required. This conversation would be greatly facilitated if the Confessing Church of Germany should speak very frankly – not only about the crimes of the nazis, but also especially about the sins of omission of the German people, including the church. The Christians of other countries do not want to take a pharisaic attitude. But they hope that it will be openly said – what is said so impressively in Bonhoeffer's poem – that the German people and also the church have not spoken out with sufficient clarity and with sufficient emphasis.

I did not know at that time whether the leaders of the post-war church in Germany would agree with such views. That question was soon answered. In August 1945 the Evangelical Church of Germany chose for their new council men who had taken a clear and courageous stand during the church conflict. Most of the men whose words and actions during the Hitler period had caused concern and met with suspicion in the ecumenical movement were forced to resign.

So it was clear that as soon as possible representatives of the ecumenical movement should have serious conversation with the new leaders of the German church. But who should go? Bishop Bell would of course have to take part for he had remained all through the war the trusted friend of the Confessing Church in Germany. He wrote on August 10th 1945: 'The sooner that an official church delegation can go to Germany, the better. I understand how terribly isolated and impotent the Germans feel. I would of course do my best to go and see German church leaders in whatever way seems likely to be most useful to the church.'

The Dutch churches proposed that the first group to go should be mainly composed of churchmen from the countries which had been occupied, for the most acute and urgent task of reconciliation had to do with the relations between their countries and the German people.

It was not easy to get the delegation to the same place on the same date. Various types of permits had to be acquired from the military authorities, travel by military transport had to be organized. It was somewhat of a miracle that it proved possible to bring together a group representing the churches of the United States (Dr S. M. Cavert of the Federal Council, Dr S. C. Michelfelder of the American Lutheran Church), of Great Britain (the Bishop of Chichester), of France (Pastor Pierre Maury), of Holland (Dr H. Kraemer) and of Switzerland (Dr A. Koechlin) in addition to me. The Norwegian representative whom we expected did not succeed in reaching Germany in time for the meeting. We had heard that the new Council of the Evangelical Church of Germany would meet on October 17th in Stuttgart. It had been impossible to warn them that we were coming. So our arrival caused considerable surprise and also much joy.

During the journey to Stuttgart some of us had talked at length about the purpose of our visit. It was clear that we should aim at the resumption of full ecumenical relationships. But how could this be done? On the one hand, we could not make a confession of guilt the condition for a restoration of fellowship, for such a confession could only have value as a spontaneous gesture; on the other hand, the obstacles to fellowship could only be removed if a clear word were spoken. Pierre Maury gave us the right phrase. He suggested that we should say: 'We have come to ask you to help us to help you.'

When we arrived in the largely destroyed city of Stuttgart we heard that in the evening there would be a special service in the Markuskirche where Bishop Wurm, Pastor Niemöller and Bishop Dibelius would speak. Bishop Wurm spoke warm words of welcome to the World Council delegation. Pastor Niemöller then preached on Jeremiah 14.7-11: 'Though our iniquities testify against us, act, O Lord, for Thy name's sake . . .' It was a most powerful message on the meaning of repentance. Niemöller said that even in the church it was not sufficiently understood that the last twelve years had been a visitation from God. It was not enough to blame the nazis. The church also had to confess its guilt. Would the nazis have been able to do what they had done if church members had been truly faithful Christians? He spoke of the tremendous suffering that had been brought to Poland, Holland, Czechoslovakia, France, Norway, Greece and other countries. The only hope left was that a new day would be prepared by men who had the love of Christ in their hearts.

Hearing that sermon I felt a sense of liberation. If the German church would speak this language all obstacles to fellowship would be overcome. We would not enter into another period of sterile discussions about war guilt as we did after the first world war.

On the next day we had the first meeting between the World Council delegation and the members of the Council of the Evangelical Church of Germany. It was not a meeting of strangers, for these eleven German churchmen had never ceased to feel deeply attached to the ecumenical fellowship and we who had come from abroad, were glad to recognize the men who had been engaged in a costly battle for the integrity of the Christian church. So when Bishop Theophil Wurm opened the meeting and said that it was a great thing that we had the opportunity to manifest the unity of Christians in spite of all that had happened between our nations, he spoke for us all.

I explained why the World Council had sent our delegation. We had come to re-establish fraternal contact. We had not forgotten our debt of gratitude to the Confessing Church. We remembered the witness up to the point of ultimate sacrifice rendered by men like Dietrich Bonhoeffer. We were glad that the leadership of the church was now in the hands of men who had stood for the freedom of the Word of God and for the exclusive submission of the church to its Lord. There were however still obstacles to be removed and questions to be answered. I picked up the phrase of Maury: the delegation asked the German church leaders to help the other churches in such a way that the other churches could help the German church.

Pastor Asmussen spoke next and his words were decisive for the further conversation. He said that what had to be cleared up had to be cleared up between the Christians of Germany and God himself. Years ago he had decided that at the first moment when he would meet brothers from the other churches he would say to them: 'I have sinned against you as a member of my nation, because I have not shown more courage.' He knew that this kind of confession could be misunderstood. But this was not an hour for clever diplomacy, but for 'foolishness in Christ'. Pastor Niemöller said that the voice of the conscience of the German church should now speak. The church knows that it shares in the guilt of the nation and prays that God may forgive that guilt. This forgiveness must be the new source of power in the church and lead it back into the fellowship of the *Una Sancta* so that all together would be enabled to create something new in the world.

The first to answer on the WCC side was Dr Kraemer of Holland. He said that there was no hatred in the hearts of the Christians in Holland. Those who had suffered much had learned to be merciful in their judgment. He hoped we could all speak together as standing before God. He had heard with deep emotion what Pastor Asmussen and Pastor Niemöller had said. He understood this as a call to his own church also, that it could only live by the forgiveness of sins. It could not be a matter of bartering. In the light of what had been said the other churches could now say to the German church that they were also ready to accept their responsibility for what had happened in Germany.

At the conclusion of the session Pastor Asmussen proposed that the Council of the Evangelical Church of Germany should meet by itself to take a decision concerning a public declaration along the lines of the conversation that had just been held.

On October 19th Bishop Wurm read to the WCC delegation the text of the declaration which had been accepted by the Council of the German Evangelical Church. The key sentences were:

> With great pain do we say: through us has endless suffering been brought to many peoples and countries. What we have often borne witness to before our congregations that we declare in the name of the whole church. True, we have struggled for many years in the name of Jesus Christ against a spirit which has found its terrible expression in the national socialist regime of violence, but we accuse ourselves for not witnessing more courageously, for not praying more faithfully, for not believing more joyously and for not loving more ardently. Now a new beginning is to be made in our churches.

Pastor Pierre Maury was the first to respond. He said that the ecumenical delegation desired to accept this declaration without pharisaism. This word would help the other churches to carry on their struggle for justice. The other churches would not say: 'Now at last the Germans have repented', but rather consider the German declaration as a call to renewal of their Christian life and to the common task of re-christianizing Europe. Bishop Bell said that in united loyalty to Christ the churches should now work together for a just and peaceful order. I added that it was now the responsibility of the other churches and of the World Council of Churches to ensure that the declaration would not be exploited for political ends.

Pastor Asmussen announced that the Council of the German Evangelical Church had decided to join the World Council of Churches. Bishop Wurm and Pastor Niemöller would represent the German Evangelical Church at the first post-war meeting of the Provisional Committee.

It was inevitable that the 'Stuttgart Declaration' should lead to much controversy in Germany. There were headlines in the press stating that the Protestant churches had acknowledged Germany's war guilt. Thus the impression was given that the church had given the victors a good pretext for imposing a hard peace and another 'Versailles'. It was even more disquieting that within the church there were so many voices stating that all the crimes had been committed by a small number of wicked men, that the German nation did not bear responsibility for these crimes and that in any case all nations were equally guilty for the suffering which the war had caused.

But the German churchmen who had signed the Stuttgart declaration stood firm. Asmussen, Lilje, Niemöller and others insisted in their sermons and addresses that the confession of Stuttgart was to be understood as a word spoken before God and in the context of the Christian fellowship. Niemöller made the point that Christians in other countries had not reacted in a self-righteous way. On the contrary, the declaration had led them to examine their own actions and to ask what was their own guilt.

Niemöller was right. Soon after the meeting in Stuttgart I had occasion to read the declaration of the Evangelical Church of Germany to the first post-war assembly of French Protestantism in Nîmes. The Assembly expressed its gratitude and sent a reply stating that this declaration made it possible to restore full fellowship between the churches of Germany and France and to undertake together the task of reconstruction. The Synod of the Netherlands Reformed Church sent a message to the Evangelical Church of Germany saying that the Stuttgart declaration had been a truly Christian and liberating action. The Dutch church desired also to confess that in the struggle against national socialism it had not been sufficiently faithful and courageous. It added that the Confessing Church in Germany had been one of the means by which the church in the Netherlands had come to understand the significance of a faithful witness. Similar expressions of gratitude came from the churches in the United States and in Great Britain.

It was due to the Stuttgart meeting that the ecumenical movement could now go ahead and turn to the future. If that meeting had not been held or if it had not succeeded in restoring fraternal relations, it would have been impossible to create the necessary spiritual conditions for the inauguration of the World Council at Amsterdam in 1948.

At the same time a real contribution had been made to a renewal of normal relationships between Germany and other nations. Speaking at the Assembly of the Lutheran World Federation in 1952, in Hannover, Wilhelm Kopf, the Prime Minister of Lower Saxony, said that the meeting in Stuttgart had been the first important step in gaining for Germany a place once more among the nations of the world.

In October 1970 German television invited five men who had been present at Stuttgart in 1945, together with some younger men, to participate in a television round table discussion about the abiding significance of the Stuttgart declaration. The five were: Gustav Heinemann, who was now President of the German Federal Republic, Martin Niemöller, Wilhelm Niesel, Hanns Lilje and I. The old-timers told again the story of the meeting in 1945. The younger ones raised pertinent questions concerning the relevance of the Stuttgart declaration for the present situation in the church and in the world. But the most important moment came towards the end when the convener asked President Heinemann whether his recent official visits to Norway and to the Netherlands had anything to do with the Stuttgart confession. Heinemann said: Yes, for the result of the 1945 declaration had been the restoring of the relationships between Christians, but much remained to be done to arrive at relations of confidence between the German nation and the nations which had suffered under the German occupation. His approach to the people of Norway and of the Netherlands had been made in the spirit of the Stuttgart declaration.

I told President Heinemann how impressed I was by this example of the way in which an act of reconciliation which has taken place within the church, can contribute to the healing of the community of nations.

28 | *A New Beginning*

IN FEBRUARY 1946, in Geneva, the Provisional Committee of the World Council could at last hold its first post-war meeting. There had not been a full meeting of the committee since 1939. All of us on the committee had looked forward to this reunion, but had also wondered what problems of mutual understanding we would have to face after having been separated for so many years and after having gone through such diverse experiences. But the meeting proved to be more harmonious than any we had held. There was such joy in discovering that in our completely different surroundings we had all tried to hold on to the same realities, and especially to the reality of our oneness in Christ, that we quickly understood each other again without difficulty. Bishop Berggrav became the spokesman of all when he said in his sermon in the St Peter's Cathedral:

> Here I have a confession to make: I wondered anxiously what it would be like to meet today with friends from all the different parts of the Christian world. The surprise, for me at any rate, was that it was no surprise. It was quite natural. Natural because we have lived together more closely during these five years than we did when we could communicate with the outside world. We have prayed together much more, we have listened together much more to God's Word, our hearts have been alongside one another. I find nothing strange in seeing here today Boegner, Canterbury, Chichester, Indians and Chinese. It is just the manifestation of what we already knew, that the universal fellowship of God's churches is no longer weak but has been established by him, and through it the experience of the war now lives and works. The time is past when Christian fellowship in the world was a groping experiment. Christ has said to us during the war: 'My Christians, you are one.' Thank God, for it is not the general rule in the world that living fellowship can be taken for granted after the peace.

The one shadow over the meeting was that several of the men whose contribution could have been decisive were no longer with us. We wondered what William Temple, William Paton, William Adams Brown, Dietrich Bonhoeffer would have brought to the meeting. But some of the early pioneers were there:

John R. Mott, now over 80, but energetically working for the bringing of the younger churches into the World Council; Archbishop Germanos and Professor Alivisatos, persistently seeking to ensure that the Orthodox churches should take their full place in the movement; George Bell of Chichester, who could compare this meeting to the first post-war meeting in 1919, and who because of his own share in maintaining fellowship between Christians in Germany and the ecumenical movement, had special reason to rejoice that this time the war guilt problem did not divide us. There were other men who had helped to keep the World Council alive in war-time: Marc Boegner who presided over the meeting with a rare combination of authority and humour, Alphons Koechlin who had represented the committee during the years of separation and maintained the independence of the World Council. There were the men who had become flag-bearers of the resistance of the church to national socialist ideology: Martin Niemöller looking thin after the years in a concentration camp, Bishop Wurm who had given the 'silent' church in Germany a voice, Hendrik Kraemer, the spokesman of the movement of renewal of the church through prophetic witness in Holland, Bishop Berggrav, the leader in the struggle of the Norwegian church for its spiritual independence. It was a great moment when Berggrav and Niemöller, who had never met but been so deeply interested in each other, shook hands in my room.

We gave one full day to a survey of the situation of the church in different countries and different parts of the world. There was no triumphalism, least of all from the countries where the church had been engaged in a sharp conflict with the political powers. For we all realized that the story of the church in war-time was a story of some strength but also of much weakness, of moments of obedience but also of times of lack of courage. But we also heard from many places, including Asia and Latin America, of new opportunities arising out of the great shaking of the foundations.

The service in St Peter's Cathedral summed it all up. The vast church was overcrowded. The organ filled the great space with joyful sound. A long and colourful procession filed up the nave slowly. Men who had wondered whether they would ever see each other again walked side by side. Archbishop Germanos read the New Testament lesson in Greek. Archbishop Fisher and Dr Koechlin said the prayers of intercession. Then came three short sermons by Chester Miao (China) in English, Bishop Berggrav in German and Martin Niemöller in French. All spoke of the struggle of Christians to remain faithful in times of pressure and of the renewal which brings together in Christ those who have done each other grievous wrong. Kathleen Bliss said rightly: 'The real meaning and purpose of this world gathering was made plain in this service.'[1]

In my report to the meeting I dealt only briefly with the past. I said: 'For those who have had the privilege to be intimately associated with the Council in war-time, these years will always stand out as the time when the ecumenical task was spiritually easy and simple because, in spite of the enormous technical difficulties, the marching orders were so very clear and the basic unity of the defenders of the faith was so deeply felt.' I noted that during the war fifty churches were added to the list of churches accepting membership in the Council. Now our task was to secure the full participation of churches which had not yet responded. I raised the question whether we should not prepare for a meeting between delegates of the Orthodox Church of Russia and of the WCC, and also send a delegation to the Greek-speaking churches. On the basis of previous discussions I proposed that the first Assembly should be held in 1948.

It was a productive meeting. Specific plans were made for the Assembly. The setting up of the Reconstruction Department, of the Youth Department and of a body to deal with international affairs was approved. The plan for the creation of the Ecumenical Institute was also accepted. I was delighted when Dr Cavert suggested the name of Dr Kraemer as its first director, for with his world-wide experience, his status as a layman and his passion for the renewal of the church he was just the right man. As his countryman and friend I could hardly have made the proposal myself.

Who was to take the place of Archbishop Temple as Chairman? There were several, in fact too many, possibilities. Then, rather unexpectedly, it was proposed not to have one chairman, but a group of five presidents. The meeting became convinced that this would have the great advantage of demonstrating 'to the churches as well as to the world that the great confessional and denominational families are united in their desire to constitute the World Council of Churches'. So Dr Boegner, Dr Mott, Archbishop Germanos, Archbishop Fisher and Archbishop Eidem were chosen and a tradition was thereby established which was later followed by the World Council Assemblies.

There was a good deal of discussion about the right of the Provisional Committee to issue a message. There were those like Dr Kraemer and Dr Niemöller who spoke with strong conviction about the obligation of the WCC to give a prophetic witness. There were others, including the Archbishop of Canterbury and Bishop Berggrav, who warned against the assumption that the WCC could be the voice of the Christian church, for that would give the wrong impression that it had been authorized to speak for the churches. I took the line that we should speak when we had been given something urgent and important that we could say together, and only if that were the case. But a message was finally adopted. It spoke of the world's crisis and referred especially to the new situation created by the dropping of the first atomic bombs a few months earlier. 'Man's triumph in the release of atomic energy threatens his destruction. Unless man's whole outlook is changed our civilization will perish.' It urged the nations to heed the warning: 'I have set before you life and death: therefore choose life.'

Specific resolutions were also adopted on the transfer of populations and on anti-semitism. With regard to this last subject the committee recognized with thankfulness the faithful witness of many Christians, who at peril to themselves had made their protest against anti-semitism and given shelter to its victims.

But it also acknowledged with penitence 'the failure of the churches to overcome, in the spirit of Christ, those factors in human relationships which have created and now contribute to this evil which threatens both Jewish and Christian communities'.

During the same year (1946) we made an attempt to enter into discussion with the Orthodox Church of Russia. The basic difficulty was that during the whole period between the first and the second world wars when the ecumenical movement was taking shape, the Church of Russia had been cut off from all international contacts and that it had therefore only vague and inadequate information about the nature of the ecumenical movement. But we had heard from several sides that the Moscow Patriarchate had shown interest in the World Council. Metropolitan Nikolai, who was the chief of the foreign office of the church, had said during his visit in Western Europe: 'I hope that we shall collaborate.' After consultation among the presidents of the Provisional Committee it was therefore decided to send a letter to Patriarch Alexis in Moscow. The letter expressed the sense of regret on the part of the World Council that during so many years the Russian church had not been able to take part in the ecumenical movement and said that the World Council was now anxious to make contact with that church. It concluded with the proposal that a small meeting should be held between representatives of the Orthodox Church of Russia and representatives of the World Council.

I received a telegraphic answer during the meeting of the Administrative Committee in August. Metropolitan Nikolai informed us that the meeting could take place at the end of the autumn of 1946 and asked us to wire the names of our representatives. So we appointed a delegation of seven. Bishop Bell was to be the chairman and I was to be the secretary. We proposed that the meeting should take place in Prague at the end of December. This was accepted by the Patriarchate. In the beginning of October a further letter came saying that two archpriests would be sent to Geneva to make a study of the activities of the World Council. But at the end of October Metropolitan Nikolai wired that the journey of the archpriests had to be postponed since there were visa difficulties. Furthermore, the Patriarchate said, it was not sufficiently prepared for the meeting proposed for Prague, and that the meeting should therefore be postponed until 1947. We were not able to find out which archpriests were to visit us and we received no further communications from Moscow on the subject. Later I shall describe how the situation changed in 1948. We did not realize in 1946 that it would take another twelve years before the meeting we had in mind would be held.

Fortunately it was possible to send a delegation to the Greek-speaking churches. This group, under the leadership of Bishop Brilioth of Sweden with the Rev. Oliver Tomkins as secretary, was well received and helped greatly to ensure that a number of Greek Orthodox churches were represented at the first Assembly.

One of the immediate tasks was to give definite shape to the commission on international affairs which the Geneva meeting had decided to create. This was to be a common organ of the World Council and the International Missionary Council. The Commission on a Just and Durable Peace of the Federal Council of Churches in the USA was asked to organize an international conference to elaborate a concrete plan. John Foster Dulles, the chairman of the Commission, became therefore the chairman of the conference which was held in Cambridge in August. Walter van Kirk and I served as secretaries. At that time international travel was still difficult. There were special restrictions for the Germans. Three of them were allowed to come under the condition that they should not speak in public. This was one of the reasons why, against the definite desire of the American delegation, most of the meetings were closed to the press.

It was significant that about twenty of the participants were laymen, for the whole purpose of the meeting was to arrive at a Christian approach to international affairs which would not consist of pious phrases or counsels of perfection, but of concrete proposals and recommendations growing out of Christian convictions and based on a thorough knowledge of the realities of international relations.

There were hesitations about the setting up of a permanent body for this purpose. Did it not mean that the churches were 'going into politics'? But in one sense the World Council had 'gone into politics' already in 1939 with its conference in Geneva, and it had been one of the most rewarding aspects of our wartime task to keep an international discussion going between the men of the Commission on a Just and Durable Peace in the USA, the Peace Aims Group in Britain and various groups on the European Continent. We had learned that it was not enough to produce resolutions on peace whenever there happened to be an ecumenical meeting. The world situation was so grave that only by the continuous work of people specially set aside for this purpose could we hope to make any Christian contribution in this realm. Most hesitations disappeared when it became clear that we were in the good position of having several competent men willing to devote their energies to this new venture. So the decision was taken to propose to the WCC and IMC the creation of a Commission of the Churches on International Affairs. The *New York Times* described the new commission as 'a spiritual, beneficent lobby at our international tribunals . . . recognizing no master, only the Divinity'. And this was indeed what we had in mind.

The problems which the new CCIA would have to face were already apparent at this first meeting. One of the most difficult discussions was that about the tension between the communist world and the Western world which was already beginning to appear. It is interesting to note that Dulles took, in this respect, a position rather different from his position in later years. For he not only expressed his belief that the tension between East and West could be reduced, but also used the surprising phrase: 'No political system is incompatible with Christianity.' This led to a strong reaction from Emil Brunner, who expressed his conviction that totalitarianism was indeed incompatible with Christianity. Thus at its very birth the CCIA had a foretaste of the discussions which it would have to carry on during the next decades. Kenneth Grubb and Frederick Nolde, who would carry the main responsibility for the work, would have their hands full.

It was also in this summer that we began to use the Château de Bossey. We needed a home for the Ecumenical Institute and so Robert Mackie and I had looked at a number of places in the neighbourhood of Geneva. We had come to Bossey on a very cold and dark winter day and the disorganized old house with its innumerable pictures of Napoleon had not seemed very inviting, but we had tried to imagine how it would look in spring and summer, and we had said: this is the place we need. The first meeting held in the château was that of the General Committee of the World's Student Christian Federation. Owing to the interruption of the war years this was the only meeting of the General Committee which took place during the decade when I was chairman of the WSCF. I had not been able to do much for the Federation during those ten years, except keep in close touch with Suzanne de Diétrich, who had held the fort in Geneva, and back up from afar Robert Mackie, who held the movement together from his temporary headquarters in Canada. But I was glad to find that a new generation of leaders was available who would continue the work in new ways, but in the same spirit.

In October the Ecumenical Institute was officially opened. Dr Kraemer, who had accepted the directorship but would only be able to give full time to it after January 1948, said in one of his first lectures to the students that the renewal of the church could be defined in terms which Confucius had used, namely: 'the rectifying of the names'. Its purpose was, to discover again the true meaning of the church and of church membership. And this was what Bossey tried to achieve.

But the first course was not an easy undertaking. Here they were – young men and women out of resistance movements, armies, internment camps whose nations had fought each other. For many it was rather a shock that one of the lecturers was a German. But this German – Reinold von Thadden, who had himself been in prison as a lay-leader of the Confessing Church – was just the right man to help the students to discover another face of Germany. Perhaps the most interesting series of lectures was given by Nicolas Berdyaev, then seventy-two years old but still in the centre of the spiritual struggle of the times. His analysis of communism as a blend of a humanistic conception of ends which Christians could support, with an anti-human theory of means which Christians should reject, and his insistence that Christians should show that they had a better and more radical answer, helped many to see the direction in which they should go.

Towards the end of the year I was again in Germany. The Germans were still terribly isolated and tended to concentrate all their attention on their own misery. It was eminently worthwhile to tell German young people about the rest of the world and to make them see their tragedy in larger perspective. When Robert Mackie, Hanns Lilje and I came to Tübingen we found an audience of eleven hundred students. I told them that during the last thirteen years we had heard many big words and phrases from Germany, but that nearly all had gone with the wind. Only two had remained: one was 'Barmen', the affirmation of the faith of the Confessing Church; the other was 'Stuttgart', the confession of guilt and the word of reconciliation.

From Germany I continued the journey to Prague. Professor Hromadka took me to see President Benes. The President was optimistic about the future. He said: 'The world should know that while we have close relations with Soviet Russia, the Russians do not interfere in any way with our internal affairs.' A year later his remark was no longer true, and the President himself had become one of the victims of the change of regime.

The international Christian organizations which had jointly sponsored the World Christian Youth Conference of 1939 judged it necessary to bring together as soon as possible the representatives of the younger generation to confront them with the post-war ecumenical tasks. It was something of an achievement on the part of Francis House, the organizing secretary, and his colleagues that the second World Conference of Christian Youth could be held as early as 1947 in Oslo. The Japanese delegation had not received permission to come from the Allied authorities. And there were no Russians from Russia. But nearly all the other countries were represented. The German delegates were the first Germans to come to Norway since the occupation-force had left. Happily Niemöller had come as a speaker and showed by his address that there was 'another' Germany.

I had given the closing address at the first World Christian Youth Conference and now I was to provide the link with Amsterdam 1939 by giving the opening address. I intended to describe how the deeply divided, unreconciled world denied all that we stood for as Christians, and how we ourselves had a great share in this denial in that we had tried to have the Kingdom without its righteousness. And I wanted to show how the Lord Jesus Christ overcomes our denial and allows us to start anew with him. Now on the very day of the opening there came the news that the Netherlands government had decided to start a 'police-action' in Java, and that the fighting had begun between the Dutch army and the army of the Republic of Indonesia. I felt strongly that the use of force would settle nothing and only produce a deeper chasm between the Indonesians and the Dutch. And I realized that I was now in a position in which I had never been before. I had participated in so many attempts to bring together Christians from nations which had been or were at war with each other, and I had so often urged others to admit the share of responsibility of their own nation! Now it was my turn.

I wrote to Jetty: 'For the first time in this long ecumenical history I am now myself in the terribly difficult situation of a man whose country is guilty in the eyes of the world and who is looked upon by another delegation here present – the thirteen Indonesians – as the representative of an agressor nation.' There was no time to discuss with others. I decided to add to my speech a single sentence which would at least show that I wanted to practise what I had preached. I said: 'You will forgive me if at this point I refer specially to the conflict in which my own country is involved, and if I say to our Indonesian friends how deeply I feel the burden of guilt resting on my own country for developments leading up to the terrible events taking place at the very time when we meet together.' It was inevitable that the press gave headlines to this statement. There were some strong reactions from Holland and I was taken to task by the Netherlands *chargé d'affaires* in Oslo. The sting of this rebuke was however greatly reduced when he revealed in the course of the conversation that there were prominent Dutch diplomats who agreed with my position. But the really important result was that it became possible to have searching and frank conversations between the Indonesian and Dutch delegations. We went through difficult moments together but we did not give up. The Indonesians wanted the Dutch delegates to take a definite stand against the police action. But the forty-five Dutch delegates found it extremely hard to decide how far they should go in criticizing or condemning the action of their government which was backed by a very large sector of public opinion.

Finally we were able to work out a joint statement which was presented to the conference. The statement reflects the tensions which appeared in our discussions as well as the common ground which we found. It said:

> The Indonesian and Dutch delegations at the World Conference of Christian Youth in Oslo have discussed and prayed together and are grateful that this is possible within the framework of this Conference with its title: 'Jesus Christ is Lord', precisely at the moment when the two peoples are at war with each other.
>
> The Dutch delegation confesses with distress the shortcomings of the Christians of the Netherlands. It considers the lack of true spiritual concern, of passionate prayer and of true Christian unity as contributory causes of the disaster which has come to Indonesia.
>
> The Indonesian delegation takes its stand on the conviction that the use of armed force must be halted immediately and the way of negotiation must be resumed.
>
> The Dutch delegation, convinced of the right of the Indonesian people to liberty and independence, is acutely conscious of the tremendous danger which the use of arms implies for a good relationship between the two peoples. It is convinced that every opportunity of halting the use of arms immediately must be seized in order to return to the way of negotiation.
>
> The members of both delegations desire to continue to meet each other as brothers and sisters in Jesus Christ, in order to help clear the road toward

co-operation between the two peoples on a basis of liberty and equal rights.

Toward the close of the conference M. M. Thomas of India, who would come to play such an important role in the life of the World Council as chairman of its Central Committee, spoke on 'The political message of Oslo'.[2] He said that this message consisted in the knowledge of common guilt and divine forgiveness as the basis of common life. He said about my statement: 'Some might have clapped their hands. Some might have thought of making political capital out of the statement of Dr Visser 't Hooft. I could not do either, because the righteousness of my politics and the justification of my political decision, at that very moment, had broken down into a sense of common guilt before God in Christ.'

NOTES

1. In *The Christian News Letter*, March 20th 1946.
2. This speech was printed in *The Christian News Letter*, September 1947.

29 | *The First Assembly*

IN FEBRUARY 1946 the Provisional Committee decided to hold the first Assembly in the summer of 1948. It seemed to me almost impossible to make adequate preparations in such a short time: so many churches were completely disorganized through the war, so many had gone through years of isolation. A new generation of church leaders had appeared, and most of them had little or no ecumenical experience. The whole concept of a World Council of Churches was still a strange new idea and indeed many looked upon it with considerable suspicion.

Furthermore, the Assembly was to do so many things at once. It would have to be a constituent and legislative meeting, working out a constitution, a programme and a policy for the new council. It would have to be a world-wide forum of discussion concerning the message and mission of the church. It would have to manifest that the churches were on the way to renewal and that in spite of their differences they were united in the central affirmations of the Christian faith.

That we succeeded in completing the preparations was mainly due to the fact that so many had discovered in the war years how indispensable, how urgently necessary, the ecumenical movement had become for the life of the churches. Practically all who were asked to co-operate responded positively. Church leaders and theologians and laymen who had never shown any interest in ecumenical affairs were now ready to give their time and energy. One Amsterdam delegate remarked at the Assembly that his whole library was present in Amsterdam. Even Karl Barth, who had so far remained a critical outsider and whose name had been proposed by Henry Van Dusen for the key-note address, agreed this time to co-operate.

There were many preparatory meetings on the main Assembly subjects. I remember two especially. The first was held in 1947 at the Château de Bossey and dealt with 'The Biblical Authority for the Church's Social and Political Message Today'. The leading lights were Karl Barth and Anders Nygren, the foremost Swedish Lutheran theologian. In the discussion of the relation between the Gospel and the Law, which had caused so much controversy between

Lutherans and Reformed, Barth finally said to Nygren: 'If what you have said is Lutheran, I am Lutheran' and Nygren replied: 'If what you have said is Reformed, then I am Reformed.' But when another much less open-minded Lutheran quoted at great length the confessional documents of the sixteenth and seventeenth century Barth became irritated. He said nothing, but picked up a Greek New Testament and put it on top of the book of ancient confessions. The gesture was more eloquent than words would have been.

The other meeting was held in London early in 1948, called to prepare the Assembly section on 'The Church and the Disorder of Society'. As I walked with J. H. Oldham from the Athenaeum to the place of meeting he asked me whether we could not find an expression to indicate briefly and clearly what a right ordering of society would mean from a Christian point of view. Could we use 'The Humane Society'? Or rather 'The Responsible Society'? I said that the second was just what we needed. At the meeting Oldham proposed both phrases, but I argued that 'humane' could not be adequately translated and so it became 'The Responsible Society'. Not for a moment did we think that for the next twenty years this phrase would continue to serve as a key-concept in ecumenical thinking about social problems.

During those last months before the Assembly we were still uncertain whether the Orthodox churches of Russia, Rumania, Bulgaria and Yugoslavia would send delegates to Amsterdam. The situation seemed relatively hopeful. Although the consultation which we had hoped to have with the Orthodox Church of Russia had not taken place, Metropolitan Nikolai, the President of the Department of Foreign Church-relations of the Moscow Patriarchate, wrote in March 1948 that the Orthodox Church would like to act on our request that it should participate in the ecumenical movement and would give a definite answer in April. There was no further word in April, but the newspapers reported that on the occasion of the five hundredth anniversary of the 'autocephaly' (independence) of the Church of Russia a conference of Orthodox churches would be held in Moscow in July and that this conference would have the ecumenical question on its agenda. We learned also that some very positive reports on the ecumenical movement were being prepared, one by Professor Stephan Zankov of Bulgaria, who had been an ecumenical leader since 1920, and another one by Professor Coman of Rumania, who also knew the movement extremely well. So I was surprised to hear through a Moscow broadcast at the end of July that the churches concerned had decided to decline the invitation to send delegates to the Assembly.

Just a few days before the opening of the Assembly I received a letter from Metropolitan Nikolai. It confirmed the news that the Church of Russia would not participate in the Assembly and enclosed the resolution on the ecumenical movement which the Moscow Conference had adopted. This resolution was a somewhat disconcerting document. It accused the World Council of seeking to exert 'international influence' and of thus falling into the temptation which

Christ had refused. It stated that the WCC was no longer concerned with the true unity of the church. And it criticized the Council for accepting as a condition of unity the simple recognition of Christ as Lord. The churches concerned could therefore not participate in the ecumenical movement 'in its present form'.

I found it difficult to understand what had happened. A Dutchman, Mr J. van Epenhuysen, an orchestra conductor who had joined the Orthodox Church and had participated in the Moscow meeting, came to see me and threw some light on the problem. He and a few others had tried hard to get the conference to adopt a more positive attitude to the ecumenical movement. But they had come up against a deeply rooted suspicion that the World Council was controlled by Western political influences. The report of Archpriest Razumovsky, who had described the World Council as a tool in the ideological war, had been far more decisive than the favourable reports. And when it came to the final meeting there had been no occasion for the presentation of a positive point of view.

Razumovsky's report, which I saw later, was a curious concoction of wrong quotations, misunderstandings and rumours. Thus his thesis that the WCC wanted to become a political power was based on a statement in the report of the Edinburgh Conference of Faith and Order in 1937, which he read (perhaps owing to a wrong translation in Russian) in this way: 'We do not believe that a church, corporately united, could be an effective international influence without some permanent organ of conference or council.' But Edinburgh had not spoken of 'international influence', but of 'an effective international community' and had meant of course effective in creating close relations between the churches. It was also interesting to note that one of the main sources of Razumovsky's report was the literature of the very reactionary Karlovci-Synod, which was strongly opposed to the Moscow Patriarchate, but also considered the ecumenical movement as dangerously progressive and largely dominated by free-masonry. There remained the question why there had been such a change in the attitude of the Patriarchate since the letter of March. The most probable answer was that in the spring and summer of 1948 the East-West situation had greatly deteriorated. The cold war was entering a critical phase, and this was bound to have its repercussions in the attitude of the churches concerned. The only Russian from Russia I could welcome at Amsterdam was a representative of the Tass Agency who came to complain that he had not received a ticket for the opening service in the church. I told him that I would be very glad to help him to go to church.

There was also much uncertainty about the participation of Roman Catholic observers. We had at that time no contact with the Vatican, and so I discussed the matter with some Roman Catholic friends. Father Yves Congar sent me a list of fourteen Roman Catholics who had shown active and sympathetic interest in the ecumenical movement and I received further names from other correspondents. I was assured that in most cases the persons concerned could count on the approval of their immediate superior. Invitations were sent out to ten Roman Catholics early in 1948.

In April I heard that the Archbishop of Utrecht, Cardinal de Jong, took the position – in view of the location of the Assembly – that he should choose the observers and that very few of the persons on Father Congar's list would receive his approval. I explained through an intermediary that we would be ready to consider inviting persons proposed by the Dutch hierarchy, but that it was the responsibility of each Roman Catholic who had been invited, and not of the World Council, to obtain whatever permission was required. While this discussion was still going on and before any names had been received from Utrecht the Holy Office in Rome issued a *Monitum* reminding all Roman Catholics that it was forbidden to participate in ecumenical meetings without permission from the Vatican. We were not sure whether this meant that the Vatican would give the permission to some who were considered to be 'safe', or whether it meant that no Roman Catholics would be allowed to go to Amsterdam.

In the meantime the situation had been further confused by the intervention of Mr Myron Taylor, the American industrialist who had been sent to Rome, originally by President Roosevelt, as the personal representative of the President of the United States to the Pope. He came to see me and explained that at the request of President Truman he was visiting several religious leaders. He would see Pastor Boegner in Paris and the Archbishop of Canterbury in London. He expressed the conviction that all who believed in God and in freedom should be brought together to fight communism. We should therefore invite to the Assembly representatives of national governments engaged in this fight. It was clear that he wanted to come to Amsterdam himself. He said that he had raised the question of attendance of Roman Catholics at the Assembly with Pope Pius XII and gave one to understand that though the Pope had not committed himself he might well decide to send observers to Amsterdam. He also expressed astonishment that we had not invited the leaders of Islam to participate in the meeting.

I could only tell him that he had misunderstood completely what the World Council really was. Our sole purpose was to manifest the fundamental unity of the Christian churches. Mr Taylor did not think that it was necessary to have Christ mentioned. I explained that we were trying to bring all the Christian churches together including the Eastern European churches and those of the USSR. Mr Taylor did not like this idea. I told him that we wanted to remain completely independent of all governmental influences. So between his conception of the role of the church and ours there was such a wide gulf that it seemed impossible to make him understand what we were after.

Had he really been right about the willingness of the Pope to send observers? I doubted it and told him what steps had already been taken to secure the attendance of Roman Catholic observers. Dr Boegner, whom Mr Taylor visited a few days later in Paris, followed this up by saying as clearly as possible that if the Pope had really intended to send observers he should have let the World Council know about this; we did not need the mediation of any government for the solution of such a purely ecclesiastical problem.

On June 18th all further discussion came to an end, for the Holy Office made it known that no Roman Catholic would receive permission to attend the Amsterdam Assembly. What had happened? All we heard was that there had been a very large number of requests from Roman Catholics for permission to go to Amsterdam, not only as observers, but as visitors. The Vatican had become worried about this enthusiasm and had therefore taken this negative decision.

On the day before the Assembly opened I received a visit from the Jesuit, Père Charles Boyer. He was the chairman of the *Unitas* movement with headquarters in Rome. He had attended a congress of philosophers in Amsterdam and would remain in the city during the Assembly. He would not attend the meetings, but would be glad to receive as much information as possible. Since it seemed to me important that the Vatican should get a clear picture of the Assembly I promised him that I would not only send him a full documentation, but also make sure that different participants visited him to give him a first-hand impression of the Assembly.

The Dutch Roman Catholic bishops issued a special pastoral letter on the ecumenical problem. It explained that the absence of the Roman Catholic Church was wholly due to dogmatic reasons. For unity could only be found if all Christians were to return to the Roman Catholic Church. The bishops added that they would follow the work of the Assembly with sympathetic interest and would ask Catholics to pray for it. This letter was dated July 31st and read in the Roman Catholic churches on August 22nd. But I did not receive a copy until August 31st. Cardinal de Jong explained in a covering letter that, through an oversight, the letter had not been sent in time. I answered that the letter had been immediately distributed to all delegates as soon as it had arrived.

When on the opening day the colourful procession of the three-hundred-and-fifty-one official delegates began to move into the historic *Nieuwe Kerk* I found it difficult to believe that the moment for which I had been waiting for ten years had really arrived. These men and women from 147 churches in 44 countries represented the great family in which I had been privileged to live and work. In practically every delegation there were friends with whom I shared common memories. But this time we were not only enjoying a family gathering; we were also going to commit ourselves to a common task to be undertaken through a common instrument of co-operation, fellowship and witness.

John R. Mott was of course the first speaker. He was now eighty-two years old. It did not matter that he was using once more the old phrases which we had heard so often. What mattered was that he stood there as the living incarnation of the movement which had prepared the way for this day and that he had set in motion the spiritual process which was now to find a clear manifestation. He mentioned names of innumerable men and women who had done the pioneering work. The cloud of witnesses was around him.

In fact when he came down from the pulpit he found that he had not yet mentioned all whom he wanted to be remembered and asked D. T. Niles, the next speaker, whether he would read the additional names. But Niles did not feel he could do this. It would have been too much of a good thing. And he had a different job to do. He preached a straightforward sermon on the unexpected, but very appropriate text: 'Who am I, that I should go unto Pharaoh?'

The next day was unforgettable for more reasons than one. It began with a telephone call which woke me up. An Indonesian delegate wanted to see me urgently. His message was that the Indonesian delegation had decided that their head, who had been invited to the luncheon at the Royal Palace, would not attend because of the conflict between the Netherlands and Indonesia. I tried hard to get this decision changed. It would be such a pity, on the very first day of the Assembly, to have a political incident. But my arguments did not seem to carry much weight. Then suddenly I grasped a straw. The Indonesian delegate said that they would like to talk the problem over with Karl Barth. I promised that I would find Barth for them. Stewards were sent out in different directions to find Barth. In the meantime the important first conference session began in the Concertgebouw. Even during the moments when the World Council of Churches was officially constituted I could not get the Indonesian problem off my mind. Finally a message was brought to me that Barth and the Indonesians were now meeting together and, towards the end of the morning, I received word that the problem had been solved.

What had happened? Barth explained that he had first asked the Indonesians to sing their national anthem for him. Then he had told them that as a Swiss he was also a republican. But he felt that when Princess Juliana, who was really interested in the ecumenical movement, invited church leaders to meet her, we should not disappoint her. He proposed that the Indonesian delegate should come to the luncheon and had added: 'and he should not make a deeper bow than I will make'. The luncheon proved a very happy occasion. Princess Juliana expressed strong convictions about the place of women in the church, and Archbishop Eidem of Sweden had a rather hard time explaining why (at that time) his church would not ordain women.

But I must come back to that first morning in the Concertgebouw. The resolution concerning the official formation of the World Council of Churches, presented by Marc Boegner, was accepted *nemine contradicente*. Then the Archbishop of Canterbury, who was in the chair, asked for a moment of silent prayer, after which he thanked God for his having brought us to this hour. The creation of a World Council of Churches, which had seemed such an impossibly difficult task in the nineteen thirties and which had seemed a hopeless affair in the dark moments of the world war, proved now to be such a simple and undramatic operation. But I had not much time to think about this, for I had to give the General Secretary's report. The main purpose of that report was to define (as clearly as could be done in this early stage) what the World Council aimed to be and to do. For there were all sorts of misunderstandings. I had to make it quite clear that we were not forming a 'Super-Church' and remarked that 'anyone who had worked in the ecumenical field knows that the slightest attempt to exercise such control is bound to meet with the determined resistance of our churches which share the same strong sense of independence'. I had also to deny strongly that we were pursuing political ends and said: 'Our task is to prove in word and in deed that we serve a Lord whose realm certainly includes politics, but whose saving purpose cuts across all political alignments and embraces men of *all* parties, *all* lands.' I asked how the World Council should then be defined and gave this answer:

> We are a council of churches, not *the* Council of the one undivided Church. Our name indicates our weakness and our shame before God, for there can be and there *is* finally only one Church of Christ on earth. Our plurality is a deep anomaly. But our name indicates also that we are aware of that situation, that we do not accept it passively, that we would move forward towards the manifestation of the One Holy Church. Our council represents therefore an emergency solution – a stage on the road – a body living between the time of complete isolation of the churches from each other and the time – on earth or in heaven – when it will be visibly true that there is one Shepherd and one flock.
>
> The functions of the council follow from this situation. We are a fellowship in which the churches after a long period of ignoring each other come to know each other. We are a fellowship in which the churches enter into serious and dynamic conversation with each other about their differences in faith, in message, in order. We are a fellowship in which Christian solidarity is practised, so that the churches aid their weak or needy sister-churches. We are a fellowship in which common witness is rendered to the Lordship of Christ in all matters in which a common word for the churches and for the world is given to us. We are above all a fellowship which seeks to express that unity in Christ already given to us and to prepare the way for a much fuller and much deeper expression of that unity.

I had, of course, also to refer to the absence of the Church of Russia and several other Eastern Orthodox churches. I explained what had happened before and at the Moscow Conference and added:

> The one hopeful element in the situation is that the reasons given for the negative decision are based upon a complete misunderstanding of the true nature of our movement – a misunderstanding such as can easily arise in a church whose leaders have no first-hand knowledge of ecumenical life. If we succeed, here at Amsterdam and in the coming years, in making it clear that, so far from pursuing political purposes, we have no other concern than the concern for the Lordship of Christ everywhere – in East and West – and for

his Church as the *one* Holy Church, it may yet be possible to remove the existing misunderstandings. In any case our course is clear. We should keep the door open for the Church of Russia and other Orthodox churches not already represented among us. And we should feel responsible for them as we feel responsible for each other.

With regard to the Roman Catholic Church I mentioned the recent decision of the Holy Office and added:

This decision is all the more regrettable since in recent years many Roman Catholic priests and laymen have shown a very deep understanding of the purposes and character of our movement. In fact the interest which individual Roman Catholics have shown in this Assembly and which has expressed itself in requests for invitations, in articles and in personal visits, has been one of the most striking features of the period of preparation. It remains to be seen whether the 'veto' of the Holy Office means in fact that this new and more hopeful approach is implicitly condemned or whether there is a possibility for continued conversation. From the point of view of the World Council we must hope and pray that real opportunities for fruitful contact may remain in existence.

I need not try to tell again the story of the whole Assembly, but I pick out a few events which stand out in my memory.

One of the evenings was devoted to meetings of the various confessional bodies. I was of course curious to find out what had been said at these meetings about the ecumenical movement and the World Council. So I placed myself at a table in front of the hotel where many delegates lived and asked people returning from the various meetings what had been the main point made by the speakers. The answers were strikingly similar. Nearly all reported that they had been told that their confession was really the centre of the ecumenical movement and that the other confessions would discover that some day. What, I asked myself, did this mean? Was this just the inevitable reaction of church bodies who sought to reassure themselves at the time when each confession found itself suddenly confronted with the question of its own future in an ecumenical age? It could, I thought, be interpreted in this way. But it could also mean something different – namely, that each confession had something essential to give to the ecumenical community. The great question would become whether they would all discover that in ecumenical life receiving is often more blessed than giving. The Assembly message said that as the churches had talked together, they had begun to understand how their separation had prevented them from receiving correction from each other in Christ. Would the World Council become an instrument of such mutual correction?

I had to spend a good deal of time with the Nominations Committee. This small group of seven fortunately very wise men, chaired by Bishop Yngve

Brilioth, had an extremely difficult task. Much would depend on their success in nominating the right presidents and the ninety right people to serve as members of the Central Committee. There had been a sharp debate in the days before the Assembly between those who wanted the World Council to be organized wholly on a confessional basis and those who wanted it to apply the principle of geographical representation. A compromise had been reached and it was therefore now necessary to ensure both adequate confessional representation and adequate geographical distribution. It would of course also be necessary to include a sufficient number of lay men and women. And we had to start from scratch without any tradition to build on. The task could only be accomplished through many consultations with individuals and delegations. All members of the committee shared in this process, but since I knew so many delegates personally I had to do a considerable part of the job. It was rather a miracle that the committee could present the list for the Central Committee in time and that the list was accepted.

The composition of the Presidium was also a real problem. It was soon agreed that it would be preferable to have a group of presidents rather than one single president. The nature of the council as an instrument *of* the churches rather than as an organ *above* the churches could be more clearly manifested by a Presidium. Five names were soon agreed on: Pastor Marc Boegner of France, the Archbishop of Canterbury, the Archbishop of Uppsala (Sweden) and Archbishop Germanos of the Ecumenical Patriarchate had already served. Bishop G. Bromley Oxnam of the Methodist Church of the USA was another rather obvious name. And all agreed that John R. Mott should become Honorary President. But the question came up whether the younger churches should not be represented. They did not have many delegates at the Assembly, but should the council not emphasize from the outset that it desired to become truly universal in outlook and structure? It was decided to propose a sixth president from Asia. Who should it be? Attention was called to the name of a Chinese lady who had a prominent place in academic life. But how would our Chinese friends feel about this choice? Bishop Brilioth, Bishop Henry Sherrill and I went on a night expedition to find a Chinese bishop who would be able to answer this question. We did find him, but since he was in bed the discussion had to take the form of shouting through the closed bedroom-door. It took some time to get him to understand the issue. The answer was negative. We had to start again. The committee finally decided to propose the name of Professor T. C. Chao.

The secular press gave most attention of course to the speeches of John Foster Dulles, who was at that time chairman of the Commission on a Just and Durable Peace of the Federal Council of Churches and who was later to become Secretary of State under President Eisenhower, and of Professor Josef Hromadka, the well-known theologian from Czechoslovakia. For these two speeches became in fact a confrontation between two very different Christian attitudes to the international situation. It was striking to find that both had modified their position, but in opposite directions. Dulles had been attacked at the Cambridge Conference of 1946 for not being sufficiently firm in his attitude to communism. This time he described communism as the greatest obstacle to world peace. I had known Hromadka as an admirer of President Masaryk with his strong attachment to liberal democratic ideals. But he was now pleading for a sympathetic understanding of communism as a force which embodied much of the social impetus which the church and Western civilization should represent, but had largely lost. It was clear that a great change had taken place since 1946. The days of the comradeship in arms between Russia and the West were over. The cold war with its process of polarization had begun. It would become increasingly difficult to find common ground between Christians whose thought was influenced by the prevailing political concepts of the Western world and Christians who sought to play a positive role in their communist environment.

The Assembly had to face this issue. It did so in a statement which created a good deal of debate. The third section said: 'The churches should reject the ideologies of both communism and *laissez-faire* capitalism and should draw men from the false assumption that these extremes are the only alternatives.' The words *laissez-faire* which did not appear in the original draft were added as the result of an amendment by Charles P. Taft. The real significance of this declaration was that the World Council refused to identify itself with any political or social ideology and thus to let itself be used as an instrument in the cold war. And the adoption of Oldham's phrase, 'the responsible society', provided a criterion and signpost for positive social thought and action.

It was strange how during those days the Dutch part of my life and the international part overlapped on several occasions.

On August 31st, for example, I sat with the Assembly leaders in the stadium where Queen Wilhelmina took leave of her people and where the main events of the fifty years during which she had reigned were brought back to life. And another great moment came when I accompanied Martin Niemöller to the large youth rally in the Apollohal. A German using the German language, speaking to young Dutchmen only three years after the war and receiving a warm reception – that could only happen if speaker and audience understood the reconciling force of the gospel.

Immediately after the Assembly the Central Committee chosen by the Assembly held its first meeting at Woudschoten, the centre of the Dutch Student Christian Movement. There was no hesitation about the election of the chairman. Bishop George Bell was the obvious choice not only because of his experience, but also because he had the gift of bringing men of various backgrounds and opinions together. As to the vice-chairmanship, the committee took the risk of appointing a man who was a newcomer to the ecumenical movement, namely Dr Franklin Clark Fry of the United Lutheran Church of America. His role in the Assembly had been to insist on the basic principle that the World Council should really be a council of churches, in which the churches would have the final say. Few realized that they were electing a man whose talent for chairing both large assemblies and small committees was unique. I was appointed General Secretary in the same room in which I had been appointed General Secretary of the World's Student Christian Federation sixteen years before.

During the meeting word was received that Bishop Lajos Ordass of the Lutheran Church of Hungary, whom the Assembly had elected as a member of the Central Committee, had been arrested in Budapest. It was decided to send a letter to the Hungarian authorities expressing concern and asking for information, and to request the chairman to make a protest if no satisfactory reply was received. The reply from the Hungarian government was unsatisfactory and Bishop Bell therefore sent a protest in October. Thus it was right from the start that the Central Committee was confronted with the acute problems of the post-war world. But the long and intensive discussion on the right way to deal with such a problem helped greatly to make the committee into a team which shared a common responsibility.

The Archbishop of Canterbury asked me in Amsterdam where I would go for a good holiday which I obviously needed. I answered that I had had no time to think about this. He said 'Why don't you go to my palace in Canterbury?' And so Jetty and I spent a few weeks in that vast and empty but wonderfully quiet place and had a little time to think. Pius IX had said before the first Vatican Council that councils go through three periods: one of the devil, one of men and one of God. I felt that in Amsterdam it had been somewhat different. We had begun with a very human enthusiasm about the creation of the council. Then we had had a period of confusion, which was the time when the devil had his greatest chance. But finally God had overcome our confusion and we had therefore been able to make a real covenant with each other and had agreed 'to stay together' (as the Message had said).

THE FIRST YEARS after the Amsterdam Assembly were a time of expansion of World Council activities. The Department of Interchurch Aid and Service to Refugees had to take on many new tasks. Faith and Order began to plan for the third World Conference on Faith and Order. The Study Department launched a series of new studies. The Commission of the Churches on International Affairs had its hands full with the many acute international issues of the hour. The Ecumenical Institute was now operating a full programme. The Youth Department developed a stronger and geographically wider programme. There were new developments in Asia to which I will have to come back in another chapter.

It was clear that the World Council was meeting real needs which could not have been met without it. Isolated and struggling churches were finding encouragement in the fact that they were now part of a world-wide fellowship which cared for them. In the field of reconstruction, inter-church aid and service to refugees and other people in need we found that co-operative action was much more effective than separate action. And in the realm of Christian thought and theology the Council was an indispensable instrument for a cross-fertilization between the churches and regions.

The theological climate of the time seemed to be favourable for ecumenical advance. In the introduction to the Stone Lectures which I gave in 1947 in Princeton Theological Seminary on 'The Kingship of Christ' I had noted that American Christians now realized the need for a restatement of the social gospel of the 'twenties and that European churches were at last beginning to discover their responsibility to the world. So it was now possible to get beyond the old and sterile alternative of a social gospel which was not really a gospel but a system of moral laws, and individualistic orthodoxy which was not really orthodox since it did not have the cosmic outlook of the Bible. Thus in 1950 I could say in my report as General Secretary that there was undoubtedly more convergence of theological thought in the ecumenical movement than there had been for a long time.

One impressive example of this was the study conference at Wadham College,

Oxford, in the summer of 1949 which sought to arrive at an ecumenical agreement concerning guiding principles for the interpretation of the Bible in relation to social and international life. The conference could say: 'We have found a measure of agreement that surprised us all' and submit a remarkably substantial report. Once again we were discovering that the Bible need not divide us as it had done so often in the past. The conference could conclude: 'It is an actual experience within the ecumenical movement that when we meet together, with presuppositions of which we may be largely unconscious, and bring these presuppositions to the judgment of Scripture some of the very difficulties are removed which prevent the Gospel from being heard.'

It was during this conference that some of us were invited to meet King George VI and Queen Elizabeth at an informal tea-party at St Catherine's, an ecumenical training centre in Windsor Park under the direction of my old Student Movement friend, Amy Buller. Each of us spent part of the time at the table where the Queen was presiding and part of the time at the table of the King. There was a considerable difference between the two groups. At the table of the Queen there was much serious conversation about church life. At the table of the King there was much gaiety. The King told amusing stories about his journeys. One Japanese delegate tried to bring up a more important matter and told the King that in Christian circles in Japan there was some hope that the Japanese Emperor might embrace Christianity. The reaction was rather unexpected. The King said laughingly: 'But that is just as if I were to become a Buddhist.'

In these years the World Council seemed to be making considerable progress. But there was another side of the picture. One year after the Amsterdam Assembly, at the Central Committee meeting in Chichester, I had to report:

> The very fact that the ecumenical movement has come of age and has taken more definite and substantial form means, in our present nervous and divided world, that its purposes have been widely misunderstood and that it has been the object of attacks from different quarters. It is curious to notice that the council is suspected at the same time of an over-emphasis on ecclesiastical centralized unity and of a lack of real concern about reunion; that it is considered by some to be a typical expression of the reactionary tendencies of the bourgeois world and by others as an organization which endangers the foundations of the capitalist system; or that it is alternatively considered as being manoeuvred by Social Gospel theologians, Barthians, Anglo-Catholics and Modernists. It is probably inevitable that such misunderstandings should arise when a complex movement without precedent in church history comes into being.

The most urgent task was therefore to clarify the nature, the purpose and the policy of the council. And the two questions which deserved priority were: How does the council understand its own existence and task in relation to the churches? Or, to put it in more formal words: What is the ecclesiological significance of the World Council? And what is the position of the council with regard to the ideological and political conflicts of our time and, more particularly, to the conflict between the communist world and the Western world? To tell the story coherently I will deal with these two questions separately, though in fact we were of course discussing both at the same time and at the same meetings.

The Amsterdam Assembly had not been able to give much time and thought to the question of the nature of the World Council. I had written a paper on the subject for the preparatory volume on 'The Universal Church in God's Design', but this paper had not been discussed. Most delegates did not realize what problems were involved and did not ask what implications membership in the Council would have for the conception which their church had of its own nature and of its relationships with other churches. But in the years after the Assembly many critical questions were asked. Some of the sharpest questioning came from Roman Catholic ecumenists. At a meeting in Paris in September 1949 a group of World Council representatives met with a group of very able Roman Catholics, several of whom were to become leaders in Catholic ecumenical activities. At this meeting, which I will describe in another chapter, our World Council group learned a great deal about the problems which we would have to study. It was in the light of these and other conversations that I proposed to the Executive Committee in February 1950 that we should choose as one of the main themes for the next meeting of the Central Committee in Toronto the subject: 'The Ecclesiological Significance of the World Council of Churches'. With the help of my colleague, Oliver Tomkins of Great Britain, I wrote a draft of a statement on this subject, sent this to several theologians and corrected it in the light of their comments.

From the past experience I realized that this document would not be accepted without considerable discussion, but I had not expected that it would create an explosive situation. The debate became one of the most heated we have ever had in the Central Committee. It became clear that in forming the World Council the church leaders had had different presuppositions. There were those who understood the World Council as the fundamentally adequate answer to the problem of church unity. There were others who could only regard it as an instrument for making a new approach to the problem. The first had taken it for granted that the churches in the council gave full and unreserved recognition to each other. The others believed that membership in the council did not mean that any church had to give up its convictions about the nature of the church, but rather that each member church was ready to enter into relations of fellowship and dialogue with other churches with the hope that this would lead to full recognition and full unity. The main target of the attack became the phrase: 'There is a place in the World Council both for those churches which recognize other churches as churches in the full and true sense and for those which do not.'

Henry van Dusen, of Union Theological Seminary in New York, was one of the most outspoken critics of the conception of the World Council on which the statement was based. He defended the thesis that the World Council expresses the form which unity is ultimately to take. Several speakers representing the tradition of the free churches supported this position. But then Georges Florovsky, speaking on behalf of the Eastern Orthodox churches, made a passionate plea for the principles embodied in the document. The question was whether there was a place in the council for churches which regard churches of other confessions as essentially incomplete. This was not a matter of drafting, but a matter of principle. He said he was in great distress, for if others were to consider that the Eastern Orthodox position was too extreme it might be that the time had come to part.

Pierre Maury of France made a contribution to the discussion which proved to be a turning point. He did not consider even his own church a full and true church. No family of churches should be afraid to have it stated as a fact that others did not regard their church as complete. After this several speakers agreed that the Orthodox churches were not the only ones to 'unchurch' the churches. The very originality of the World Council was precisely that it sought to create fellowship between churches who were not yet able to give full recognition to each other. Finally, after some further modification but without substantial change, the document was received and it was agreed to send it out for study and comment in the churches.

Immediately after the meeting, I wrote in *The Ecumenical Review*:

> During the course of that searching discussion, there were moments when it seemed that the council had come to a real crisis in its history. But it proved to be a crisis unto life, for at the end of the discussion all present had arrived at a deeper understanding both of the very real differences which exist between the member churches of the council in their conception of the church and also of the not less real work of the Holy Spirit by which these churches are brought into fellowship with each other.

This document, which became known as 'The Toronto statement' found much wider acceptance than we could have expected at the time. It allayed fears that the council would become a 'Super-Church' and played a considerable role in later years when the Orthodox churches of Russia and other countries had to make up their mind about membership in the council and when the Roman Catholic Church became ready to enter into relationship with the council.

The weakness of the document was that it did not speak clearly enough about the common tasks of the churches. This was to a large extent corrected when a year later in the Central Committee meeting at Rolle (Switzerland) a substantial statement on 'The Calling of the Church to Mission and Unity' was received.

I had hoped that after the war we would be able to concentrate our attention on the internal affairs of the council. The great expansion of work and the difficult theological issues that had to be faced were quite enough to keep us on our toes. But the turbulent post-war world was constantly knocking on our doors and interfering with our plans. Some of the gravest tensions in the life of the council were caused by the political and ideological divisions of the cold war period.

Before coming to these moments of tension I must provide a bit of background. In April 1949 I took part in a symposium in New York on 'Christian Responsibility in World Affairs'. Together with Arnold Toynbee, Charles H. Malik, Charles W. Ranson and John Foster Dulles, I tried to develop the implications of the Amsterdam Assembly with regard to the tensions between the Eastern and Western political blocs. I said that the first concern of the World Council in this area should be that neither the ecumenical movement as a whole nor the churches individually should identify themselves to such an extent with any social or political ideology that religion would become exploited for purely secular political ends.

Our second concern should be to defend the fundamental liberty of the church to exercise its evangelistic and prophetic functions without hindrance. The situation in several countries under a communist regime was not that the churches were openly persecuted, but that attempts were made to domesticate them so that they could no longer proclaim their convictions with regard to public issues.

The third concern of the council should be to maintain fellowship between its member churches. This would take much imagination, much mutual confidence and much patience.

The fourth concern should be to make it clear that no political or economic system had yet given a full or adequate solution to the problem of freedom and justice. Amsterdam had said that we should seek a better way. This 'third way' was of course not a mere middle way. And it was not a third political force. But it was the attempt to seek new creative solutions.

The final concern should be to do everything possible to prevent the ideological conflict from leading to war.

In April 1950 the Synod of the Evangelical Church of Germany met in the the Eastern sector of Berlin. The main theme was: 'What can the Church do for Peace?' and I had been asked to give the introductory address. The atmosphere was electric, for it was precisely on the opening day of the meeting of the Synod that in most churches in Eastern Germany a declaration was read in which the churches protested against the ideological pressure that was being exerted upon the people. The East German church stood up for the spiritual freedom and dignity of man. From the point of view of the church this was an act of pastoral responsibility, not a political choice for or against a power bloc. But would the political authorities understand this?

The opening session at which I gave my address was attended by the repre-

sentatives of the four occupation powers – USA, Great Britain, USSR and
France. To speak about peace in East Berlin seemed equivalent to carrying coals
to Newcastle, for East Berlin was covered with slogans about peace. But the very
inflation of the word also gave me an opportunity to explain what the Scriptures
said about *shalom*, as a peace which is not a peace imposed by some upon others,
but a total peace received from above, demanding sacrifice from all and including
all men.

The synod spoke out clearly. Of special significance was the word of repentance for the sins of commission and omission with regard to the Jewish people.
It was deeply encouraging that in this city of destruction and division the church
could still be a force of healing.

In the summer of 1950 the international tensions became more acute. These
tensions led in due course to a time of crisis in the World Council. The Central
Committee meeting in Toronto began nine days after the attack on South Korea.
The Commission of the Churches on International Affairs had prepared a state-
ment on the Korean question and this was submitted to the Central Committee.
The issue seemed to be quite clear. Had not the United Nations Commission in
Korea come to the conclusion that an act of aggression had been committed?
And had not the Security Council of the United Nations decided to meet this
aggression by a police measure? So there was general agreement that the World
Council should speak up for the maintenance of the principles on the observance
of which the peace and security of all nations depended.

The statement commended the United Nations, an instrument of world order,
for its prompt decision to meet the aggression, and for authorizing police action.
But it said also: 'We stand for a just peace under the rule of law and must seek
peace by expanding justice and by attempting to reconcile contending world
powers.' It happened that at this meeting there were no representatives of the
churches in Eastern Europe and only one delegate from China. During the
debate the basic assumptions underlying the statement were not challenged. The
only controversial point was whether the churches could commend the use of
force for the defence of world order. In the end only two members of the
Central Committee voted against the statement and these two were conscientiously opposed to the use of armed force in principle, anywhere and for any reason.

But this was not the end of the debate about Korea. A few weeks after the
Toronto meeting the Hungarian Church press published an open letter to me as
General Secretary of the council, signed by Bishop Albert Bereczky of the
Reformed Church in Hungary. Bishop Bereczky had become the most outspoken representative of those leaders in the Eastern European churches who
were attempting to find a *modus vivendi* with the communist regime and who
defended their policy on theological grounds. He himself came from a pietistic
background, but had come to the conclusion that by their lack of concern for
social justice the churches themselves were to be blamed for the fact that the
social revolution had been carried out by the communist movement. Now this

theology of repentance dominated his total outlook. In his open letter to me he took the line that the Central Committee had been quite wrong in its judgment. It ought instead to have addressed a strong word of repentance to the Western powers, for the origin of the trouble was the imperialistic attitude of those powers. The churches which had been silent about the sins of the Christian nations had no right now to take the side of these nations, he contended.

Soon afterwards Bishop Bereczky came to see me in Geneva. We had a long and intensive conversation. He was a man who, in spite of his unimpressive physical appearance, immediately impressed me as a very strong personality. I found that he was certainly not a mere opportunist who had adapted his outlook to the new political environment. He was passionately, almost fanatically, convinced that he had the prophetic mission to proclaim that, through the communist revolution, the churches were called to make a complete break with their past and that they should take a fundamentally positive attitude to the new communist order. He held this conviction so stubbornly that it was practically impossible to make him aware of other no less important convictions held within the ecumenical family. He knew very little about the Western European or Anglo-Saxon world and saw the whole world situation only from the perspective of the great change which had taken place in his own country and in his own life. We remained on friendly terms, but we did not make much progress in finding common ground.

In my report to the Bishop of Chichester and other World Council leaders I quote the following: 'Right at the start Bishop Bereczky explained that the one and only reason why he had written his letter was that he wanted his church to stay in the World Council. The one thing to avoid was the creation of an Iron Curtain between the member churches of the council . . .' The Bishop emphasized that 'this is a time of God's judgment upon the church and the churches must therefore strike the note of repentance'. I answered that I agreed on this point. But I remarked that repentance for the sins of the past must become concrete and must therefore mean that the church does not commit the same sins in the new situation. If the churches of Hungary had sinned by not protesting against feudalism, was there not a great danger that they were in fact repeating the same sin by not protesting against the great injustices of the present regime? The Bishop replied that a church under judgment is not in a position to make prophetic statements. On the other hand he stressed the point that in concrete cases he had more than once called the attention of the government to specific injustice and that this had not been without result.

I concluded my report by saying: 'My own impression of this conversation is that Bishop Bereczky is utterly sincere in his Christian conviction. I believe, however, that he is so deeply and one-sidedly concerned with repentance for the past that he is to some extent paralysed in his dealings with the present.'

The element of truth in this reaction to the resolution on Korea was obviously that in that resolution we had failed to show, in line with the whole tradition of the ecumenical movement, that we wanted to continue what Emanuel Mounier of France had called 'the struggle against the easy conscience of the West'. This was all the more necessary since at the end of 1950 and in the beginning of 1951 the nations seemed once again to be drifting towards war on a world scale. Nobody felt that more deeply than Bishop Bell. So he convened a special consultation of church leaders immediately preceding the meeting of the World Council's Executive Committee at Bièvres, near Paris, in January 1951.

In preparation for that meeting I wrote a memorandum in which I said that within our WCC membership we found roughly the four following positions:

(a) Those (mostly in the Western nations) who consider that the major issue of international life is the issue of aggression and violence versus law and order and who consider it imperative to support the United Nations in its effort to maintain international order as over against totalitarian aggressiveness.

(b) Those (largely in Asia but also in Western Europe) who conceive the present conflict as a conflict of power blocs which seek to use the United Nations for their own selfish ends and who believe that the church (and the World Council) should in no way identify or even seem to identify itself with one of these blocs.

(c) Those (in Eastern Europe and China) who believe in the essential rightness of the cause of the North Korean and Chinese governments and consider the action of the United Nations as an attempt to oppose the liberation of Asian peoples. Many of them feel at the same time that the intentions of the communist nations are fundamentally peaceful and they support therefore the movement of 'partisans of peace' as over against the 'warmongers' in the West.

(d) Those (in various parts of the world) who believe that a police-action such as undertaken by the United Nations means in fact war and that it is wrong for the church (a fortiori the World Council) to approve of war in any form.

The position, I continued, was now:

(a) that an important section of our membership has not understood our recent utterances as a pastoral and ecumenical word spoken with the intention to help the churches in taking a specifically Christian decision, but as a political word;

(b) that the impression has been created that the World Council has identified itself with the position of the 'Western' democracies;

(c) that in spite of the fact that the member churches in communist countries desire to maintain the ecumenical fellowship, that fellowship is in fact threatened.

I continued:

In this situation the question arises whether we have once again reached a point in the history of the ecumenical movement at which our duty to maintain fraternal relations with our member churches and our duty to render concrete witness concerning the crucial issues of international life enter into conflict with each other. It is clear that both duties are important.

The fraternal relations which we still have with churches in communist areas have exceptional value. They demonstrate to a deeply divided world that the Lord continues to gather his people. They mean for the 'Western' churches that they may share in the renewal of life which comes to the struggling churches in their conflict with a hostile environment. They mean that the churches in communist countries receive the consolation and encouragement of belonging to the world-wide fellowship which seeks to support them in their struggle. It would therefore be a true ecumenical disaster if the day were to come that all inter-church relations across the dividing line were broken off.

But it is also essential that the World Council shall continue to speak to the churches concerning the crucial issues of our time. A World Council which would cease to struggle for a concrete witness would soon become irrelevant and therefore also cease to create real fellowship. And in the situation in which we find ourselves today, in which Christian men and women in their deep uncertainty and confusion long for a word of guidance from a truly ecumenical, world-embracing perspective, it would be a very serious matter to give up our attempts to find and speak such a word.

We must therefore continue to do whatever we can to remain loyal to our two tasks. We must not choose one of the two lines of least resistance – namely, to write off the churches in communist countries and to act as the mouthpiece of the other churches, or to refrain from any relevant expression of conviction. We are still at the point at which we must accept the full spiritual tension in which God has placed us and which is our particular share of the burden which the church has to bear today. We must seek to speak with a sense of responsibility for the whole fellowship; we must seek to hold the churches together without sacrificing our right and duty to witness.

It may be that before long we will be placed in a situation in which it is manifestly impossible to do this. If so, we shall have to take a crucial decision at that time. But we have no right to create that situation or to force that situation upon ourselves.

After long discussions a letter to the member churches was drafted (which was later accepted by the Executive Committee).[1] In comparison to the Korea resolution of 1950 it was a more pastoral document which contained a strong appeal to the churches to do everything they could to ensure that armaments, whatever their necessity, should not come to dominate the whole life of national and international society. And it set the political conflict in a wider context by declaring that 'everywhere the victim is man. Often he is treated no better than an object, or at best a tool, rather than a responsible person. He hears much about peace, but, for the sake of peace, he is told either to hate or to re-arm.' The letter urged the rich nations to afford economic and technical assistance to the poor nations on such a scale as will eventually assure an effective response to the needs of the underprivileged. For 'the people have seen the vision of social justice; it is for us to help to transform it into reality'. And the letter affirmed that the saying, 'from each according to his ability, to each according to his need', has its roots in the teachings of Jesus.

This letter was on the whole well received. There were, as usual, criticisms from the right. They pointed out that the statement about ability and need was a quotation from the writings of Lenin, but the objectors did not realize that Lenin had not invented it and that the same idea could even be found in Calvin's commentary on the epistles to the Corinthians. There were also some criticisms from the left. But there were many positive reactions.

In May I received a letter from Dr T. C. Chao, one of the Presidents chosen by the Amsterdam Assembly, which showed that the crisis was by no means over. Dr Chao wrote that as a patriotic Chinese he had to protest against the Toronto statement on Korea 'which sounds so much like the voice of Wall Street' and that he wished to resign from the office of President.

It was paradoxical that in that very same year, 1951, when the relations between the World Council and the churches in countries under a communist regime were reduced to a minimum, there was one occasion on which hundreds of thousands of Christians from the Eastern and the Western side of the 'curtain' could meet together. This was the *Kirchentag* in Berlin. I had been in close touch with the *Kirchentag* movement since its beginning in Hannover in 1949, and had been a speaker at the mass meeting among the ruins of Essen in 1950. Reinold von Thadden, the father of the *Kirchentag* movement, had shared with me his vision of the *Kirchentag* as a great force of renewal which would reach the grass-roots and mobilize Christian laymen. He wanted to bring into the life of every congregation what he had learned and received in the Student Christian Movement, the World's Student Christian Federation and the World Council about a radical, world-transforming Christianity with an ecumenical perspective. And the wonderful thing was that the response of the people to the invitation was overwhelming. This Berlin *Kirchentag* had a far larger attendance than any of its predecessors. I was one of the speakers at the closing meeting in the stadium built by Hitler for the 1936 Olympic games. Every place was taken and there were almost as many people in the overflow meetings as in the stadium itself. Von Thadden rightly remarked that during these days the Iron Curtain had practically been removed. But it was also an occasion when Western Christians could learn some important lessons from their brethren living in the East. One of the participants from the West put it this way to a man from the East: 'We thought we had come to encourage you, but we go away encouraged by you.' For the

Christians who stood up for their faith in spite of all ideological pressure had found a quality of Christian life which was not often found among Christians living in easier circumstances.

The Central Committee met again in August 1951 in Rolle on the shores of Lake Geneva. In the light of all that had happened during the last year it had been decided that one of the main themes of discussion would be: 'The Role of the World Council of Churches in time of Tension.' Bishop Eivind Berggrav of Oslo, who had become a President of the World Council after the resignation of Archbishop Eidem of Sweden, was to be the main speaker on the subject. This time Eastern Europe was represented. Bishop Bereczky had come with the clear intention of continuing to challenge the action which the World Council had taken with regard to the Korea crisis and indeed the general policy of the World Council concerning international affairs.

Bishop Berggrav gave a truly pastoral address. Two characteristic sentences were: 'I find that the New Testament demands of me that I shall be willing to accept as a full brother in Christ a man who seems to me perhaps quite dangerous in his political or economic views', and: 'Do remember that even tensions may be hidden blessings'. Happily Bishop Bereczky responded at the same level. While he maintained his objections against the World Council's statements on Korea, he expressed his gratitude for Berggrav's approach and said that we had now experienced what was the soul of the ecumenical movement. The further discussion also showed that this was not an attempt to drown all real problems in a sea of sentimental brotherhood. For Bereczky was strongly challenged concerning the apparently inadequate reaction of the Hungarian churches to acts of injustice committed in their country. And Bereczky came back with his radical questions concerning Western policies. But there was no breach of fellowship. So when we had to answer the letter of Dr Chao we could say with conviction: 'We rejoice that we can together affirm our common faith and our common loyalty to Jesus Christ, our Lord and Saviour. And we express the hope that in spite of all that has happened and may happen, we will remain united in the oneness of Christ and in intercession for each other.'

A further complicating factor at this time was the activity of Myron Taylor, still acting on behalf of President Truman. After the failure of his approach to the World Council in 1948 which I have described already, the President and Mr Taylor had worked out a new proposal. The President would invite the heads of the Christian churches to come to Washington and to work together on a joint statement concerning peace and concerning common resistance to communism. When Mr Taylor submitted this proposal to two of the presidents of the World Council, Pastor Marc Boegner in Paris and the Archbishop of Canterbury in London, both turned it down. It was inconceivable that church leaders should come to Washington to work out a common statement under the auspices of the President of the United States. Pastor Boegner had had occasion in 1950 to tell President Truman personally that the churches were working for peace, but that they could not possibly participate at the request of a temporal power in a crusade the political and religious character of which would endanger their spiritual independence.[2] But Mr Taylor returned to the attack. The form which the proposal now took was that the Pope and the leaders of the World Council of Churches should produce a common statement along the lines of President Truman's ideas. In the summer of 1951 he met in London with the Archbishop of Canterbury, the Archbishop of York, the Bishop of Chichester and Presiding Bishop Sherrill of the Protestant Episcopal Church in the United States. The difficulty on this as on earlier similar occasions was that it was not clear what President Truman and Mr Taylor had in mind. The Archbishop of Canterbury wrote: 'He (Mr Taylor) never made up his mind whether he wanted the Christian leaders to be peace-makers or leaders of a crusade.' He could give no assurance that the Pope would be willing to co-operate in this plan. In these circumstances the Anglican leaders came to the conclusion that the plan ought to be abandoned.

Now it happened that in 1950 the Synod of the Reformed Church of France had adopted a resolution requesting the World Council of Churches to appeal to the churches outside its constituency to agree that all churches together should co-ordinate their efforts and unite their prayers 'so that the peace of God may come upon the nations'. This request had been considered by the World Council's Executive Committee, but after a long discussion the committee came to a negative conclusion. For in the light of the information available through several channels it was quite clear that it would be impossible to get agreement on any substantial appeal between the Vatican, the Moscow Patriarchate and the World Council of Churches. So the report of the Executive Committee to the meeting of the Central Committee in the summer of 1951 contained this sentence: 'For the World Council of Churches to seek to join with great churches outside its membership in a general peace appeal now is not a practicable policy and its pursuit would not help the general situation.'

When Mr Taylor saw this report he must have taken this sentence, which was originally simply an answer to a member church of the World Council, as a public repudiation of the plan on which President Truman and he were working. On September 28th President Truman reacted sharply. He said publicly that he had for some time tried to bring the leaders of the churches together, but that they had been unable 'to say, with one voice, that Christ is their Master and Redeemer and the source of their strength against the hosts of irreligion and danger to the world and that will be the cause of world catastrophe'. Very soon afterwards the President announced that he would propose the appointment of an ambassador to the Vatican. The reaction of the Protestant churches was however so strong that within three months the proposal was withdrawn.

My role in this tangled episode was to disentangle the various developments. At the end of a long letter to Franklin Clark Fry in which I tried to analyse what had really happened I wrote: 'The misunderstanding which has arisen between

President Truman and the church leaders is not half as serious as the misunderstanding which would have arisen if we had given any encouragement to Mr
Taylor in his confused plans of mixing up Church and State.' Fry expressed his
agreement in much stronger phraseology than mine.

I believe that it was in this same period that I received a discreet inquiry
whether we would be interested in having an ambassador from the USA
accredited to the World Council in Geneva. I replied that I could only give a
very provisional reaction, which was that I had no idea what to do with such an
ambassador. Fortunately no more was heard about this. For was it not like asking
the manager of a chinashop, after he had had a visit from a bull, whether he
would like to have the bull as a permanent guest?

But there were other suitors as well. The World Peace Council, which was
advocating some of the main aims of Soviet foreign policy, had sent us a number
of communications asking the World Council of Churches to participate in its
activities and to support its policies. But this would also have meant giving away
the independence of the World Council. It was however agreed that some of the
leaders of the CCIA and I, as General Secretary, should meet with the President
of the World Council of Peace, Monsieur Joliot-Curie, and some of his
colleagues. This meeting took place in Paris, in November 1951. We had a frank
and interesting discussion in which it became clear that while we were all
deeply concerned about disarmament, about the control of atomic weapons and
about the peaceful co-existence of different political and social regimes, there
were vital differences between the basic conceptions and the approaches of the
two bodies concerned. I considered it quite a compliment when one of the
delegates of the World Peace Council said to me: 'Our meeting with you has
been much more peaceful than our meeting with the Quakers.'

In such manner did the World Council try to find its own way through the
virgin-forest of international politics during the years of the cold war.

NOTES

1. *The Ecumenical Review*, April 1951, p. 267.
2. See his article in *Le Figaro*, November 11th 1951.

AT THE TIME of its inauguration in 1948 the World Council was still very largely Western in its composition and orientation. Asia, Africa and Latin America had been represented by able delegates at the first Assembly, but there were so few of them, and the post-war problems of the West had demanded so much attention, that the Assembly had not yet adopted a truly ecumenical, world-wide perspective. It was especially urgent to give a much greater place to Asia. For it was precisely in these post-war years that Asia was going through the greatest transformation of its history. As Dr Panikkar, the Indian historian and diplomat, put it, the end of the 'Vasco da Gama period' had come. After 450 years, during which the life of most Asian nations had been dominated by Western political, cultural and religious influence, the Asian peoples had become independent and were beginning to take their own place in the life of the world. Asian Christianity was therefore clearly confronted with a new task.

But could we really speak of an Asian Christianity? The result of missionary work in Asia carried out by a large number of missionary societies of different Western countries had been that each Asian church had a much closer relation to a specific Western church than it had to other Asian churches. The effective channels of communication were those between the younger churches and the sending churches in the West with which they were connected. The Asian churches had not yet discovered each other.

The first ecumenical job to be done in Asia was therefore to initiate a process of sharing between these churches. In 1948 Stephen Neill, at that time associate general secretary of the World Council, discussed the matter with a group of East Asian church leaders who had come together in Manila. It was agreed that the World Council and the International Missionary Council should convene a representative conference in Bangkok in 1949 to work out concrete proposals. Charles Ranson, the General Secretary of the International Missionary Council, and I were to attend this meeting together. We decided to use this opportunity to make a common visit to the Indonesian churches. Ranson's presence would underline the fact that I was coming in the first place as the representative of the World Council of Churches rather than as a Dutchman, and I could help Ranson through my many contacts in the country.

We arrived at a crucial moment in the history of Indonesia. The second 'police action' had led to an uneasy armistice in May 1949. One part of the country was being governed by the Indonesian republic of Dr Sukarno with its seat of government in Jogjakarta and the other part was still under Dutch administration centred in Batavia (soon to become Djakarta). But the Round Table Conference in The Hague had just decided that sovereignty would be transferred to the United States of Indonesia at the end of December. Thus our visit in November came at a moment when on one side of the demarcation line there were the problems of the last days of colonial rule and on the other side those of the first stage of independence. We wanted of course to visit Christians in both conditions.

In Djakarta church leaders from all parts of the country were meeting to form a Council of Churches of Indonesia. We were struck by the fact that the meeting was dominated by the younger men who had received a better education and felt more at home in the new world. The issue of the full independence of the churches was no longer an open question. Missionaries would be welcome, but it was clearly understood that their role was to be purely advisory. And there was a strong desire for church unity. Ranson and I asked whether the strong emphasis on the churchly character of the council would not lead to a down-grading of evangelism. But the subsequent development showed that the Indonesian churches were deeply aware of their missionary calling.

I visited the High Commissioner of the Crown, Mr Antonius Lovink, with whom I had worked together in the early days of the 'Swiss Road', in 1942 and 1943. He received me in the same palace in which my wife's uncle, Governor General de Jonge, had received us in 1933. I remembered how convinced our uncle had been that Dutch rule over Indonesia would last indefinitely. Now there remained just a few weeks before sovereignty would be transferred to the Indonesian people.

Lovink was worried about the immediate future. Was there not a danger of a breakdown of law and order? It was, he said, extremely difficult to know what advice should be given to the Dutch people in the more disturbed areas of the country. I could only express my deep sympathy with him at a time when he was carrying such an impossibly heavy responsibility.

We succeeded in getting permission to fly across the demarcation line to Jogjakarta, the seat of the Republican government. We were well received by the church leaders and the representatives of the governmental office for religious affairs. President Sukarno gave us an unhurried audience. We told him about our mission and about the forthcoming Bangkok Conference. He spoke with the self-confidence and the straightforwardness of a leader who had reached his main goal. His interest in and knowledge about Christian leaders was remarkable. He asked us about John R. Mott and about C. F. Andrews, the English friend of Mahatma Gandhi. When we brought up the question of religious liberty he said that in the new Indonesia all religions would enjoy full freedom. That was implied in the first of the five basic principles of the republic, the Pantja Sila. Missionary activity would continue, provided that the missionaries were wanted by the religious communities. He brought up the issue of communism and stated rather surprisingly that there were more communists in the United States than in Indonesia. They would have freedom of expression, but if they caused disturbances, they would feel the iron hand of the state.

He showed us his collection of paintings and said 'I am crazy about paintings.' I remember especially some extremely impressive and haunting pictures of Indonesian guerilla-fighters.

During this first meeting Sukarno did not make on me the impression of a great demagogue. He was not giving himself airs. I even wondered whether he might become another Nehru. The Sukarno whom I was to meet later, after he had been in power for several years, would make a very different impression.

In conversation with the pastors of the Church of Central Java we learned how they had been hurt by the fact that the Dutch, the people from whom they had received the Gospel, had bombarded Jogjakarta on a Sunday morning and that a large group of young men had been arrested by Dutch soldiers at the end of a church service. I could only answer that there were Dutch Christians who did realize what these things meant for them and felt deeply about it themselves. We came very close together. When they asked me to close with prayer I was glad to have the chance of praying with them in Dutch for their country.

In East Java we had to face a delicate problem. The Christians in that area were deeply concerned about the tragedy that had taken place in the Christian village of Peniwen. Dutch soldiers had shot six male nurses of the Christian hospital, although there was no proof that these men had been involved in any form of guerilla activity. Now I had heard already in Djakarta that leaders of the republican army wanted us to act as a 'commission of enquiry into the atrocities committed by the Dutch army'. This was of course out of the question, for it would have made our visit a highly political rather than an ecumenical affair. So when the leaders of the East Java church told us that they had made the necessary arrangements for a visit to Peniwen, Ranson and I reacted that we could not accept this proposal, for our visit would surely be exploited for political purposes. But they were so unhappy about our refusal and felt so strongly that our coming to East Java would be meaningless if we did not go to Peniwen, that we changed our minds. We asked however for a definite promise that the only information given to the press would be given by the church itself and that it would be made quite clear that the visit would have a fraternal Christian and not a political character.

I described the visit in my travel diary in this way:

Off we go with three cars. Near the end of the Dutch-occupied territory held up and sent back to a captain, who refuses to take responsibility to let us go on, makes nasty remarks about the T.N.I.[1] and sends us back many miles to the commander of the battalion. At that moment we all thought that we would never get to Peniwen. But the commander proves to be a most understanding person. We tell him the whole story. He warns us against the risks involved. Peniwen is TNI-territory and it may be quite unsafe. But we answer that we have in our party several men of considerable influence in TNI circles and that the TNI will surely put its best foot forward. The other risk is that we may be used for propaganda. But we tell him that we have a definite promise from the Javanese Christian leaders. So he allows us to go on. We pass into territory. Since the road is destroyed we leave the cars behind and begin our walk of 7 kilometres. In front wild-looking TNI soldiers with stenguns and several with long black hair. (Charles calls them the 'glamour-girls'). A TNI officer says: 'That is in order that the monkeys may not be frightened when we live in the woods.' But in fact it is because of the oath not to cut one's hair till freedom is achieved.

Beautiful (but terribly warm) walk through the Javanese countryside. Sawahs, clean dessas, fine views of the mountains; everywhere curious faces (when have they last seen white men on a peaceful visit?). At last quite high up Peniwen, one of the largest Christian villages in Java. Friendly greetings everywhere. Crowds assembled, at first a little shy, later surrounding us on all sides. Reception in the big parsonage. Lots of TNI officers, nearly all of them Christians. (The 16th brigade of Warouw contains many Menadonese and Ambonese.)

Mardjo Sir[2] plays the game and explains to all that we have come to make a fraternal visit to the Christians of Peniwen, not for political reasons, and that no one is to write in the press about us except the synod. This seems to be acceptable. We go to the big church. Some 500 to 600 people stream into the church. In front the elders, most impressive looking very old Javanese wise men. On the left the TNI officers. On the right the women, many with small children. Even a friendly dog walks around during the service. We sing 'The Church's One Foundation' which Mardjo Sir has brought back from the Amsterdam Assembly and translated. Short address by the local pastor (I Cor. 12) and by Mardjo Sir who speaks on Christian unity. I also make a short speech on the common membership in the Body. You are part of that body together with Christians of all nations. Other Christians know about your suffering. But when Christians suffer they come to know the Spirit, which consoles us. This at Mardjo Sir's request in English. He whispers that they think that I come from Switzerland. But he adds that I may pray in whatever language I like. So I pray in Dutch for the congregation of Peniwen, for those who have suffered, for those who are the cause of this suffering, for the Indonesian church and nation. Charles speaks briefly in the same spirit. More singing and the short service is over. It should be noted that the programme for the service which was shown to us upon arrival contained also: statement on the events at Peniwen in February 1949. But Mardjo Sir had cut that out of the programme in view of our understanding. After the service pictures of our party surrounded by the Peniwen crowds. Then a meal. Conversation with TNI Christian officers who say that Warouw remains an active Christian who always carries his New Testament. It is not true – they say – that he has communist leanings. Optimism about the future. I make a short speech in Dutch to thank the TNI for their courtesy and friendliness. The commander answers that they had expected such a visit long ago and that they are glad that we have come at last. We go to the special graveyard where the six victims (male nurses of the clinic) have been buried and see the small hospital which is in bad condition. But not the slightest attempt is made to turn the visit into a demonstration. More pictures. We leave, a very cordial 'Come again!', children follow us part of the way. Once again seven kilometres in steaming heat and once again longhaired TNI in front with dangerous looking stenguns. The Javanese Christian leaders deeply grateful for this day. 'This is a blessing for us', says Mardjo Sir.

Ranson went to Menado and I visited faraway Amboina, an almost wholly Christianized part of Indonesia where the visit had a festive character. I was received at the airport by two flute orchestras and a choir. When I had to speak in an isolated village I made the mistake of presenting myself as a postman from the world-wide fellowship of Christians. The trouble was that they had never seen a postman.

Then together again to Sumatra. For the third time we had to cross a demarcation line to get to the heart of the Batak country on the shores of the magnificent Toba lake. We were deeply impressed by the vigour of the Batak church, which was just holding its general synod. It was still a rapidly growing church. We preached to very large congregations. But the church had to face grave problems. With their congregations now totalling one thousand they needed far more pastors than they had. They hoped that they could get help from other churches, but were at the same time afraid that help might mean foreign influence.

We visited their school for the blind, where the pupils sang for us a hymn describing their longing for a world where there would be no more darkness. We were so moved that we tried to sing for them as best we could 'The Church's One Foundation'. Their reaction showed that they understood the message we wanted to convey.

The Batak church leaders accompanied us to the demarcation line where an enterprising Chinese had opened a small restaurant with the well-chosen name: 'Neuteral'. I do not know whether this name was meant to be Indonesian or Dutch or Esperanto. But it was clear that customers from both the Indonesian and the Dutch armies were welcomed. Each group however practised complete apartheid. So when our little party, composed of the different races and nationalities sat down at one and the same table, we created a mild sensation. We felt that this little demonstration of Christian living together in a divided world was a good final summary of the mission which we had been privileged to fulfil in Indonesia.

The Bangkok Conference which came next, was the first meeting of church-leaders from all over East Asia. It had both the qualities and the defects of a *première*. There was the joy of getting to know fellow-Christians with similar problems and similar concerns. And there was the lack of experience in the technique (and language) of ecumenical communication. The leadership was in the competent hands of Dr Rajah B. Manikam of India and Dr S. C. Leung of China, who lived in Hongkong. Practically all East Asian countries were re-presented, but the Chinese churches had sent a message saying that they were unable to send a delegation, although they felt closely bound to the ecumenical movement. I was somewhat disappointed to find that the conference had so little to say on the issue of the relevance of the Christian message to the cultural heritage of Asia. Paul Devanandan of India gave a brilliant address on the sub-ject, but the following discussion was meagre. My impression was that this was due to the fact that the Asian churches were now inclined to take a defensive attitude. In the process of nation-building after independence the traditional cultural heritage of each country was being rediscovered and the national religions were asserting themselves. This created a more difficult situation for the Christian minorities. So the churches were rather afraid of being over-whelmed by the surrounding culture.

But I believed that the way forward was – as Devanandan had shown – not to take a merely defensive attitude, but to come to grips with the new situation. At the time when the Asian cultures had to face the new problems arising in a dynamic modern society, Christianity could and should render its witness *within* these cultures.

The conference was much more creative in the field of social ethics. The committee on 'The Church in Social and Political Life', ably led by M. M. Thomas of India, produced a remarkable report[3] which contained one of the best statements on the Christian attitude towards communism that had ever been made by an ecumenical meeting. It described communism as a judgment on the churches for their failure to stand for social justice, but it emphasized at the same time the inherent weakness of communism, in that it lacked a concep-tion of the independence of moral reality over against power.

The most important decision of the meeting, adopted unanimously, was to recommend to the International Missionary Council and the World Council of Churches that a joint secretary of the two organizations be appointed to work among churches and Christian councils of Eastern Asia, to help the churches to share more fully their thought and experience and to establish closer contacts between these churches and councils and the world-wide ecumenical movement. It was added that this joint secretary should be an Asian. This recommendation was later accepted by both the IMC and the WCC so that Dr Manikam of India could begin his pioneering work in East Asia in 1951.

After the conference Ranson and I made a short visit to Hongkong where we met many Chinese Christians and missionaries who had just come out of China. It was difficult to get any clear picture of the situation of the church in China for the revolution was still in its early stage, the policy of the new government with regard to religion had not yet been worked out and the Chinese Christians seemed to have different views as to the attitude they should take. But it was clear that the churches in China were entering into a time of trial.

Ranson went to Japan and I went to Burma. Burma was going through a national crisis. Civil war had broken out in several parts of the country. There were simultaneous insurrections started by the communists on the one hand and by the Karen ethnic minority on the other. Now the main strength of the Protestant churches was precisely in the Karen area, and many leaders of the insurrection were Christians. So the relations between the Buddhist Burmese and the Christian Karens had become strained. The Buddhist majority felt that Karens were playing into the hands of the communists and thus endangering the newly gained independence of the nation. The Karens did not trust the Buddhist government and did not believe that it would grant them true autonomy and religious freedom.

I had a long conversation with Prime Minister U Nu. To reach his residence I had to pass through several barriers guarded by machine-gunners. But he himself seemed to be a genuine peace-loving Buddhist. He was deeply concerned about the worsening of the relations between the Buddhists and the Christians and assured me that he believed deeply in religious liberty. On the basis of conversations I had had with Christian friends and especially with the courageous Mrs Ba Maung Chain, who was constantly working for peace, I raised the question whether it would not be possible to invite a group of neutral persons, preferably from other Asian countries, to act as mediators. But the Prime Minister felt that this would be a dangerous precedent and that the people of Burma had to solve their problems themselves. I was more successful when I called attention to the fact that the Baptist pastor who had represented the Burma Baptist Church at the Amsterdam Assembly had been in prison for a year and that no trial had taken place. The Prime Minister promised to look into the case, and the pastor was indeed released soon after my visit.

The Christian leaders to whom I reported my conversation with the Prime Minister felt that in spite of what he had said the only hope for peace was that there should be strong pressure from other Asian leaders, and that the man who because of his prestige had most chance of success was Pandit Jawaharlal Nehru. So they asked me to take this up with Nehru, and I agreed to do so.

I went again to visit the famous Shwe Dagon Pagoda which is one of the most important Buddhist centres in the world. I had three surprises. In one of the temples I found Dutch tiles representing the city of Dordrecht from which my family had come. I was shown a pagoda which was set apart for the Moral Rearmament movement for, as the priest pointed out, 'There is no difference between the principles of Moral Rearmament and those of Buddhism.' And I was introduced to the General Secretary of the World Buddhist Association, a 'colleague' whose professional problems were probably quite similar to mine.

When I came to New Delhi I tried to get a private appointment with Prime Minister Nehru. Instead, I was invited to a luncheon in the garden of his residence with a good many other people. Nehru was obviously in the mood of a man who had to cope with an overwhelming task and wanted to use the hours away from his desk as hours of relaxation. He said that luncheons were held in the garden because that was his only chance of coming into the garden. When the secretary of an international student organization was presented to him and explained its aims, Nehru became impatient with the fine phrases used by his guest and interrupted him saying: 'But what are you *doing?*' When the well-known politician, Krishna Menon, arrived Nehru embraced him and said: 'Menon, you are just an inverted snob.' So it was not easy to get him to listen to the proposal concerning Burma which I had promised to submit to him. His answer was that the fighting in Burma had been meaningless from the very beginning, that he would be ready to go to Burma for a short visit to help in the pacification of the country, but that he could only do so if he were invited by the Burmese government. This seemed to me an encouraging answer and I transmitted it immediately to Mrs Ba Maung Chain in Rangoon. But the invitation was never issued and the civil war in Burma went on for a long time.

I attended the second synod of the Church of South India in Madras. I was glad to get to know this church at first hand, for it had and still has a unique place in the ecumenical movement. It had brought together in one church congregations of Anglican, Methodist, Presbyterian and Congregationalist background. The outcome of this attempt to unite traditions which had seemed to be incomparable with each other would certainly have a considerable influence on the future of the movement towards church unity. Now the church had been in existence for two-and-a-half years. For my sermon at the opening service in Madras Cathedral I took as my text: 'For we share in Christ, if only we hold our first confidence firm to the end.' I spoke of the common danger in the life of the World Council and of the Church of South India. Now that we were no longer moving in the sphere of ideas but in the sphere of everyday realities we might easily lose the original confidence with which we had started. But I found that much of the *élan* with which the church had been formed was still present. I was specially impressed with the remarkable new liturgy for the communion service which was used for the first time at this meeting. And I found that there was no reason to fear that episcopacy as understood in this church would lead to a prelatical and authoritarian form of church government, for there was a healthy democratic atmosphere in the meetings.

From Madras to Travancore, the state where the Syrian Orthodox Christians form such a large part of the population. I arrived at a critical moment in the life of the Syrian Orthodox Church. A serious conflict had arisen between those who desired complete autonomy for the church in Travancore and those who defended the right of the Patriarch of Antioch to govern the church. This conflict had gone on for almost four decades and had created much friction and bitterness. Now a group of young people had formed a 'Peace League'. They had succeeded in creating a strong movement in favour of reconciliation. So the bishops had at last agreed to meet together to arrive at a solution of the conflict.

The young leaders of the Peace League told me what had happened during the three days preceding my arrival. I wrote their story down as follows:

The Peace League makes all necessary arrangements for the meeting. Two hundred picked volunteers of the League surround the Mar seminary (where the bishops are in conference). No one is to be allowed into the seminary whom the League does not trust as a constructive element in the situation. The bishops agree on the two principles that the Patriarch of Antioch is the head of the Church and that the Jacobite Syrian Church in India must have its own Catholicate. But they do not agree on more detailed arrangements. At this point the League intervenes and gets two laymen from each side together to draw up an agreement. The bishops are not willing to accept this statement. This is the critical moment. Processions around the seminary with shouts of 'Blessed are the peacemakers', 'Peace or Death'. Spontaneously the 200 volunteers declare that they will fast unto death unless the agreement is signed. The penitential psalms are recited. At last the bishops sign. General rejoicing.

Now that it was all over, the Peace League leaders wondered whether they had done right. Had they exerted too much moral pressure? I took the line that the danger of their attitude seemed to lie in their 'peace at any cost' slogan. Peace is not the highest ideal for the Church. Should they not become a *Life*-movement rather than a *Peace*-movement? The great need was for spiritual revival, for evangelism, for volunteers for the priesthood. Those who are willing to fast unto death for the Church should be willing to devote their lives to the Christian ministry. We had a very searching conversation on these matters and prayed together.

I was so deeply impressed by these fully committed young churchmen that I promised them that in my contacts with church leaders I would back up their peace efforts as strongly as I could. So when I dined with the Catholicos, the head of the church in Travancore, and later with Mar Julius, the delegate of the Patriarch of Antioch, I emphasized strongly that the unity of the Syrian Orthodox Church was not only important for the life of the church itself, but also for the whole Christian cause in India and in Asia generally. In further meetings with the ministers of the Travancore government and with businessmen I found a strong desire for peace in the church and for a renewal of its life. One of the men, the editor of a newspaper who had already spent years in prison because of his political convictions, said that he would be willing to return to prison for the sake of peace in the church.

This journey was concluded by a visit to Ceylon. My friend, D. T. Niles, had obtained permission to use, for youth meetings, the big church built by the Dutch in the eighteenth century, but now out of use and in a state of decay. I was the first Dutch pastor to preach there since the end of the eighteenth century. But I did not speak to Dutch soldiers and civil servants or Ceylonese who had come in order to please the authorities and who sat stiffly on their benchs. I spoke for young Christians sitting on mats, a company made as colourful as a tulip field by the saris of the girls and wholly spontaneous in their reactions. As Jetty and I later looked around in the church we found the tomb of a member of her family who had been commander of Jaffna and had died there at the age of thirty-nine, in 1737.

Two years later in 1952 the third World Conference of Christian Youth was held in Kottayam, in the South Indian state of Travancore, the home of the ancient Syrian Orthodox Church. I was one of the speakers. The eager interest of the Travancore people in our meeting was overwhelming. The delegates stayed with local families, visited congregations, and every night the main square was filled with thousands of people who came to hear what the young Christians from all over the world had to tell them about their faith, their problems, their hopes. During the conference the nineteen-hundredth anniversary of the coming of St Thomas to India was celebrated. The festival began with a procession of all conference delegates, many of them in national costumes, and preceded by two towering elephants carrying icons of St Thomas. In this solemn atmosphere the brass band introduced a note of gaiety by playing tunes belonging to the repertoire of student festivities rather than to ecclesiastical ceremonies. At the meeting place the crowd was so large that the speakers had to shout at the top of their voices. Leaders of all the different Christian churches – Syrian Orthodox, Uniate, Assyrian, Mar Thoma, South India and Roman Catholic – were present. The addresses were characterized by a sober note. The Catholicos of the Syrian Orthodox Church said: 'I see before my eyes a replica of the ecumenical movement. During the nineteen centuries of our existence we had not been blessed with an occasion like this. Let this be a prologue to the fulfilment of our Lord's desire that they all be one.' Dr John Matthai, the Syrian Orthodox layman who had been Minister of Finance in the Indian government, called on the church to re-christianize itself in order to fulfil its calling. I thanked the Travancore Christians for the faithfulness which they had shown through the centuries and expressed the conviction that their preservation surely meant that God desired to use their church as an instrument of witness in India and in Asia.

The Central Committee of the World Council of Churches met in Lucknow immediately after the Kottayam meeting. We were the guests of Isabella Thoburn College, of which Sarah Chakko, the first woman to become a President of the World Council, was the Principal. We were not prepared for two complicating factors: an epidemic of influenza which resulted in our Philippine delegate, a medical doctor, having to take care of thirty or forty cases of 'flu at the same time, and the ubiquitous monkeys. My room was near a main road. One evening I heard moans such as men utter who suffer from acute pain. Had there been an accident? I could see nobody in the road. After a while I discovered a monkey on a roof holding his stomach which had obviously absorbed more than it could stand.

Dr Radakrishnan, the President of India, and Prime Minister Nehru came to speak to us. I was once again impressed by Nehru's personality. He had now become the most powerful man in India and played an important role in world politics. But one had the feeling that in his case power had not been a corrupting influence. He was big enough to refrain from demagogy. Speaking without any notes he gave us an incisive and comprehensive report on the international situation as he saw it. The discussion with Dr Radakrishnan was not easy. On the one hand he seemed to come close to the Christian position, but when it came to the deepest issues he asked us Christians to give up our central affirmations and to accept a broad religious relativism.

This was the first meeting of our Central Committee in Asia. Sarah Chakko (whom we were not to see again since she died soon afterwards) said at the closing service that this meeting was for her the fulfilment of a long-felt desire, for the Council had been too Western in its orientation and needed to be confronted with the Asian situation.

By 1956 the time had come to consider whether the relationship which had been developed between the churches in Asia should receive a permanent organizational expression. As East Asia secretary of the International Missionary Council and the World Council of Churches, Dr Rajah B. Manikam had succeeded in giving the East Asian churches a new sense of belonging together, and this had found expression in the sending of Asian missionaries to other areas in Asia. What should be the next step? There were different opinions. All agreed that Asia should have its own regional ecumenical body. But some Americans and Asians were working on the creation of an Asia Council on Ecumenical Mission which would take over the administration of the work in Asia for which assorted European and American mission boards had been responsible. Others thought in terms of a council which would concentrate on co-ordination and stimulation rather than on administration. At another consultation in Bangkok in 1956 it was finally agreed that the question of the future shape of ecumenical co-operation in Asia should be submitted to a representative conference of Asian churches and councils of churches.

Out of this consultation came a considerable advance in the planning of the integration of the International Missionary Council and the World Council of Churches. In order to escape from the heat of Bangkok we held a number of the discussions on this subject in the swimming pool of the Royal Sports Club. The cool water had a most beneficial effect on our thinking!

In the following year, 1957, the representative meeting of the churches and councils of churches from that vast area between Japan and Pakistan or between Korea and Australia was held at Prapat in the highlands of Sumatra, the territory of the Batak Church. The degree of hospitality we received was illustrated by the fact that the civil war which was going on in the region observed a cease-fire for the duration of our meeting. The conference was preceded by a *Kirchentag* attended by many tens of thousands of Batak Christians. The task of our preacher, D. T. Niles of Ceylon, was not made any easier by the fact that the crowd was looking forward to the great moment when President Sukarno would arrive. When he came there was great excitement. He knew exactly how to awaken the patriotic emotions of his audience. Sitting near him I could feel the electric current established between the leader and the mass.

Later on that day the President held a reception for the conference delegates. Just before he came in an adjutant appeared to see whether the arrangement of the room was to his liking. He discovered just above the President's chair a Dutch advertisement for Heineken's beer. When he removed this with some difficulty I could not help turning to my neighbour and saying: 'There goes the last vestige of Dutch culture!'

The Prapat conference was wholly in the hands of the Asian churchmen. The representatives of Western missionary societies and of the international bodies took the back seats in a literal and in a figurative sense. The dominating theme was 'The Common Evangelistic Task in Asia'. It was now clear that the initiative in missionary work would henceforth be taken by the Asian churches and that the task of the sister churches in other continents would be a supportive one. It was decided to set up an East Asia Christian Conference as an organ of continuing co-operation among the churches and Christian councils in East Asia. Australia and New Zealand were 'adopted' by the Asians.

Were we witnessing an ecclesiastical edition of the Bandung Conference of 1955 where statesmen of twenty-nine Asian countries had affirmed the solidarity of the Asian peoples over against the West? Some messages received from political leaders spoke indeed of the analogy between Prapat and Bandung. But there was an important difference. The Asian Christians at Prapat certainly believed that their churches and their countries should draw together, that they had common problems and a common task. But there was nothing exclusive or introverted in their sense of solidarity. And one strong argument for their regional ecumenism was that it would make the voice of Asian churches more clearly heard in the worldwide ecumenical movement.

On the Sunday the conference delegates visited various Batak congregations. I went by boat to the island of Samosir. The Toba Lake is the most beautiful lake that I know anywhere in the world. There is a pristine purity in the proportions and colours of the scenery that makes one think of the very beginnings of creation when God saw the world 'and behold it was good'. The congregation expressed their hospitality by the fine singing for which the Batak people have a special talent.

The proposals of the Prapat conference were so well received that in 1959, at Kuala Lumpur in Malaya, the inaugural assembly of the East Asia Christian Conference could be held. In one of the 'John R. Mott Lectures' which I gave at that meeting I expressed my gratitude that the East Asia Christian Conference had come into being before the World Council of Churches held its Assembly in Asia. For the World Council would not come to a geographical area named Asia where there happened to be a number of member churches. It would come to a family of churches which had a common understanding of their task and a common contribution to make to the larger family.

In 1959 I went by the polar route to Japan to represent the World Council at the celebration of the centenary of the member churches of the National Council of Churches in Japan. The spirit of the meetings was realistic rather than triumphalistic. For the expectations which had been entertained at various times, and especially after the second world war, that large numbers of Japanese would turn to Christianity had not been fulfilled. There had never been a mass movement to the churches as in many other Asian regions. As I visited the impressive headquarters of some of the so-called new religions which express traditional Japanese piety in new forms and which regularly hold assemblies of some hundred thousand adherents, I realized that in Japan the Christian church will for a long time remain a small minority.

However small the numbers the quality of Christian thought and Christian life in Japan was impressive. In no other country outside Europe could one find such awareness of all the modern trends of theology. And Christian laymen could be found in many positions of leadership. But I asked the question whether it had not been too easily taken for granted that Japan was becoming a 'Western' country and that a 'Western' type of Christianity would meet its spiritual need. Had sufficient attention been given to those elements in Japanese life which had not changed?

For even during a short stay one could notice that the modern Japan had not really replaced the old Japan. My friend, Mrs Takeda Cho, Professor of Sociology, threw a great deal of light on the situation when she explained that the Japanese were really living in a two storey-house. There was the storey of traditional Japanese life and there was the storey of modern civilization. And the staircase between the two stories had not yet been built.

I had told my Japanese hosts that my great-grandfather had visited Japan in 1834, twenty years before Japan ceased to live in splendid isolation from the rest of the world. At that time the Dutch were the only foreigners who had permission to maintain a small commercial settlement in Japan. My great-grandfather had been the captain of a Dutch frigate which had made the long journey of fifteen months to the East Indies, to Japan and back to Holland. We have still in the family several fine Japanese paintings, on one of which the ship is seen as it lies at anchor near the island of Decima, in the bay of Nagasaki.

My Japanese friends invited me immediately to visit Nagasaki. In spite of the atomic bombardment there was still a good deal to be seen of the period of Dutch-Japanese commerce. I was taken to the oldest restaurant in the city. The hostess told us that in the old days this had been a favourite place of the Dutch officers. Looking at the considerable display of different dishes I asked her whether any of these foods had been introduced by the Dutch. She asked me whether I recognized any of them. I pointed to a sort of meatball and asked her what it was called. The Japanese word was clearly derived from the Dutch.

In 1966 just before I retired from my post as General Secretary of the World Council, I went to Asia to attend the Hongkong Conference of the East Asia Christian Conference. The Indonesian church leaders invited me to visit Indonesia on my way to Hongkong. I knew that I would receive a friendly reception but I was not prepared for the very warm welcome given me. There was no longer the slightest need to feel self-conscious about being a Dutchman in a country which had liberated itself from Dutch rule. The time had come to start a new chapter, but we could build on old friendships which had been maintained in the most critical period. I was asked to preach in Dutch in one of the large churches in Djakarta. No Dutch sermon had been preached in the city for eight years. At a reception given by the Council of Churches Dr Johannes Leimena, the vice-premier with whom I had closely collaborated at the time of the 1933 World Student Christian Federation conference in Java, was the main speaker. I had heard how at the time of the crisis, in 1965, when communist leaders attempted a *coup d'état* and brought strong pressure to bear on Sukarno to join them, Leimena had been instrumental in convincing Sukarno that it would be folly to take the side of the revolutionaries against the legal government and the army. Leimena was willing to tell me the full story of the dramatic events on the air-base when he had to argue with Sukarno and had finally succeeded in taking him to the presidential palace in Bogor. I could only comment that by his energetic intervention he had almost certainly prevented a major international crisis. For, in the light of the Vietnam situation, it was not difficult to imagine what would have been the reaction of the countries most concerned, if Indonesia with its strategic position had been taken over by an extreme leftist government.

My friends had arranged that I should be received by President Sukarno. The audience took place at 7.30 a.m. at the same palace in Djakarta where I had been received in 1933 and 1949 under very different circumstances. The occasion was like the *petit lever du roi* at the French court, in that we assisted at the President's breakfast, but the difference was that as the temperature rose a uniformed lady attendant took off the President's shirt and shoes so that only his undershirt and pants remained. The company consisted of our group of churchmen, a French painter, a Dutch journalist and an Indonesian general. Dr Leimena tried to steer the conversation towards the issues of Indonesian national life and of the international situation. But the President would not hear of this and said: 'Why are you always so serious, Leimena?' He seemed to be unable to fix his mind on any other subject than his own prestige. He spoke of his collection of paintings and showed us a recent French painting which he had acquired. Why did the young people attack him for his interest in paintings and criticize him for his interest in feminine beauty? The Roman Catholics were among his strongest critics. He would write to the Pope to get them to stop their campaign. He was something of a painter himself. One of the group asked him to show his own work. He took two sheets of paper, drew on each a woman's head, signed the drawings and gave them to the French painter and to me. The point to which he returned again and again was that he was so badly misunderstood by the younger generation.

It seemed to me almost unbelievable that this egocentric man with his self-pity who seemed to have lost touch with reality was the same Sukarno who in 1949 and 1957 had made on me the impression of a most energetic and dynamic political leader. He had completely changed and it was clear that he could no longer lead a great nation in a critical period of its existence.

I had told the President that I would love to see again the mountain residence in Tjipanas, where Jetty and I had lived in 1933 and which we had loved for its extraordinary beauty. He gave orders that the place should be opened up for our party. I found the pavilion in which we had lived exactly as it had been thirty years ago. I walked around in the gardens which were as lovely as ever. But this time the main building housed the Indonesian part of the President's collection of paintings. It was more than doubtful whether he should have spent so much money on art, but it was clear that he had the eye and taste of the great collector.

I heard a good deal about the terrible massacres which had taken place after the failure of the *coup d'état* and in which hundreds of thousands of communists or people suspected of communist leanings had been killed. Should the World Council and other international bodies have raised a strong protest? The difficulty was that it was practically impossible to pin down the responsibility for these atrocities. Neither the government nor the army as such seemed to have encouraged the culprits. So to whom should any protest be addressed? Some of the regional churches had spoken courageous words at the critical moment. All Indonesians with whom I talked were deeply unhappy about this dark page of their national life.

The most impressive element in the situation was the quite extraordinary growth of the Protestant churches in Sumatra and even in Java. Those Dutchmen who had prophesied that when the Dutch left the advance of Christianity would cease had been quite wrong. The problem was now how to help the fast-growing churches to receive and instruct the converts. There was a fine spirit of solidarity. Young people from Java offered their services to the Sumatra churches. And the whole Christian movement in Indonesia had strong leadership. I was particularly impressed by some of the laymen who were deeply convinced that the missionary witness belonged to the very essence of Christianity and defended therefore the right of the church to evangelize in spite of political pressure to freeze the present situation. General Simatupang, the former chief of staff of the Indonesian army, now gave practically his full time to the Indonesian Council of Churches and helped the churches to think out their grand strategy with regard to mission and service. Other Christian laymen, such as Dr Tambunan, held responsible posts in the new government. Christians were deeply engaged in the struggle to build the Indonesia of the future.

From Indonesia I went to Hongkong to participate in the study meeting of the East Asia Christian Conference on the theme: 'Confessing the Faith in Asia Today'. We lived in Kowloon, the most Chinese part of the colony. I made long walks through the colourful narrow streets in order to get a 'feel' of Chinese life. Owing to my illness in Indonesia in 1933, my plan to visit China then had not materialized. The old and the new China were both represented in the city and lived side by side in an uneasy relationship. Christian friends, some of them recently arrived in Hongkong, told me of the effect of the 'cultural revolution' in the People's Republic on the life of the churches. It was clear that organized Christian life in China was coming to an end. The few remaining churches were being closed. If Christianity were to survive it could only do so as a movement in the catacombs. I thought of the days when we had great expectations for the churches in China and when Chinese Christian leaders had brought an impressive contribution to our ecumenical meetings. And I wondered whether China would see another renaissance of Christianity, as had happened before, or whether it would become like North Africa where Christianity had had a period of great vitality and later been almost completely eradicated.

The meeting of the East Asia Christian Conference dealt with a subject which had fascinated me ever since my first journey to Asia. I had been shocked to find how uncritically and unimaginatively Western forms of theology and church life had been transplanted to Asia. The criticism which had come both from outside and inside the churches that Asian churches were a foreign import was by no means unfounded. And now that the Asian cultures reasserted themselves this foreignness of the church was all the more serious. Attempts had been made to interpret the Christian message in Asian categories and forms. But none of these had been very successful. The Asian churches were rightly afraid that the outcome might be a new form of syncretism, that is, the indiscriminate mixture of various religions. Syncretism was indeed one of the greatest spiritual temptations of our time, not only in Asia but also in the West. I had written a small book on the subject[4] in which I had tried to show that biblical Christianity and syncretism are clearly incompatible. But if in Asia and other parts of the non-Western world the answer could neither be the copying of the Western tradition nor the mixture of Christianity with non-Christian conceptions, what was the right way for the churches? This was the problem which the meeting had to face. I spoke therefore on 'Accommodation, true and false'. Yes, the

Christian message had to find a different and relevant form of expression in Asia. But there were norms of accommodation which we find already in the New Testament when St Paul and St John carried the gospel from a Palestinian environment into the Hellenistic world.

The conference did not itself produce an Asian theology. But it did indicate the direction which the churches should follow in confessing the faith in Asia. The churches should not think in terms of survival, but should render a relevant witness to their nations as these were rebuilding their national, social and cultural life. They were to confess their faith not in order to define the truth held by one church over against another church, but to clarify together the meaning of the gospel in the concrete religious and cultural situation of Asia. And the criterion should be a biblical theology.

In the following years I had a chance to help in the follow up of the line which the Hongkong meeting had taken. The Theological Education Fund, an agency working under the auspices of the World Council, asked me to chair a committee which was to consider the future of this body which had already done so much to raise the quality of theological education in Asia, Africa and Latin America. Our group came to the unanimous conclusion that in the next period the Theological Education Fund should concentrate on the creation of centres in which theological educators and others would make a thorough study of the ways and means by which the Christian message could become effectively related to the cultural and social realities in these various continents. Our proposal was accepted by the Division of World Mission and Evangelism of the World Council of Churches.

NOTES

1. Indonesian army.
2. Moderator of the East Java Church.
3. See *The Ecumenical Review*, Spring 1950, p. 278.
4. *No Other Name*, London and Philadelphia, 1963.

I HAD LEARNED at Amsterdam in 1948 that the administration of a World Council Assembly was the toughest part of the General Secretary's job. But I had no idea that the second Assembly would present even more problems and crises than the first.

In retrospect the reasons why the Assembly of 1954 in Evanston was more difficult are quite clear. The first Assembly had a sufficient *raison d'être* in the creation of the World Council of Churches itself. It had the momentum and inspiration of a new departure in church history. Whatever weaknesses it had would be forgotten and forgiven if it succeeded in bringing the World Council into being. But the second Assembly would have to show that the coming together of the churches made a real difference and produced concrete results in their life and witness. That was a tougher proposition.

Furthermore, we had now to meet in an even more explosive international political situation and in the very country in which that situation had produced the most nervous reactions. In 1953 and 1954 'McCarthyism' was the central issue in the USA and it was inevitable that in view of the presence of delegates from Eastern Europe and of the World Council's refusal to identify itself with any political orthodoxy or ideology we would become a target for the witch-hunters.

Again, the theme chosen for the Assembly – of the Christian hope – led in the three years before the Assembly to a general theological debate which seemed at certain moments to lead to increasing dissension rather than agreement.

Preparations began as far back as 1950. At its Toronto meeting the Central Committee decided that since 'the world is full of false hopes, of fear and of despair' the main theme of the Assembly 'should be along the lines of the affirmation that Jesus Christ as Lord is the only hope of both the Church and the world'. And, on the proposal of Dr Henry P. Van Dusen,[1] it was agreed 'that the Study Department Committee take steps to form a commission of not more than twenty-five of the most creative thinkers of the churches to work on the preparation of a document which will be the basis for the consideration of the main theme of the Assembly'.

Few, if any, realized the difficulty of the task which we had agreed to undertake. Professor James Hastings Nichols, writing after the Assembly, expressed
his admiration for the courage which the World Council had shown in tackling
this theme and added: 'Where angels and denominations fear to tread there goes
the World Council.' But I am far from sure that the Central Committee would
have taken this decision if it had realized what a theological tempest it would
have to face.

When the Advisory Commission on the theme of the Assembly held its first
meeting in 1951 two things became clear. First of all that we could not fulfil our
task without raising some of the most central and controversial theological issues.
The eschatological problem – that is the problem of the relation of the Kingdom
of God to human history and of the ultimate hope to the proximate hopes – is the
key-problem of modern theology and had dominated the ecumenical discussion
ever since the Stockholm Conference of 1925. It was true that in the 1930s and
1940s the gulf between 'otherworldly' and 'this-worldly' interpretations of the
Christian faith had been bridged to a considerable extent. But the suspicion that
the 'Europeans' were not really concerned with the issues of life in the present-
day world and that the 'Americans' were activists without theological substance
had by no means disappeared.

In the second place we found that the more 'creative' Christian thinkers are,
the less chance there is that they will reach a common mind and arrive at an
agreement.

I wrote immediately after that first meeting: 'We had to go through deep
waters and there were moments when it seemed that the task would have to be
given up.' Was it not fantastic to expect that Karl Barth and Reinhold Niebuhr,
Emil Brunner and Georges Florovsky, Hendrik Kraemer and Henry Van Dusen
would find a common word on such an extraordinarily difficult theme? Several
of them had more than once crossed swords with each other. So it was not
surprising that during that exploratory meeting they reacted to each other 'with
cautious defensiveness and hostile aggressiveness'. Fortunately, there were also
some effective bridge-builders. So we succeeded at last in working out a first
report which was to serve as a basis of discussion in the churches. This document[2] showed only too clearly that we had not really arrived at a clear agreement
and that we had not yet reached the point at which we could really speak out
with a common voice on this most difficult subject.

But this very weakness had the good result that many churches and many
individuals felt it necessary to send in their criticisms. So the second meeting of
the commission in 1952 had a good deal of useful material to work with. That
meeting was much more peaceful. The members had come to know each other.
There was less nervousness and more humour. This time we not only compared
our own theological positions but, with the help of the philosopher Donald
Mackinnon and the philosopher-theologian Roger Mehl, we also tried to define
the Christian attitude to the three modern alternatives to the Christian hope:

The presidents' table at the Amsterdam Assembly. Visser 't Hooft is in conversation with the Archbishop of Canterbury (Geoffrey Fisher). Beside him are John R. Mott and Archbishop Germanos.

Dag Hammarskjöld visits the Evanston Assembly (*sitting third from the left*).

The Russian Church becomes a member of the World Council, 1961.

Pandit Jawaharlal Nehru and Raj Kumari Amrit Kaur visit the New Delhi Assembly, 1961. On the extreme right is Bishop Dibelius of Berlin.

Marxism, scientific humanism and democratic utopianism. This second report[3] represented the first crystallization of a common mind. Once again there was very widespread discussion in the churches.

By the summer of 1953 the time had come to draw up the final report to be submitted to the Assembly itself. All energy had now to be concentrated on production. But since the group had now become accustomed to team-work the task could be accomplished in time. Towards the end of the meeting we felt that the document lacked a strong concluding word. Who was to write this? It was unanimously decided to ask Karl Barth to undertake it. He remained in his room for a good part of the day and when he read his pages on 'The Sum of the Matter' we all said, 'This is it', and no one asked for any substantial changes. That could hardly have happened in 1951.

The real difficulty remained, of course, that an ecumenical document which represents the outcome of a spiritual struggle cannot have quite the same significance for those who have not shared in that struggle as it has for those who have participated in its creation. For it is impossible to convey through such a document the sum-total of discoveries which the members of the group have made during their period of dialogue and common work. We had the feeling that something very important had happened among us. As Paul Minear put it: 'What had seemed impossible at first had become not only a possibility but an actual fact: a common mind and attitude toward hope, a hope which leads us closer to our Lord.' We had broken through the deadlock of the debate between a purely futurist and a purely 'realized' eschatology, between a fundamentalist and a modernist approach, between quietism and activism. But would the Assembly make the same discoveries that we had made?

At first it seemed that this was not the case. The discussion of the report led to considerable confusion. Many criticisms seemed to cancel each other out. The committee which had to draw up the statement in which the Assembly would express its reaction to the report had a hard time and its draft statement had to be revised three times before it was finally accepted. The statement as adopted recognized that the report exhibited a substantial ecumenical agreement, but stated frankly that in the discussion at the Assembly sharp theological differences had been expressed. The report of the Advisory Committee could not be the only word of the Assembly on the theme of hope. But it was sent to the churches with a commendation of the Assembly as 'a creative and provocative ecumenical statement of Christian hope for this day'.

Had we made a mistake in asking the young World Council to tackle such a tremendous task? I do not think so. For as Samuel McCrea Cavert, my colleague in the WCC's New York office, pointed out after the Assembly, the discussion of the Evanston theme proved to be 'a stimulus to continuing theological reflection and study' and showed 'the importance of a vertebrate system of Christian belief'. The task of the ecumenical movement was surely not to produce some easy and vague compromise theology, but to confront all churches with the substance of the Christian faith. At an early stage of the World Council, Evanston helped to convince many that the ecumenical movement was not a movement of superficial relativism, avoiding all really important issues, but a movement striving for unity through the renewal of the churches by a common rediscovery of the full richness of the faith.

The discussion on the theme led to an incident which was much discussed after the Assembly. The report of the Advisory Committee had not spoken explicitly about the place of Israel in Christian eschatology. A study group in Basle had called attention to this omission and a number of delegates had made the same point in the discussion groups at the Assembly. So the first draft of the statement on the report of the Advisory Committee had made reference to this problem 'and spoken of the ultimate fulfilment of God's promises to the people of Ancient Israel'. But in the first discussion in the plenary meeting, delegates from the Near East proposed that the reference be deleted since it would be understood as a reference to the state of Israel. This proposal was not accepted. But in the second discussion the matter was brought up again and from a different point of view. Charles P. Taft, prominent American layman, expressed his strong disagreement with the reference to Israel since it seemed to single out the Jews and this would jeopardize the personal relations of Christians with their Jewish friends. A telegram from Dr Charles Malik of the Lebanon also urged us to omit any mention of Israel. But a number of European delegates, such as Dr Hendrik Berkhof of Holland and Dr Pierre Maury of France, spoke strongly in favour of retaining the sentence concerning Israel. It was not a political statement, they said; it was a re-affirmation of the biblical teaching as given in St Paul's Epistle to the Romans. A vote had to be taken. The result was 195 to 150 for elimination of the word about Israel. A group of delegates returned on the next day to read a special declaration explaining why they could not leave out Israel in speaking about Christian hope. And it was decided that the whole question would have to become a subject for ecumenical conversation and study.

What had happened? As the crucial vote was taken and I could clearly see from the platform what side the various national delegations were taking I said to myself: the spectre of Hitler is present. Not in the sense that anyone was infected by Hitler's anti-semitism. No, in a quite different way. I saw that the churchmen from countries which had been, for longer or shorter periods, under the national socialist regime had practically all come to feel that Israel had not only a central place in the past history of salvation, but also in the future of salvation. As they had had to face the demonic hatred of the Jews they had found deep meaning in St Paul's interpretation of the destiny of Israel in the ninth, tenth and eleventh chapters of the Epistle to the Romans. Those who had not been so close to the terrible drama of the extermination of Jews in Europe could not see it this way. They felt that to single out the Jews, to give them a special place inhistory, was – in spite of all good intentions – a sort of discrimination. It was their votes, together with the small number of votes from Near Eastern Christians who were afraid of political misunderstandings, which constituted the majority.

There were some emotional reactions to the vote. But there was really no reason for anyone to feel self-righteous. The minority had to admit that before the days of Hitler they had practically all, including Karl Barth himself, interpreted St Paul's teaching on this point in a more or less allegorical rather than a historical way. And the majority had to learn that the minority had not the slightest intention of discriminating against the Jews, but was motivated by shame that the churches had not understood in time the full spiritual dimension of the Jewish question. This process of clarification would however take time. We would have to wait till the third Assembly to arrive at a common statement on the subject.

But I was not allowed to give undivided attention to such theological discussions. We were meeting at a time when the cold war was going strong and when the United States was obsessed by the issues which Senator Joseph R. McCarthy had raised. The American churches had become deeply involved in the nation-wide debate. Bishop G. Bromley Oxnam, our American World Council President, had in July 1953 appeared at his own request before the 'Committee on un-American Activities' and fought a courageous battle against the hysterical accusations made against him and the churches in general. The National Council of Churches had set up a Committee on the Maintenance of American Freedom under the chairmanship of Bishop Henry Knox Sherrill, another strong supporter of the World Council. Our Executive Committee had, at its session in August 1953, seriously considered whether it would be possible to hold the Assembly in the United States. Bishop Oxnam reported that the Secretary of State, Mr John Foster Dulles, had assured him that all bona fide delegates would receive entry visas. And although it was realized that we were likely to meet various difficulties, we decided that we should go ahead.

In November 1953 I went to the United States on an exploratory visit. McCarthyism was still going strong, but the opposition to the witch-hunt was becoming more vocal. The press tried to get me to express my opinion on the debate. I made a rather general statement about the impression which the attacks against freedom of opinion was making in Europe and I did not mention McCarthy. But the *Washington Post* brought it out under the headline: 'World Church Head assails McCarthyism'.

During this visit Bishop Oxnam and I went to the White House to invite President Eisenhower to address the Evanston Assembly. We were received in the most cordial manner. Our mission was to explain just what the Assembly would be: a gathering of people of many nationalities with the most diverse points of view. The president proved to be deeply interested and said that in principle he was willing to interrupt his holiday in order to visit us at Evanston. On the following Sunday Mr and Mrs Eisenhower came to the National

Presbyterian Church where I preached on the theme of the Assembly. I don't know whether I succeeded in explaining the importance of the ecumenical discussion on the Christian hope. His only comment afterwards was: 'That was a good thought.'

In my report to the Executive Committee meeting in Germany, in February 1954, I said that I had become convinced of the importance of holding the Assembly in America at this particular moment. A great spiritual struggle was going on in the country and the churches were playing a decisive role in that struggle. By bringing in the ecumenical dimension the Assembly could render a real service to the American churches at a critical moment of their history.

In the spring of 1954 I went to New York to work with my colleague Robert Bilheimer on the final preparations for the Assembly. Jetty accompanied me. On the boat I received a telegram warning me that I should be very careful in my statements to the reporters who would meet the boat. This seemed rather ominous. I wondered whether I would not get in trouble with my passport, for this carried a Russian visa given for a visit to Eastern Germany. The officer looked at the passport very carefully and especially at one page. I could not see what page it was. Was it the one with the Russian stamp? He suddenly turned to me and said: 'Have you ever seen a mynah-bird?' I asked him to repeat the question, for it did not seem to make sense. 'Well,' he said, 'I see you have been in India and so have I. It was in India that I bought a mynah-bird which speaks even better than a parrot. Don't forget to buy one when you go to India again.' My wife and I decided to celebrate this event by a special visit to the Zoo to look for the first time of our life at a mynah bird.

But soon there arose more difficult passport troubles. Although it had been agreed that all delegates appointed by the churches should receive visas for Evanston, it was obviously difficult to get all the government departments concerned to collaborate. There was even a moment when trouble arose about the visa of Gustav Heinemann of Germany. I don't know exactly who made the trouble, but I hope that the person concerned has lived long enough to read in his newspaper that the man whom he considered suspect in 1954 is now the President of the Federal Republic of Germany. The most difficult problem was, however, to get visas for the delegates from Hungary. Dr Franklin Clark Fry and Dr O. F. Nolde had to go to Washington to convince the government. Finally the visas were granted, but with the restriction that these delegates would not be allowed to visit any part of the United States except the Chicago area. An obvious result of this decision was that the spotlight of public attention was focussed on these Hungarians and I had to spend a good deal of time trying to help them in their problems of public relations. During the Assembly a member of the United States Congress, who headed one of the investigation committees on communist activities, requested the five Hungarian delegates to appear before his committee. They were of course greatly upset about this. We had long discussions with them and the conclusion was that Dr Fry answered for the

Hungarians, saying bluntly: 'These men are here exclusively for church conferences and this fact heightens the clear impropriety of your proposal.'

In these matters the press, which had no fewer than 646 representatives at the Assembly, played a helpful role. Charles Parlin, as chairman of the Press Committee, had the policy of sharing our problems with them and the great majority responded by a fair and honest appraisal of our work.

In the uneasy atmosphere in which the Assembly had to be held it was most helpful that President Eisenhower came to address us. Together with the President of Northwestern University I went to meet the president at the military airport, some distance from Evanston. The first moment was somewhat disconcerting. For after greeting us the president used an expression which is more often heard in military than in ecclesiastical circles and continued: 'What have I got on my pants?' Some of the eye-medicine which his doctor had given him had made a stain on his white pants. The three of us sat side by side in an open limousine. The president began to tell various stories. But as we passed villages we found groups of people shouting, 'Hi, Ike!' And every time Ike got up with his tall body, so that he towered above us, shouting: 'Hi, folks!' 'It is strange,' he said, 'I cannot remain seated when people greet me.'

But with so many interruptions it became somewhat difficult to pick up the thread of the conversation again and again. There was no question but that he was genuinely interested in what the ecumenical movement was trying to do. But it was also clear that he had only very vague ideas about the role of the churches. His one basic concern, to which he came back again and again, and which he also expressed strongly in his address to the Assembly, was that all over the world men who believed in the power of prayer should join in praying for peace. It was clear that in this matter he spoke out of a deep conviction.

Dag Hammerskjöld, Secretary General of the United Nations, also came to address us. He was in a sense a member of the family, for he had been on terms of intimate friendship with the Søderbloms at the time when Archbishop Søderblom was preparing the Stockholm Conference of 1925. His address ended on a striking note. He referred to a statement in the report of the Advisory Committee on the main theme which spoke of the centrality of the cross of Christ. And he went on: 'The cross, although it is the unique fact on which the Christian churches base their hope, should not separate those of the Christian faith from others, but should instead be that element in their lives which enables them to stretch out their hands to peoples of other creeds in the feeling of universal brotherhood which we hope to see reflected in a world of nations truly united.' It was not until after his death when his journal *Markings* was published that I understood that that sentence expressed the deepest motivation which had enabled him to carry on his impossibly difficult task.

I had of course to spend a great deal of time on the question of nominations. The most difficult point was the composition of the Presidium. The Structure and Function Committee had decided to propose to the Assembly that the

Presidents should be ineligible for immediate re-election when their term of office came to an end. The strong argument for this proposal was that the office of President should not be held always or for a very long period by the leaders of the same churches, and that different regions and churches should be represented when their turn came. But this proposal was strongly attacked by the Bishop of London and other (by no means all) delegates from the Church of England. They considered it essential that at least at this second Assembly the Archbishop of Canterbury should be re-elected. The issue led to a vigorous debate, in which it became clear that the great majority of the Assembly was in favour of the proposal of the Structure and Function committee. Among those who opposed the Bishop of London there were several prominent members of the Anglican Communion. The Archbishop of Canterbury himself had made it clear to some of us that he was not worried about the proposal. So the important principle that in its Presidium, as in all other parts of its life, the World Council should seek to be both geographically and confessionally representative was established.

The Bishop of London seems to have over-estimated my role in this matter and to have thought that this decision, in fact taken after prolonged debate in the whole Assembly, was largely due to my work behind the scenes. For he made the public comment after the Assembly that it had been a combination of 'German theology, American money and Dutch bureaucracy'. I told my friends that I was greatly tempted to send him a message proposing that Anglican prelacy should join with the three decisive forces which he had mentioned. Was it the Dutch bureaucrat in me which made me resist that temptation?

Another difficulty arose as the Nominations Committee sought to work out the list of the new Presidents. In the committee there was strong backing for the name of Bishop Otto Dibelius of Berlin. His name had become very well known outside Germany. But there were a good many delegates who preferred the choice of Dr Reinold von Thadden, President of the German *Kirchentag*. Their strong argument was that there should be at least one layman in the Presidium. But Dr von Thadden felt that he would not be able to add this additional responsibility to those he was already carrying. In the meantime a request that a layman should be included in the Presidium was signed by sixty delegates and in the light of this it was decided to postpone the final vote so as to reconsider the matter.

During the discussion I discovered that our press people, not realizing that there was any difficulty, had assembled the six presidents on the committee's list to enable the press photographers to make the first pictures of the new presidium. I had to do something about this. We could hardly afford to have pictures in the press of a presidium which had not been elected and might be changed. But I got to them just too late. The papers carried a picture of me standing in front of the six trying to convince the photographers that they should not use their cameras.

On the next day the original list was adopted. Speaking on behalf of the sixty petitioning delegates, Professor d'Espine of Switzerland said that it was a question of principle and not of personalities, and that it was necessary that the council be aware of the vital importance of participation by lay men and women in the council's leadership.

There were many other crises. After the Assembly I drew up a list of seventeen of them. Those that had to do with the Eastern Orthodox churches, with the Dutch Reformed churches of South Africa and with the Roman Catholic Church can best be mentioned in the chapters dealing with these churches.

In describing this Assembly in terms of its crises I have of course misinterpreted it. For the Assembly is in the first place an assembly of and for the delegates and they can give their full attention to the task of elaborating section statements and committee decisions. But I have not misrepresented my activity during this Assembly, which was largely in the nature of trouble-shooting.

I would of course have preferred to participate more fully in the production of the reports. But there was this consolation: As crisis after crisis was solved it became very clear that a strong uniting force was operating among us. Bishop Hanns Lilje called it: 'the majesty of the cause'. It was more than mere 'co-existence'. The section on international affairs was correct in replacing that far too static concept by the expression, 'living together in a divided world'. We were learning gradually how to live together. The 'staying together' which had been the key-idea of the first Assembly could now be interpreted as 'growing together'. The World Council ship had been shaken by the storms of the season, but it had shown that it was seaworthy.

NOTES

1. At that time President of Union Theological Seminary and chairman of the World Council's Study Department Committee.
2. *The Ecumenical Review*, October 1951, p. 71.
3. *The Ecumenical Review*, October 1952, p. 73.

33 | *The Impact of Eastern Orthodoxy*

THE EASTERN ORTHODOX churches had played an important part in the creation of the ecumenical movement. As early as 1920 in its remarkable encyclical concerning the creation of a 'League of Churches' the Ecumenical Patriarchate of Constantinople had spontaneously provided an initiative which, together with similar initiatives coming from Uppsala and from New York, gave the movement its broad basis and its first impetus.

At the meeting of the various sectors of the movement which I attended in the 1920s and 1930s the Orthodox churches were well represented. Several of their leaders, such as Archbishop Germanos of the Ecumenical Patriarchate, Professor Hamilcar Alivisatos of Greece, Professor Stephan Zankov of Bulgaria and Bishop Ireneus of Novi Sad (Yugoslavia) were among the most trusted and influential leaders. But as a result of the political repercussions of the second world war the situation changed considerably. The Moscow Conference of Orthodox church leaders stated in 1948 that the churches represented at the conference felt obliged 'to decline the invitation to participate in the ecumenical movement in its present state'. This meant that not only the Church of Russia, which had so far not been able to play any role in the ecumenical movement, but also the Orthodox churches of Rumania, Bulgaria, Yugoslavia and Poland remained outside the World Council of Churches. Thus by the time of the Amsterdam Assembly in 1948 the only Orthodox churches with which we had normal relations were those of the ancient Patriarchates (Constantinople, Antioch, Alexandria and Jerusalem), of Greece and of Cyprus. In fact there were just two sizable Orthodox delegations at Amsterdam: the delegation of the Ecumenical Patriarchate of Constantinople and the delegation of the Church of Greece.[1]

This created a difficult situation for all concerned. At Amsterdam and at the following meetings the Orthodox delegates felt rightly that with such an inadequate representation they could not possibly make the contribution to the ecumenical dialogue which they were entitled to make in view of their place in church history, in view of their present significance, and in view of their numerical importance. And although those of us who were responsible for the policy of the World Council were keenly aware of this problem we found it practically impossible under the given circumstances to ensure that the voice of Orthodoxy should not be drowned by Western and mainly Protestant voices.

Under any circumstances the dialogue between Eastern and Western Christians was a difficult matter. After a separation of some thousand years each regional family of churches had developed their own spirituality, their own style of life, their own categories of thought. There were few in the West who had made any study of Orthodox Christianity and even fewer who had had any direct personal contact with it. Nor did many Eastern church leaders understand post-reformation church history in Western Europe and America. There was also the deep suspicion in the East that Western Christianity was a proselytizing force undermining their churches. And there was the Protestant irritation when it seemed that Orthodox ecclesiology was no more tolerant than the traditional ecclesiology of Rome, with which Protestants were very familiar.

But now this difficult relationship was further complicated by the fact that in the years following the Assembly of 1948 so few Orthodox churches could participate, which made it hard to demonstrate that the Orthodox churches could be and should be fully at home in the World Council. I could not help wondering whether it would be possible to hold any Orthodox churches in the World Council. There seemed to be a real danger that the World Council would become less ecumenical in scope than the pre-war ecumenical movement had been.

During this critical period I was greatly encouraged by the attitude of a number of Orthodox leaders who took a stand for the continuation of Orthodox participation. There was for example Archbishop Germanos, the Exarch of the Ecumenical Patriarch in Western Europe. He had drafted the Constantinople encyclical of 1920 and had in that same year been the leader of the first Orthodox delegation which participated in meetings of the ecumenical movement. He had played a prominent part in the Life and Work and Faith and Order movements. At the Amsterdam Assembly he did everything that could be done to create relations of confidence between the Orthodox delegation and the delegations of other churches. I found him a wise and friendly elder statesman who was always willing to give helpful advice. His death in 1952 was a great loss. During the last year of his life he had translated into Greek the Toronto statement of 1950 which was of decisive importance in removing misunderstandings about the World Council which had arisen in some of the Orthodox churches.

Equally important was the stand taken by Professor Hamilcar Alivisatos of Athens. He was also a founding father of the ecumenical movement and had attended practically all important meetings of the movement since 1920. I had been in close touch with him since my first visit to Greece in 1929. Now he used his very influential position in the Church of Greece to defend the World Council against those who were suspicious of its intentions. He went out of his way to create opportunities for Greek churchmen to come to know the Western churches and for Western churchmen to discover Greek church life.

Professor Stephan Zankov of Bulgaria had an even more difficult position. He had also been an active participant in the ecumenical movement before the second world war. Through his books and lectures he had helped many in the Western churches to begin to understand the specific genius of Eastern Orthodoxy. When I visited him in Sofia I found the walls of his study covered with pictures of the many ecumenical meetings he had attended. So he was deeply distressed to find that, owing to the political and ecclesiastical developments during and after the second world war, his church was no longer participating in the ecumenical movement, and that he was cut off from his many friends in other churches. But he did not give up hope. He did what he could to remove the misunderstandings about the World Council which had arisen in Eastern European churches and bombarded me with letters urging that the World Council make a determined effort to enter into conversation with the Moscow Patriarchate and the churches which were co-operating with that Patriarchate.

The fourth and the most important name which has to be mentioned in this connection is of course that of Patriarch Athenagoras of Constantinople. What his consistent support of the ecumenical cause has meant for the movement should become clear in the following pages.

Soon after the Amsterdam Assembly in 1948 I visited Greece. I found that the church leaders there were concerned about the whole problem of the relations between the Church of Greece and the World Council. The most revealing discussion took place in a beautifully situated monastery near Athens, where I met the bishops and theological professors who were mainly responsible for the thinking out of the ecumenical policy of the Church of Greece. They told me that questions were being raised about further participation in the World Council. Even the friends of the World Council wondered whether it would be possible to continue to co-operate. Could the Ecumenical Patriarchate and the Church of Greece go ahead on the ecumenical road when all the other Orthodox churches stayed out? I answered that several of those Orthodox churches might well be glad to know that Constantinople and Greece kept the Orthodox flag flying in the World Council of Churches. They expressed also the fear that the discussions on issues of faith and order would lead to compromises which would endanger the integrity of the Orthodox churches. I stated that the true Faith and Order method was to state disagreements as clearly as agreements.

I felt of course that the basic issue was the issue of the Orthodox conception of the church. So I asked the group to tell me whether the Orthodox churches could recognize the non-Orthodox churches as real churches. The result was a heated debate among the Greek theologians themselves, carried on in Greek. Translation was forgotten. So I had to ask meekly whether this meeting was not called to have a discussion with me. When an attempt was made to summarize the discussion it appeared that this was really an unresolved problem. There was of course no uncertainty about the Orthodox Church being the true church, but there were different nuances with regard to the implications of this belief for an evaluation of the non-Orthodox churches.

I left Athens with the impression that, in spite of the real problems which we had to take very seriously, the Church of Greece would continue to co-operate with the World Council.

From Athens to Istanbul. It was a joy to meet again Patriarch Athenagoras who had been enthroned as Ecumenical Patriarch of Constantinople at the beginning of the year. In the twenty years since I had been his guest at Corfu I had only seen him briefly at meetings in America, but he treated me as an old friend. The quite unimpressive surroundings in which he now had to live seemed to underline the impressiveness of his personality. And it was clear that he wanted to give to the word 'ecumenical' in his title its full content and meaning. He thought in terms of the total Christian cause and this all the more so since he lived in a country in which Christians were a small minority.

After the conversation of two hours which I had with him I wrote in a report to Geneva:

> He speaks about our work with an enthusiasm, as if he were a World Council secretary. And it is quite clear that he means it. Thus he said after luncheon to the members of the Holy Synod that there ought soon to be an ecumenical meeting somewhere in Orthodox territory . . . Well, we have a real friend in the Phanar.

In Cairo I met both the Greek Orthodox and the Coptic Patriarch and found both of them willing to collaborate with the World Council. The Greek Orthodox Patriarch of Alexandria put me on the spot when he asked me whether the World Council would support his request to the United Nations that the relics of St Nicholas and St Mark be returned to Alexandria. Remembering my visit in 1930 to Bari, where the relics of St Nicholas were kept, I doubted whether there was any chance that the request concerning St Nicholas would be considered. And Venice would feel even more strongly about the relics of St Mark.

A remarkable contribution to deeper understanding between the Eastern and Western parts of Christendom was made by the St Paul's Festival in Greece in 1951. Professor Hamilcar Alivisatos had had the excellent idea of celebrating the nineteenth centenary of St Paul's arrival in Greece with a pilgrimage to the places which St Paul had visited. The participants from many churches lived together on a ship, and this facilitated the close contact between them. Many learned lectures were given, but perhaps the most impressive aspect of the festival was that in so many places the Greek people made the festival their own. For them we were not merely taking part in a commemoration of events which belonged to past history, but in a demonstration of gratitude for a living heritage. All this was summed up on the last evening when the pilgrims, surrounded by a large crowd, met on the Areopagus. The mighty Acropolis towering above us had become a venerable piece of history, but the unpretentious Areopagus was the pulpit from which a living message was announced.

The festival gave me a wonderful opportunity to get to know the leaders of the various Orthodox churches. I divided my time between conversations on church affairs with the older generation and swimming with the younger generation in many places with familiar biblical names. Some raised their eye-brows and seemed to think that this was not the right style of pilgrimage. One of the best moments came on the Sunday when we reached Lindos on the island of Rhodes. I arose early and climbed through the narrow streets with their brilliantly white houses to the top of the Acropolis with its marvellous view over the blue Aegean sea. I heard some voices behind the pillars of the temple. Someone was reading aloud. Suddenly I recognized the words. It was the seventeenth chapter of Acts read in Swedish. I joined my Scandinavian fellow-pilgrims and found it moving to hear St Paul's words about the unknown God in that most appropriate setting.

The visit which I made in 1951 to the Near East was largely focussed on the refugee problem, but also provided opportunities for contacts with Eastern churches. We began with visits to the refugee camps, truly a disconcerting experience. In 1948 when the state of Israel was born these refugees had left their homes in the territory taken over by Israel. They had expected that they would soon be able to return. But they had to wait for a political settlement. And no such settlement had come or was even in sight. The help given by the United Nations and the voluntary organizations, including the World Council, enabled the refugees to get a bare subsistence. But the real problem was that their future was so utterly dark.

In a camp near Jericho the camp-leader made a speech in Arabic in which I recognized the word 'Satan'. I thought that he referred to the Mountain of Temptation which we could see in the distance. But the translation showed that I was wrong. He had adapted a saying of Churchill and said: 'In order to return to our homes, we would be willing to make an alliance with the devil.'

The desperation of the refugees became very clear also in a camp near Bethlehem. When our party arrived the people came rushing down the hills and shouted what seemed to be violent protests and threats. It looked as if we had a riot on our hands. A speech in English by a white man would be no good. So I asked our Indian colleague, Sarah Chakko, to address the crowd. There she stood in her Indian sari and began to speak in a firm quiet voice about the refugees in her own country, about their sufferings and about the desire of the churches to help all men everywhere who had lost their homes. When the speech was translated into Arabic the crowd calmed down and a man spoke up saying: 'We are sorry. We thought you came from the United Nations. We did not know you were men of God.'

The conference held at Beirut on the following days sought not only to determine how the churches could best help the Near Eastern refugees, but also how the refugee problem could be solved. We were at that time still hopeful that through the intensive co-operation of all concerned – the Arab states,

Israel, the Western governments and the international organizations – it would be possible to give these 800,000 people a normal existence. But it was 'hoping against hope' for political passions were already rising to such a feverish level that rational discussion of the problem became almost impossible.

After the conference we went to Israel. The crossing of the frontier at the Mandelbaum Gate was the entrance into a totally different world. The explosion of energy and the imaginative and intelligent way in which the new national life was being organized was extraordinarily impressive. But there seemed to be little awareness of what was happening a few miles further on beyond the frontier. I had a memorable conversation with Martin Buber, the philosopher-theologian who seemed to incarnate the ancient wisdom of Israel. He was aware of the long-range problem. He sought to apply his 'dialogical principle' of the I-Thou relation to the Near Eastern situation. He believed deeply in the mission of Israel to be 'a blessing among the nations' and to act as a bridge between the Western and the Arab world. If men could be found on both sides who could take such an approach there seemed to be a chance for a peaceful solution. We Christians, with our shameful record with regard to both the Jewish and the Arab world, had no right to judge or to condemn. But precisely because we were so deeply involved we had to be actively concerned about peace between Israelis and Arabs. I wrote at that time:[2]

> So far most Christians who have shown interest in the Near East have done so as partisans, and have identified themselves with the cause of the Arabs or with the cause of Israel. We need desperately a non-partisan Christian approach to the whole problem of human relations in the Near East. We need to prove that there are Christians who do not think in terms of the defence of interests and rights, or even causes, but who simply care for the men and women for whom Christ died.

In 1955 Jetty and I made a more leisurely visit to the Near East. The two places which left the deepest impression were Mount Gerizim and the Litho-strotos. The Samaritans had pitched their tents on Mount Gerizim for they were preparing the celebration of their Easter festival. They looked like the Assyrians on the ancient mosaics. When my colleague, Christopher King, who had visited them several times, told them who I was, they began a long discourse to show how much Christians owed to the Samaritans. What about the good Samaritan? And did we not remember that when Christ healed ten men who suffered from leprosy only one returned, and that he was a Samaritan? And down there in the valley at Jacob's well had not a Samaritan woman given a drink of water to 'your Messiah'? I was surprised by their knowledge of the New Testament. Their purpose was of course to get help for their people. I promised that our relief-workers would look into their situation.

The Lithostrotos is the place where, according to the gospel of St John (19.13), Jesus stood before Pilate. When Père Vincent of the *Ecole Biblique* in

Jerusalem explored the ancient Antonia fortress he found an ancient pavement with inscriptions made by Roman soldiers and he became firmly convinced that this was the pavement mentioned in the story of the passion. It is not certain that Père Vincent was right, but in any case this is a place where one gets that shock of confrontation with the reality of the biblical story which one does not easily get in the Church of the Holy Sepulchre. For here you can see; it must have been like this: soldiers concentrating on the game, for which they have scratched lines in the stone, while Jesus faces the decisive hour.

We attended the Eastertide services of the various Christian churches in Jerusalem. The most impressive was the feast of the washing of the feet in the Armenian cathedral. It was distressing to find that the churches in Jerusalem seemed to live still in the pre-ecumenical age and that it was the Mohammedan governor of Jerusalem who had to keep the peace between them. But this visit to the Near East ended at a conference in Beirut at which representatives of the younger generation of the member churches in the Near East met under the auspices of the World Council's youth department. Here something new was being born. Here there was a common concern for the Christian witness and Christian action. The day of renewal of life was being prepared in the oldest churches of Christendom.

During the next few years the position of the Orthodox churches in the ecumenical movement remained very difficult. They represented at that time a minority of the membership and felt overwhelmed by the Western and Protestant churches. And this had again a discouraging effect on their willingness to participate. Thus at the World Conference on Faith and Order in Lund, in 1952, there were only nine Orthodox delegates. And at the second Assembly of the World Council in Evanston in 1954, with its 502 delegates, the Orthodox had twenty-nine representatives. It was not surprising that on both occasions these delegates felt it necessary to make special statements concerning their doctrinal and ecclesiological position, in which they expressed their reservations concerning a number of affirmations in the reports adopted by the meetings concerned.

Looking back on those years it seems to me that three factors were decisive in keeping the Orthodox churches in the World Council. In the first place the Toronto statement of 1950 made it clear that the World Council would not impose on its members any particular conception of the church or of church unity; and that there was a place in the Council for those churches which recognize other churches as churches in the full and true sense, and for those who do not. For this meant that the World Council recognized the specific position of Orthodoxy. In the second place the consistent, patient and determined support given to the World Council by some of the Orthodox leaders, and especially by Patriarch Athenagoras, helped greatly to maintain the Orthodox churches in the wider fellowship. The Patriarch's decision taken in 1955 to appoint a permanent representative of the Ecumenical Patriarchate at World Council headquarters in Geneva and his choice of Bishop Iakovos (later Archbishop Iakovos), a warm friend of the ecumenical movement, to be the first such representative had far-reaching effects on the relations between the World Council and Orthodoxy. And in the third place the practical demonstration of solidarity through inter-church aid, service to refugees and in other ways was another important factor.

The great disaster which befell the Greek Orthodox Christians in Istanbul in 1955 provided a test case for this solidarity. In September of that year riots took place in the city which caused great damage to the Orthodox churches, schools and hospitals. I asked Ray Maxwell, our staff member concerned with aid to Orthodox churches, to go immediately to Istanbul to get the full facts, to convey a message of deep sympathy to the Patriarch, and to find out what action we should take. His report, which we sent to the churches and to the press, helped to make Christians in the West realize the seriousness of the situation. I issued a public statement saying:

> What has happened to the Greek Orthodox Church in Istanbul is even worse than the first reports gave us to understand. It is one of the worst calamities that has befallen any Christian church in our time and adds a further tragic chapter to the story of the sufferings of the Eastern Orthodox churches. That such a crime against the church should be perpetrated at a time when we speak of human rights is hard to believe and to understand. The Christian world will want to express its solidarity with its brethren in Istanbul in every possible way. It will also be aware of the obligation to insist that full compensation be given in so far as there can be compensation for the historic treasures which have been destroyed. It will also want to express the conviction that steps must be taken to avoid the recurrence of such violence and to secure the respect of the rights of a religious minority. Every church in the World Council cannot but feel that the burden which this member-church must carry is also its burden.

Our Division of Inter-Church Aid appealed to the churches to raise funds for the Christians in Istanbul and received a good response. And the Commission of Churches on International Affairs took action at the governmental level. But that was not enough. It was even more necessary to give to this church in its hour of crisis the spiritual and moral backing of the total ecumenical family. So we decided to send an ecumenical delegation to Istanbul. Its report[3] concluded with these words:

> We believe that we have been able to assure the Christian people of Istanbul that their brethren the world over are sharing their burden and so fulfilling the law of Christ. Had there not been a World Council of Churches it would have been necessary to call one into existence for such a situation as this. But the World Council does exist, and this tragic moment has proved a supreme opportunity to display before the world the reality of the fellowship which binds the Churches together in a bond of fellowship and love.

Speaking on behalf of the Ecumenical Patriarchate Metropolitan James of Philadelphia said at the meeting of the Central Committee in 1956:

> The Ecumenical Patriarchate is grateful to the World Council of Churches not only for the solidarity and fellowship expressed in its trouble and calamity, but also because it has had another experience of the necessity of the ecumenical fellowship as it had the vision to describe it in its Encyclical of 1920.

But the situation of the Ecumenical Patriarchate remained precarious. The problem of the future of Cyprus created considerable tension between Turkey and Greece. There were rumours that the Patriarchate might be forced to leave Turkey. At the meeting of the Executive Committee of the World Council in February 1957 the situation was discussed at considerable length and it was agreed that the World Council should give full support to the Patriarchate in its desire to remain in the city in which it had carried on its widespread ministry for sixteen centuries. It was also decided that the two officers of the Commission of the Churches on International Affairs, Sir Kenneth Grubb and Dr O. F. Nolde, together with the General Secretary, should make a direct approach to the Turkish government.

The three of us travelled to Turkey via Greece. In Athens we had occasion to have conversations with the Archbishop, with other church leaders and with diplomats which gave us the necessary background for our *démarche* in Turkey. The most interesting conversation was the one we had with King Paul. He received us informally in his residence outside Athens and showed deep interest in our mission. When the time to take our leave approached I asked him what specific arguments he would use, if he had to convince the Turkish government that the Ecumenical Patriarchate should remain in Turkey. He smiled and said that that was too big a question to be answered on the spur of the moment. I thought of course that my question would remain unanswered and was therefore most surprised when the next day a courier from the palace arrived at the restaurant where we were taking luncheon and brought me an *aide-mémoire* from the King. He had continued to think about the problem and put down in a clear manner the main points he believed we should make.

We had difficulty in making contact with the Turkish government, but we succeeded finally in seeing the Acting Minister of Foreign Affairs and also the Governor of Istanbul. Our impression was that the situation was somewhat less acute than we had anticipated. But it was nevertheless useful to make it clear to the Turkish government that there was in the churches of many countries a real concern about the well-being of the Ecumenical Patriarchate.

It happened that we were at the Patriarchate on the Sunday when the feast of Orthodoxy is celebrated and Orthodox Christians come to express their attachment to the Patriarch. We were impressed by the calm dignity which he maintained in the midst of the troubled situation of his church and by his determination to continue to work for reconciliation between the Greeks and the Turks.

In the years following the Amsterdam Assembly of 1948 I heard little about the churches in Russia. In this period of cold war very few churchmen from other countries were permitted to visit Russia. Some Russians living in Western Europe came to share what they knew, and on one occasion I met in Berlin a Christian from Russia who gave a most impressive account of the spiritual renewal which was taking place in many parts of the country and who expressed the conviction that there was now more true Christianity in Russia than there had been before the revolution. But for the time being it seemed to be impossible to establish any contact with the Patriarchate of Moscow or with the leadership of other churches in Russia.

In these circumstances Pastor Martin Niemöller's visit to Russia at the beginning of 1952 broke new ground. In the cold war atmosphere of those days his readiness to enter into conversation with Russian churchmen was widely interpreted as an irresponsible political move, but we knew that his concern was above all a truly ecumenical one. A few days after his return he gave us a full report at the meeting of the World Council's Executive Committee in Lambeth Palace. The visit had been undertaken as a private visit at the invitation of Patriarch Alexis. Niemöller had been deeply impressed by the intensity of devotion in the services which he had attended and particularly by the new emphasis on preaching. Dr Niemöller did not minimize the negative aspects such as the pressure of propaganda and the prohibition of religious education. But he felt that the churches were truly Christian churches in giving priority to the service of Christ.

In his discussions with the Patriarch Niemöller had mentioned the problem of relationships with the World Council of Churches. He had found that the Patriarch was not well informed about the council but had sensed a tone of regret on his part that the Church of Russia was not a member of the council. And he had been impressed by the clear indications that church people in Russia were eager to have spiritual fellowship with Christians of other countries.

Two years later when Bishop Bell and I visited Hungary we received an oral message from Metropolitan Nikolai, the head of the Foreign Relations Department of the Moscow Patriarchate who had been in Hungary in the week before our visit. He had asked the Hungarian church leaders to tell us that he would be glad to receive full information about the work of the World Council and that he hoped the time would come when closer contact could be established between the Church of Russia and the council. We answered that we also hoped that in the not too distant future it would be possible to arrange for conversations between the two bodies.

A few months later, in the summer of 1954, the second Assembly of the World Council was held in Evanston. The political climate was by no means favourable for any action towards closer relations with the churches in Russia. But Bell had the imagination, the courage and the tenacity required to convince the Assembly that a new approach should be made to the Russian churches.

With the help of a small committee he drafted an appeal to the governments, to the peoples and to the churches concerning the international situation. This appeal spoke of the steps which governments should take in order to reverse the trend towards war; it mentioned specifically the responsibility of the churches in those countries between which tension exists to visit one another and to promote the reconciliation of the nations. Now Bishop Bell proposed that this appeal should also be presented to the churches not related to the World Council, including the churches in Russia and in other lands. The Assembly adopted these proposals, alongside a further resolution which recorded the concern and sorrow of the Assembly over the continuing sufferings and disabilities of fellow Christians in many parts of the world.

Thus the Assembly had definitely agreed that the time had come to seek to establish contact with the churches in Russia. But how should this be done? At the meeting of the Central Committee just after the Assembly this question was hotly debated. Many desired that a delegation composed of three World Council representatives should go to Moscow. Some others felt strongly that no such personal contact should be made. Archbishop Michael of the Greek Orthodox Church (who had been chosen as one of the Presidents of the World Council) moved a resolution to express sympathy with the persecuted churches under communist regimes. It was pointed out that the Assembly had already expressed its sympathy with Christians who suffer pain and trial. But the Archbishop insisted that his resolution be put to the vote. We had come to a deadlock. The presidents, the chairman and the general secretary were asked to withdraw to discuss the matter with Archbishop Michael. But we did not succeed in convincing him that his proposal was out of place at this particular moment. So the motion was put, but it was not adopted. There was still further discussion as to how the Assembly appeal should be presented to the churches of Russia. Should a delegation go to Moscow or not? Bishop Otto Dibelius of Berlin made it known that he would be willing to approach the Russian Orthodox bishop in Berlin. It was finally decided that Bishop Bell, Dr Franklin Clark Fry and I should have power to decide how the decision of the Assembly concerning the transmission of the appeal to the non-member churches should be implemented.

We three came to the conclusion that it would be best to begin with an approach to Bishop Boris in Berlin, who represented the Moscow Patriarchate in that city, and that Bishop Dibelius and I should represent the council. We made the visit to Bishop Boris in October 1954. Provost Heinrich Grüber, who was the liaison officer of the German Evangelical Church with the East German authorities, accompanied us. We were well received. Bishop Boris explained that the Russian Orthodox Church was a strongly hierarchical church and that he had therefore asked the Patriarch of Moscow to authorize him to receive our delegation. The Patriarch had given a favourable answer. We explained what action the Assembly had taken and called special attention to the work of the section on International Affairs, to the 'Appeal' of the Assembly and to the resolutions concerning suffering churches and religious liberty. Bishop Boris promised to forward these documents to the Patriarchate and stressed that in the present circumstances personal contacts between World Council leaders and leaders of the Russian Orthodox Church were specially important.

This proved to be the beginning of a new chapter in our relations with Russian Orthodoxy. In February 1955 I received a full reply signed by Metropolitan Nikolai, the head of the department of foreign affairs of the Church of Russia.[4] The letter gave general approval to the Evanston appeal, but urged the World Council to revise its attitude to the World Council of Peace with which the Russian Orthodox Church was co-operating. At the meeting of the Central Committee in Davos 1955 the Executive Committee submitted the draft of a reply to the Moscow Patriarchate. This draft had been prepared by Bishop Bell, Bishop Dibelius, Professor Josef Hromadka and Bishop James of Philadelphia. The main point in it was that the time had now come 'to give our conversation a wider range and that we should concentrate on the deeper aspects of co-operation between churches as churches and on fundamental issues of Christian faith and conscience, and on this foundation turn again to questions of the actions of Christians in the world'. The draft proposed that personal meetings should be arranged between representatives of the Orthodox Church of Russia and representatives of the World Council of Churches. The prolonged debate concerning this draft led to its approval *nemine contradicente*.[5] The Central Committee was ready to take the road leading to ecumenical fellowship with the Church of Russia.

Metropolitan Nikolai answered that the Patriarchate welcomed the proposal for a meeting between their representatives and those of the World Council. A delegation of the National Council of Churches of Christ in the United States went to Russia in March 1956 and our committee chairman, Dr Franklin Clark Fry, who was a member of that delegation, agreed with Metropolitan Nikolai that the two of them would propose the holding of a meeting composed of three or five representatives of each side at the end of January 1957. Paris was mentioned as a possible place of meeting. The Central Committee approved this plan at its meeting in Hungary in the summer of 1956. But the events which took place in the autumn of 1956 changed the situation. On November 5th the officers of the World Council issued a statement on the Hungarian crisis supporting the demand of the Hungarian people to determine freely their own government and their own form of society. I sent a copy of this statement, together with other statements of the officers on the Suez crisis, to the Moscow Patriarchate. Again I cabled the Patriarchate that we would find it necessary to discuss the role of the churches in international crises with particular reference to the Suez and Hungarian crises. This cable crossed with a letter from Metropolitan Nikolai asking that the proposed meeting be postponed for some time in order that the representatives of his church might prepare themselves better for the meeting.

It was not until 1958 that a new date was set. Agreement was reached that the

first meeting should take place in Utrecht (Netherlands) from August 6th to 9th.
Dr Fry, Metropolitan Iakovos of Melita and I were to represent the World
Council.

Dr Fry had warned the Executive Committee that rapid progress could not be
expected. The conversations would be cumbersome because they would have to
be conducted entirely through interpreters. Moreover the Orthodox Church of
Russia had never yet participated in the ecumenical movement. There would be
no formal negotiations. The meeting would be of a purely exploratory character.

This prognosis proved to be correct. When we met in the same Hôtel des
Pays-Bas, in which the delegates of the 1938 conference on the constitution of
the World Council had stayed, we found that it took time to get on the same
wavelength. At first the tone was diplomatic and formal. But both Metropolitan
Nikolai, who did most of the speaking on the Russian side, and Dr Fry introduced a more friendly and informal element in the proceedings. The common
meals, which were largely used to tell stories, helped greatly. Metropolitan
Nikolai's most remarkable contribution at this point was the account of a church
choir in the Caucasus, all members of which were over a hundred years old.
Then there was the exchange of presents. On the first day the Russians distributed gifts. On the second day we reciprocated. We thought that this settled the
matter of presents. But on the third day the Russians came with another suitcase,
the contents of which were distributed. And since this was the last day they had
won this *combat de générosité*.

It became clear that while the Russian church leaders were now ready to
revise the verdict of the 1948 meeting in Moscow, some of the issues raised at that
time were still much on their mind. Did the World Council not neglect the
fundamental issue of church unity? And was there no danger that (especially in
view of its present basis) the World Council would lead to a lowest common
denominator form of ecumenism? The answers we gave to these questions
seemed to remove the misunderstandings to a considerable extent.

I had to introduce the subject: the World Council and world peace. My main
emphasis was that we were working for peace based on justice and freedom,
and that we did so on specifically Christian grounds and in complete independence from governmental policies or ideologies. The Russians agreed that the
churches had to work together for peace and made a statement about their own
position on the defence of peace. But there was at this time no discussion of such
controversial matters as the World Council of Peace or the Hungarian situation.

The participants had to produce a communiqué, and this proved to be much
more difficult than I had anticipated. Every sentence which I proposed was
scrutinized with the greatest care. The result was that the communiqué looked
to the press and to our Central Committee members like a very vague document.
In fact it was quite remarkable that after this first meeting we could say so much
about common aims and concerns. Since it was said in the communiqué that the
Russian delegates would report back to their Patriarchate (and to the other

churches which had participated in the 1948 Moscow conference), 'in a spirit of full sympathy with the fundamental principles of the ecumenical movement', we had found a good foundation for future developments.

A concrete proposal of the consultation had been that observers from the Orthodox Church of Russia should be invited to attend the meetings of the Central Committee of the World Council. This proposal was approved on both sides, and so at the meeting in Rhodes in 1959 Archpriest Vitaly Borovoy was present as an observer.

That meeting in Rhodes was the first Central Committee meeting in an Orthodox country. Rhodes belongs to the ecclesiastical jurisdiction of the Ecumenical Patriarchate, and our hosts were that Patriarchate together with the Church of Greece. So I used this opportunity to underline the great debt we owed to the Ecumenical Patriarchate. In my General Secretary's report[6] I recalled the fact that exactly forty years ago the Holy Synod of Constantinople had decided to propose to the other churches that a league or council of churches should be created and that this has been the very first church initiative of this kind in history. At that time this idea and a very similar plan proposed by Archbishop Søderblom seemed too revolutionary to be carried out. The importance of the Constantinople proposal was, however, not only that it formulated a plan which was realized in 1948 when the World Council of Churches was formed. It was also that it called upon 'all churches of Christ of different confessions throughout the world' not to look upon each other as strangers and foreigners, but as relatives and as part of the household of Christ and 'fellow heirs, members of the same body and partakers of the promise of God in Christ'. I concluded:

> It seems to me that meeting as we do on the territory of the Ecumenical Patriarchate, forty years after the time when this encyclical was drafted on the island of Halki, we have reason to think with deep gratitude of the Orthodox church leaders who thus broke new ground for the ecumenical idea and became pioneers of the World Council which was organized many years later.

The main theme of the Rhodes meeting was 'The Significance of the Eastern and Western Traditions for Christendom'. The discussions on this theme, the Orthodox services, the visit to the island of Patmos with its unforgettable beauty, where St John wrote the Book of Revelation, helped the Central Committee members to a better understanding of the spirit of Eastern Christendom.

In December 1959 I went to Russia with five other members of the World Council staff. After those many years of worrying, hoping, discussing about the churches in Russia and their relation to the ecumenical movement I would at last get to know them personally. I found it a fascinating visit. We were the guests of the Patriarchate of Moscow and were received with that rather overwhelming hospitality of which the Russians have the secret. Thus I was given a suite of five large rooms in the solemn Sovietskaya Hotel in Moscow. And at the many very long meals one had to learn to say *niet* to hosts and waiters. But the truly heart-warming hospitality was that given by the faithful at the many services which we attended. They were so obviously happy to meet fellow Christians from other countries and waved their handkerchiefs so energetically when we brought them a message of fellowship. The length of the services – some of them lasting four hours – was a test of spiritual endurance, but the wonderful singing helped greatly.

Patriarch Alexis received us in his palace in Zagorsk. He had come from one of the leading families of pre-revolutionary Russia and spoke French as easily as Russian. So the conversation was easy. He asked me many questions about the plans of the World Council and about the place of the Orthodox churches in it. It was clear that he had not yet made up his mind about future relations with us, but he was genuinely interested.

With Metropolitan Nikolai, the head of the Foreign Department of the Church of Russia, we dealt with the concrete issues of common concern. We were not yet at the stage of discussing the entrance of the church into the World Council, but had to find ways and means for the Russian church to get to know our work and for the council to become better acquainted with Russian Orthodoxy.

We had similar discussions with the leaders of the Russian Baptists, who proved to be very ready to establish closer links with the council, and with the leaders of the Lutheran Church in Latvia.

During the whole period of our visit we were accompanied by a group of five Russian churchmen. The fact that we were continually together during visits to churches and museums, in trains, cars and planes, and especially during long meals, meant that we got to know each other very well. The leader of this group was the young Archimandrite Nikodim, who was the assistant to Metropolitan Nikolai in the Department of Foreign Affairs. He and I spent many hours together during our journeys and he bombarded me with questions about the other churches and the ecumenical movement. My friend, Alexandre de Weymarn, who had come along as my interpreter, had a hard time keeping up with this unending cross-examination. But it was worthwhile, for Archimandrite Nikodim became soon afterwards the leader of the Foreign Department of the Orthodox Church and again, later on, Metropolitan of Leningrad. He told me years after our visit that he had been quite sceptical about the ecumenical movement but was 'converted' by our visit.

There was furthermore the Archpriest Vitaly Borovoy, who had already been in Geneva and had shown great understanding of the problems and possibilities of the World Council. Most often our meals began with a period of telling stories. When we had laughed enough we would turn to more serious subjects. Thus we had great discussions about the missionary task of the church in the modern world. Ought the church not to use new missionary and evangelistic methods to reach outsiders? Our Russian friends always came back to the point that the church itself is the great evangelistic fact and that by living its own sacramental life it performs at the same time its missionary task. But I was not convinced that this was an adequate answer to the problem of the church's life in a thoroughly secularized society.

We saw many beautiful things: the famous Roublov icons, the Kremlin churches, the treasures of the Hermitage. And it was of course for me a specially great event to see for the first time the quite exceptional collection of Rembrandt paintings in the Hermitage. The 'Return of the Prodigal Son' was even more impressive than I had anticipated. As long as that was hanging in the Hermitage a powerful answer was being given to the exhibits in the anti-religious museum.

In other ways, too, the Russians remained confronted with reminiscences of their Christian past. At the Bolshoi theatre during the Romeo and Juliet ballet there was a moment of such true devotion that one of my colleagues remarked: 'That could have been danced in a church.' And there were of course the icons in the Kremlin and the museums. Interestingly enough even the very modern metro made its Christian contribution: in one of the stations one could see St Alexander Nevski bearing a standard with a picture of our Lord.

We had interesting conversations with government officials. One of these men explained the merits of their system of separation of church and state and asked whether I was satisfied with the situation of the church as I had seen it. I answered that I had had a good many favourable impressions and mentioned some of them. But there were also other impressions, which I could summarize by saying that I wished that the separation between church and state were carried out more consistently. What did I mean? Well, there was the question of freedom for the churches in their approach to youth and freedom to construct church buildings in the new city quarters. At this point my neighbour said that while we had different ideas we could be friends and have a drink together.

The visit to Soviet Armenia began in a plane in which the temperature was incredibly cold when it was on the ground and incredibly hot when it was in the air. So we spent the night covering and uncovering ourselves. We were extremely well received in the ancient Armenian capital city of Etchmiadzin from where we could see the biblical Ararat. The Catholicos (who is the head of the Armenian church) showed deep interest in ecumenical affairs. He asked many questions and made it clear that he wanted to enter into fraternal relations with the council. We were present at the service during which a new altar was consecrated in the cathedral and at the solemn dinner following that ceremony. The addresses reflected the strong conviction that for the Armenians, who had formed the first Christian nation of history, the church would remain the centre of their national life.

At the final dinner in Moscow Patriarch Alexis spoke with appreciation of the work of the World Council. He stressed that the strength of the Russian church lay in its liturgy and common prayer, in its sacramental life through which the

Lord himself was really present. This was the reason for the vitality of the Russian church which surprised those who looked at it from the outside.

I said that the Orthodox Church, as well as other churches in the Soviet Union, had shown in troubled times that they lived by that power which comes from the Holy Spirit and this power is eternal and ever creative. We desired to receive from the Orthodox Church the fruits of its rich history and contemporary Christian experience. We had found a common spiritual language and it had therefore not been difficult to agree on the next steps which were to be taken. We believed that these relationships would become increasingly profitable for both sides.

When I reported my impressions of the visit to Russia I said that we had come back with questions rather than answers. A Russian churchman had said, 'The Russian Orthodox Church has passed her examination'. That was true in the sense that in spite of all the pressure upon it the church had not collapsed. It remained a tremendous fact that the Russian church existed. But had this not been just the first examination, and would there not be a second one during which the church would have to show whether it had a relevant message for the secularized masses?

In the chapter on the New Delhi Assembly I have already told how the Orthodox churches of Russia, of Rumania, of Bulgaria and of Poland were admitted to membership in 1961. A year later the Georgian Orthodox Church came in together with the Armenian, Estonian Lutheran, Latvian Lutheran and Baptist churches of Russia. When in 1965 the Serbian Orthodox Church also entered the council we could say that practically all of Eastern Orthodoxy was included in the World Council family of churches. We had reached an important milestone. Now the great question was whether the membership of the Orthodox churches could be made truly meaningful for them and for the council itself.

In 1963 the monastic community of Mount Athos celebrated its thousandth anniversary. Mount Athos is a conspicuous promontory in Northern Greece with beautiful scenery where monks of different Orthodox nations live in twenty large monasteries and very many small communities or hermitages and form a self-governing republic. No women are allowed to enter this self-contained world. The Orthodox call Mount Athos 'the Holy Mountain'. I had always wanted to visit this unique place where history has stood still and where one can get a glimpse of the Eastern Christian world as it lived and prayed centuries ago. Now to visit this monastic world, known as a place of total seclusion, with a large company of pilgrims from many churches and countries, was certainly not the best way to discover its real significance. How deeply our visit disturbed the quiet life of the monks came out especially in the fact that we were the first visitors in the history of Mount Athos to be transported in motor cars. At one point I saw a poorly clad monk jump away into the bush, as if he had met with the devil himself.

There were impressive services. When in the Central church at Karjes the creed was read by King Paul in front of the patriarchs of many Orthodox churches and the troops surrounding the church presented arms, we seemed to be back at the time of the Constantinian era when church and state were closely intertwined and the *basileus* had an ecclesiastical as well as a civil dignity.

Some of the best moments were those when I could slip away from the crowd, get at least a glimpse of the utter quiet of the place, and try to imagine what it would mean to spend one's life meditating in such lovely solitude. But I am afraid that I could not really imagine what life would be like if one would never see a woman or a child and if one would never hear the noise of mass media or of political conflict.

There were a good many signs that the future of the monasteries on Mount Athos was not bright. It was especially sad to visit one of the Russian monasteries and to find in it only three or four very old and weak monks. I asked some of my Greek friends to support the request of the Church of Russia to the Greek government to admit to Mount Athos monks from Russia for these Russian monasteries.

The closing services and ceremonies took place at the famous Megisti Lavra (the Great Monastery) with its fine collection of ancient manuscripts. According to the plans we were to have a final meal in the beautiful dining hall with its sixteenth century, brightly coloured frescoes. We were already seated when it was announced that our ship would have to leave soon. We had to go down to the harbour on foot. I saw my chance for a quick swim and was soon in the water. Then back to the path leading to the harbour. There I met the head of the Benedictine order who was having difficulty in descending the rough path and was supported by an Italian journalist. I offered to help on the other side. So I arrived at the ship holding my underclothes, wet from my swim, in one hand and steadying the leader of one of the most ancient orders of christendom with the other.

In 1964 the World Council held its first meeting in Russia. The Executive Committee had been invited to meet at Odessa. I was asked to preach in one of the Moscow churches on the Sunday before our meeting. This was a most exceptional invitation for which the personal approval of the Patriarch had been required. The church in which I preached was appropriately in the 'Lefortova' part of Moscow, named after the Lefort whom Peter the Great made an admiral, the only admiral Geneva has ever produced. The church was full and my sermon, translated by Archpriest Vitaly Borovoy, was several times interrupted by audible signs of approval. At the end there were shouts: 'Where does this little father come from?' To be called *Batouchka* was really like being adopted into the family of the faithful in Russia.

We were well received in Odessa and had a good meeting of the Executive Committee. One of the main themes, to which I will come back, was the role of the World Council in the light of the discussions on ecumenism at the second Vatican Council. Dr Nolde presented an interesting statement on religious liberty, one of the main points of which was that full freedom of religious propaganda as well as freedom of anti-religious propaganda should be ensured so that a frank confrontation could take place.

I had some interesting discussions on this subject with Russian government officials. Since we were in the period of the Olympic winter games I made the point that just as in a ski race everybody had the same chance, so believers and atheists should be allowed to compete in complete freedom. Why did the Russian government, then, introduce so many administrative measures which curtailed religious liberty? The answer was that now the majority of the people were atheistic. A Russian churchman entered into the conversation and said: 'The administrative measures often lead to the strengthening rather than the weakening of faith.' In another conversation a government official said: 'The churches are afraid of the secularization process.' I answered that this was unfortunately true, but that the secularized world was also afraid of Christianity. So we agreed that we should overcome our fear on both sides.

In Zagorsk Franklin Clark Fry and I received the degree of honorary professor of the Theological Academy. We were asked what other places we would like to visit and expressed the desire to go to the Pechora monastery. After some hesitation we were allowed to go there with a small party of four people. This monastery in the neighbourhood of the ancient city of Pskov is one of the few monasteries in Russia which is still in full operation. We were glad we had come. On this sunny winter's day this ancient place, with its churches, catacombs and fortress walls, and its spirit of worship, presented a most typical picture of what we think of as Holy Russia. And we were received with the greatest warmth. The fifty monks with whom we had our dinner listened with profound interest to the speeches about the ecumenical movement given by Fry, Bishop Emilianos and me.

In Leningrad we visited many churches and asked everywhere how many people attended the services on Sundays and weekdays. Counting it all up we came to the conclusion that in Leningrad at least the average church attendance was not much below that of some cities in Western Europe.

Once again I was impressed by the persistent signs of Christian influence in Russian culture. We were shown the official film of the siege of Leningrad: towards the end of that film it is shown how Rembrandt's marvellous painting of the Prodigal Son is brought back to the Hermitage gallery. Another form of Christian witness was the Dostoyevsky Museum where it becomes so very clear that Dostoyevsky's central concern was concern for the gospel of Christ.

The time had now come to make closer acquaintance with the Eastern European churches which had recently joined the World Council. I took part in visits of small delegations to Rumania, Yugoslavia and Bulgaria.

In Bucharest we stayed at the patriarchal palace. Patriarch Justinian proved to be a most dynamic type of church leader. Even Dr Fry, who knew something about energetic church management, was impressed by the ability and vigour which the Patriarch showed in organizing the life of his church. It was also noteworthy that he had established excellent relations with the other churches. As he showed us around the palace he called attention to the rooms which were reserved for the leaders of the Lutheran and Reformed churches. Again we were glad to find so many monasteries in full operation. Patriarch Justinian believed deeply in the mission of the monks, who were on the one hand to be active in social and manual work and on the other to intercede 'for those who do not know how to pray, who do not want to pray, who cannot pray and especially for those who have never prayed'.

The visit I made to Yugoslavia in 1964 was different in that my main task was to hand over to the municipality of Skoplje one hundred and twenty-five new bungalows which had been built with the $600,000 contributed by the member churches of the World Council on the basis of the appeal issued at the time of the earthquake disaster which had ruined the city. We had the definite impression that this ecumenical action meant at the same time an improvement in the relations between church and state in Yugoslavia. In Belgrade I had several conversations with Patriarch German about the relations of his church with the World Council, preparing the way for its entrance into membership which took place in 1965.

When I visited Bulgaria with a World Council delegation in 1964 I found that a good many of the church leaders were exceedingly well informed about the ecumenical movement. The work of Professor Stephan Zankov had borne fruit. During the years when the Church of Bulgaria had been cut off from ecumenical life he had continued, in and out of season, to speak up for the cause of Christian unity. He was now an old and sick man, but he was deeply moved by the visit of ecumenical leaders. His life work had not been in vain. A few months later he died.

Now that World Council delegations had visited the Eastern churches the heads of several of these churches came to Geneva in order to get better acquainted with the work of the council. Patriarch Alexis of Moscow was the first to come. As we drove through the city he told me that he had not been in Western Europe since the end of the nineteenth century when his parents had taken him to Switzerland and southern France, but he still recognized some parts of the city. He was obviously happy about the fraternal relations of his church with the ecumenical movement and enjoyed the visit so much that he expressed the desire to spend a holiday in Switzerland. But this plan could not be carried out.

The meeting in the Ecumenical Centre at which we welcomed the Patriarch was attended by the President of the Geneva government and the ambassadors of Russia representing their country in Berne and in Geneva. I said in my address that we lived in a time of increasing secularism and that the Christian church had to accept confrontation with many ideologies. But all concerned should ensure that at no point should this confrontation be made more difficult by using methods of constraint. This we asked not only for the sake of the church, but for the sake of peace; for there could not be peace without mutual confidence, and there could be no confidence without respect for the deepest convictions of other people.

I added that we were glad that through our new fraternal relationship we were also able to work for a true international reconciliation. This had been shown recently when in this same place we had discussed the issues of disarmament with the official government representatives of Russia, the United States and the United Kingdom. I also thanked the Patriarch for the support he had given to the ecumenical movement.

Other visitors – Patriarch Justinian of the Rumanian church, Catholicos Vazken of the Armenian church and Patriarch German of the Serbian church – came after I retired as General Secretary, but I had occasion to greet them and to talk about common memories. And when Patriarch Athenagoras of Constantinople could at last fulfil his wish to visit both Rome and Geneva I had opportunity to address him in the St Peter's Cathedral of Geneva. I spoke of the role which the Ecumenical Patriarchate had played in the creation of the ecumenical movement in the 1920s. Following that tradition Patriarch Athenagoras had consecrated his whole life to the cause of unity. Coming to the World Council of Churches in Geneva he was really like a farmer visiting his own fields to see whether the seeds he had sown were growing well. He had reminded us that of the various forms of dialogue the dialogue of love was the most important.

I had occasion to make a good many visits to Patriarch Athenagoras at Istanbul. The narrow streets leading to the Phanar where the big car of the Patriarchate was always in danger of colliding with overloaded carts drawn by horses or donkeys, the rather solemn meals with the metropolitans bearing the historic names of the most ancient centres of Christianity and, very especially, the overwhelmingly warm reception by the Patriarch himself – became very familiar. Visiting him was not like having an audience, but like having a long unhurried meeting with a pastor and friend. The main subject of conversation was generally that of Christian unity. 'When does a man express his deepest desire?' asked the Patriarch. And he answered himself: 'When he formulates his last will. And where do we find the last will of our Lord? In the high-priestly prayer in the seventeenth chapter of St John. Now, that prayer is all about unity and love. That is what we have so often forgotten in our theological quarrels. That is what the ecumenical movement must bring back.'

He rejoiced in the fact that more and more churches were joining the World Council. He said: 'You brought the Orthodox churches in.' I answered: 'No, that was your achievement.' For with his great faith in the ecumenical cause he had stood by the World Council in the period when it had few strong advocates in the Orthodox world.

He made it very clear that in spite of all difficulties the Ecumenical Patriarchate should remain in Istanbul. Western diplomats who suggested that the

Patriarchate should be transferred to another country did not understand the significance of the great tradition of Constantinople as an ecclesiastical centre. The maintenance of this tradition was in no way a danger for Turkey. On the contrary the Patriarchate could be an advantage to Turkey in its relations. If the Patriarchate were ousted, Turkey would be weakened. He went therefore out of his way to improve the relations between the Patriarchate and the Turkish people.

He spoke often of his desire to meet the Pope. And when that meeting had taken place, he said that it had been like a dream. We lived in a time of miracles. We should now really look forward to the time when all Christians would break the bread together. He however would not live to see that day.

In 1968 I went to Moscow to participate in the commemoration of the restoration of the Patriarchate which had taken place fifty years ago. The services in Moscow and Zagorsk during which Patriarch Alexis was surrounded by five other Orthodox patriarchs were deeply impressive. Thousands of believers for whom there was no place in the churches stood outside so as to be as much involved as possible in the feast of thanksgiving. One wondered what the people of Moscow thought when they saw the fleet of sixty cars full of clergymen of many churches on their way to the Zagorsk monastery.

I stayed at the new Hotel Russia, from which I had an unforgettable view of the Cathedral of St Basil with its innumerable towers, each one of a different shape and colour. And when I went to the opera, Don Carlos, in the Kremlin theatre and watched the scene during which the stage was dominated by an enormous crucifix and the heroine sang her prayer it seemed to me again that the Christian message which was being pushed out of the front door was always coming back through the back door.

There were opportunities for long conversations with Archbishop Nikodim and with representatives of the governmental commission on religious affairs. I was again impressed by the fact that the men of the government were remarkably well informed about ecumenical problems. And I wondered whether any governmental offices in the West were making as thorough a study of our World Council literature.

A few weeks later at the fourth Assembly of the World Council at Uppsala (Sweden) we had for the first time a really adequate representation of the Eastern Orthodox churches. The Orthodox contribution became a vital part of the total life of our meeting.

Similarly, in the work of the World Council staff, the Orthodox now have a real place. We have not succeeded in getting enough Orthodox staff members, but those who have joined us are men with a unique gift of interpreting the Christian East to the Christian West and vice versa. Dr Nikos Nissiotis from Greece, Father Vitaly Borovoy from Russia and Metropolitan Emilianos of the Ecumenical Patriarchate do not allow us to forget that without the full contribution of the East we cannot be truly ecumenical.

This does not mean that we have gone very far with the dialogue between East and West. But we have now after many centuries of hostility, of indifference, of misunderstanding, the chance to arrive at a real meeting and a fruitful exchange of the spiritual gifts of each. Reinhold Niebuhr has recently said that in the West the sense of history and of mystery was on the decline. That seems to me very true. Now the East has preserved exactly those two dimensions of the faith. On the other hand, Orthodoxy needs to enter into a real confrontation with the modern world such as the Western churches with their concern for the world are seeking to realize. In any case the doors between these two spiritual worlds are now open. The question is whether the next generation will have the imagination to use this great opportunity.

NOTES

1. Several Russian Orthodox leaders from the Russian emigration in Western Europe were included in the Constantinople delegation. There were also delegations from Eastern churches not in communion with Constantinople, such as the Church of Ethiopia and the Orthodox Church of Malabar (India).
2. *The Ecumenical Review*, July 1951, p. 406.
3. *The Ecumenical Review*, January 1956, p. 188.
4. See *The Ecumenical Review*, July 1955, p. 389.
5. See *The Ecumenical Review*, October 1955, p. 64.
6. *The Ecumenical Review*, October 1959, p. 70; see also p. 79.

IN THE FIRST years after the Amsterdam Assembly of 1948 Africa did not play a considerable role in the life of the World Council. In most African countries the churches had not yet become autonomous and so they could not join the council. The one exception was South Africa where we had at that time five member churches, two of which were Dutch Reformed and Afrikaans speaking.

At the first full session of our Central Committee in 1949 in Chichester (England) the Commission of the Churches on International Affairs raised the question whether the World Council should take action concerning the racial situation in South Africa. On the proposal of Bishop W. J. Walls of the African Methodist Episcopal Zion Church (USA) it was decided that the CCIA should develop a study on inter-racial relations with special reference to South Africa. One of the proposals which the CCIA made at the next meeting in 1950 was that the World Council should send a delegation to South Africa to discuss the racial problem with the South African churches. Dean Benjamin Mays (of the USA) urged strongly that such a delegation should be multi-racial in character. It was decided to ask the churches in South Africa whether they were ready to invite an ecumenical delegation, and it was added that the Central Committee favoured a multi-racial delegation.

One year later again I had to report to the Central Committee that none of our member churches in South Africa felt that the sending of a delegation was practicable in the present circumstances. The two Afrikaans-speaking churches had added that the sending of a multi-racial delegation would create special problems. But all churches were ready to receive a representative of the World Council. The Central Committee thereupon expressed its regret that a multi-racial delegation seemed to be impractical at this time and its hope that such a delegation could be sent later on. And it was decided that the General Secretary should visit South Africa as soon as possible.

I spent five weeks in South Africa in 1952. The programme included visits to each of the four provinces of the country and also to Basutoland. There was practically no time for sight-seeing, but I did get visual impressions of the many facets of South Africa: rich fertile areas with orange plantations and vineyards, but elsewhere eroded hills where only the skeleton of the earth was left; attractive villas with fine gardens, but also the terribly monotonous locations where the black workers had to live; city centres as modern as anywhere in the world but also most primitive and poor villages.

I met representatives of all the main sections of the country: Afrikaans-speaking, English-speaking, Bantu, Coloured (in South Africa this means the people of mixed ancestry) and Indian. It was amazing to find that each of these groups seemed to live in its own closed world and that there was practically no dialogue or communication between them. I wrote in my report to the Central Committee:[1]

> As one moves, as I did, from Afrikaans homes to English homes, then again to a Bantu or an Indian milieu, it is almost as if one crosses several borders and visits a number of different countries, each with its own assumptions, its own outlook upon the world and often, though not necessarily, its own prejudices.

Thus I was in the strange situation that before long I seemed to have more reliable information about the true feelings of the different groups than most of the people who had lived in the country since their birth. None of the images which each had of the others seemed to correspond to the realities. The Afrikaans were not as cocksure and dogmatic, the English-speaking not as imperialistic and hypocritical, the Bantus, the Coloured and the Indian not as primitive, passive and satisfied as they were made out to be.

In the nature of the case I spent a great deal of time with the Afrikaans-speaking community. They were now in the key position. Their churches were closely connected with the government and the ruling political party. They supported the philosophy of apartheid. In my dealings with the Dutch Reformed church leaders I was greatly handicapped by the fact that only one of the four federated Dutch Reformed churches (the Dutch Reformed Church of Transvaal) and one smaller Afrikaans church (Hervormde Kerk) were members of the World Council, and that precisely at the time of my visit a noisy campaign against the World Council, with the usual accusations concerning its modernism and leftism, was in progress. But it was a considerable advantage that I could speak to the Afrikaners in Dutch and they could speak Afrikaans to me. I gave a number of my addresses and sermons in Dutch. I found that Afrikaners, even though they know English, open up in a quite different way when they can use their own language.

In this connection I was surprised to find that there was often a very considerable divergence between the official position of the churches and the opinions which my Afrikaans-speaking hosts expressed in private. There were of course conversations during which I had to listen to an exposition of the apartheid doctrine in unadulterated form. But there were many other conversations in which men who held prominent positions in the Afrikaans-speaking

Frederick Nolde and Visser 't Hooft greet U Thant in the Ecumenical Centre at Geneva in 1966.

Eugene Carson Blake and Visser 't Hooft greet the Ecumenical Patriarch of Constantinople in Geneva in 1967.

With President Kenneth Kaunda of Zambia and the former Archbishop of Uppsala, Gunnar Hultgren, during the Uppsala Assembly, 1968.

Opening service for the Central Committee of the World Council in Canterbury Cathedral, 1969. Patriarch German of Yugoslavia is next to Visser 't Hooft.

community spoke of their perplexity concerning the race question and of their doubts concerning the policy of the government. A well-known older pastor received me with the words: 'You have now been long enough in this country to have discovered that we are all suffering from a bad conscience.' Another pastor said at the start of our conversation: 'If I were a Bantu in the present situation I would have become a communist.' There were a few Dutch Reformed church-men who had the courage to challenge openly the theological arguments used to support apartheid. Thus the senior theologian, Professor B. B. Keet of Stellenbosch, said in his addresses and articles that the church was not to adapt itself to the state and to society, as it was in danger of doing, and that it had no right to use the Bible to justify current racial policies. Similarly Pastor Ben Marais in Pretoria had just written a book showing the fragility and theological inadequacy of the theories underlying the dominant Dutch Reformed position on race. But such men were few. The great majority felt that even if they had their personal doubts about the line which the church and the government were taking, threats to their survival coming from the side of the English speaking, of the Bantu majority and of world opinion were so great that they simply had to present a common front.

I had to admit that the position of the Afrikaans-speaking people was often misrepresented. I had read many times in the world press that the Dutch Reformed church based its position on the story of the cursing of Ham, one of the sons of Noah, who was supposed to be the ancestor of the black people. But no responsible Dutch Reformed theologian holds such a view today. Again, it was commonly thought that these churches interpreted apartheid as permanent domination of the blacks by the whites. In fact one could read in one of the documents of the Bloemfontein Conference of Dutch Reformed churches the following sentence: 'No people in the world worth their salt will be content indefinitely with no say, or only an indirect say, in the affairs of the state or in the socio-economic organization of the country in which decisions are taken about their interests and future.'[2] Again, the outside world had not taken sufficiently seriously the new interpretation of apartheid as 'distinctive development' or 'development according to kind'. But I became convinced that from the point of view of the World Council a number of serious questions had to be raised about the position of the Dutch Reformed churches. It was the basic concern of the ecumenical movement to demonstrate that Christians are members of one and the same body. Now these churches did not desire this, but by their strong emphasis on separation of the races in the life of the churches they were in fact obscuring that central element in the New Testament teaching. I said in my report: 'The important thing is to manifest to a world in which the races live in tension, that in Christ their tension is overcome.'

As to apartheid I had come to understand that much depended on the specific definition given. The Dutch Reformed churches had committed themselves to the view that it should be understood as a 'Process of development which seeks to lead each section of the population in the clearest and quickest way to its own destination under the gracious providence of God'. They believed that the only way to do this was to achieve a total separation of the races. Bantus would govern themselves in their own territories and would no longer be used as workers in the white territories. But was this really a possible solution? The minister of internal affairs had told me that such a plan could perhaps be realized in two hundred years, but that for the moment it was just a dream. And business leaders had explained to me that the inexorable economic development led in the opposite direction, and that the influx of black labour to the urban centres would certainly have to continue. So it looked as if the present form of apartheid, which meant in fact that the Bantu had no say about his own destiny, would simply continue. How could a Christian church accept this? And was it not a very serious fact that in this way the Bantu was not given any tangible reason to hope for a better day? As I raised such questions I had of course some unpleasant moments, but I must say that on the whole the Dutch Reformed leaders were quite willing to discuss those matters. Dr C. B. Brink, one of the most influential Dutch Reformed leaders, said in a meeting: 'Visser 't Hooft likes to use shock tactics.' That was true, for this seemed to be the only way to come to a clarification of the situation.

The English-speaking churches took a different line. They affirmed that the church should be multi-racial and that, as they put it in the report of the South African Christian Council, 'the unity in Christian fellowship must inevitably spread into fellowship in secular activity'. But this conviction was not sufficiently demonstrated in the daily life of the church. Common worship services were quite exceptional. And the leadership of these churches was almost wholly white. Though the official church declarations spoke in favour of the building of a multi-racial society, it was clear that the majority of their membership was not ready for any fundamental change in inter-racial relations.

Fortunately, some of the English-speaking church leaders and laymen were in the front of the battle for inter-racial justice. I was especially impressed by Senator Edgar H. Brookes, who had given his whole life to the solution of the race problem. I asked him whether the situation could not be compared with King Canute trying to hold back the waves. He answered: 'But King Canute could get back to dry land. The time factor is so important. If we could work on the problem for several generations we could solve it. But do we have that much time?'

It was not surprising to find that the Africans who were willing to talk openly were very pessimistic. To them apartheid meant the continuation of a caste society in which they would have to remain the proletariat. Industrialization and urbanization led to the disintegration of Bantu society. Large numbers of Africans had to leave their homes in the reserves and were not allowed to bring their family to the towns. The inevitable result was the collapse of moral standards and the increase of crime. Many white church leaders were concerned about this, but industry and business were unwilling to make the necessary sacrifice to stop this disastrous process. I talked with some of the prominent leaders of the African National Congress. Several of them were active Christians. None of them was an advocate of violence. They were deeply discouraged by the fact that all attempts to arrive at a real dialogue between representative Bantus and the government had failed. What policy should they adopt now? More light was thrown on this question when I came to Durban. At the International Club in that city I met Chief Albert Luthuli and Manilal Gandhi, the son of Mahatma Gandhi. Chief Luthuli, who was the president of the Natal branch of the African National Congress and was later to receive the Nobel Peace Prize, also came to the inter-racial meeting of pastors to which I spoke, for he was an active church member. The longer one talked with him the more ludicrous it seemed to be that in certain political circles he was considered as a communist and a terrorist. For he was still hoping for a peaceful solution of the race problem on the basis of democratic principles and there was not the slightest sign of racial antagonism in his attitude.

The three of us – Chief Luthuli, Arthur Blaxall of the South African Council of Churches and I – visited Manilal Gandhi at the Phenix settlement which his father had founded in 1904 and where he had started the *satyagraha* (non-violence) movement. Manilal Gandhi had tried to continue the work of his father and had fought a battle for inter-racial justice with strictly non-violent methods, but had had little success. It was all the more admirable that he showed no sign of bitterness. I described the visit in my travel diary as follows:

> The Gandhi family receives us cordially. On the walls pictures of Mahatma Gandhi, Nehru, Tagore and Radakrishnan. As we sit down to luncheon Manilal Gandhi requests me to ask the blessing. Mrs Gandhi serves us, but the son Aron and the very bright and gifted daughter Sita sit at the table with us. The conversation becomes extremely animated when I ask whether the present moment is really the right moment to start passive resistance. The otherwise quiet Manilal Gandhi becomes eloquent: 'No, the people are not yet ready for true passive resistance. They do not know the ethics of non-violence. What is the use of calling for ten thousand ignorant volunteers? Give me ten really convinced people who are ready to go the whole way. But I have not even ten.' Chief Luthuli who is a man of astounding good humour is on the spot. He argues that the leaders of the African National Congress are trying to explain to the people what non-violence means, but he admits that few really understand it. As to the question of the right time he realizes that there is a danger that premature action may solidify the ranks of the Nationalist party, but after all there is so little difference between the two main parties in their attitude to the non-European. Something must be done.

It was a strange experience to be suddenly involved in such a serious and searching debate between an Indian spiritual leader and a Zulu chief and to be taken into their confidence. I could only admire Manilal Gandhi for his strong adherence to the principles which his father had taught him. But I felt also deep sympathy with Albert Luthuli who found himself confronted by a tragic dilemma.

Before I left South Africa it was agreed that I would give the leaders of the South African member churches an opportunity to make comments on my report before its publication. I did this soon after my return. Although at many points the report raised critical questions these leaders felt that it was not unfair and that it was a useful contribution to the ecumenical discussion.

The next stage was the submission of the report to the Central Committee at its meeting in Lucknow, in January 1953. The committee said that it was glad to recognize that a constructive conversation had begun between the South African member churches and the World Council concerning the Christian attitude to the race problem. It adopted again a strong resolution condemning enforced segregation in the life of the church and all forms of discrimination based on the grounds of race. And it confirmed a former decision that one of the six sections of the second Assembly of the World Council should deal with the subject of 'Intergroup Relations: The Churches amid racial and ethnic tensions'. The preparatory commission for this section, which was ably chaired by Roswell P. Barnes (USA), had three South African members: Ben Marais, Alan Paton (the author) and Z. K. Matthews (the Bantu leader). At the Assembly I could not participate in this section, but I became involved in its heated discussions when the South African Dutch Reformed delegates came to me complaining that their position was not taken seriously. One of them said: 'They have asked the last drop of blood from us.' They intended now to make a statement to the Assembly saying that they had come to the conclusion that the World Council did not desire to have any further conversation with the Dutch Reformed churches of South Africa. Roswell Barnes and I explained that this was certainly not the case. The section report and the resolutions had no mandatory power over the member churches, but each member church should be willing to reconsider its own policies in the light of the findings of the Assembly. We arrived at an agreement. In the main resolution which would urge the churches to renounce all forms of segregation and discrimination and to work for their abolition within their own life and within society we would seek to introduce a recognition that for some churches the immediate achievement of this objective was extremely difficult, and that the fellowship of the ecumenical movement was such as to offer to these churches the strength and encouragement to overcome these difficulties. This was accepted by the section. The Dutch Reformed delegates made a public statement saying that they could not consider the report and the resolutions as the last word on the issue of race relations, that they would however not vote against it, and that they would urge their churches to study the report.

During the next few years we did not make further public pronouncements on the South African situation, but we tried through visits and correspondence to stimulate the process of reflection on the basic issues – a process going on in the South African churches, including the Dutch Reformed churches. There were encouraging developments. I could report to the Executive Committee in 1957 that when the government had proposed a law with strict rules concerning the church attendance of Bantus all the churches had protested. But there was no fundamental change in inter-racial relations.

In March 1960 the disturbances at Sharpeville, during which a number of Africans were killed, led to the declaration of a national state of emergency in South Africa. World opinion was deeply shocked. The officers of the World Council felt that in this situation, in which strong tensions arose between the member churches in South Africa and between some of those churches and the churches of other countries, priority should be given to personal contacts. I asked the South African churches whether they were ready to receive the visit of a World Council representative. This was accepted, and Robert Bilheimer, an Associate General Secretary, went to South Africa in April. The main result of the conversations he had with South African church leaders was the proposal that the World Council should take the initiative for the calling of a consultation which would provide opportunity for a thorough discussion of the race problem in South Africa, between the member churches in South Africa, between white and black church leaders, and between the South African churches and the World Council. In May Franklin Clark Fry, Ernest Payne and I sent a letter to the member churches in South Africa proposing a consultation on five subjects: the factual understanding of the situation in South Africa, the action taken by the churches to establish justice in race relations, the meaning of the Gospel for relations among the races, the implications of the rapid social change which was taking place and the interpretation of the present emergency. All member churches accepted the proposal in principle, but formidable obstacles had to be overcome before the plan could be carried out.

There was, first of all, the fact that in an interview with a *New York Times* correspondent the (Anglican) Archbishop of Capetown (Joost de Blank) had expressed the opinion that since they had failed to condemn apartheid the Dutch Reformed churches of South Africa should be expelled from the World Council. In a letter to Franklin Clark Fry the Dutch Reformed churches said that as a result of this interview the impression had been created that the proposed consultation would deal specifically with this question of expulsion. Dr Fry could answer that no request looking towards the expulsion of the Dutch Reformed churches had been received by the World Council. The next problem was that the Bishop of Johannesburg, Ambrose Reeves, who had been appointed a delegate to the consultation, but was at that time in Great Britain, had not been allowed to return to Johannesburg. A common approach of the churches was made to the government to ask for a re-entry permit for him. This was refused, but the solidarity of the churches had been sufficiently demonstrated. It was largely due to the persistent and imaginative work of Robert Bilheimer, who had to fly several times to South Africa, that those problems were solved.

In my report to the Central Committee in St Andrews, in August 1960, I described the role of the World Council in this matter as follows:

> We should have done far more than we have done to arrive at a deep understanding of the complex problems of human relations in South Africa. We will therefore have to be good listeners, but that does not mean that the role of our delegates will be a passive role. Our delegates will not be empty-handed when they go to South Africa. They will come with the convictions held in the ecumenical fellowship as most clearly expressed in the report of the Second Assembly at Evanston. Our hope must be that through such a meeting of minds we will not only help to create more real ecumenical fellowship between the churches of all races in South Africa and between them and the World Council, but also and especially make a substantial contribution to the cause of justice and freedom for all races of mankind.

The following were chosen to represent the World Council: Franklin Clark Fry (USA), Ernest Payne (Great Britain), Wilhelm Niesel (Germany), Bishop Lakdasa de Mel (Ceylon), Charles Parlin (USA), Sir Francis Ibiam (Nigeria) and I. Unfortunately Sir Francis Ibiam had to inform us just before the meeting that, owing to his election as governor of the Eastern Province of Nigeria, he could not carry out his intention of attending the meeting.

We met for a full week in December at the Cottesloe College Residence of the University of Witwatersrand. There were some eighty participants and the meeting was fully inter-racial. The churches had sent their most prominent leaders. There were men who had close connections with the government, but there were also strong critics of apartheid like Alan Paton, whose passport was taken away just before the meeting, and Z. K. Matthews, a leader of the African National Congress, who was not allowed to leave the country. It was truly a unique occasion for dialogue between people who had had little or no opportunity to meet each other.

The meeting was well prepared. Each participating church had been asked to prepare memoranda on the subjects of discussion. Many of these documents were of very high quality and provided a solid basis for the work of the meeting. It was most encouraging to find in the memoranda of the Dutch Reformed churches, on which some sixty professors, pastors and missionaries had worked, a number of statements which represented the most advanced thinking in these churches and which amounted to demands for very considerable changes in the policy of the government with regard to the Africans and the Coloured.

It was unanimously decided that Franklin Clark Fry should chair the consultation and that the World Council delegates would chair the groups on the five topics. My task was to give the daily bible studies and to serve as consultant on the small committee which would draft the findings of the consultation.

The opening speech of Franklin Fry was a masterpiece. He dealt openly with the suspicion that this consultation was really a tribunal before which certain churches stood on trial. He said:

> Is there going to be pressure? If you mean, against your convictions, the answer is no. It is not the function of the World Council to exert pressure upon the convictions of any church. What power could we wield, if we wanted to? If however pressure means the pressure of God's word, the answer is yes; this pressure is equally upon us all.

The group went to work. There were a few who spoke the language of political meetings and repeated familiar slogans, but the great majority entered into a process of give and take and of discovering new perspectives. White churchmen had the opportunity to hear much about the realities of the situation among the Bantus and the Coloured. Afrikaners and English-speaking began to revise the image they had of each other. This was the kind of Christian dialogue which was so very badly needed in South Africa. The remarkable thing was that after a while the sharp lines of demarcation between the various delegations became less pronounced. We were helped by the fact that we could participate in common worship, including a communion service at which white and black ministers administered the sacrament, and that we had all our meals together. There were only a few white delegates who practised apartheid during meals.

The drafting committee had now to begin its work. It was unanimously agreed that no statement would finally be included in the report which would not be supported by eighty per cent of the members present and voting. This was to ensure that nothing would be said that would be unacceptable to one of the major groupings. So our drafting committee had to discover on which points an almost complete agreement could be reached. This we did largely by picking out the most constructive and forward looking positions which were contained in the memoranda submitted by the Dutch Reformed churches.[3] In this way a number of important points could be made about the need for more consultation between the various racial groups, about mixed marriages, about common worship, about migrant labour, about job reservations, about the representation of the coloured people in Parliament, and about the right of all people to participate in the government of the country. In some cases we even used the exact wording which was found in the Dutch Reformed memoranda. An important example of this was the point on participation in government. One of the memoranda of the Dutch Reformed Church contained an affirmation on this subject which had within the context of the South African situation most far-reaching implications. It said: 'It is our conviction that the right to own land and to participate in the government of which he is a subject, is part of the dignity of the adult man, and for this reason a policy which denies to the economically integrated non-white people the right to participate in the government of the country cannot be justified.' This sentence became one of the key sentences of the draft which we submitted to the consultation.[4] When our draft was submitted to the plenary meeting we found to our relief that every one of our points received the approval of more than eighty per cent of the delegates. The only delegation which voted against a number of the findings was that of the small Hervormde Kerk which was 'more royalist than the king' in its defence of total apartheid and voted even against the principle that 'no one who believes in Christ may be excluded from any church on the grounds of his colour or race'.

But the great majority of the delegates of all races, including those who had come from abroad, were deeply grateful that we had been able to find so much common ground and to render a common witness. Archbishop de Blank made an impressive statement expressing regret for words which had been spoken in the past and thanking the Dutch Reformed churches for the patience which they had shown. The Moderator of the Dutch Reformed Church of the Cape, Dr A. J. van der Merwe, said that his church had also its share of guilt for the tensions which had developed and that a new era in the relations between the churches in South Africa could now begin.

The significance of the Cottesloe statement[5] must of course be understood in the light of the South African situation. It represented an agreement between churchmen from very different backgrounds. Each delegation would have liked to say more at specific points. To many people outside South Africa its recommendations might seem commonplace, but in South Africa it represented a possible way of overcoming the deadlock and it would give hope to the many who had become hopeless. 'Do you realize that this statement contains dynamite?' asked one of the reporters at the press conference after the meeting.

So the World Council delegates left South Africa with the feeling that the ecumenical method had once again proved to be the right one and that in view of the great influence which the churches could exert in South Africa there was reason to hope for a real breakthrough in the inter-racial situation.

But we had underestimated the strength of the forces which were opposed to any new deal with regard to race relations. A veritable campaign was organized against 'Cottesloe'. A Dutch Reformed journal wrote: 'We cannot remember that in recent years any event in, or in connection with, the church has created so much debate and so much confusion.' Prime Minister Verwoerd[6] made it very clear that he considered Cottesloe as an attempt by foreigners to interfere in South African affairs. He could not believe that an organization like the World Council of Churches could make any permanent impression on the thinking and action of South Africans. And he went so far as to describe the statement of the highly representative consultation as just an expression of view by individuals of some of the Dutch Reformed churches. A clear indication of things to come was given when he added: 'The churches have in fact not yet spoken. Through their synods at which the members as well as the whole of the clergy will be represented, the voice of the churches has still to be heard.'

The Dutch Reformed delegates who had participated in the consultation tried hard to combat the misunderstandings and deep suspicions which had arisen with regard to the role of the World Council. In their report,[7] which told the whole story of the preparation for the consultation and of the consultation itself and which contained the full text of the memoranda they had submitted, they said clearly that the South African churches had asked the World Council to take the initiative for the calling of the consultation. And they added: 'The chairman of the consultation and the other World Council representatives who chaired the study groups have been impartial and fair. In the last analysis our delegates and not the World Council must accept responsibility for the findings which have largely been taken from the memoranda which the two Dutch Reformed churches have drawn up independently from each other.' But their testimony was drowned in the great clamour of voices shouting that the cause of the Afrikaans people was in danger.

The machine of the ruling political party worked effectively. The small Hervormde Kerk condemned the Cottesloe statement and decided to leave the World Council. The Federal Council of Dutch Reformed Churches declared that the tendency of the statement as a whole was to undermine the policy of apartheid and that the consultation had dealt with matters which were not within the competence of the churches. Thus the Dutch Reformed churches of Transvaal and of the Cape were put in a most uncomfortable position. To approve Cottesloe would mean to enter into opposition against the government and against the party to which the vast majority of church members belonged, and it would mean at the same time a break between the Dutch Reformed churches. So the inevitable happened. At the Synod of the Transvaal church and of the Cape church the defenders of Cottesloe lost the battle, and both synods decided to terminate their membership in the World Council. I have always wondered whether the majority of the delegates realized that they were not voting against positions imported by the World Council and imposed on their churches, but against the convictions expressed by the best minds of their own churches and submitted at Cottesloe by their own trusted leaders.

Was the Cottesloe story then a story of complete failure? I did not think so. I wrote at that time:[8]

> The fact remains that this witness and the attitude which the World Council has taken with regard to race relations has encouraged many, particularly among the non-white Christians, who had begun to feel hopeless about the role of the Christian church. And it should be remembered in the churches of the World Council that not only in the present member churches in South Africa, but also in the churches which have left us, there are many men and women who are deeply conscious of belonging to the world community, gathered by the same Lord, whose task it is to make the transcendent power of Christ tangible and visible in deeds of justice and fellowship through which the estrangement of the races can and must be overcome.

> Some of these men and women felt so deeply that the Cottesloe consultation

had shown a truly Christian way to overcome the tragic deadlock that they organized a Christian Institute to continue the struggle for inter-racial justice. Pastor Beyers Naudé, a former moderator of the Dutch Reformed Church of Transvaal, who had been one of the most active members of the consultation, took the initiative and persisted, in spite of strong opposition, in leading it with great wisdom and courage. Through the Christian Institute and also through the Christian Council in which the English speaking churches co-operate, Cottesloe has continued to challenge the Christian people of South Africa.

I must now turn to other countries in Africa which had very different problems. In 1952 I spent some time in Ethiopia. The ancient Church of Ethiopia had joined the World Council in 1948. This had been largely due to the personal interest of Emperor Haile Selassie in the ecumenical movement. In the nineteen twenties the Emperor had come to know Archbishop Søderblom of Sweden, who had made a great impression on him and who told him of his ecumenical plans. But the Ethiopian church had remained isolated. There was a strong fear of proselytism by Catholic or Protestant churches. While the younger generation was educated in English by Indian and Canadian teachers and thus brought in contact with the modern world, the church had not yet begun to adapt itself to the new situation. I wondered whether it would not be possible to help the church by providing an ecumenical team of advisers, but did not find much response. The Emperor was aware of the problem. The church which he attended was the only one in the country to use the national language, Amharic, rather than the ancient liturgical language, Geez. Moreover he had made arrangements for the sending of students to Eastern Orthodox theological schools.

My audience with the Emperor was a solemn affair. He stood at the end of a great hall wearing his uniform, very erect and motionless. The instruction was to make three bows, one at the entrance, one in the middle, one in front of the Emperor. This was not difficult as one entered the hall, but quite difficult when one had to leave. I thanked him for the interest he had shown in the World Council, expressed the readiness of the Council to help the Church of Ethiopia in any way that would be acceptable and said that we hoped that Ethiopia would continue to grant religious freedom to all confessions. I also reminded the Emperor of his visit to Geneva in 1936, at which time I had on behalf of an international delegation expressed deep sympathy with his country. The Emperor spoke of his gratitude to God for his return to the country. He had been glad to hear of the formation of the World Council of Churches and desired that the Church of Ethiopia should participate in it. With regard to religious liberty he considered that religion was a matter between God and each individual person.

Ethiopian churchmen explained to me the tradition of the church to which they were deeply attached. The most interesting item was that the true Ark of the Covenant was in Ethiopia. For after the visit of the Queen of Sheba to King Solomon the Queen had borne a son, and this boy had visited his father in Jerusalem. He had seen the Ark of the Covenant and expressed the desire to have a similar ark. The carpenter did such a good job that the two arks were indistinguishable. The ark which remained in Israel was lost, but the ark which came to Ethiopia still existed and it was certainly the original one. Such traditions showed that the church of Ethiopia lived in a world far removed from the modern civilization which was now being introduced into the country.

In 1958 the Assembly of the International Missionary Council was held at the University College near Accra in Ghana. We were so busy with the problems concerning the future of missions and specifically concerning the proposed integration of the International Missionary Council and the World Council of Churches that we had little time left to get to know the country. But Kwame Nkrumah, who had become Prime Minister in 1957, came to address us and some of us had the opportunity of meeting him. He paid a tribute to the missionaries who had worked in Ghana: yellow fever had decimated them and their families; they belonged to the martyrs of Christianity as surely as those who faced persecution for their faith. Nkrumah's main preoccupation now was that since the hold of tribalism was slackening and young people came to the towns in great numbers the old social disciplines were growing weaker. In the task of educating young people for genuine maturity missions could play a great role. In the past the missionary societies had sent out a number of able ethnologists. What was needed today were missionaries who had a knowledge of sociology.

I made a short visit to Sierra Leone where I stayed with the governor, Sir Maurice Dorman. Although independence was in sight, the traditions which British governors had upheld during the great days of the Empire were still maintained. I had to borrow the dinner jacket of my friend John Karefa Smart, the minister of mines. But there was a delightful mixture of formality and informality and an easy mixing of black and white. On a Sunday morning I preached the sermon in the Anglican cathedral. The service had great dignity and the faithful, dressed in their best Sunday clothes, were extremely quiet. If the faces had not been black one could have imagined that one was in Canterbury or Chichester. As I left the church a friend from New Zealand asked me whether I would be interested in visiting an African independent sect. I accepted immediately, for I had heard so much about these sects that I was eager to get a personal impression of their life. When we got out of the car we heard sounds of music and shouting. In the small building which we entered we found a crowd of men and women who were dancing, jumping, singing and cheering. A small organ was playing syncopated music. We were warmly welcomed by the leader dressed in a pink gown who called himself 'the apostle'. He gave some explanations about the teachings of his sect and offered me an African costume. I was asked to put this on immediately. And would I be willing to bring them a spiritual message? There I stood dressed as a Yoruba. The sermon became the shortest one I ever delivered. For as soon as I had said something which they were glad to hear, the dancing and jumping began again. I said for instance: 'I find that you Africans have really understood that the gospel is good and joyful news.' After any such sentence I would have to wait the next few minutes to allow them to prove what I had said by hallelujahs of the voice and of the body.

I came away from that experience with the conviction that the churches in Africa would have to take the question of africanizing their ways of worship and of evangelism far more seriously than they had done so far. It was not necessary that the cathedral service should follow the pattern of the sects, but it was necessary to bring into the life of the churches that truly African intuition that worship has to do with the whole of man, with his body and with his soul.

From Sierra Leone I went to Ibadan in Nigeria where, under the auspices of the International Missionary Council, representatives of the churches from all over Africa were brought together to get to know each other, to discuss their common problems and to consider in what ways they could establish a more permanent link among themselves. Ibadan is the most African of the big cities in Africa and we lived in African style. As in the first all-Asia meetings which I had attended, the conference was dominated by the surprise and joy of meeting fellow-Christians who had the same convictions, the same concerns. One delegate said: 'By discovering each other we have discovered ourselves.' The little hut in which I stayed was near the one occupied by Alan Paton, the South African author of *Cry the Beloved Country*. We spent a good many evenings together. He believed strongly that, as he put it in his address to the conference, the church as the guardian of justice, love and truth, should rejoice in the liberation of human energy and talents which was taking place in Africa, but that it would also have to oppose the excesses and cruelties of nationalism in its worst manifestations and any seeking for revenge.

The conference was not yet ready to make a definite plan for the organization of an All Africa Conference of Churches. There was still a good deal of fear, not so much among the Africans themselves as among the missionaries, that ecumenical bodies were a danger to the purity of the faith. But a continuation committee was created and this committee could prepare the way for the setting up of a more permanent structure of continental co-operation.

At the New Delhi Assembly in 1961 ten more African churches joined the World Council. Africa was at last beginning to play its role in the ecumenical movement. We chose our first African President – Sir Francis Ibiam of Nigeria. Now we needed a strong African on our staff. I thought of Professor Z. K. Matthews who had impressed me at the time of the Cottesloe Consultation of 1960 as an extremely able and wise spokesman for the Africans. He was a lawyer who had become principal of the University College of Fort Hare in South Africa, where so many of the brightest young men from different parts of Africa had been studying; but since he was also a leader of the African National Congress of South Africa he had had to leave the college. What a pity that a man of such ability and of such spiritual integrity, whose one desire was to arrive at a just and peaceful solution of the race problem, was pushed aside by the rulers of the country. Would he be willing to join our staff? We could always try. I was delighted when he accepted our call. In many places in Africa the new leaders as well as the new church leaders respected him as their *guru*. And his work as secretary for Africa of our Division of Interchurch Aid, Refugee and World Service gave him a chance to make a great contribution to the up-building of the new Africa.

The churches of Africa were now ready to take the next step on the ecumenical road. In 1963 two All Africa Christian conferences were held. The first was the youth assembly in Nairobi; the second the inaugural assembly of the All Africa Conference of Churches in Kampala.

It seemed to me that the young people were considerably ahead of the older generation. They expressed themselves more freely. They were more clearly aware of the common problems which the African countries would have to solve. Their complaint was that there was too much 'negative preaching' in the churches. Instead of being told what Christians should not do, they wanted to hear what positive social ethic the churches could offer as a foundation for the building of the new African society. And they were impatient about the lack of real progress of the movement towards church unity.

It was not difficult to understand them. When at the beginning of the Kampala conference each delegate had to say which church or which missionary society he represented, my colleague Bishop Lesslie Newbigin said to me, 'A real cacophony'. What could all these divisions and subdivisions mean for Africans who were confronted with new issues that had little to do with the old controversies? The urgent problems were surely the ones which the young people had discussed, such as the formation of an educated ministry, the working out of relevant social ethics and the working out of truly African ways of worship and witness. The whole position of the church in Africa was changing rapidly. Many services and opportunities, which until recently were offered by the churches alone, were now being offered by the new states and other agencies. An African sociologist said rightly: 'From now on the church must shine in its own light.' It would have to rely wholly on the intrinsic quality and the relevance of its message and its example.

The Kampala conference did not solve these problems, but it expressed the conviction that the African churches should stand on their own feet, that the time had come to express their 'selfhood', and it created the All Africa Conference of Churches which could become a precious instrument in helping the churches to fulfil their common mission in Africa. It would at the same time enable the African churches to make their voice heard in the ecumenical movement.

The situation in Southern Africa and particularly in South Africa, Angola, Mozambique and Rhodesia, became increasingly alarming. So in 1964 the

World Council's Department on Church and Society, together with the Mindolo Ecumenical Foundation (Kitwe) and the South African Institute of Race Relations, organized a consultation held in Kitwe (Zambia) on 'Christians and Race Relations in Southern Africa'. Daisuke Kitagawa, who had done a remarkable job as the first World Council Secretary on Racial and Ethnic relations, was in the chair. Some seven countries from Southern Africa were represented. The strong delegation from South Africa was largely composed of men who had welcomed and persistently advocated the policies outlined by the Cottesloe Consultation of 1960.

But the situation had changed since 1960. This came out in the impressive address by Professor Z. K. Matthews on 'The Road from Non-violence to Violence'. He described the tragic fate of the men of his generation who had believed that, as the Africans adapted themselves more and more successfully to the new ways of life, they would be accorded more and more recognition as fellow-citizens of the white man. He enumerated the attempts made by the African National Congress ever since 1912 to get a hearing for the cause of the African people. Innumerable deputations, petitions and resolutions had been addressed to the government. But it had become a story of the refusal of dialogue, of missed opportunities for co-operation, of disappointment of all hopes for a democratic solution of the problem of race relations. Until recently all the outstanding leaders of the Africans had stood by the policy of non-violence in achieving their aims. But as this policy appeared to the ordinary man not to yield any results, the leaders who stood for non-violence and for co-operation between black and white on the basis of equal opportunity were being replaced by leaders who did not hold this view.

Z. K. Matthews moved us profoundly because in telling this story he showed us the anguish of his own mind. He had himself always thought in terms of non-violence and co-operation. To him, as to his friends Luthuli and Xuma, this had seemed the Christian way. But what could one say to the younger generation who retorted: 'What have you achieved?' Could one simply go on urging them to stand by the methods of persuasion and discussion in the face of increasing and relentless force? At no time did Z. K. Matthews advocate the use of force. But he did show that we would have to consider again what the Christian attitude should be with regard to violence.

I had the difficult assignment of speaking on 'The Christian's Role in Transforming Society'.[9] I tried to formulate the main insights which we had received in the ecumenical discussions concerning 'The Responsible Society'. Coming to the race problem I said:

> In our day and generation all men are forced to choose between two world views, the one according to which the civilization dominated by the white race must hold the fort and defend its interests at whatever cost against the other races; the other according to which the world must now become a

multi-racial international society with equality of opportunity for all. The ecumenical movement has definitely chosen the second world view.

I had of course also to deal with the question of resistance and violence. My point of departure was the position of Calvin, worked out by John Knox and the Scottish confession of faith of 1560 according to which one of the good works which Christians are to undertake for the sake of their neighbours was the defence of the oppressed and the repression of tyranny. There were various forms of resistance: spiritual, legal, illegal and violent. I spoke of the dangers of violent resistance. It could create such a deep chasm, I said, that a peaceful solution would become impossible. The deepest separation between peoples is a river of blood. We could not absolutely exclude the possibility that in certain situations Christians might have to participate in violent resistance. I mentioned the case of those Christians in Germany who had felt obliged to do so during the days of the second world war. But Christians should never resort to violence before having counted the heavy cost and before being quite certain that this was the one and only possibility of serving the cause of justice. In most situations there were far more possibilities for non-violent resistance than most people realized.

The group dealing with 'Justice in the Political Life of Southern Africa' adopted most of the points which Z. K. Matthews and I had made and included them in the report.[10] But several members from South Africa, among whom were Pastor Beyers Naudé and Professor A. G. Geyser, declared that they felt bound to dissociate themselves from any suggestion that the use of industrial disruption, the invoking of sanctions or other forms of international intervention or the use of internal violence are permissible methods to secure social justice. This was noted in the official report.

The urgency and complexity of the problem of violent resistance was brought home to me when Eduardo Mondlane made a short visit to the consultation. He was the son of a Mozambique chief who had been educated by the Swiss Reformed missionaries. He had been a youth consultant at our Second Assembly at Evanston in 1954. His studies in the USA had been so successful that he had become a professor in Syracuse University. Afterwards he had held a prominent position on the staff of the United Nations. But he had come to the conviction that he should give his whole energy to the cause of the liberation of his people, and so he had left the comfort of a good job and became the leader of the Mozambique liberation movement (Frelimo). He was very ready to discuss the moral and spiritual problems with which he was now confronted. He said that he and his friends had not chosen violence. They were reacting to a form of oppression which was in fact a form of violence. At any time they were ready to enter into negotiations with their opponents. I spoke to him of the dangers of violence. But I did not feel free to condemn his choice. Was he not a striking illustration of what Calvin had said about the role of 'lower magistrates' in resisting oppression? Could we Dutchmen continue to sing our national anthem with its praise of William the Silent for his commitment to the cause of 'removing tyranny' and say to Mondlane that he was wrong? And had I not approved the actions of my friends, Dietrich Bonhoeffer and Adam von Trott, when they had made a similar choice?

Mondlane came to see us several times in Geneva. He participated in the World Conference on Church and Society in 1966. Three years later he was assassinated. I cannot think of him as a terrorist. He was a Christian who had had to make an impossibly difficult choice in what German theology called a *Grenzfall*[11] – that is, a case on the borderland – and who had made that choice with full awareness of the sacrifice involved. I was glad that the World Council had shown enough imagination to make him feel that he belonged fully to the ecumenical family.

The Kitwe consultation had considerable repercussions in South Africa. Professor A. D. Pont of Pretoria published a series of articles in which he accused certain 'fellow-theologians' of being traitors to their church and their country. It was quite clear that these theologians were Pastor Beyers Naudé and Professor A. G. Geyser. One of the main accusations was that they had attended a secret meeting at Mindolo (Kitwe) in order to conspire with Pan-Africanism, a communist inspired movement which aimed at chasing the white man out of Africa barbarously and murdering him. In this connection sentences from my address in Kitwe were quoted out of their context. This led of course to a great discussion in the press. Pastor Beyers Naudé and Professor Geyser introduced a libel action against Professor Pont and against the editor of the paper in which the articles had appeared. When the editor made a public apology the case against him was withdrawn. But Professor Pont did not apologize for his false accusations and insults. The case attracted a good deal of attention. I gave the lawyers of the plaintiffs a full account of what had really happened at the Mindolo (Kitwe) Consultation. Professor Pont lost the case. The judgment of the Supreme Court of South Africa gave a fair description of the role of the World Council of Churches with regard to the Cottesloe and Mindolo meetings.

It was time that a major meeting of the World Council should take place in Africa. Our African president, Sir Francis Ibiam, invited the Council to hold the 1965 meeting of the Central Committee in Enugu, the capital of the province of which he was the governor. The African churches were well represented. Two African church leaders, S. H. Amissah, the Ghanaan secretary of the All-Africa Conference of Churches, and A. Adegbola of Emmanuel College gave the main addresses. I was also impressed by the ability of the young group of ministers and officials of the provincial government. There seemed to be good reasons to be hopeful about the future of the country. It was all the more sad to find later on that Nigeria was torn apart by a bloody civil war.

The Central Committee expressed again deep sympathy with the victims of unjust accusations and discriminatory laws in South Africa and Rhodesia, as well as in every other country, and supported the appeal for funds for their legal defence, and aid for them and their dependents.

But it was clear that the real issue before us was not just an issue of civil rights, but of international social justice. I said therefore in my report to the Central Committee:

> The interdependence of our modern world, the conviction that the needs of all can be met, the emergence of a new sense of dignity and a new hope among underprivileged masses, the emergence of so many new nations which desire to build healthy national societies – all these have made the international, intercontinental social problem the most inescapable issue of our times. As we meet in Africa many of us will be made even more conscious of its reality than we were before.

NOTES

1. *The Ecumenical Review*, January 1953, p. 174; also published separately.

2. *Die Naturellevraagstuk*, Bloemfontein, 1950, p. 120.

3. The memoranda submitted by the Dutch Reformed Church of the Cape were published in Afrikaans in the Acts of the Synod of that church held in October 1961, pp. 245–61.

4. The memorandum had spoken of 'economically integrated' non-white people. Cottesloe spoke simply of 'non-white people'. The Dutch Reformed delegates who voted in favour of this point in the report of the consultation declared that they had done so with the understanding that participation in the government of the country referred, in the case of white areas, to the Africans who are domiciled in the declared white areas in the sense that they have no other homeland.

5. *The Ecumenical Review*, January 1961, pp. 244–50.

6. In his New Year radio message for 1961.

7. Printed in the Acts of the Synod of the Dutch Reformed Church of the Cape, October 1961, pp. 241–75.

8. *The Ecumenical Review*, July 1961, p. 517.

9. Published in *Race Relations in Ecumenical Perspective*, July 1964 (World Council of Churches).

10. *Christians and Race Relations in Southern Africa*, Department of Church and Society, World Council of Churches, 1964, pp. 11ff.

11. See, e.g., Karl Barth, *Kirchliche Dogmatik* III: 4, pp. 510–15; and Helmut Gollwitzer, *Forderungen der Freiheit*, pp. 385–8 (Engl. trans., *The Demands of Freedom*).

AFTER THE Evanston Assembly of 1954 the ecumenical ship seemed to have reached somewhat stiller waters. The great world powers again entered into conversation with each other and their leaders met in Geneva in 1955. The new approach made by the World Council to the Moscow Patriarchate met with a positive reaction. So the Central Committee decided in 1955 to accept the invitation of the Hungarian member churches to hold its 1956 meeting in Hungary. We realized, of course, that this first meeting in a country under a communist regime might well lead to complications. But, as I had been able to find out during visits there in 1954 and 1955, there was in the churches of Hungary a strong and widespread desire for direct personal fellowship with the ecumenical family. We might be able to help in a difficult situation, and we might at the same time make our contribution to the transformation of the cold war into a relationship of constructive international dialogue.

So I returned rather hopefully in March 1956 from the meetings in Australia and New Zealand where we had made our plans for that year. But I found our office in a mood of crisis. Two days before my return Archbishop Makarios, the head of the Church of Cyprus and also ethnarch of the Greek-speaking Cypriots, had been deported by the British authorities. The Greek Orthodox churches were reacting in the sharpest possible way. A stream of telegrams was pouring into the office containing protests against this 'sacrilegious' act and demanding that the World Council intervene immediately.

This was indeed a crisis. It was not only that the cohesion between the member churches of the council was threatened; the whole relationship between the Eastern and Western churches which had been built up during the last thirty years seemed to be at stake. If the World Council were to keep silent at this moment, the solidarity between East and West, which had been a keynote of the ecumenical movement, would be shown to be verbal rather than real.

The normal procedure would be for the chairman, vice-chairman and the general secretary to put out a common statement. But I found that the chairman, Dr Fry, was travelling in Russia. A statement signed by the vice-chairman and the general secretary would give the impression that the chairman was unwilling to sign. So I decided that this was one of the rare occasions when the general secretary had to stick his neck out. And I issued a statement to the press making the following five points: First, that I could at this time give only a personal expression of opinion. Second, that this act against the head of an ancient church was very deeply resented throughout the Eastern Orthodox world and that it endangered the efforts of the World Council to bring 'Eastern' and 'Western' churches together. Third, that Christians of other churches should express their deep sympathy to the Orthodox Church. Fourth, that our Commission of the Churches on International Affairs had already, in 1954, declared that it recognized the right and fitness of the people of Cyprus to determine for themselves their future status, and that the conflict should be settled by negotiation and not by acts of violence on one side or the other. Fifth, that responsible public opinion in many countries considered that the deportation of Archbishop Makarios was not in line with the best traditions of British statesmanship, and that the return of the Archbishop from exile was an essential preliminary to the continuation of negotiations.

This statement was well received in the Greek Orthodox churches and in the Greek press. But what would British church leaders say? In the Cyprus debate in the House of Lords, on March 15th, 1956, both the Archbishop of Canterbury and the Bishop of Chichester took part. Archbishop Fisher found it shocking that an Archbishop (that is Archbishop Makarios) should take the lead in a political matter and involve himself in all the passionate partialities which political incitement always involves. He did not express a definite judgment concerning the rightness or wrongness of the deportation, but proposed various steps to get out of the present deadlock. Bishop Bell quoted from my statement but went farther than I had gone, saying that the deportation was a blunder, an opinion that was also expressed in a somewhat milder way by Earl Attlee, the former Prime Minister. At a later stage of the debate the Marquess of Salisbury, speaking for the government, attacked the Bishop of Chichester and said that the issue was whether Archbishop Makarios should have been allowed to ferment and organize terrorism. Was not Bishop Bell subordinating everything to the continuation of the World Council of Churches, so that nothing mattered but that? At this point the Archbishop of Canterbury interjected the following statement: 'May I say that I entirely agree with the noble Marquess on this matter? I am very sorry that the right reverend Prelate (the Bishop of Chichester) quoted the Secretary of the World Council of Churches who, I think, exceeded all his rights in issuing this statement at all.'[1] Archbishop Fisher followed this up by a letter which was a rap on my knuckles. He said that he took very strong exception to my statement and that it was improper of the secretary of the World Council to declare, with all the prestige of his office, upon the merits or demerits of British statesmanship without the full approval of the officers of the World Council and of the British member churches.

That was about the strongest reprimand I had ever had from the head of a church in the council. Had I really gone too far? From a formal point of view Archbishop Fisher was right. But this had been a situation in which considerations concerning the substance and consequences of the matter seemed to have greater weight. The Eastern Christians had seen this action as directed against the head of an Orthodox church. In the light of their history they did not make a sharp distinction between ecclesiastical and political action. And was that distinction always made in the West? Had not Mr Winston Churchill in 1944 insisted that Archbishop Damaskinos should become the Regent of Greece?

In any case the Makarios crisis did not lead to a lasting estrangement between the Eastern and the Western churches. Professor Hamilcar Alivisatos wrote from Athens: 'I would like to assure you that any feeling of isolation there might have been here, has been dispelled by the encouragement which your sympathy and that of the Bishop of Chichester carry.'

The meeting of the Central Committee in Hungary in the summer of 1956 was surrounded by an atmosphere of eager hospitality. When on the two Sundays the committee members returned from their sometimes arduous journeys to the congregations in different parts of the country, their stories were quite unanimous. They had all been received in the warmest possible manner. Hungarian Christians had shown how deeply they appreciated this opportunity to realize that they were part of the world-wide Christian fellowship. At the same time the visitors had gained a new understanding of the difficulties, but also of the new spiritual insights, which the life of the church in a communist society could bring.

The Hungarian government received us at a luncheon in the impressive building of the Parliament and gave us all desirable facilities for the meeting. In our discussions we did not avoid the difficult issues. One of the main themes of the meeting was: 'The Churches and the Building of a Responsible International Society'. It seemed at first that the variety of convictions in our midst was such that we would not be able to express a common mind. One draft after another for a statement was rejected. But finally we could adopt a common text which contained a number of most relevant points. One was that when one nation dominates another politically, or economically, the dependent subject people is deprived of the possibility of developing a fully responsible society. Another dealt with the necessity of discontinuing, limiting or controlling nuclear tests. Again another spoke of the freedom men should have to choose by whom and in what way they wished to be governed, to obey the dictates of their consciences, and to worship, to witness and to have their children educated in church, school or youth meeting.

During the days of the meeting the leaders of the Lutheran World Federation were negotiating with President Horvath of the State Office for Church Affairs about the rehabilitation of Bishop Lajos Ordass of the Lutheran Church of Hungary. I was asked to participate in these meetings. The issue was whether Bishop Ordass would again be allowed to function as an active bishop. He had been condemned on charges which had to do with foreign exchange transactions but of which we considered him innocent. Franklin Clark Fry was the able, patient and tenacious spokesman of the Lutheran World Federation. President Horvath defended the governmental point of view with equal stubbornness. But finally certain points of agreement were found. A legal process for the rehabilitation of the bishop had begun. The possibility that he should at some future time function again as bishop would be considered. This was in the circumstances as much as could be hoped for.

My impression at the end of the Central Committee's sessions was that our coming to Hungary had been meaningful. Professor Josef Hromadka said that the members of the Central Committee were now nearer together than they had been in 1948 at their first meeting. Professor Laszlo Pap, speaking on behalf of the Hungarian churches, said: 'I can testify that your coming and living with us has made a very big impression in our congregations.'

I had once told Bishop Bereczky that I was very fond of Hungarian gypsy music. He had not forgotten this. On the last evening a first-rate Hungarian band played us *czardas* after *czardas*. And a Hungarian rhapsody of Liszt played on the cymbalo was a worthy climax of the remarkable hospitality we had received.

On October 15th Professor Pap came to visit me in Geneva. We talked of course about the developments in church and state in Hungary. The main news was that Bishop Ordass had been rehabilitated and that in the Lutheran Church considerable changes in procedure and church discipline were being discussed; similar developments were expected in the Reformed Church. But there was nothing in his report that could be understood as an indication that any major change might soon take place in the political situation. So the news which came through in the last week of October – that big demonstrations had taken place in Budapest – came to us as a complete surprise. When the fighting began and the life of the country became disrupted, our first reaction was to organize a relief action. My colleague, Dr Edgar Chandler, flew to Vienna on October 30th and on the next day the first trucks carrying food and blankets left for Hungary. On October 31st I had a telephone conversation with Professor Pap in which I asked two questions: What can the World Council do to give effective help to people in need? And what is happening in the life of the church? Pap urged us to intensify the relief programme and told me what changes were being made in the leadership of the church.

But on this same day we had suddenly to shift our attention to another crisis. The Anglo-French attack against Egypt had begun. This was a no less ominous development. In a cable to Fry I expressed the conviction that the World Council should remind the churches of some of the affirmations of the Evanston Assembly on the use of force in international relations and call attention to the repercussions which the intervention would have for the relations between the continents. Fry agreed in principle.

I will not easily forget that Thursday morning when five of us held a permanent emergency meeting in my office. Telephone from New York: Frederick Nolde, the Director of the Commission of the Churches on International Affairs, asks whether he should come to Geneva. Telephone conversation with Pap about developments in Hungary. Telephone with our vice-chairman, Dr Ernest Payne, about a possible statement on Suez. Telephone from the Bishop of Chichester to exchange views on the Suez crisis. One of the very encouraging elements in the situation was that on the same day the Archbishop of Canterbury made a remarkably strong speech in the House of Lords. He said that Christian opinion was terribly uneasy and unhappy over Britain's decision to use force against Egypt. He called attention to the hostile reactions which the government's action had received in all parts of the world. And he raised this grave question: 'Are we doing the right thing by the highest and wisest standards that we as a nation know?' The Standing Committee of the British Council of Churches also issued a similar clear statement and the leaders of that council called on the Lord Chancellor and expressed to him the deep concern of Christian opinion in Britain regarding events in the Middle East.

We worked on a draft statement, secured the agreement of Fry and Payne, and released the following on November 2nd:

> The Chairman and the Vice-Chairman of the Central Committee and the General Secretary of the World Council of Churches request all member churches of the World Council in this grave situation in the Middle East to remember what the churches said together about international order, and most recently at the Second Assembly of the World Council at Evanston. We direct particular attention to the passage in the Evanston report where the churches state that 'no nation in a dispute has the right to be sole judge in its own cause', where they call upon the nations to 'pledge that they will refrain from the threat or the use of force against the territorial integrity of any state' and where they affirm that 'any measures to deter or combat aggression should conform to the requirements of the United Nations charter'. Finally we ask the churches to pray to Almighty God that he will guide the governments and the peoples in the way of peace.

But we had to turn our eyes again to Hungary. In the days following the creation of the new government great changes were taking place in the life of the churches. A number of church leaders resigned. Bishop Lajos Ordass became again the leading figure in the Lutheran Church and Bishop Laszlo Ravasz in the Reformed Church. New plans were made with regard to religious education, youth work and social work. What we heard gave us the impression that a day of renewal had come to the churches in Hungary. So I sent several messages of sympathy and encouragement in which I spoke of the new era opening up in the life of the churches of Hungary. These messages were published and the German edition of the Ecumenical Press Service quoted also a remark which I had made to the staff – namely, that I was glad that the meeting of the Central

Committee in Hungary had helped to prepare for that new day. This remark, which of course referred to the impact which our meeting had made on the life of the churches, was later misinterpreted in Hungarian political circles and taken to mean that our meeting had paved the way for the political uprising in the country. It was certainly a fact that for the Hungarian churches the Galyatetö meeting had been an opening of windows, but it was also a fact that none of the participants had conceived the meeting as an attempt to set the stage for the overthrowing of the regime.

On Sunday, November 4th, the Russian army occupied Budapest. We could no longer communicate with the Hungarian churches. We could only redouble our efforts to help the refugees who were pouring into Austria by sending more relief workers to Austria and by organizing the emigration of the refugees to other parts of the world. And we could try to express our sense of solidarity with the Hungarian Christians and their nation. Together with Dr Nolde, who had arrived from New York, our staff group worked on a draft statement. The chairman and vice-chairman gave their consent readily and on November 5th the following statement was issued:

Christians throughout the world are profoundly shocked and sorrow-stricken at the tragic reversal suffered by the Hungarian people, who had clearly asserted their desire for freedom and independence in national and church life. The Chairman and Vice-chairman of the Central Committee of the World Council of Churches and the council's General Secretary call to the attention of the member churches the immediate relevance of certain statements in the appeal to churches and governments adopted by the Evanston Assembly. They refer particularly to the claim that fear and suspicion cannot be replaced by respect and trust unless powerful nations remove the yoke which now prevents other nations and peoples from freely determining their own government and form of society. We urge the member churches to continue to seek this objective. As also stated at Evanston, Christians must stand together with all who, in the struggle for freedom, suffer pain and trial. Our unity in this fellowship will remain unbroken whatever happens and will also find expression in prayer for the people of Hungary in their hour of trial and for the churches in their witness to our crucified and risen Lord.

> Franklin Clark Fry, *Chairman of the Central Committee*
> Ernest Payne, *Vice-chairman of the Central Committee*
> W. A. Visser 't Hooft, *General Secretary*

The following weeks brought naturally all sorts of reactions to our statements on the two crises concerning the Middle East and Hungary. Some of the most difficult discussions were those with pastors and leading laymen of the Reformed Church in France, who felt that with regard to the Suez conflict we had far too easily sided with the United Nations. Dr Nolde and Sir Kenneth Grubb went to see church leaders in Paris and helped to clarify misunderstandings.

In relation to the situation in Hungary we had to deal with two completely opposing attitudes in our constituency. There were those who felt that we ought not to have spoken as we did, because this could only strengthen the anti-communist complex of the West. Karl Barth took this line. And there were those who felt that from now on all relations with the churches in Eastern Europe should be broken off. I believed that both attitudes were wrong. After having spoken out on the Suez crisis we could not have kept silent on the Hungarian crisis. We had had to make it perfectly clear that the World Council stood for basic convictions quite apart from purely political considerations. But we had to work at the same time for the maintaining of fraternal relations between the churches in all countries and it was now more essential than ever to remain in contact with the churches in Eastern Europe.

Before that turbulent year 1956 was over I had to give attention to another equally critical situation. French church leaders asked me to go to Algeria where the situation was going from bad to worse. I spent only twelve days in Algeria and Tunisia, but it was long enough to get a feel of the tragedy of the situation. The gulf between the French and the Algerians was widening every day. On both sides fear and resentment were growing. The French pastors and laymen with whom I spent most of my time were men who loved the country and its inhabitants, and who felt deeply frustrated about the deadlock in human relations. There were very few places where personal contacts between Algerians and French were still maintained. In the primitive cabin of the Sisters of Grandchamp, a Protestant order working in one of the poorest shanty-towns, I spent unforgettable hours with Algerians who spoke with deep feeling of their desire for freedom. And in the heavily guarded *Kasbah* I was taken to a small club, organized by a Christian layman, where men of the two nationalities were still able to communicate with each other and where I heard many stories about the suffering and injustice caused by the violent conflict. It was a relief to go along to Tunisia, which had already gained its freedom. President Bourguiba received me cordially and we discussed the issues of religious liberty. He made it clear that he would stand by the declaration on human rights of the United Nations.

In the letter which I sent to all the Protestant pastors in Algeria and Tunisia I asked them to see the Algerian situation in the light of the world situation. Many Frenchmen seemed not yet to have understood the deeper significance of the nationalist movement among dependent peoples. It was normal and desirable that peoples should become conscious of their own identity, for that was really a discovery of their human dignity. I proposed that greater attempts be made to create personal contact between Christians and Islamites. There were almost no Christian Algerians. So the only way of bridging the gulf between the nationalities was for Christians to enter into direct relations with believers in Islam. In the present situation this should not take the form of missionary work in the traditional sense. What was required, first of all, was an approach based on the desire to get to know one's neighbour.

In Tunisia I found that some younger intellectuals were keen on contacts with people from other countries – and especially people from small countries without much political power. So I proposed that the World Council should set up an international team which would go to Tunisia for the purpose of establishing such contacts and rendering whatever help in the field of development the Tunisians desired to have. This team was actually formed and has worked in Tunisia for many years.

Our Executive Committee met in February 1957. I had to report that the churches in Hungary, and especially the Reformed Church, were in a very critical situation. President Horvath of the governmental office of religious affairs had made strong accusations against the World Council of Churches and against those Hungarian church leaders who had been in close touch with the World Council at the beginning of November 1956. The telephone conversations which Pap and I had had at that time and about which we had spoken openly were now believed to be part of a vast conspiracy. Mr Horvath had stated that in these conversations I had made an offer of five million dollars a year to the Reformed Church on the condition that the church would follow my instructions and support the 'counter-revolution'. He had added that the Central Committee meeting in Hungary had also been used as an occasion for political plots.

Though these accusations were fantastic and groundless we had to take them seriously. For they could have serious repercussions for the life of the church and for some of its leaders. So it was decided that Dr Eugene Carson Blake, representing the Executive Committee, and I should have a personal meeting with Mr Horvath. It was agreed that the meeting should take place in Prague. When the time came to leave for Prague the Czechoslovakian visas had not arrived. I left Geneva anyway and met Dr Blake in Zürich. We decided to take the risk of arriving in Prague without the required visa. It took a good deal of explaining and telephoning but finally, thanks to the help given by Professor Hromadka, we were allowed to leave the Prague airport for the city.

I had known Mr Horvath for many years and we had had many friendly conversations. But at this meeting the relations were cold and formal. Dr Blake made it clear that the World Council had three concerns: the first had to do with the accusations which the Executive Committee had heard with amazement; the second had to do with the problems of the Reformed Church; the third had to do with the personal situation of a number of church leaders. I then gave an account of the action which the World Council had taken with regard to the crisis in Hungary.

In the following discussion it became clear that the basic problem was that expressions which we had used in a church context had been interpreted by the Hungarian authorities as references to political activity. Thus the Central Committee had at its meeting in Hungary insisted on the necessity of student work and student movements. We had of course in mind that permission should be granted to start again a Student Christian Movement. But Mr Horvath had thought that we were partly responsible for the student protest meetings which had inaugurated the October rising. Similarly, my message to the church, saying: 'We stand ready to help', which had simply meant that we would use the resources of inter-church aid to meet the needs of our fellow Christians in Hungary, had been taken as an offer of political support to a 'counter-revolution'.

A good part of the discussion had to do with what President Horvath called the 'illegality' of the actions of several church leaders. I asked whether Mr Horvath, as a member of a revolutionary party, did not agree that in certain exceptional circumstances legality was not the highest and decisive criterion.

After six and a half hours of discussion President Horvath stated that he found the result of the meeting somewhat meagre. But the important thing was that we were again on speaking terms and that we had been able to register the strong concern of the World Council that the Hungarian churches should have a leadership which would be fully trusted by the congregations.

The Central Committee meeting in Yale Divinity School in New Haven, Connecticut, in the summer of 1957, gave specific approval to the actions which had been taken with regard to the crises in Hungary and in the Middle East. But that was not the end of the affair. The old wild accusations concerning the counter-revolutionary activities of the World Council – and especially of its General Secretary – appeared again and again in some Hungarian and Chinese publications. The Chinese version in the Christian periodical *Tien-Feng* (June 24th, 1957) was that 'Visser 't Hooft sent instructions from Geneva to Pap to be sure and overthrow the supporters of the People's Government as well as leaders of the Peace Movement and restore to high positions those fascists who before 1945 have usurped the important offices of the church' and that 'the General Secretary of the World Council of Churches and his company utilized their ecclesiastical connections with Hungary to have a hand in the Hungarian events and rendered harm to the Hungarian nation, the Hungarian people and the Hungarian churches' (December 23rd, 1957). It was decided that we should make a last effort to explain what had really happened. So Dr Ernest Payne, our vice-chairman, was asked to write an article in *The Ecumenical Review* (April, 1958). The article had the appropriate title 'Some Illusions and Errors'.

Other international tensions with which I had to deal in the following years are described in other chapters. There were happily also more encouraging developments.

I think of the two consultations on disarmament held in Geneva in 1962 and 1964. The Commission of the Churches on International Affairs had been at work on disarmament problems for a long time, and the Central Committee had, on several occasions, spoken out on the dangers involved in the armament race and on the testing of nuclear weapons. In 1957 the Central Committee commended to the churches a CCIA statement on Atomic Tests and Disarmament and requested them to communicate it to their governments. That statement asked the governments concerned to stop, by international agreement, the testing of nuclear weapons. But during the following years little or no progress was made in the discussions on this matter between the great powers. In 1961 when Russia resumed tests and in 1962 when the United States started another series of tests we, that is the officers of the World Council, made public statements expressing our grave concern. The New Delhi Assembly had recommended in 1961 that we should try a new type of approach, namely, to hold a consultation between Christians from various countries, together with the specialists who represented the governments most concerned in the negotiations on disarmament. The question was of course whether those busy men would be willing to meet with the church leaders. They did come to our modest chalet in Malagnou which was still our headquarters at that time. We heard representations from the leading figures of the disarmament negotiations: Ambassador Tsarapkin of Russia, Mr Alexander Akalovsky of the United States, Sir Michael Wright of the United Kingdom and Baron von Platen representing Sweden and the eight non-aligned powers. With this background the churchmen sought to define what the task and message of the churches should be in this field. They urged again that a treaty to cease nuclear weapons testing be concluded at the earliest possible moment. This statement was confirmed by the Central Committee and widely distributed.

There were not many places in the world where this type of constructive dialogue between men living in completely different political environments was taking place. I said in my report to the Central Committee:

> The coming in of a number of large churches living in Eastern Europe increases our responsibility for constructive action with regard to the ideological and political tension between the largest power-blocs. Our great advantage in doing this is that as Christian churches we share a common faith and we meet therefore as brothers in that faith and not as representatives of rival ideologies. That is not to say that we find it easy to arrive at a common mind about the tough issues of international relations. But it does mean that, as has been shown in New Delhi and at the disarmament consultation under the auspices of the CCIA in Geneva, we can arrive at common conclusions about a number of important issues and thus make a common witness to the world. And though so far, on such a crucial matter as the cessation of atomic tests, our repeated warnings have not yet been heeded, we must not become weary, we must continue to speak out, we must combat the hopelessness and defeatism that is so widely prevalent and continue to believe that a clear testimony concerning peace and justice will finally meet with a response in the hearts and minds of men.

A year later the Moscow treaty on the banning of nuclear weapons tests in atmosphere, in outer space and under water was signed. We were glad to feel that we had been able to make a contribution to this encouraging development. And the officers sent to leaders of the three governments concerned an expression of gratitude for this first step in breaking the nuclear impasse.

But the treaty dealt only with one aspect of disarmament. So in 1964 another consultation was held with the disarmament specialists. We agreed that further progress could be made through international agreements on the simultaneous decrease of the stock of nuclear arms. But we had to admit that there was little chance of progress unless greater confidence could be established. And that could only be done through the solving of the most acute international problems.

I must mention another crisis which led to much controversy in our midst. In October 1962 the tension between the Russian and American governments about Cuba became acute. The development of Russian military bases on the island led to sharp reactions in public opinion in the United States. On October 21st Dr Nolde, the director of the CCIA, gave an address in Washington the main parts of which had been discussed beforehand with the officers of the World Council. He recognized that the transformation of Cuba into a Soviet-supported enterprise was a danger to the North American hemisphere but added that the United States had bases on foreign soil closer to Russia than Cuba is to the United States. His main emphasis however was that any military action to be taken should be in accordance with the charter of the United Nations.

On October 22nd President Kennedy announced that the United States was going to impose a quarantine on Cuba. It seemed to me clear that we could not remain silent in this situation. For the unilateral decision to impose a quarantine was surely not in line with the United Nations charter. Moreover the World Council Assemblies had again and again spoken out against attempts to change an unsatisfactory situation by force and, at the time of the crises over Hungary and Suez, we had taken our stand precisely on these principles. Would we not be inconsistent if we did not take the same line this time? So with the help of Geneva colleagues I drafted a statement. I read the statement over the telephone to Dr Fry and Dr Payne, who proposed minor changes. It was my impression that Dr Fry was in close touch with the office of the CCIA and that I could therefore assume their agreement unless I was advised to the contrary. But I failed to check up on this point. The statement was issued to the press on October 23rd in the following form:

> Taking their stand on statements made by the World Council of Churches assemblies, committees and officers of the World Council of Churches have on several occasions expressed their concern and regret when governments have taken unilateral military action against other governments. The officers of the World Council of Churches consider it, therefore, their duty to express their grave concern and regret concerning the action which the USA government has felt it necessary to take with regard to Cuba and fervently hope that every government concerned will exercise the greatest possible restraint in

order to avoid a worsening of international tension.

Franklin Clark Fry – Ernest Payne – W. A. Visser 't Hooft

Our colleagues of the CCIA felt that owing to the lack of consultation they were being put in a most difficult situation. They considered that the statement was incomplete and therefore too one-sided. We agreed therefore that the members of the UN Security Council should receive the statement together with the section on Cuba in Dr Nolde's speech of October 21st. In this way the submission to the Security Council contained four considerations: warning against unilateral action, need for the greatest possible restraint, recognition that the Soviet-supported enterprise in Cuba constituted a danger and the claim that any military action to be undertaken should be in accordance with the United Nations charter.

The statement was strongly disapproved of by a number of church leaders and approved by others. And it led to much debate in the public and secular press. In a few cases member churches dissociated themselves from our action. We were accused of being fellow-travellers. These critics did not seem to have noted that on November 7th we had sent a message to the Indian churches with regard to the border dispute between India and China, in which we had said that at this critical hour for the life and spirit of India involved in a struggle to defend its national security, the officers of the World Council desired to assure the Indian churches of their profound sympathy and expressed the hope that a just and peaceful settlement would be reached.

The real issue was whether in our statement on the Cuba crisis we had given too much emphasis to the legal aspect of the matter. At this point I saw eye to eye with my colleague, Dr Nolde, who asked our critics whether this apparent departure from the United Nations charter did not constitute a disproportionately high price when viewed from the standpoint of mankind's efforts to progress towards an international order, on the basis of international law and operating through international institutions.

Since there had been so much questioning about the action of the officers, I drafted in the following months a memorandum on 'Statements of the Officers in Times of Crisis'. I said that in the context of the World Council a statement by the officers did not pretend to be a statement on behalf of all member churches, but was an attempt to interpret in a particular situation the convictions formulated by our assemblies, an attempt which had no other authority than the weight which it carried by its own truth and wisdom. We found ourselves often in a real dilemma. For as a body called into being to create fellowship between the churches we should give a high priority to the concern to maintain fraternal relations between the churches. But we had in the history of the ecumenical movement learned together that it was the duty of the churches to speak out and to speak out together, when the very foundations of the international order were shaken. Some said to us: if you continue to make statements on very controversial international issues, the World Council will disintegrate. Others replied: the World Council will become completely irrelevant if it has not the courage to take a stand on the great issues of international life. The World Council's leaders should do all they could do to maintain the fellowship between the churches which was still precarious. But they should not forget that the fellow-ship had a content. It was based on common convictions and existed in order to render a common witness. And the common convictions should not only find expression in the form of very general common principles, but also in the form of concrete statements with regard to specific international crises. We had to live with this dilemma. But it was up to the Executive Committee to tell us whether it wanted to limit the freedom which the officers had in this matter according to our present rules.

After full discussion the Executive Committee expressed the conviction that the present rules provided adequate guidance, but stressed also that the officers should make every endeavour to consult the chairman and director of the World Council section most concerned. I think that this was the right decision. It was in the nature of the case that you could not elaborate a 'crisology'. But it meant that in the present period of history when crises happened so often the officers continued to carry a heavy responsibility.

NOTES

1. *Hansard*, House of Lords, vol. 196, p. 569.

THE ISSUE DOMINATING the second Assembly had been whether the World Council could maintain its cohesion and integrity in spite of theological tensions in its own life and of political division in the world around it. The central question of the third Assembly was rather whether we were able to become a World Council in the full sense of the word. Our going to Asia was not merely a matter of choosing another part of the world for our meeting. It was a symbol of the fact that we had to become less Western and more truly universal.

In my address to the Assembly I used the text which the pioneer missionary William Carey had used in 1792 for a sermon which inaugurated a new period in the expansion of Christianity – a text from the prophet Isaiah (54.2): 'Enlarge the place of thy tent, and let them stretch the curtains of thy habitations; spare not, lengthen thy cords and strengthen thy stakes.' I mentioned several reasons why we were called upon to enlarge our vision. The first was that

> the longing for Christian unity has ceased to be a concern of the few and has become a preoccupation of the many ... The principle which in the early days of the ecumenical movement seemed revolutionary, namely that churches between which there were profound divergences could nevertheless be on speaking terms with each other, is now widely accepted and applied. The nearness in time of the Pan-Orthodox meeting in Rhodes, of this World Council Assembly and of the second Vatican Council has made the impression that we live in the day of general ecumenical mobilization.

I mentioned further the coming together of the World Council of Churches and of the International Missionary Council, the very considerable expansion of our membership and the new relations with the Roman Catholic Church.

An important difference between the second and the third Assembly had to do with the change in leadership. At Evanston the generation of the great old men who had given shape to the ecumenical movement in the 1920s and 1930s had still been much in evidence. Bishop George Bell (Chichester), Pastor Marc Boegner of France, Archbishop Yngve Brilioth of Sweden, Dr Alphons Koechlin of Switzerland, Bishop Eivind Berggrav of Norway had still participated in the leadership of the meeting. Even our great-grandfather John R. Mott had been present to remind us of our heritage. But in New Delhi there were no more than five or six men who had held responsible positions in the pre-war ecumenical movement and none of them was in the leadership of the Assembly. There was however a different link with the pre-war tradition. This was the group of at least thirty men and women from all parts of the world who had participated in the World Christian Youth Conference at Amsterdam in 1939 and whose life had been deeply influenced by that experience. Many of them had given a large part of their life to service in some part of the ecumenical movement. And now they were carrying considerable responsibilities in the Assembly, as delegates, as advisers or as staff members. They had become the shock-troops.

This changing of the guard meant that I now represented the elder generation. After being regarded for some thirty years as a representative of a new genera-tion I found it rather hard to get accustomed to the change.

The three crucial issues on which the Assembly had to take action – namely, the question of integration between the World Council and the International Missionary Council, the admission of the Orthodox Churches of Russia, Rumania, Bulgaria and Poland, and the amplification of the 'Basis' (the first article of the Constitution) – had been on the agenda of the Central Committee for several years and had been thoroughly canvassed. So they did not lead to any prolonged controversy in the Assembly.

The merger of the World Council and the International Missionary Council was the logical result of a long process begun in 1938 when the two bodies agreed to set up a joint committee of which the first chairman was Dr John R. Mott, and when William Paton, secretary of the IMC, became Associate General Secretary of the World Council. In 1948 the two councils had decided to describe themselves as being in association with each other. There were of course many organizational problems to be overcome, and there was at first reluctance in some of the constituent councils of the IMC, who did not quite trust the World Council for theological reasons, and in some of the Eastern Orthodox member-churches of the World Council, who were afraid that the World Council would become involved in proselytizing activities. But the patient work of the Joint Committee, which was later chaired by Dr John A. Mackay and finally by Dr Henry Pitney Van Dusen, and which had a very wise executive secretary in Dr Norman Goodall, produced its results. In Asia and in Africa our membership was increasingly overlapping. The activities of the two councils had become increasingly inter-dependent. We were together responsible for the Commission of the Churches on International Affairs and for the setting up of the East Asia Secretariat. So many people were involved in the life of both bodies! And the leaders had so many common memories, so many common experiences, so many common tasks!

By the time of the Assembly there were not many left who did not agree that the World Council needed the contribution of the missionary forces in its everyday life and that the missionary movement needed to be more directly concerned with the effort to manifest the unity and universality of the church. By way of anticipation Bishop Lesslie Newbigin, the General Secretary of the IMC, and I walked side by side in the procession towards the opening service of the New Delhi Assembly. The decision to approve the integration was adopted without any opposition, and the chairman, Archbishop Iakovos of the Greek Orthodox Church, could declare that the two bodies had now become united. The two streams which had come from the same source, namely the World Missionary Conference of 1910 in Edinburgh, had become one single stream.

Another difficult question on which the New Delhi Assembly had to express its judgment was whether the Basis of the World Council – that is, the definition of its nature given in the first article of its constitution – should be amplified or not. Two proposals had received considerable backing. According to the first, which came from Norway, the words 'according to the scriptures' should be inserted. The second one, which came from the Eastern Orthodox churches, was that the Basis should become explicitly trinitarian. It was, however, not quite clear what was meant by a trinitarian basis. Did it mean that we should use the word 'Trinity' or use one of the traditional formulations concerning the Trinity? If so, there would probably be a good deal of opposition from the churches which wanted to avoid difficult, technical theological terminology.

Light was thrown on this during the visit of the World Council staff group to Russia in 1959. At one of the leisurely and copious breakfasts in Leningrad the conversation turned to the question of the Basis. Father Vitaly Borovoy, professor of the Leningrad Academy, remarked that the progress which was taking place in the life of the World Council should also find expression in a further development of the Basis. I asked what he had in mind: Would not a doctrinal formulation of the dogma of the Trinity turn the Basis into a fully-fledged creed? Professor Borovoy and Dr Nikos Nissiotis, our Greek Orthodox colleague, answered that it was not necessary to have in the Basis a doctrinal formulation, but that there should be specific reference to God and to the Holy Spirit as well as to Christ. So I wrote on the back of the menu the following formulation:

> The World Council of Churches is a fellowship of churches which believe in Jesus Christ, our God and Saviour and which under the guidance of the Holy Spirit seek to fulfil together their common calling to manifest their unity as children of our heavenly Father.[1]

Father Borovoy and other Orthodox friends said that this was indeed what they meant. So I took this formula to the Executive and Central Committees. After further discussion it was decided to add also the words 'according to the scriptures' and to bring in the trinitarian dimension at the end, so that the Basis would be as follows:

> The World Council of Churches is a fellowship of Churches which confess the Lord Jesus Christ as God and Saviour according to the Scriptures and

therefore seek to fulfil together their common calling to the glory of the one God, Father, Son and Holy Spirit.

It is remarkable that the proposal to amplify the Basis in this way had considerable repercussions in three different directions. It helped to give the Eastern Orthodox churches greater confidence in the World Council and to bring in the many Orthodox churches which had not yet become members. It reassured the more 'evangelical' elements in the constituency of the International Missionary Council who had hesitated about integration with the World Council. And it played an important role in the evolution of the attitude of the Roman Catholic Church to the World Council.

At the New Delhi Assembly some delegations voiced their reservations concerning the proposal. Their main criticism was not directed at the additions which were widely accepted, but at the expression 'the Lord Jesus Christ as God and Saviour'. For it was felt that these words seemed to minimize the humanity of our Lord. The defenders of the proposal felt, however, that in the context of the amplified Basis there was much less danger of such a misunderstanding. The result of the ballot was that 383 votes were cast in favour of the proposal, 36 against the proposal, with seven abstentions.

The third crucial issue at New Delhi was that of the admission of new churches. Twenty-three churches had applied for membership. Eleven of these were African churches. This was important, for it was high time that Africa, which had so far only played a minor role in the movement, should make its voice heard among us. For the first time two Pentecostal churches had applied; this meant that we were entering into contact with a young and vigorous type of Christianity which had so far kept aloof from ecumenical life. Even more important for the future were the applications from the Eastern Orthodox churches in the Union of Socialist Soviet Republics, Rumania, Bulgaria and Poland. For their admission would mean on the one hand that Eastern Orthodoxy would no longer be in the position of a minority which had difficulty in making its voice heard, but have a strong place in the council, and on the other hand that churches in countries under communist regimes would have a much larger representation than they had ever had before.

The story of the development of the relationships between the Orthodox Church of Russia and the World Council is told in another chapter. The Central Committee had become convinced that these new Eastern Orthodox applications as well as all others should be accepted. But would the Assembly agree and give us the required two-thirds of the votes of the member churches?

In international life the cold-war atmosphere had by no means completely disappeared. Some newspapers had carried warnings against the acceptance of churches which according to their opinion would exert a nefarious influence in the World Council. Furthermore, opposition had been voiced by individuals and groups within some of the member churches.

In my report to the Assembly I had said:

A tremendous opportunity is offered to us, the opportunity to ensure that a real spiritual dialogue shall take place between the Eastern churches and the churches which have their origin in the West. If we accept this opportunity our ecumenical task will not become easier but we shall surely be greatly enriched. In this respect the strengthening of our stakes will be especially necessary since we have not only to contend with the ancient divergences between the Christian East and the Christian West, but also with the modern tensions between the political East and the political West. But what right have we to refuse this task if it is laid upon us? We can only pray that we may be worthy of such a great responsibility.

And just before the voting took place I said on behalf of the Central Committee:

In this matter the committee and its officers have sought to give absolute priority to the question: How can the cause of Christ and in particular the cause of Christian unity be served best? It (the committee) has become impressed by the desire for fellowship with Christians from other churches which lives in the churches of Russia. It has become convinced that for the sake of the Church of Christ it is important that fellowship should be established between the churches of Russia and other churches. In this matter we have been encouraged by the fact that the leaders of the Orthodox Church of Russia have made such a thorough study of the work of the Council and have come to know the principles and procedures which govern the life and work of the Council.

The result of the balloting was that all twenty-three applications were accepted. For the Orthodox Church of Russia there were 142 affirmative votes, 3 negative and 4 abstentions. I was especially grateful for the fact that practically all churches in the United States had voted in favour of admission, for they would have the most difficult time in explaining the deeper meaning of this vote to people inside and outside the churches whose thinking was dominated by the ideological East-West conflict.

It was a remarkable moment when the twenty-three leaders of delegations of the new member churches came up to the platform to receive their badges as official delegates. Archbishop Nikodim, who was the leader of the Russian delegation, remarked that it was almost like an ordination.

This time the discussion on the Christian attitude to the Jewish people, on which the Evanston Assembly had not been able to find a common affirmation, led to a resolution which was adopted without opposition. We had learned our lesson. We knew that we could speak out together against anti-semitism, but that we had as yet no common mind about the theological questions of the destiny of the Jewish people or about the deeper significance of the creation of the state of Israel. So a resolution was proposed which was wholly concentrated on the issue of discrimination and which made the important point, that the historic events which led to the crucifixion should not be so presented as to fasten upon the Jewish people of today responsibilities which belong to our corporate humanity and not to one race or community.

In the discussion an attempt was made to bring in the more specifically theological dimension. I spoke strongly against this and tried to explain that such an attempt would only result in the kind of stalemate which we had had at Evanston. In private conversation with the Swiss delegate who proposed this theological amendment I succeeded in convincing him to withdraw the amendment. So the resolution was accepted. I was criticized by some of my friends for interfering in this matter. I should not have put such pressure on the Assembly, they said. But I did not and do not plead guilty. For I knew only too well that if the debate had not been concluded at that session there would have come pressure upon some delegations from outside the Assembly, and we would once again have divided counsels. Our one chance to arrive at a positive result was to act speedily on the points on which we could agree among ourselves. The resolution was well received and found an especially favourable echo in Jewish circles.

Another encouraging development, which for obvious reasons was treated as a confidential matter, was the bringing together of the delegations from Indonesia and from Holland. I found each eager to talk with the other. The relationships between the two countries had greatly deteriorated. Diplomatic relations had been broken off and there was the danger that the conflict about West Irian might lead to military confrontation. The Christians on both sides who had been bound together by bonds of friendship and common experience, but were now cut off from each other, were glad to seize the unique opportunity which the Assembly offered them to enter into frank conversation with each other. There remained considerable disagreement about the political issues involved, but there was a determination to maintain fellowship at all cost. Some of us remembered how once before, in 1947 at Oslo, the ecumenical movement had held us together at another critical moment in our relationships. This meeting at New Delhi showed that as soon as the present crisis was over we would again begin to be able to work together. And that is what actually happened in the following years.

I had again to spend a great deal of time with the committee on nominations. The choice of members for the Presidium and for the Central Committee was becoming more and more difficult, for there were now many more churches which had to be taken into account. At the same time, now that the World Council was better known, there were many more people who considered membership in the governing bodies of the council as a distinction worth competing for. Not all went so far as the delegate who came to say: 'I am the best candidate from our delegation', but there were many indirect approaches. Fortunately we had a strong and independent committee with a chairman,

Professor Willy Tindal from Scotland, who did not let anybody else make up his mind for him.

The choice of Presidents did not prove too difficult. The new Archbishop of Canterbury was chosen not in the first place because of his status, but because of the real contribution he had made to the ecumenical dialogue in the realm of Faith and Order. Archbishop Michael Ramsey made it clear to me that he did not want to be embroiled in administrative affairs but that he would like to help in theological matters. This time we proposed also the name of a layman, Mr Charles Parlin of New York, who had already rendered very great services to the World Council. The choice of Martin Niemöller was widely appreciated. In proposing him we had of course thought in the first place of his role in the time of the church struggle and his pioneering in opening up avenues of communication with the churches in Russia. We did not realize that he would also play an important role in the field of World Council administration and finance.

The most difficult nominations problem was over the chairmanship of the Central Committee, a most influential position. The appointment had to be made by the Central Committee itself. The task of bringing in nominations for chairman and vice-chairman was entrusted to a nominations committee with the Bishop of Winchester as convener. The committee faced a dilemma. Should the principle of rotation or the principle of continuity prevail? I reported to the nominations committee that I had discussed the matter with a number of Central Committee members and had asked them for suggestions, but that there seemed to be no strong support for new candidates. The non-American members were on the whole in favour of the re-appointment of Dr Fry as chairman for they appreciated his firm way of presiding over the meetings. Some American members took a different view, for they considered that with regard to relations between the churches in the United States Fry's attitude was often too authoritarian. The Bishop of Winchester's committee reported that it had come to the conclusion that the main consideration at this time was to secure continuity of leadership by men whose wisdom, experience and proved capacity for leadership commanded the most whole-hearted confidence. So they recommended that Dr Fry be invited to serve again as chairman and Dr Ernest Payne again as vice-chairman. This proposal was accepted and both Fry and Payne accepted.

It has been said by some that the nominations at this and other assemblies were 'prefabricated'. This is true only in so far as the process of discussion concerning nominations has to begin a long time before the Assembly. But it is quite untrue if it is taken to mean that a few people had made up their mind before the Assembly about the nominations and sought to impose their choice on the Assembly. In fact the nominations procedure was one of unending consultations, of constant revision of original proposals, of assessing again and again the confessional and geographical factors involved. The outcome of such a process is never what one person or one group of persons has 'prefabricated'. It is always a surprise comparable to the outcome of a complicated chemical process in which many different ingredients have become mixed together.

From my point of view the New Delhi Assembly was an easier Assembly than the two preceding ones. Robert Bilheimer was in charge of the administration, as he had been in Amsterdam and in Evanston. He had become a master in the art of assembly organization. Dr Fry was a presiding officer who could deal with every possible or impossible situation. It was a joy to work with them.

Our Indian colleagues, above all Korula Jacob, the secretary of the local arrangements committee, had done well. The great conference building, the Vigyan Bhavan, was by far the most suitable place for an assembly that we had yet found anywhere. The various embassies, including those from countries of Islamic tradition and those of communist regimes, offered much hospitality. I felt certain that never had the New Delhi diplomatic corps heard so much discussion of religious themes as it did in those days. I recall especially the amazement and amusement on the face of the wife of the ambassador of a communist government when she received a young monk from her own country. But the most generous hospitality of all was given by Rajkumari Amrit Kaur, that truly great lady who came from a Christian princely family, who had been closely associated with Mahatma Gandhi and who had served for many years as Minister of Health in the Indian government.

Prime Minister Nehru came to visit us. He looked a good deal older than at the time of our meeting at Lucknow in 1953. He spoke again in that straight-forward, non-rhetorical way which made his words so convincing. When he described the problem of the politician whose personal views were often un-acceptable to the masses of the people, and who had therefore to accept com-promise, we realized what he had gone through during his many years in high office. His main warning was against the cold-war approach to international affairs. He expressed his satisfaction that the Assembly had not shrunk from facing the complex problems of our time in a positive spirit.

The Indian press gave us remarkably good coverage. Its interest was awakened when it became known that more television and radio teams would come to India for this occasion than had come for the visit of Mr Khrushchev. And we were fortunate in having Bishop Lakdasa de Mel of Ceylon as chairman of the press and public relations committee. It was a joy to watch his handling of the press conferences. He had an exceptional gift for breaking the ice between the hundreds of journalists with their critical questions and the 'victim' on the platform who had to provide the answers. His humour created an atmosphere in which the press became part of the common enterprise.

I had to find time during the Assembly to satisfy the boundless curiosity of the reporters of *Time* magazine. For *Time* had decided to combine its report on the Assembly with a cover story about me. On the way to New Delhi in Karachi I had been asked by a *Time* photographer whether he could take some pictures of me. The man stayed for several hours and made 120 pictures which were to serve as a basis for the painting to be made in New York. At New Delhi I was subjected to many hours of interviewing. No detail was too insignificant to be mentioned in the long, cabled reports to *Time*'s headquarters. Henry R. Luce, the boss and editor-in-chief, came to New Delhi to get a personal impression of the Assembly. He asked me to bring a number of Assembly leaders together at dinner so that he could pick their minds. I was surprised that he did not ask questions himself, but wanted me to lead the discussion. He did not at all make the impression of a great *entrepreneur* with the self-confidence that comes from success. He seemed rather to be shy in the presence of the theologians and church leaders. But there was no doubt about his interest in our work.

The issue of *Time* with the cover-story reached New Delhi during our Central Committee meeting after the Assembly. I was relieved to find that it gave a positive evaluation of the Assembly and that what the *Time* reporters had picked up from my colleagues, from my family and from me was on the whole accurate. I liked the description of my role in the Assembly as '*guru*, watchdog, trouble-shooter, father-confessor and cheer-leader'. It was a strange experience to walk through New Delhi and to find my face looking at me from the news-stands.

When the Assembly was over I had that strange feeling of emptiness which comes when the event on which one has concentrated all one's attention for a long time has suddenly become a part of history. All the more so, since at the time of the next Assembly I would no longer be General Secretary.

The inherent weaknesses of such a vast gathering in which people of the most diverse backgrounds had to arrive at a common mind in sixteen days had again become apparent. But was there any other way in which we could keep the World Council close to the churches? Franklin Clark Fry was surely right when he said in his closing speech: 'The assets of this procedure, the democratic sounding of the mind of the church, have outweighed the obvious liabilities of throwing open discussion to so many with such disparate viewpoints.'

What had been the specific significance of this Assembly? The combination of two factors: the induction of so many non-Western churches and the holding of the meeting in Asia had clearly demonstrated that we were now entering into a more truly world-wide period of our life. From now on we would have the duty and privilege of thinking in terms of all the cultures into which the Christian church had penetrated, but many of which it had not yet taken seriously. The Archbishop of Canterbury said to me in New Delhi that he found the ecumenical movement now much more mature, and that one reason for this maturity was that 'we had left the European ecumenical palaver behind us'. We were forced to think henceforth in terms of the whole world.

It was only a beginning. New Delhi had but touched on the tremendous issue of how to avoid simultaneously the old syncretism between the Christian faith and Western culture, and a possible new syncretism between the faith and Eastern cultures. Similarly we had only begun to face the issues of world-wide social justice. Sam Cavert, who had been associated with the ecumenical movement since its beginnings, wrote in the report of the Assembly: 'They (the churches) were not only determined to stay together (as at Amsterdam) and to grow together (as at Evanston) but to move out together into the world's struggle for social justice and international peace'.

I hoped that he was right.

NOTES

1. In the excellent study on the history and significance of the Basis by Wolfdieter Theurer (*Die Trinitarische Basis des Oekumenischen Rates der Kirchen*, 1967) this formula is reproduced (p. 175) without the words 'our God and Saviour'. This is due to an error of transcription in the letter which I wrote on the subject to Dr Franklin Clark Fry and Dr Ernest A. Payne.

37 | *The Ecumenical Mobilization of the Roman Catholic Church*

IN THE PERIOD immediately following the creation of the World Council the Roman Catholic Church and the World Council did not know what to expect of each other. There were many unanswered questions and many uncertainties. Those of us most involved in the World Council wondered whether the Vatican had nothing else to say about the constantly growing movement for unity than it had said in the very negative encyclical, *Mortalium Animos* of 1928 and in the equally negative decisions of 1948 concerning participation of Roman Catholics in inter-church meetings. Would the Roman Catholic authorities not take account of the new inter-confessional relationships which had been established during the war in prisoner-of-war camps, among refugees or in resistance movements? Would their attitude to the ecumenical movement not be influenced by the fact that Roman Catholic church leaders and leaders of other churches had defended their Christian convictions together in the struggle with national socialist paganism? And would they not be impressed by the writings of their own Roman Catholic ecumenists whose number was rapidly growing and who had entered into fruitful dialogue with their counterparts of other confessions?

But the Roman Catholics had also a number of questions to ask. What was the real nature of this new World Council of Churches? Was it an attempt to set up a centre of unity which would be able to offer an alternative to the only effective centre of world-embracing unity which had existed so far, namely the Roman Catholic Church? Or was it based on a genuine desire to bring all the churches together? Which particular conception of the church and of church unity actually dominated the thought and policy of the Council? These were questions to which the Amsterdam Assembly had not provided clear answers. It was obviously necessary to discuss all these questions with Roman Catholic theologians who were informed and concerned about the ecumenical movement. So in 1949 an important, and of course unofficial and confidential, meeting was held at the Istina Centre in Paris. Ten men who were fully involved in the work of the World Council met with an equal number of Roman Catholic 'ecumenists', including the father of Roman Catholic ecumenism, Père Yves Congar O.P., Père Jean Daniélou S.J. (who was to become a cardinal), Père Jérome Hamer

O.P. (later the Executive Secretary of the Vatican's Secretariat for Unity), Père Maurice Villain S.M., an indefatigable advocate of ecumenism and Jean Guitton, the author. The reason why the Roman Catholic group was wholly French-speaking was that French Catholicism was, in the ecumenical field, far ahead of other parts of the Roman Catholic Church.

The discussions were exceedingly frank. In my opening statement I dealt first of all with a number of misinterpretations of the World Council which we had found in Roman Catholic publications. It was not true that the churches in the council 'despaired about unity' and were therefore concentrating on co-operation in the moral and social field, as Père Boyer, the editor of the periodical, *Unitas*, had written. It was not true that the council was dominated by Barthian theology, as others had declared. The important thing to remember about the council was that it was a meeting place of many conceptions of the church and many conceptions of unity. One could not describe the council in terms of the 'normal' categories of theology. The council had to deal with an abnormal situation and had therefore to describe itself in 'abnormal' categories which did not fully correspond to any of the traditional forms of thinking about the church.

During the discussion on these questions many misunderstandings were cleared up. The pertinent questions raised by our Roman Catholic partners, with their keen awareness of problems concerning the nature of the church, helped us of the World Council to realize that we had to make an effort to define much more clearly what the World Council was and what it was not than we had yet done. Thus the Istina meeting became an important stage in the preparation of the statement on the nature of the World Council which was submitted to and adopted by the Central Committee of the Council in Toronto in 1950.

The other series of questions relating to the Roman Catholic attitude to ecumenism were also fully discussed. Père Congar gave a penetrating analysis of the Roman Catholic position. There were more possibilities for Roman Catholics in the ecumenical movement, he said, than one would assume from a perusal of the official documents of the hierarchy alone. The encyclical, *Mortalium Animos*, could no longer be considered as an adequate answer in the present situation. There was in the Roman Catholic Church a constant dialogue between the centre and the periphery and the centre had often responded to initiatives of the periphery. Père Congar said that there were unchangeable elements in the church but also many elements which could be reformed. The new Roman Catholic theology desired to go back to the original sources of the faith, he reported, and in so doing it found much common ground with the Protestant biblical theology. In the concept of the *vestigia ecclesiae* (which means that other churches have at least traces of the true church) could be found a starting point for the rethinking of relations between the churches.

The last point was fully discussed. Père Daniélou said that our common task was to arrive at a dynamic conception of the *vestigia ecclesiae* for these traces of the church could be developed and lead to greater agreement.

We also discussed how far we could go together in common prayer and theological co-operation. It was agreed that at present common public worship was impossible, but that informal prayer in interconfessional groups was not excluded. As to theological co-operation, Roman Catholic theologians could attend informal groups and could contribute to ecumenical discussion by preparing publications on the subjects which were being discussed in the World Council.

This had been a most useful meeting, but I wondered whether the Vatican would show any sign of a better understanding of the ecumenical movement.

Before long this question received an answer. Early in 1950 the Holy Office in Rome issued an 'Instruction' on the ecumenical movement which dealt, at considerable length, with the issues arising in the new situation. The tone of this document was different from that of the 1928 encyclical. The ecumenical movement was no longer dismissed as a pernicious heresy, but appreciated as the outcome of a desire for unity which had been inspired by the Holy Spirit. The Vatican had recognized (as Père Boyer, at that time the semi-official spokesman of the Vatican on ecumenical matters, put it a few years later) that 'in the World Council a new force has emerged and it would not be wise not to take account of it'.[1] At the same time the emergence of the ecumenical movement was considered as an event taking place 'outside the church' (that is, outside the Roman Catholic Church). Unity could only be thought of in terms of the return to the Roman Catholic Church. Strong warnings were given against a 'dangerous indifferentism' and against 'the spirit of a so-called eirenicism' which looked in vain 'for a progressive assimilation of the various creeds'. Nevertheless gatherings at which Catholics and non-Catholics met as equals to discuss matters of faith and morals were not absolutely forbidden, but might only be held with the approval of the competent ecclesiastical authority.

Thus the door was set ajar. I issued a statement on the subject, and the World Council Executive Committee, in July 1950, expressed its general agreement with the line I had taken. The statement was as follows:

> I have been asked to comment on the Instruction concerning doctrinal conversations between Roman Catholics and Protestants which has been issued by the Congregation of the Holy Office of the Vatican. My comments can only be of a personal and unofficial character since the Central or Executive Committees of the World Council have not yet considered this document. I can summarize my remarks in the following points:
>
> 1. The very fact that such a document is issued at all is a clear indication that the ecumenical movement has begun to make its influence felt among the clergy and laity of the Roman Catholic Church. We can only rejoice that such is the case.
>
> 2. As the document itself points out, meetings between Roman Catholics and representatives of other confessions are regularly held in many places. These

meetings are generally of an informal character and are intended to lead to better mutual understanding and to frank discussion of points of friction.

3. According to the new instruction, all such meetings will henceforth have to be directed and supervised by the hierarchy. Thus they will lose that informal and spontaneous character on which much of their value depended. There will be less room for the pioneers.

4. Moreover, the ecumenical contacts will be supervised from the viewpoint expressed in the document, namely, that the only purpose of ecumenical contacts can be the return of all Christians to the Church of Rome. At this point the document remains below the level reached by certain members of the Roman Catholic hierarchy who have declared that union cannot take place in the form of a victory of one body over another as happens in the secular realm. The churches in the World Council have a different conception of true unity, namely, that (in the words of the Amsterdam Assembly) they are to be bound closer to Christ and therefore closer to one another.

5. Unless I am mistaken, this document is the first in which the Holy See permits explicitly, though with certain restrictions, that Roman Catholics and Christians of other confessions may pray together. This is a step forward.

6. It is also important that inter-confessional meetings on social questions are allowed. This should facilitate effective common action wherever Roman Catholics and Christians of other confessions are ready to make a common stand for social justice.

7. Christians outside the Roman Communion should continue to pray that the Roman Catholic Church may be led to a wider and deeper conception of Christian unity.

In one important respect my prognosis proved to be wrong. I had been too pessimistic in saying that there would be 'less room for the pioneers'. I ought to have had greater confidence in the upsurge of ecumenical concern in many parts of the Roman Catholic Church. For in the nineteen-fifties it became increasingly evident that, especially with regard to ecumenical questions, Roman Catholicism was no longer as monolithic as it had been before or at least had appeared to be. True, the encyclical *Humani Generis* of 1950, with its condemnation of 'false eirenicism' and its strong warnings against the new theology, seemed to put new obstacles in the way of ecumenical dialogue. And the proclamation in the same year of the doctrine of the bodily assumption of Mary made the impression that the Roman Catholic Church took no account of the convictions of the other Christian churches. But the Roman Catholic ecumenists continued to fight for their good cause.

It was at that time that I visited the Abbé Couturier in Lyons. He was now an old and sick man, but he was more convinced than ever that his life-work to establish a truly ecumenical movement of prayer for unity had received divine blessing and he was greatly encouraged by the response which had come from Christians of all confessions.

In 1952 a development took place which at that time attracted very little attention, but which was to have far-reaching consequences for the ecumenical movement. Two Dutchmen, Father J. G. M. Willebrands (later Cardinal Willebrands) and Father Frans Thijssen approached Father Yves Congar with the proposal to set up a permanent body which would bring together the Roman Catholic theologians who were engaged in studies in the field of ecumenism. Later in that year the Catholic Conference on Ecumenical Problems was founded in Fribourg. Afterwards Father Willebrands, who had become secretary of the conference, and Father Thijssen went to Rome to discover whether they would be allowed to enter into contact with the World Council. There they received encouragement from Father Augustin Bea (later Cardinal Bea) who was at that time the father-confessor of Pope Pius XII.

Soon afterwards the two Dutch fathers came to Geneva to see me. This was an important moment in the relations between the World Council and the Roman Catholic Church. I could say to them that although we realized that the new body which had just been organized had no official status, it would be a great advantage for us to be in conversation with a responsible body of Roman Catholic ecumenists. As to the method of co-operation it was agreed that for the time being the most effective way of co-operation would be for the Roman Catholics to study some of the same themes on which the World Council was working and so make their contribution to the ecumenical dialogue.

This was the beginning of the co-operation between Father Willebrands and me, a co-operation facilitated by the fact of our common background in the same province of Holland. We had to proceed very carefully and without any publicity. We had no idea that the time was not far off when we would be co-operating openly at the official level. I found Father Willebrands a man with deep convictions about our common ecumenical task and with a fine combination of vision and realism.

It was encouraging to find that at the Lund World Conference on Faith and Order in 1952 several Roman Catholic observers could be present with the permission of the ecclesiastical authorities. But two years later, at the time of the Second Assembly of the World Council in Evanston, the paradoxical character of our relations with the Roman Catholic Church again became evident.

The Catholic Conference on Ecumenical Problems had decided to make its own contribution to the work of the Assembly and had asked Father Yves Congar to write a first draft of a paper presenting the Roman Catholic conception of the main theme, 'Christ the Hope of the World'. This paper was revised in the light of comments of other Catholic ecumenists. When I received it, I made it available to the Assembly delegates and commented in my report to the Assembly that this was a substantial and valuable contribution to our discussions.

We had thought that in line with the instruction *Ecclesia Catholica*, and with the precedent of the Lund Conference on Faith and Order, it would be possible to have some Roman Catholic observers at the Assembly. But the American Roman Catholic hierarchy adopted a negative decision on this subject. When I told a European bishop about this veto, he said: 'Well, they are Irish, are they not?' No doubt this bishop has learned since that some Roman Catholic church leaders of Irish descent have become active in ecumenism. But the remark was interesting in that it showed that in 1954 the European Catholic hierarchy had a much more positive ecumenical attitude than the American hierarchy.

Some Roman Catholic priests from Europe had gone to the United States with the expectation that they would be able to attend the Assembly as representatives of the press. But Cardinal Samuel Stritch, Archbishop of Chicago, in whose archdiocese Evanston lies, decided that this would not be allowed. So these priests went to stay in a place just outside Evanston and received their information through visits of Assembly delegates or by means of the telephone.

Some six weeks before the Assembly Cardinal Stritch issued a pastoral letter on 'church unity'. He repeated the well-known arguments why the Roman Catholic Church could not participate in ecumenical gatherings. A journalist showed me a copy of this letter before it appeared in the press, so that I could prepare an answer and have it published simultaneously with the Cardinal's letter.[2] I said that I appreciated the tone of the letter but that at certain points it gave a caricature of the goal of the World Council, for example when it spoke of 'some sort of man-made unity of Christian sects'. I expressed surprise that the letter did not refer to the Instruction, *Ecclesia Catholica*, which had left the door open for the participation of individual Roman Catholics in ecumenical gatherings, if the necessary ecclesiastical authorization had been given. I concluded: 'The World Council will therefore continue to seek opportunities for such unofficial contacts. In this it is encouraged by the great interest which Roman Catholics in several countries have shown in its work.'

Is it worthwhile to tell this rather sad story? I believe it is, for it is against the background of the 1954 situation that the full significance of the revolutionary developments of the nineteen sixties becomes clear.

But we are still in the nineteen fifties, a period of contradictory developments, some leading to increased tension, others to a *rapprochement* between the World Council and the Roman Catholic Church. Thus the Roman Catholic writers on ecumenical subjects, whose number was steadily increasing, represented, as I wrote in 1956,[3] 'variations in ecumenical attitudes within the one Roman Catholic Church' which 'seem to be no less considerable than those within the World Council with its many member churches'. Some looked on the World Council as a strange, disturbing and possibly dangerous phenomenon. Others said naively that this search for unity would of course lead to a massive return to the Roman Catholic Church, since it alone possessed already the unity required. But there was also a growing number of Roman Catholic ecumenists who made a very real effort to understand the nature of the World Council. Father Congar, Father Hamer, Father C. J. Dumont of Istina in Paris, Father Maurice Villain of France, Canon Gustave Thils of Belgium and others rendered a great service by their constructive criticism, for they challenged us to think through the deeper issues concerning the nature and work of the World Council to which the theologians in the membership of the World Council were not giving sufficient attention. But we could not help wondering whether the attitude of these men could be considered as representative for their church, for in those years some of these ecumenical pioneers were facing grave difficulties with their ecclesiastical authorities. On our side, my German colleague, Hans Heinrich Harms, spent much time in maintaining contacts with the Roman Catholic ecumenists and went several times to Rome to make discreet inquiries about possible improvement of our relations with the Roman Catholic Church.

One of the most persistent controversial issues was that concerning religious liberty. Ever since its first Assembly the World Council had taken a strong stand on religious liberty. The Commission of the Churches on International Affairs had played a significant role in the formulation of the article of the United Nations Declaration on Human Rights dealing with this subject. So when the World Council received complaints concerning oppressive measures taken against churches it felt obliged to take action. Two of the most acute situations were those of the Protestant churches in Spain and in Colombia. The Executive Committee spoke out repeatedly against infringements of their religious freedom and the Central Committee decided in 1957, on a motion of Dr Geoffrey Fisher, Archbishop of Canterbury, 'to arrange for a study to be made of religious liberty arising in Roman Catholic and other countries'.

In many Roman Catholic periodicals this resolution was interpreted as an attack on the Roman Catholic Church. But there were a number of Roman Catholics who made a real effort to remedy the situation. I remember especially the occasion when I received an SOS from Spanish Protestants. There was the very real danger that the work of their church would be completely paralysed. I asked a Roman Catholic priest who was well-informed about the Spanish situation to come to see me. I said that I not only wanted to help the Spanish Protestants but also wanted to avoid a public controversy which would do real harm to the relationship between the Roman Catholic Church and other churches. Could he possibly take some action? He did not promise anything except that he would think about the matter and come back within a week. When he returned he told me that he had first gone to the Swiss Foreign Office. The fact that a Roman Catholic priest had come to ask for support of the Protestants in Spain had made such an impression that they had promised to take diplomatic action. Then he had gone to his bishop, who had promised to make an approach to the Spanish ambassador at the Vatican. The storm blew over.

The study on religious liberty, for which the Central Committee had asked in 1957, became an objective approach to the underlying theological and sociological problems. This was largely due to the fact that just at that moment the right man for this task appeared on the scene. One of my Genevese friends asked me to receive a former Spanish Jesuit who had left the Roman Catholic Church and who was eager to work for the ecumenical movement. I was somewhat suspicious, for I knew only too well that most men who leave the church in which they have grown up are unable to develop a truly ecumenical attitude. But when I came to know Dr Angel Carrillo de Albornoz I found that there was in him no trace of aggressiveness against the Roman Catholic Church. He had felt obliged to give up his responsible position in the Vatican because he could no longer subscribe to all the tenets of the Roman Catholic faith, but he remained grateful to the church for having given him spiritual nurture and he wanted to avoid any action which could be harmful to it. I asked him at first to help us in getting better informed about the theological developments in the Roman Catholic Church and became increasingly impressed by the fairness of his judgment and the extent of his knowledge (he had four doctorates, none of them honorary). Thus it was natural that Dr Carrillo was asked to undertake a thorough study of the issues of religious freedom. The memoranda and books he wrote were extremely well received by Roman Catholics as well as by Protestants and Orthodox and helped greatly to prepare the way for the new statement on religious liberty which the Second Vatican Council made. The end result was that this problem which had created so much misunderstanding between the churches was no longer a cause of division.

In those years we had no official relations with the Vatican. So the fact that Bishop Otto Dibelius of Berlin, one of the Presidents of the World Council, visited Pope Pius XII in 1955 created a mild sensation. Many articles were written by journalists who tried to guess what great issues the two church leaders had discussed. I was of course eager to know more about this meeting. Soon after it, being alone with Bishop Dibelius in the car which drove us from Sydney, Australia, to the place where our Executive Committee would meet, I asked whether he felt free to give me some account of the meeting. He said that he would be glad to. I expected some interesting revelations. The bishop began by explaining that men of his generation had learned that when one visited a sovereign the right etiquette was never to bring up a subject of conversation. Now the Pope was a sovereign and so Dibelius had left the steering of the conversation to him. The Pope had first asked him whether he liked the climate in Rome. The bishop said that he found that climate very pleasant. The Pope had then asked whether he agreed that communism constituted a real danger to Christian civilization. The bishop had said that this was indeed his opinion. And then, he concluded, it was time to go. I thought of all the clever guesses of the journalists everyone of which had been wrong. The time for real ecumenical dialogue at the top had obviously not yet come.

Pope John XXIII succeeded Pope Pius XII in October 1958. A few months later, on January 25th, 1959, he announced his intention to call an Ecumenical Council. This created a great sensation. Pressmen telephoned to say that the Pope had spoken of an invitation to other churches to seek together the basis of a return to unity. They wanted to know what the response of the World Council would be. I could not believe that their interpretation was correct and that Pope John intended to call all the churches together with the aim of arriving at full unity. So I avoided committing myself until I could get more precise information.

On the next morning I had to begin a series of lectures at the Ecumenical Institute in Bossey on 'The Relations between the Roman Catholic Church and the Ecumenical Movement'. The audience consisted of students from many countries and churches, including two Roman Catholic ecumenists. We decided to replace the first lecture by a general discussion about the significance of Pope John's surprising announcement. All sorts of theories were advanced as to the intentions of Pope John. Several believed that he would really seek to bring leaders of all the churches together.

Two days later reports from Rome began to speak a rather different language. The key phrase was now that one of the objectives of the Council would be to invite the separated communities to seek unity. I made therefore a statement calling attention to the considerable difference between the two interpretations which had been given and added: 'Much depends on the manner in which the Council will be called and the spirit in which the question of Christian unity will be approached. The question is: How ecumenical will the council be in composition and in spirit?'

When the World Council's Executive Committee met two weeks later we were still quite uncertain about the nature and subject matter of the proposed Ecumenical Council. So the committee said that it had not enough precise information to make a formal statement on the subject, but that it gave general approval to the statement I had made.

We were at that time not the only ones who were uncertain about the council plan. In a report written in March of that year I wrote: 'It is remarkable that in many conversations Roman Catholic friends, instead of telling us what the Ecumenical Council is going to do, ask whether we have any idea what it might do.'

In other respects, also, this year 1959 was a year of considerable confusion with regard to our relations with the Roman Catholic Church. At the meeting of the Central Committee of the World Council of Churches in Rhodes several Roman Catholic priests were present as 'journalists', for at that time the question of the attendance of Roman Catholics as observers had not been solved. One of these priests proposed to the large delegation from the Eastern Orthodox churches that a special meeting be held to explore the possibility of contacts between Eastern Orthodoxy and Roman Catholicism. The World Council leaders were not informed, and were greatly surprised when press reports began to appear which gave the impression that the Central Committee meeting had been used to start official or semi-official negotiations between the Roman Catholic Church and the Eastern Orthodox churches. An inaccurate report from the Vatican radio complicated matters still further. All this led to a great deal of misunderstanding. It was quite normal that informal conversations between Roman Catholic and Eastern Orthodox theologians should take place, but it was regrettable that this was done in such a way that mutual confidence was weakened rather than strengthened. Father Willebrands helped greatly to restore the good relations by publishing a very objective account of the so-called 'Rhodes incident'.[4]

The event showed again that there was a need for the clarification of the World Council's relations with the Roman Catholic Church. And this happened even sooner than we had expected.

In June 1960 Father Willebrands, with his colleague Dr Frans Thijssen, came to see me in Geneva and brought me news about far-reaching developments in Rome. Pope John had decided to create a Secretariat for Unity and had asked Cardinal Augustin Bea to be the head of it. The Cardinal wanted me to be directly informed about this before the public announcement was made and had therefore asked Father Willebrands to visit me in Geneva. This was indeed important news. I had so often complained that although we had many contacts with individual Roman Catholics, there was no address or office in the Roman Catholic Church to which we could turn to discuss problems of relationships at an ecclesiastical and representative level.

Father Willebrands brought a second message. The cardinal had added that he would be glad to meet me in the near future. In the circumstances it would have to be an unofficial meeting without any publicity. It was therefore preferable not to meet in Rome or in Geneva. Would I be willing to see him in Milan in September? I accepted at once. In the light of the later developments it seems almost ridiculous that this meeting was so secret that I did not even tell my wife Jetty or my colleagues about it, and that the concierge of the convent where we met in Milan was not even allowed to ask my name. But we were at the beginning of a new development and had to be careful to make sure that in this delicate process of establishing relationships we would not be disturbed by the kind of public discussion which could so easily have complicated our difficult task.

In the conversation among the three of us – the Cardinal, Father Willebrands and me – it was not difficult to find a common wavelength. The cardinal spoke of himself as a man who was really a professor of Old Testament and who was rather surprised to have become a prelate. In the course of his biblical studies he had come to know and to appreciate Protestant scholars working in the same field. He looked like a benevolent patriarch of great age, but the keenness of his mind showed that he still had the vitality required to undertake the new pioneering task with which he had been entrusted.

The main point of the meeting was to establish a personal rapport. This was not difficult, for Cardinal Bea was one of those rather exceptional people who, even when you meet them for the first time, give you the feeling that you have known them for many years. He spoke of the great change in the attitude of the Roman Catholic Church to the other churches. The Vatican no longer considered the ecumenical movement as tending to 'indifferentism' or 'relativism', and believed that the Holy Spirit was at work in it. The principles concerning relationships which we had formulated at the World Council meeting at St Andrews in the summer were quite acceptable. We had said there that the fact that a dialogue was now possible with the Roman Catholic Church should be warmly welcomed and that the change which was taking place in our relation-ships was a change in procedure and climate and did not mean that the funda-mental differences which existed between the Roman Catholic Church and the churches in the World Council had been solved.

The three of us had a useful preliminary discussion about the question of inviting Roman Catholic observers to the third Assembly of the World Council at New Delhi and, conversely, of inviting observers from non-Roman Catholic churches to the second Vatican Council.

I was of course glad to hear that Father Jan Willebrands had been appointed as executive secretary of the new Secretariat for Unity. He and I had been co-operating since 1952 and we had no difficulty in understanding each other. I liked his frankness and I appreciated especially that he was at once a progressive ecumenist looking for ways of making a real advance towards unity and a realist who knew that, in order to have results, an ecumenical policy, like every other policy, must be the art of the possible and not a castle built in the air.

One of the first questions Willebrands and I had to work on was whether the Roman Catholic Church would be willing to send observers to the third Assembly of the World Council in New Delhi in 1961. It took a good deal of time before we received a reply. Cardinal Bea told me later on that he had had to overcome considerable opposition before a positive conclusion was reached. And the Secretariat for Unity was not allowed to send its most prominent representatives. In the light of what had happened in 1948 at Amsterdam and in 1954 in Chicago the presence of Roman Catholic observers at New Delhi was however a significant step forward. In my report to the Assembly I said that we were pleased to welcome these five observers sent by the Secretariat and expressed the hope that our Assembly and the second Vatican Council would not seek their own advantage, but only seek to serve our common Lord.

The next important question was how the observers from the other churches who were to attend the second Vatican Council were to be chosen. Monsignor Willebrands came to discuss this matter with me: we came to the conclusion that the best procedure would be to invite both the World Council of Churches and the confessional federations or alliances to send observers. I therefore made the necessary arrangement for a meeting between Monsignor Willebrands and the executive secretaries of these confessional bodies, and this led to the acceptance of the invitation by most of them.

The World Council also accepted the invitation. In doing so it made clear that its observers would have no authority to speak officially for the World Council or its member churches or to engage in any negotiation on their behalf. These words show that at that time there was a good deal of uncertainty as to the implications of sending observers. I went even farther and told our observers that their task was to observe and not to make observations.

But things worked out very differently. Our observers, among whom I must mention especially Dr Lukas Vischer of Switzerland and Dr Nikos Nissiotis of Greece, did indeed observe the work of the council and sent very substantial reports which kept me and other World Council leaders well informed about developments. But before long the observers were also engaged in a constant dialogue with the council fathers. And they were asked by the Secretariat of Unity to comment frankly on the documents under discussion. In many cases these comments had a considerable influence on the wording of the constitutions and decrees. A Roman Catholic theologian, who served as a consultant at the council, said that if an edition of the council documents could be issued in which all passages that had been changed in the light of the remarks of the observers were printed in red the result would be a most colourful production.

It was however not only in Rome that the dialogue was pursued. During the world conference on Faith and Order in Montreal in 1963, a conference attended by many Roman Catholic observers, guests and journalists, a rally was held in the University of Montreal at which Paul Emile Cardinal Léger, Archbishop of Montreal, Principal George Johnston of the United Church and I were the speakers. I spoke of the deep astonishment that such a meeting was now possible. At last we could not only speak with each other and give a common witness, but also pray together openly and publicly for the unity of the church.

It seemed that we had arrived at a period of acceleration of ecumenical developments. We had become accustomed to say: The Roman Catholic Church *and* the ecumenical movement. Now we had to learn that the Roman Catholic Church was becoming an active participant *in* the ecumenical movement. This was all to the good, but it meant that we were confronted by completely new questions and new tasks.

I was of course especially concerned about the consequences of this development for the life of the World Council of Churches and made a number of addresses on the abiding task of the World Council as a body in which no church is 'more equal than the others' and all seek together to advance towards unity. This was taken by some as a sign that I was becoming nervous about a possible shifting of the centre of ecumenical initiative from Geneva to Rome. It is true that I was far from happy when I read again and again articles giving the impression that the real ecumenical movement had begun when the second Vatican Council had been called. But this was not the decisive issue. My basic concern was to show that the Roman Catholic Church and the World Council of Churches were not comparable entities. The Roman Catholic Church was a church and the World Council was a council of churches which did not identify itself with the tradition of one church or group of churches, but was the servant of all its member churches. Writing about 'the dangers of ecumenical geometry' in 1964 I said:

> The expression that the centre of the ecumenical movement is shifting is equally inadequate to describe the realities of the ecumenical situation. For what meaning must we attach to it? Does it mean that the eyes of the world have recently been more on the second Vatican Council than on any activities of the World Council? But that is so obvious and so natural that no further explanation is needed. When the largest Christian church in the world, which has lived in isolation from the other churches, decides to enter into relationships of conversation with these churches and develops its own ecumenical programme, this is such an important development that all who are concerned about Christian unity must give their closest attention to it . . .
> Or does the shifting of the centre mean that 'Geneva', which had the initiative, must now accept that the initiative will henceforth come from Rome? To those who think in these primitive terms, we must say that Geneva has never had the initiative, for the initiatives (very specially with regard to the question of reunion) come from the churches, and the role of the council is to facilitate and to co-ordinate those initiatives. At the same time it is more than doubtful that the other churches will agree from now on to leave the main initiative to Rome or to any other single church. And the very suggestion that the initiative has passed or should pass to one church tends towards further division rather than increased unity.
> The truth is that the centre of the ecumenical movement cannot shift because it has no earthly centre. Its earthly expression is multilateral. The one centre of the ecumenical movement is our common Lord. And the only possible ecumenical geometry is that which Archbishop Søderblom used to express in the figure of the circle with Christ in the centre and all churches moving towards that centre and so coming closer together. Pascal has taught us the dangers of the *esprit de géométrie*. He tells us that we must not deal geometrically with the *choses fines*. Is it not clear that ecumenical realities are in a very special way *choses fines* and that therefore we should deal with them according to their own nature?

In this complicated situation with its great opportunities and its real dangers, the co-operation between the leaders of the Secretariat for Unity in Rome and those of the World Council became increasingly significant. During the council sessions my colleagues Lukas Vischer and Nikos Nissiotis were keeping in close touch with the Secretariat. I had occasion to visit Cardinal Bea several times and had a good many discussions with Bishop Willebrands. We found that they were

deeply aware of the reactions of the other churches and understood the nature
of the World Council. They did everything they could do to ensure that the
decree on Ecumenism which was being discussed by the Vatican Council would
provide a sound basis for new, positive and constructive relationships between
the Roman Catholic Church, the other churches and the World Council of
Churches.

But what form would such relationships take? In April 1964 we met in Milan
to discuss this question. The Secretariat was represented by Cardinal Bea,
Bishop Willebrands, Father Jérome Hamer and Father Pierre Duprey and the
World Council by Lukas Vischer, Nikos Nissiotis and me. It was a refreshingly
un-diplomatic meeting. We had now come to know each other sufficiently well
to be able to have a completely frank discussion. All the real difficulties were
mentioned. We spoke of the delicate issues of proselytism and mixed marriages,
of re-baptizing and of religious liberty. But in every case our common intention
was to find constructive solutions.

The basic problem was of course whether the World Council and the Roman
Catholic Church had the same conception of ecumenism. I said that we were
glad to find that our Catholic partners emphasized strongly that the centre of the
ecumenical movement was Jesus Christ himself. But what was the relation
between this affirmation and the other oft-repeated statement concerning the
central role of the papacy with its universal jurisdiction? Cardinal Bea spoke of
the universal significance of the papacy which no other ecclesiastical office had in
the same way. For the moment we could only note that this was a problem which
would need much more discussion.

We turned to the problem of relationships in the immediate future. Membership of the Roman Catholic Church in the World Council was not a practical
possibility at the moment. In so far as the World Council was a 'community of
dialogue' the Roman Catholic Church had no objection to membership. But the
question was whether the World Council was not more than this and whether it
did not have 'churchly' characteristics, and this created a problem for the
Roman Catholic Church. We discussed in a very positive way the possibility of
participation by Roman Catholic theologians in the work of Faith and Order.
The idea of exchanging 'ambassadors' was rejected, for this would make our
relations too formal and introduce a principle which was foreign to the World
Council. It was felt that we could keep in close touch by frequent visits to Rome
and to Geneva. Finally, we evolved a plan to have three working groups, one on
principles of common action, one on theological studies and one on practical
problems arising in church relations.

In the summer these proposals were submitted to a meeting of church leaders
who were specially concerned with the relationships of their churches to the
Roman Catholic Church and to the World Council's Executive Committee, and
the proposals were found acceptable.

In August 1964 Pope Paul VI issued his first encyclical. In it he laid strong emphasis on the necessity of dialogue with Christians who do not belong to the Roman Catholic Church. He expressed the conviction that the basic problem in this dialogue was that of the papal primacy. I commented[5] that it was encouraging to find that the Pope spoke so strongly of the need of dialogue, but that the Pope's conception of dialogue was not quite the same as that which we had used and practised in the ecumenical movement. According to the encyclical dialogue was mainly a form of communication of the truth which the Roman Catholic Church held. We understood dialogue as a process of sharing in which all receive and give and in which all are enriched and transformed. I added that the central importance given to the issue of the papal primacy seemed to mean that for the time being we should think in terms of better relationships rather than in terms of full union.

Several Roman Catholic friends told us afterwards that our reaction to the encyclical was understandable, but that we should not regard it as a final Roman Catholic word on the subject of ecumenical relations, because it was really the intention of the Pope to offer a real dialogue.

Another difficult moment came when, during the third session of the Vatican Council, just before the final vote on the Decree on Ecumenism, a number of changes were made in that text. It was announced that these changes had been suggested 'authoritatively', that is, by the Pope. Several of these suggestions gave the impression that what was offered with one hand was taken back by the other. The first reaction of the non-Roman observers, and even of a good many Roman Catholic ecumenists, was one of great concern.[6] They wondered whether it would still be possible to continue the ecumenical conversation. But the fact remained that the new decree represented a decisively important new development in the attitude of the Roman Catholic Church to other churches. As Lukas Vischer put it in those days, all would depend on the interpretation of the text. So we felt that there was good reason to go on with the plans which we had worked out with the Secretariat of Unity.

On the way to Nigeria, where the Central Committee was to meet next, I called on Cardinal Bea and Bishop Willebrands in January 1965 to ensure that we had a clear common understanding concerning the proposals which would be made to our Central Committee and to the authorities of the Roman Catholic Church. The plan was now to set up one single joint working group composed of eight representatives of the World Council and of six representatives of the Roman Catholic Church. The reason for the larger representation of the World Council was that it would have greater difficulty in getting the variety within its membership adequately represented. The task of the working group would be to work out the principles on which further collaboration should be based and the methods which should be used.

In my report to the Central Committee I referred to the recent developments in the second Vatican Council. There was reason for both expectation and disappointment. There was real renewal and there was opposition to this renewal.

But the acceptance of the Decree on Ecumenism had created a new situation. The Roman Catholic Church and the other churches had thus become more than ever before 'their brother's keepers'. A mere polite and passive co-existence would not be sufficient. The time had come to engage in an intensive conversation between the World Council and the Roman Catholic Church.

Lukas Vischer gave a detailed and realistic report on the third session of the Vatican Council so that the Central Committee was fully informed.

The proposals concerning the setting up of the Joint Working Group were well received. Spokesmen of different confessions expressed their satisfaction that we had reached this stage in ecumenical relations.

The Central Committee had thus made a specific proposal to the Roman Catholic Church. The official answer came soon afterwards and in a most impressive way. Cardinal Bea had accepted an invitation from the churches in Geneva to hold, in February, a public conversation with Pastor Marc Boegner. I asked him to visit the World Council's headquarters. The presence of a Roman cardinal at the Ecumenical Centre attracted of course a good deal of attention and it was before a full house that Pastor Boegner, as a former President of the World Council, and I welcomed him. I spoke of the very important role which the Cardinal had played in the development of the new fraternal relations between the Roman Catholic Church and the World Council and particularly in the preparation of the new Decree on Ecumenism. I said: 'We realize that this was no easy task. You were obliged to shoulder the burdens of the pioneer. You must allow us to say how much we honour the man who is its spiritual father.' I also said that we could not subscribe to all statements in the new decree, but that two things in it seemed to us of special importance. The first was that the decree stated clearly that the progress of ecumenism depended upon the renewal of the life of the churches, and declared that the Holy Scriptures are an outstanding means for obtaining true unity. The second point was that the decree rejected any form of 'ecumenical confusion' and described the ecumenical quest as a loyal dialogue in which genuine differences were taken seriously. The time had now come to explore together how we could arrive at real collaboration. In the world which was coming into being the churches would not be able to help the nations in their spiritual and moral distress unless they were willing to work closely together.

Cardinal Bea said that this meeting had historic importance. A long process of preparation had been necessary to reach this point. Then he announced that 'the Holy See greets with joy and willingly accepts the proposal made by the Central Committee of the World Council of Churches to set up a mixed committee, consisting of eight members of the World Council and six members of the Roman Catholic Church, to explore together the possibilities of dialogue and collaboration between the World Council and the Roman Catholic Church'. I replied that the proposal made by the Central Committee had not been unexpected for the cardinal, but that the fact that the Roman Catholic Church and the World Council had now publicly expressed their desire to develop relations with each other was a historic event. Now the work could begin.

Pastor Boegner said:

> When I think of the complete ignorance of one another which existed in the churches in the long centuries following their separation, when I think of the lack of comprehension . . . and when I experience in Rome and elsewhere the totally new climate which has appeared in recent years, once more I believe in the work of the Holy Spirit, and in the miracle of the grace of God.

Later I heard these two men discussing their birth years. They found that they had both been born in 1881. I reflected that even patriarchs could be pioneers.

The Joint Working Group held its first session in May 1965 at the Château de Bossey. Bishop Willebrands and I were asked to be joint chairmen. This was the first and probably the last time that two Dutchmen presided together over an ecumenical body. There was a very full agenda, for many departments of the World Council had already begun to collaborate with corresponding agencies of the Roman Catholic Church and it was necessary to define the principles and methods of our relationships. At the same time more fundamental questions, such as the varying conceptions of ecumenism and the nature of ecumenical dialogue, were taken up. Since most of the participants had worked together before and had come to trust each other we met as servants of a common cause rather than as wary church politicians, and it happened not infrequently that some of the Roman Catholics and some of the World Council representatives made common cause against other Roman Catholics and other men of the World Council.

The second session of the Joint Working Group was held in November 1965 in Ariccia near Rome. Just before the meeting I went to see Bishop Willebrands at the Secretariat for Unity to discuss the agenda. When we had finished our discussion I asked whether the council was meeting that morning. Yes, the session had just begun. Could I perhaps attend and so get a personal impression of the council? Certainly. Bishop Willebrands brought me to St Peter's and I soon found myself sitting among the observers in the very centre of that vast basilica.

I was glad to have this opportunity to see the council with my own eyes and to feel its atmosphere. Karl Barth had tried to convince me more than once that I ought to attend all the sessions as an observer, but I had replied that the general secretary of the World Council had too many other responsibilities and that he should not get so directly involved in the discussions in Rome, that he would to some extent commit the World Council before its governing bodies had had a chance to decide what their policy would be. But I had said before the opening of the Vatican Council: '*nostra res agitur*'. What was happening in the St Peter's had profound and far-reaching significance for the whole ecumenical movement.

And in a certain sense we – that is, the men who had tried to give shape to that movement – shared responsibility for this great event in church history. Had Joseph Cardinal Ritter of St Louis not been right when he said that Pope John had been divinely inspired when he called the Vatican Council and that 'some of the inspiration that came to Pope John from heaven came via the World Council of Churches'?[7]

Our involvement was underlined by the fact that it was precisely during my short visit that the first draft of the decree on religious liberty was distributed to the council fathers, for the contents of that decree had been deeply influenced by the many discussions which men of the World Council had had with Roman Catholic theologians on that subject and its acceptance would mean that one of the most painful problems in our relationships would be largely solved.

There was also the fascinating visual impression. Facing the places of the observers sat the cardinals according to their age and, further on in the nave, the bishops in longer rows, all in their robes, so that the whole cathedral was full of colour and made one think of a great festival rather than of a solemn synod.

In September 1966 Cardinal Bea and I received the Peace Prize of the German Book Trade at a solemn meeting in the Paulskirche in Frankfurt. The laudations emphasized that the prize was given to us jointly as a recognition of our common work for religious peace and for reconciliation between the churches which was at the same time a contribution to world peace. Cardinal Bea and I spoke of the relation between the unity of the church and the unity of mankind. It was a fine opportunity to show to an extremely varied audience that the ecumenical movement was not an introverted ecclesiastical affair but had a world-embracing vision. On the evening of that day a 'service of the word' was held in which both of us preached briefly.

I saw Cardinal Bea for the last time in Rome in September 1968. He looked very frail. He had resigned from his many functions in the Curia except the presidency of the Secretariat for Unity which was nearest to his heart. He was happy about the outcome of the World Council Assembly in Uppsala, which had been held in the summer and at which Roman Catholic observers and guests had played such an important role. We laughed together about the time when our meetings had been 'top secret'.

The cardinal died a few weeks later. I was asked to represent the World Council at the Requiem held in the St Peter Basilica and celebrated by Bishop Willebrands. After the service the representatives of the other churches and of the World Council were invited to visit the Pope. Metropolitan Meliton of the Ecumenical Patriarchate, speaking on behalf of these representatives, said that Cardinal Bea had belonged to us all. The Pope talked with each of us individually. I was impressed by his personal interest in the life and work of the people whom he had come to know. I told him that Pastor Marc Boegner was seriously ill. The Pope spoke of his affection for Dr Boegner and added: 'Please tell him that I will pray for him.' Then he asked where I lived since my resignation. I said that I remained in Geneva where I had lived so many years. He commented: 'Then you remain the guardian angel of the World Council.'

Bishop Willebrands became cardinal in 1969. In the evening of the day before he received the cardinal's hat his Dutch relatives and friends gave a party in his honour at which I was asked to be present. It was an occasion to reflect on the mysterious ways of providence which had used the two of us, sons of the Northern province of Holland, to work together on a common task of world-wide dimensions.

In the years immediately after the second Vatican Council opportunities for personal contacts with Roman Catholics became a normal part of ecumenical life. Doors were opened which had been closed for centuries. Things became possible which I had not expected to see during my life time, and impressive experiences befell me. In 1967 I received a honorary doctorate in theology from the Roman Catholic University of Louvain in Belgium. Now the university in Leiden, from which I had my original doctorate, had been created in the sixteenth century to do for the Reformed Church what Louvain had done for the Catholic Church. It had taken three hundred years to reach the point at which a doctor of theology of Leiden could become a doctor of theology of Louvain.

Another surprise was the reception I received in Madrid in 1969. Over the years Spain had caused me many headaches. I had often had to make statements criticizing the way in which the small Protestant minority was treated. So I could hardly believe my eyes when I found that, as I left the airplane, I was met by a delegation of ecclesiastics headed by the Bishop of Saragossa who had come to welcome me as Honorary President of the World Council of Churches. And that was not all. When I gave a lecture in the Jesuit Hall, the Bishop of Saragossa presided and the Archbishop of Madrid also sat on the platform. The Spanish hierarchy had obviously decided to take the second Vatican Council seriously. At the ecumenical service in the Reformed Episcopal Church the Bishop of Saragossa was again present and gave a fraternal greeting.

I found it a fascinating experience to get better acquainted with the complex life of Roman Catholicism in its period of *aggiornamento*. It was at first a surprise to meet priests who described themselves as 'low-churchmen' and who took a more radical position with regard to ecclesiastical institutions than I did. But there was also the opposite experience. At an ecumenical meeting, organized during the Olympic games in Grenoble, at which I spoke together with Orthodox and Roman Catholic speakers, young Catholic rightists protested so loudly and so effectively against the presence of 'heretics' that the meeting seemed to convey a message of discord rather than unity. A Catholic priest said to me: 'Sometimes I think that there are two Roman Catholic churches.' He was rather surprised when I answered: 'I have the impression that there are four.' I explained my point in this way: There are those who do not accept the renewal which the second Vatican Council has brought. There are those who feel that the council has gone as far as is required and desirable and that no one should go further for the present. There are those who believe that the council is just 'the beginning of a beginning'. And there are the radicals who want a complete revolution of the church's doctrine and life.

It was remarkable that, since a similar variety of attitudes could be found in the other churches, there arose alliances across confessional boundaries between those who had the same conception of the renewal of the church. I often found myself in far deeper agreement with those Roman Catholic theologians who sought to re-interpret the faith in modern terms, but did so on the basis of biblical theology, than with men of my own confession who were merely defending the formulations of the past or who were more concerned about adaptation to the modern world than about faithfulness to the original message.

In the spring of 1969 it was announced that the Pope would visit Geneva. The International Labour Office was celebrating its fiftieth anniversary and its director, David Morse, had invited the Pope to address the conference held on that occasion. As soon as this became known Eugene Blake requested the Pope to use this opportunity to visit the World Council. Now the coming of the Pope to the International Labour Office was an interesting event, but his coming to the World Council was not only interesting but had great symbolical significance. A colleague reminded me that in the 1950s, at a time when many church leaders came to visit us, I had made the remark that if this trend continued, some day the Pope would visit us, too. And the staff had laughed then because the idea seemed quite absurd. Now, in 1969, it was unthinkable that the Pope should come to Geneva and not visit the World Council. The visit to the World Council attracted very considerable attention in the press and in public opinion. A staff member of the International Labour Office said facetiously to a World Council secretary: 'You have stolen our Pope', but if there was a culprit, it was church history rather than the World Council.

The main hall of the Ecumenical Centre was of course filled to capacity when the Pope arrived. Eugene Blake made the address of welcome and described the great changes which had taken place in the relationships between the Roman Catholic Church and the World Council. The Pope spoke with visible emotion about this meeting as 'a prophetic moment'. The World Council was 'a marvellous movement of Christians who had been scattered and who were seeking to reconstitute their unity'. He said that the question of the membership of the Roman Catholic Church in the World Council was not yet ripe, but would have to be studied very carefully.

There was one phrase which led to considerable discussion afterwards. The Pope had said: 'My name is Peter.' Some felt that this was unfortunate, for it seemed to imply that even on this ecumenical occasion he felt obliged to make the claim to universal leadership and jurisdiction which was precisely the great obstacle to unity. Others, including myself, felt that it was just as well that, since this was clearly his deep conviction, it should have been stated openly. For this was really the paradoxical position in which we found ourselves: there were still deep differences between us, but we were nevertheless held together by a common faith and a common calling. And it was a reason for profound gratitude, that the man who called himself Peter – and those who did not call him Peter, but respected him as the leader of one of the great branches of Christendom – could now pray together for unity.

The Pope crossed the lake by boat to the park where he would celebrate the mass. Some of us were included in his party. As the boat began to move, some thirty or forty larger and smaller motorboats followed us, producing such waves that all of them danced madly on the water. There was much blowing of horns and shouting, and so our ecclesiastical party became suddenly part of a gay regatta. Most of us, including the cardinals, laughed at this strange spectacle. But Paul VI remained the Pope and made the same official gesture to the yachtsmen which he had made at the solemn occasions earlier in the day. I realized that he considered himself a man set apart, who must at every moment be aware of the dignity of his office.

A number of expectations I had with regard to ecumenical developments have not been fulfilled. But in this matter of the ecumenical mobilization of the Roman Catholic Church much more has happened than I ever dared to expect. Not infrequently we hear complaints that the ecumenical movement does not really move forward. But for those who have known the movement in its early stage, or for those who are younger but have a sense of history, this story of the breaking down of one of the greatest walls of separation in Christendom is clear proof that (to use Galileo's words) *e pur si muove* (it moves anyway).

NOTES

1. Quoted in Bernard Leeming, *The Churches and the Church*, p. IX.
2. See *The Ecumenical Review*, 1954–5, p. 169; and *The Evanston Report*, p. 15.
3. 'Notes on Roman Catholic Writings concerning Ecumenism' in *The Ecumenical Review*, 1955–6, p. 192.
4. *Vers l'Unité chrétienne*, January–February 1960; see also *The Ecumenical Review*, October 1959, p. 103.
5. Ecumenical Press Service, August 13th 1964.
6. Antoine Wenger, *Vatican II : Chronique de la troisième session*, p. 303.
7. Religious News Service, February 14th 1963. Cardinal Willebrands made a similar statement in *Vers l'Unité chrétienne*, March–April 1965, p. 17.

38 | Summing Up

IN THE LATIN oration delivered by the public orator in the convocation at Oxford in 1955, in which I received the honorary degree of doctor of divinity, it was said that like Odysseus I had seen the cities of many peoples and learned their ways. The reason why I could learn the ways and the mind of many peoples was that in most places I was not treated as a foreigner, but as a member of the family. That was one important result of the ecumenical movement. I was often astonished to find how soon the barrier which exists normally between the insider and the outsider was overcome and how I was expected to share fully in the discussion of all burning issues, even those which seemed to be very much in the realm of internal affairs of the churches or the nations. This was of course especially true in the countries which I visited more often. The second and third visits were much more fruitful than the first. I found also that contacts made in the language of the people concerned went much deeper than those during which my partners in conversation had to use a foreign language. In the places where English, French, German or Dutch were the main language, or at least the *lingua franca*, the people I worked with seemed to forget that I was a visitor and made me feel at home among them. Thus in the days of the church conflict in Germany I was treated as a member of the Confessing Church and, later on, when Reinold von Thadden created the *Kirchentag* as a movement of renewal among the laity of the German churches, I was asked to participate in drawing up the plans for that new and promising enterprise. In Great Britain Oldham introduced me to that very select and rather formidable group of British thinkers, called the 'Moot', who were tackling the long-range cultural and spiritual problems of modern society. In the United States I took part in various groups working on theology and the strategy of missions and of the ecumenical movement. In India I had deeply interesting discussions with the group around Judge Chenchiah which aimed to make Christianity more truly indigenous. In France I shared in the attempts to formulate a Christian position with regard to the spiritual temptations of the Vichy-period. And in Indonesia (where the older generation had been educated in Dutch) and among the Afrikaners in South Africa, I found that the Dutch language was a great help in getting a much more intimate relationship with the people I met.

I have always felt rather miserable when I had to speak through an interpreter. For even a good interpreter seemed to be a screen between me and my audience. And I have often wished that I had learned more languages at the time when the learning of new languages is still relatively easy. The philosopher Wittgenstein has said: 'The frontiers of my language are the frontiers of my world.' That is perhaps an exaggeration, but it is true that the world outside the reach of the languages I speak can never be as real to me as the world with which I can communicate directly.

If one spends practically one's whole active life in international work there is of course a danger that one may become an uprooted cosmopolitan. The international servant remains, even in our modern interdependent world, a man or a woman without a clearly defined place in society. He has no local habitat. He belongs to all countries and therefore to no country in particular. While for most men the world outside their own country remains a strange, unreal and rather foolish world, where one finds hotels, campings and beaches and foreigners, it is for the international servant his proper field of work. He can talk about his problems with the other members of the international, rather esoteric, profession whom he meets in airports and at conferences. When he tries to tell people living in their own national situations about his experiences and his concerns, he meets at first with polite attention, but before long they turn the conversation back to the most recent subject of local or national interest.

I found, however, that the ecumenical movement itself provided a soil in which I could strike root. Not only on the staff in Geneva but all over the world there were a certain number of people who sought to live as members of a supra-national family held together by a common faith and by the common task 'to hold the world together'.[1] This family had a strong sense of cohesion. At the same time I had opportunities to maintain contact with my home country (not least of all by reading my Dutch newspaper every day), and many doors were opened to me by Genevese friends so that I could not complain of being removed from the realities of either national or local life.

At first sight it would seem that I have had the same kind of job during thirty-four years, for I became the general secretary of the World's Student Christian Federation in 1932 and I resigned as general secretary of the World Council of Churches in 1966. But in reality there was considerable variety in my tasks and responsibilities. There was of course the difference between the informal contacts which the secretary of a student movement maintains with his constituency and the more formal relations which the general secretary of a new World Council of Churches has with the leaders of the churches. But an even greater difference was that between the times when I had to work with a very small staff and the times when I was responsible for the leadership of several hundreds of colleagues. I had to learn like St Paul (Philippians 4) what it is to be brought low and what it is to have plenty. After the crisis of the late 'twenties and early 'thirties the budget of the World's Student Christian Federation had to be cut by more than fifty per cent and I was left with one half-time collaborator. And soon after I had become General Secretary of the World Council of Churches (in process of formation) the second world war obliged us to cut its budget, so that by 1941 the total was only about twenty-three thousand dollars; on this we could maintain a staff of only four executive secretaries and five stenographers.

But during most of these years and especially after the second world war I had the good fortune to be at the centre of a process of growth and expansion. In the period from 1945 to 1948 we made a great leap forward. By the time of the first Assembly the total number of persons working in the World Council head-quarters had risen to a hundred and forty-two. We had of course left the modest villa in Champel and moved to Route de Malagnou where we worked happily but not very comfortably in a picturesque compound with an ancient Swiss chalet, one larger house (later two), a gatehouse and several wooden barracks. This was like a sudden spring-time when everything starts to grow at the same time and the gardener has to be everywhere. The Department of Inter-Church Aid and Service to Refugees had to undertake a host of new tasks and widened its field of activity; the Study Department worked on a number of new themes; Faith and Order prepared its third World Conference; Church and Society began to tackle the problems of rapid social change. And several new departments had to be set up such as those for Evangelism, for the relations of men and women in church and society, for the laity. Under the inspiring leadership of the two lay theologians and theologically gifted laymen – Hendrik Kraemer and Suzanne de Diétrich – the Ecumenical Institute became what I hoped it would become – an energizing centre and laboratory for the whole movement. In 1951 it added to its list of courses the annual session of the Graduate School of Ecumenical Studies, organized in collaboration with the Faculty of Theology of the University of Geneva. We were now eager to buy the old Château de Bossey, which we had rented, and transform it considerably, but this could only be done if we could get another large donation. Could we go back to Mr John D. Rockefeller Jr.? I had been told that it was his practice not to give more than one donation for the same purpose. But at a dinner in New York at which I sat next to him he showed so much interest in the Ecumenical Institute that I decided to approach him again. Before giving an answer he wanted to get an independent judgment on the work and organization of the Institute. So he sent Arthur Sweetzer, whom I knew from the League of Nations days, in Geneva. Sweetzer told me that no one at Bossey was to know the purpose of his visit. So I had to tell my colleagues at Bossey that a somewhat strange American would visit them who had an in-satiable curiosity about the Institute and might ask the most unexpected questions. Sweetzer's report was completely positive and the gift we received enabled us to make Bossey the permanent home of the Institute and an adequate instrument for its work.

In the years after the Evanston Assembly expansion took another form. The points of growth were development of regional ecumenical bodies in Asia, Africa and Latin America, the preparing for the integration of the World Council and the International Missionary Council, the establishment of closer relations with the Orthodox Church in Russia and the exploration of possibilities of dialogue with the Roman Catholic Church.

The staff had now grown so much that we had to begin to think about a more adequate headquarters building. In 1958 the Central Committee took the courageous decision to raise two and a half million dollars (later three million) in order to build a new ecumenical centre for the World Council, the Lutheran World Federation and the World Presbyterian Alliance. I doubted whether it would really be possible to raise so much money. But the response from large and small churches and from individual donors was most encouraging. Bishop Henry Knox Sherrill, chairman of the committee responsible for the raising of the fund, gave inspiring leadership to the campaign. It was of course by no means easy to get international agreement on the building plans. The most difficult problem was that of the ecumenical chapel. So many different traditions had to be kept in mind. And there were the protagonists of the most modern form of architecture, and also some who would only be happy with a neo-Gothic style. There was a difficult moment when our building committee felt that it had to reject one of the plans for the chapel, for, while it was interesting from an architectural point of view, it was not acceptable from the point of view of most of the liturgical traditions represented in the Council. How was I to explain this to the architect concerned? Rembrandt came to my help. I told the architect that when Rembrandt had painted the 'Night Watch' he had indeed produced a masterpiece, but the musketeers who had commanded the picture had certainly felt that he had not given them the simple group portrait which they desired to have. We were perhaps like the musketeers. We wanted a building that would be suitable for our purposes rather than an exceptional one. We had to give priority to the purposes for which the building would be used rather than to architectural originality.

By 1964 we could leave the Route de Malagnou and occupy our offices in Grand-Saconnex. In my traditional song at the Christmas party of that year I sang:

> Grand-Saconnex Palace, the central see
> Of the pan-Christian Oikoumene.
> Don't blame us if sometimes we can't resist
> To feel a little bit triumphalist.

In fact many of us were sorry to leave the Malagnou campus with its happy-go-lucky atmosphere where the World Council had spent the good years of its youth. But we had grown up. And we had reason to be grateful that supporters of the World Council all over the world had given us a building which enabled us to perform our new tasks in a new period of the council's life. We had at last our own chapel, a sizable conference hall, an adequate library, a cafeteria and sufficient office space for the two hundred and seventy-six members on the World Council headquarters staff and for the expanding staff of the Lutheran World Federation, the World Presbyterian Alliance and other bodies which were planning to join us.

I must now try to describe my work as General Secretary of the World Council. Since I was the first general secretary of an ecumenical body the like of which had not existed before, there was no tradition or precedent to give me guidance concerning the nature of my function. And those who had worked out the plan for the World Council of Churches had, perhaps wisely, left the job undefined. So I had to discover by trial and error just what role the general secretary could and should play.

One thing was very clear, and that was, that my task had a great many different aspects.

I had to be an administrator. As the organization grew there were the usual problems of structure, of finance, of personnel. Since I had never worked with a large staff or with large budgets I had to rely strongly on colleagues and committee members who were much more competent than I. We had, of course, the usual problems of financing a rapidly expanding operation, but the member churches proved willing to provide the necessary support. At this point I must speak of the debt of gratitude the World Council owes to the American churches. In the years after the first Assembly about seventy per cent of our income came from the churches in the United States. And in spite of strong efforts to raise the contributions of the other churches, by the time of the New Delhi Assembly the American churches were still contributing more than half the cost of the common undertaking. There were of course objective reasons for this, but it remained a highly unsatisfactory situation. Now it was remarkable enough that the American churches were willing to bear this disproportionate share of the total burden. But it is even more remarkable that there was never any suggestion that those who made the greatest contribution should have the greatest influence. The report on programme and finance submitted to the New Delhi Assembly says about this possible danger: 'There is no evidence in the history of the ecumenical movement that the financially stronger member churches have acted upon that false worldly assumption.' I can confirm that judgement on the basis of my experience during the whole period of my general secretaryship.

I had of course to give much time to policy-making. Urgent questions had to be answered concerning membership, concerning the relations with the confessional organizations or with regional councils of churches, concerning the relations with the missionary movement as it was organized in the International Missionary Council, concerning the implications of World Council membership for the relations between the member churches, concerning the World Council's responsibility with regard to the major issues of international relations. But the aspect of policy-making which I found most interesting and rewarding had to do with the function of the World Council in helping the churches to rethink their mandate and to find new ways of fulfilling their task in the modern world.

It was clear that the World Council could only win the confidence and loyalty of the churches if it showed them that certain of their main tasks could be accomplished better through collaboration in the council rather than by separate action and if it served as a pace-maker and path-finder, stimulating the churches with new ideas. The worst thing that could happen to the council would be that it should come to be considered as just another cog in the ecclesiastical machinery. My role was not to invent brand-new ideas, but to discover the most forward-looking initiatives in the life of the churches and to seek to make them fruitful for the whole ecumenical family.

This was a part of my task which I enjoyed greatly. When, for example, new insights about the place of the laity or about the co-operation of men and women or about the role of the churches with regard to rapid social change or about church unity percolated from World Council consultations through to the member churches I felt that the council was fulfilling its true task. When a church leader said to me that most of the new ideas on which his staff were working had come from the World Council I felt we were on the right track. But the trouble was that we could never stand still, for one had to prove again and again, through the quality of work of the council, that it was truly worth-while for the churches to give it their full support.

I had furthermore to be the chief liaison officer between the World Council staff and the member churches and also between the staff and the governing bodies of the council. This was by no means an easy task. The dilemma in which I found myself was that, on the one hand, the World Council was sup-posed to be more than just a common denominator of the life of the member churches and should aim to show the way towards new forms of witness and action; but that, on the other hand, the slightest suggestion that the World Council was trying to impose any particular ideas on the churches was bound to meet with immediate resistance. All member churches, those of a strongly hierarchical character as well as those with great international independence, agreed that the World Council should scrupulously respect the full autonomy of each member church. I could therefore never appreciate the joke made by Bishop Berggrav and others, that I was more a general than a secretary. For I knew that the quickest way to lose my job as secretary was to act like a general.

It was therefore essential to remain in very close touch with the chairman and vice-chairman of the Central Committee: George Bell and Franklin Clark Fry from 1948 to 1954 and Fry and Ernest Payne, the Baptist leader in Great Britain, until my resignation in 1966. No decisions of importance were taken without consulting them. These men came to know everything about the World Council there was to be known. They thought in terms of the movement as a whole, but since they carried responsibility in their own churches they could also look at our problems from the perspective of the member churches. So their critical judgment helped greatly to ensure that the council would remain the servant of its member churches.

I had also to be the council's minister of external affairs. There was the relation to the churches which had not joined the council in 1948, a large number of Eastern Orthodox churches, many churches in Africa and of course the Roman Catholic Church. And there were the relations with the international governmental and non-governmental organizations. My colleagues of the Commission of the Churches on International Affairs did most of the daily work in this last-named field, but I had to keep in close touch with them and to maintain sufficient contact with these various bodies to remind them that the World Council, as a whole, desired to be present on the scene where decisions about international affairs were taken.

Another important task was that of interpretation of the nature and work of the World Council and of the ecumenical movement in general. In the early years there was much misunderstanding concerning their purposes. The movement was developing before there had been time to think out all the deeper issues concerning its meaning and its purposes. So I had to do a great deal of speaking and writing on ecumenical problems, to give attention to the editing of *The Ecumenical Review* and to relations with our department of information.

The lectures I had to give each year at the Château de Bossey for the students of the Graduate School of Ecumenical Studies, from its beginning in 1951, were a good opportunity to oblige me to formulate in theological terms what I had learned in my daily work.

Finally, I was the father of a large family of men and women from many nations and churches who were working for the World Council at its head-quarters and who had not only the usual problems of human relations which arise in every staff, but also the problems of understanding between people of different national and confessional backgrounds.

These men and women worked for the World Council because they believed in the purposes of the ecumenical movement. When it was suggested that, as the council grew, it was becoming bureaucratic, I could not help smiling, for my problem was not how to wake up a staff of sleepy bureaucrats, but rather how to get a group of impatient and energetic people, full of new ideas about the task of the church, to co-operate with each other and with the churches which we had to serve and whose power of absorption was far from unlimited.

In my report on the programme and policy of the World Council of Churches submitted to the first Assembly in 1948 I had said:

A council secretary serves all member churches and does not represent the interests of one confession or nation. But he is not and must not be de-confessionalized or de-nationalized, for a secretariat composed of men who try to suppress their own convictions could hardly be called ecumenical in the true sense of the word. The secretariat must, therefore, as far as possible reflect both the divergences and the unity which exist among the member churches. If it does, the secretariat becomes itself a significant experiment in ecumenical relationships.

It seems to me that this has actually happened. We remained a group of men and women with very different theologies and different social or political ideas and we had many intensive debates among ourselves. But all tried to see their own task in the context of the mandate of the ecumenical movement as a whole, even if this meant that they might get out of step with their own churches or their own nations.

It is tempting to mention the names of the men and women who have served on the World Council staff and to whom I owe a great debt of gratitude for the contributions they have made to our common thinking, or for the large share which they have had in the development of the World Council and for their friendship. But I would not know where to begin and where to end.

I would have to enumerate all those who have participated in the work of the general secretariat as associate general secretaries or as assistant general secretaries, but I would also have to speak of the heads of departments, of the directors of the Ecumenical Institute and of the CCIA, and of the executive secretaries of the New York office. And even so the list would be incomplete. For there were men and women in all categories of the staff to whom I owe much because of their initiatives, or simply because of their loyal support.

Many of them could have had easier and more lucrative jobs. Most of them had to travel a great deal and for them as well as for their wives and children the long absence from home meant a real sacrifice. But they wanted to participate in the building up of a movement which could help to give the church a better instrument for the service of the Kingdom in the world. In any case I believe that these many colleagues with whom I worked between 1938 and 1966 know that I have always had a bad conscience when achievements of the World Council were attributed to the work of the captain rather than to the co-operative endeavours of the team as a whole.

In my own family we had of course to cope with the problem of disruption of family life caused by the many and sometimes extensive journeys which I had to make. Jetty accompanied me three times on journeys to Asia and also three times on journeys to the United States. But that meant separation from the children. After one of these journeys we found that the children, who had gone to Holland with a Swiss nurse, had forgotten all their Dutch, because the nurse had insisted that they should speak only French. In most cases, however, Jetty remained at home with the children. It was perhaps useful that as long as we were married we had never known any other life than the life of ever-recurring separation and reunion. The compensation was that home-coming was a real festival and that we enjoyed all the more the holidays which were mostly spent in the Swiss mountains. But Jetty had in this respect the most difficult burden to bear, especially in the time when the children were growing up and she did so with courage and without complaining.

I must now speak of the chairmen with whom I have had the privilege of co-operating.

In international ecumenical bodies the role of the chairman is even greater than in other organizations. The ecumenical chairman must not only have the general ability to lead a discussion, he must also have the *charisma* to transform a group of men and women with the most diverse spiritual backgrounds and completely different assumptions about the rules and the style of debate and decision-making, into a company of people who trust each other and work together to reach agreement. I have worked with six different chairmen. They were very different men, but all had that rare gift of ecumenical leadership.

In the days of my work with the YMCA my chairman was John R. Mott. He gave to every meeting which he chaired the character of a decisively important event in the history of the Kingdom of God. He made you feel that you had been recruited for the *militia Christi*. Each question was put in a vast context. Now this had an inspiring effect on large assemblies, for in this way the participants were helped to transcend their limited horizons. But it did not always work in committee meetings. When conflicts arose, especially conflicts with a theological aspect, the massive generalizations of Mott proved inadequate. He once said in such a meeting: 'Gentlemen, your refined theological distinctions escape me altogether.' But the fact remains that he never allowed us to forget the universal dimensions and the tremendous urgency of the ecumenical task. I looked up to this pioneer, who was thirty-five years older than I, as a pupil does to his master.

Francis Miller, another American layman, who was my chairman during the ten years when I worked for the World's Student Christian Federation, belonged to my own generation. So our meetings became meetings of contemporaries who had the same concerns and the same wavelength. Francis brought us his passionate conviction about the need to overcome the international disorder by the creation of what he called a Christian World Community. The Federation was to provide the nucleus for such a community. This would be done by a process of cross-fertilization between all types of Christian thought. So as chairman he sought to give everyone a full opportunity to express his conviction. It must have been somewhat unexpected for him that, through Pierre Maury and me, one of the dominating trends in the Federation became the new dialectical theology of Karl Barth, but he made a real effort to understand us and we respected him as a strong leader in the field of international and inter-racial relations.

Then, in the period of preparing for the creation of the World Council and the first six years of existence of the Provisional Committee for the World Council, my chairman was William Temple, Archbishop of York and later of Canterbury. It was due to his authority as a theologian, a churchman, a prophet of social justice and perhaps even more to his human qualities that he became the undisputed leader of the ecumenical movement. He never exploited the unique position which he occupied. On the contrary he was sometimes criticized for being too patient with people who were wasting the time of their fellow-members in our meetings. His most outstanding gift was in formulating the agreement of a meeting in which very divergent opinions had been expressed. He himself called this his 'parlour trick'. During the meeting he would scribble some sentences and then ask whether the following statement could perhaps be accepted as an expression of the common mind. I have often tried to use his method in difficult situations, but I have never come anywhere near his performance in this field.

My next chairman was Pastor Marc Boegner of France. As chairman of the Administrative Committee he presided over a number of meetings in Geneva during the war, and as chairman of the Provisional Committee, starting in 1946, he was in the chair of the important meetings after the war which had to prepare for the first Assembly in 1948. His chairmanship was characterized by great courtesy and patience. For the Anglo-Saxons, accustomed to a well-defined method of procedure, his French style of presiding without recognizable rules remained rather impenetrable, but it was generally accepted because all respected his personal authority. He did not intervene much in the debates, but would express his own strong convictions about the ecumenical movement in opening and closing speeches of great eloquence. I owe him a great debt of gratitude for the encouragement and support he gave me in the years when I was so largely cut off from the church leaders who had been appointed to bring the World Council into being.

In 1948 George Bell, Bishop of Chichester, was unanimously elected as first chairman of the Central Committee of the World Council. It was an obvious choice. For thirty years he had been at the centre of the ecumenical movement and he had shown during the years preceding the second world war, and even more during that war, how deeply he believed in the prophetic and reconciling task of the world-wide Christian community. George Bell's concept of chairmanship was that of a father of a family rather than of a keeper of hard and fast rules of procedure. He would let the discussion go on till all had a chance to express themselves and the possibility of an agreement appeared rather than hold to the time-table. When in 1954 he reported to the Assembly on the work of the Central Committee his main emphasis was on the 'steady growth of mutual trust' among the Central Committee members. He said: 'In subjects which ordinarily afford ample ground for controversy, whether political or theological, complete freedom, frankness and charity have prevailed. . . . It has been a great privilege to be the chairman of such a brotherhood of Christians.' And it was a very great privilege for the World Council that in its early years, when most Central Committee members were inexperienced in the art of ecumenical dialogue and co-operation, we had a chairman with the *charisma* of creating that spirit in the movement.

It was also characteristic of George Bell that he never came to a meeting without having something in his pocket. It might be some new proposal about the refugee situation, some new statement about the hydrogen bomb or some other urgent matter. And he succeeded generally in convincing the committee that it was right to follow his lead, because all realized that his concerns were those of a sensitive Christian conscience.

At the Evanston Assembly of 1954 Franklin Clark Fry of the United Lutheran Church in America was chosen to succeed George Bell. He had already served as vice-chairman since 1948. At that time he was a newcomer to the ecumenical movement and had a rather critical attitude to it, but it was thought that by giving him a place of responsibility he might become a constructive supporter and help to overcome hesitations in some of the Lutheran churches. This strategy was completely successful. During the next twenty years Fry gave much of his astounding energy to the Council. It was to a large extent due to the quality of his leadership as chairman in the eventful years from 1954 till his death in 1968 that the Council gained the confidence of the member churches and attracted so many new members.

Fry felt at home in the chair of committee meetings or assemblies because he, knew all there is to be known about the technique of chairmanship. Moreover, he had an astoundingly quick intelligence. He surprised me often by whispered comments showing that he knew what a man was going to say before the man had actually spoken. This had of course also a dangerous side, for committee members who were not so intelligent were sometimes frightened by him and this all the more so, since he was known to make sarcastic remarks about their idiosyncrasies. But his ability as chairman was so obvious and he was so successful in transforming what might seem to be an almost hopeless disagreement into a common decision, that it was very generally agreed that he was the right man in the right place. He could be the very formal chairman and find his way through the labyrinth of amendments and sub-amendments, but he could also suddenly bring in a clever joke, which he enjoyed with loud laughter and slapping of his thigh. There have been times when he and I did not see eye to eye. He was a denominational church leader who had become more ecumenical. I was a student movement leader who had become more church-minded. But while we were different, we respected each other and generally found enough common ground to co-operate closely together.

As to the members of the World Council Presidium, the six who are elected at each assembly, I found that their role was more important than was generally realized. It is true that Archbishop Fisher of Canterbury said at the end of his own period: 'We have been elected to do nothing and we have done it well.' But his own contribution to the life of the council spoke louder than this witticism. And why should there have been such keen interest in the election of the Presidents at each of the assemblies, if the Presidium was nothing but a facade? By the support given to the World Council in their own churches or regions (as

Archbishop Germanos and Archbishop Iakovos did in relation to the Eastern Orthodox churches), by their participation in World Council meetings, by acting as hosts to such meetings (as Sarah Chakko did in India, Sir Francis Ibiam in Nigeria and Bishop Oxnam in the United States), the Presidents became an indispensable part of the World Council's organization. And several of them, notably Pastor Boegner, Bishop Sherrill, Bishop Oxnam, Martin Niemöller and Charles Parlin served at the same time as chairmen of standing committees which played an important role in defining World Council policy.

In the years of preparation, of formation and of probation of the World Council of Churches the theologians also made an important contribution to its life. It was a time of theological renewal and creativity. Karl Barth and his friends had inaugurated the new era in which theology became once again conscious of its specific task. But before long other important voices joined in the great international debate: Reinhold Niebuhr and Paul Tillich in the United States, the Anglican theologians in England, the Eastern Orthodox in Athens and Paris, the Lutherans in Scandinavia and Germany, the advocates of the new theology in the Roman Catholic Church. And in one way or another, through their attendance at World Council meetings or through their writings, most of these theologians became involved in the ecumenical movement. It proved possible to get theologians out of the isolation of their study in order to enter into fruitful dialogue with each other and to attempt to arrive at a common witness to the modern world.

My own place in the theological world has always remained rather ambiguous. Since I came to know most of the leading theologians and many became my friends I was treated as a member of the theological 'tribe'. And I could often serve as a go-between, trying to act as an interpreter between theological schools and to remove misunderstandings. In my writing and speaking I gave a considerable place to theology. But in reality I never became a theologian in the full sense of the term. A general secretary has too many irons in the fire to give undivided or even thorough attention to theology. I have read a good many theological books, but I can also make a long list of important theological volumes which I have never been able to study. So it has happened often that I have felt at a loss when the more technical and more refined theological issues were being discussed. My own writings on theological matters are not original contributions to theological thought, but interpretations across confessional and linguistic frontiers of thoughts which I have picked up from the theological path-finders. I have often been given credit for contributions which were really borrowed feathers. It is impossible to tell your audience or your readers just where you discovered each idea and in many cases you do not even remember exactly where it came from. But I know, for instance, that I owe a great deal to Dutch theological books which have never been translated.

As the years passed I did not change my opinion that Karl Barth had a unique position in the theological world. He continued to be the dominating theologian of our generation. This did not mean that I accepted every position he took, but that I had to listen carefully to him. The real difficulty I felt in my relations with him was that he did not seem to understand the difference between the position of an independent theologian who could speak out on his own accord and that of a council of churches which could only speak on the basis of an agreement between many different positions. Eduard Thurneysen, Barth's companion in arms since the early days of dialectical theology, in whose judgment I had very great confidence, often helped to explain my position to Barth and Barth's position to me. In the years after the second world war Barth began to take a much more constructive attitude to the ecumenical movement. It was a pleasant surprise to find in the volume of the *Church Dogmatics*, which appeared in 1959,[2] a very positive evaluation of the significance of the ecumenical movement as one of the signs of a new turning of the church to the world. Barth closed that reflection by saying that if the nations would work as seriously at the problem of international understanding as the churches worked at the problem of church unity the world would be a better place to live in. But in the *Palais des Nations* no efforts were made comparable to those made in *Route de Malagnou 17*. Today readers of the *Church Dogmatics* may find that reference to Route de Malagnou rather mysterious. It is the old address of the headquarters of the World Council of Churches.

I felt that this praise coming from our most consistent critic deserved an answer and so I wrote a little poem in German. Part of the poem can be translated as follows:

> Poor Palace of the Nations
> You have not got a clue
> The place of inspirations
> Is Route de Malagnou.
>
> Thus gives the great Carolus
> Praise to Oikoumene,
> This Barthian obolus
> Produces heavenly glee.
>
> Is there not ground for fearing
> That ecumeniacs
> Will henceforth be appearing
> Megalomaniacs?

In a later conversation, in 1963, Barth began to apologize for the fact that he had not been able to finish his *Church Dogmatics*. Thinking of the twelve considerable tomes which had already appeared and which took up so much space in the bookcases of the theologians I said that he had given us quite sufficient food for thought. Barth replied that most of the medieval theologians who had tried to produce a *summa* had never completed their work and that most of the cathedrals had also remained unfinished. That answer revealed indirectly that he was not too deeply impressed by or worried about the suggestion made in the 1960s by so many younger theologians that the Barth-period had come to its end. When I spoke at the memorial service in Basle after his death in 1968, to express the gratitude of the World Council for the truly pastoral and ecumenical service which Barth had rendered to the churches all over the world, I concluded that we were not taking leave of his witness, for such a clear and faithful witness would be rediscovered again and again in the years to come.

But I must not only speak of clergymen and theologians, for I owe also a great deal to the laymen who have helped to build up the Council. We never succeeded in fulfilling J. H. Oldham's strong desire that one-third of the bodies governing the World Council should consist of lay persons, men and women. But we have had in the Central Committee and in other committees a number of laymen who have kept us in touch with the world outside the church and helped greatly to make the council the servant of the church as a whole, rather than a trade union of professional church leaders.

I think of the creative role of Frederik van Asbeck of the Netherlands and Sir Kenneth Grubb in the CCIA. 'Church and Society' could not have done its pioneering job without such men as M. M. Thomas of India, C. L. Patijn of the Netherlands, T. B. Simatupang of Indonesia, André Philip of France. The Department on Co-operation between Men and Women was set up by Sarah Chakko of India. Charles Taft, Francis P. Miller, Nathan Pusey, Charles Parlin from the United States, Kathleen Bliss from Great Britain and Reinold von Thadden from Germany were among the most active members of the Central Committee.

By their leadership, not merely in practical affairs but in the spiritual realm, these laymen kept the clergymen and theologians in their proper place. When I walked out in a solemn procession from an ecumenical service at which M. M. Thomas had spoken I said to the layman walking beside me: 'When our laymen preach such excellent sermons, what are we theologians good for?' He looked at my ecclesiastical gown and doctor's hood and answered promptly: 'For the procession!'

At this point I must speak of a prominent lay woman who had no formal relation to the World Council, but was passionately interested in its purposes. I mean Princess Wilhelmina of the Netherlands.[3]

Her place in the ecumenical movement was quite unique. Other royal persons or heads of state had shown interest in the movement. But Princess Wilhelmina became an active and vocal participant in its life. In one of her letters to the World Council she said: 'After my abdication I felt it my duty to serve Christ universally and to guide men all over the world from their diversity to Christ in unity.'[4] To this calling she devoted all her great energy and will-power. From 1950 till her death in 1962 she sent out a stream of messages, letters or brochures about the urgency of the cause of Christian unity. And many of these were addressed to the World Council. There was a time when at practically every important ecumenical meeting we received her strong exhortation.

What she had to say was very simple and straightforward. She believed with all her heart that Christ offered us a complete renewal of life. The churches had complicated the original gospel. The men who had really helped her to understand that gospel were not church leaders or theologians, but lay evangelists like John R. Mott, independent preachers like Franc Thomas, who held his meetings in a concert-hall in Geneva, Sadhu Sundhar Singh, who went around in India giving his witness to Christ in the manner of an Eastern holy man. She had not forgotten that the Christian statesman, de Savornin Lohman, whom she had greatly admired, had said: 'Not the Church, but the Kingdom of God;' and 'The Church separates, the Gospel unites.' So now she was quite sure that her vocation was to urge all Christians and especially the churches

> to put aside their problems and everything that divides them and to seize this moment to prove that their love for him (Christ) is stronger than all discussions and deeply stirred by the distress into which mankind has fallen, to put up an impressive token of their faith over against all spiritual evil that threatens mankind with destruction, by founding a unity which includes them all.[5]

She did not find it easy to express herself and her messages were often vague and repetitive. But the two points which she wanted to get across most of all were quite clear: first, the time had come to stop talking about unity and 'to found the Universal Church on earth'; secondly, the scandal that Christians were separated at the communion table should cease immediately.

We tried, of course, to convince her that we had the same goal in mind, but that by forcing the pace we would do more harm than good. But this did not impress her. Her holy impatience remained as strong as ever.

In 1954 just before the second Assembly at Evanston she asked me to come to see her and we had a long conversation. She had still that same rather severe dignity. The hard years had sculptured her face. She was now an old lady, but she had not lost her vigour and was as determined as ever to fight for her strong convictions.

No time was lost in small talk. She had done her homework and read the preparatory material for the Assembly. But she had not found in the literature a clear answer to the one decisive question: Would this opportunity be seized to declare once and for all that the divisions between Christians had been overcome and that all should be in full communion with each other? I seemed once again to be in the position of the student before the examiner. The tone was friendly, but the questions were sharp. I tried as best I could to explain how the World Council sought to approach the question of unity. We believed that unity had to grow out of the actual living and working together of the churches. We were moving forward. I described the ecclesiastical and theological realities as they were at the moment. But these matters were outside her horizon and did not really interest her. It was all or nothing. If you really believed in renewal and unity you had to say: full unity right now and without any reservation.

In the next few weeks she continued to exert the pressure. In a letter written in April she said that the failure of the churches to manifest the oneness in Christ that is the sure mark of the Christian church showed in the present dangerous world situation an irresponsible attitude, for that situation required an example of concord. And she wrote a memorandum with the title, 'Thoughts which have come to me as I reflected about the Evanston Assembly'. In it she urged that Evanston should not 'weave a veil of theological thinking between Christ on the one hand and contemporary man and society on the other, which makes it harder for men to come spontaneously to the Prince of Life'.

I answered that we shared fully her deep concern for church unity. That was the very *raison d'être* of our work. But unity could not be forced. We had learned that it could only come as the result of a spiritual process. But that process was indeed going on.

It was impressive that in spite of all disappointments she did not cease to be actively concerned with the ecumenical movement. In 1958 this concern led to a letter addressed to the Presidents and all members of the Executive Committee in which she criticized two current developments. She disapproved of the approach which the World Council made to the churches in Eastern Europe, because these churches had not protested against the iniquities which had been committed in their countries. And she found it unacceptable that the World Council was seeking funds for a new building at the time when funds were required for refugees. We explained at length why we believed it to be our duty to enter into conversation with the Eastern churches and why we had to build an adequate headquarters building for the council. But I doubt whether our arguments convinced her.

In the last years of her life she asked me to help her to make contact with leaders of the younger churches. Philip Potter of the West Indies, D. T. Niles and Selvaretnam of the Christian Ashram in Ceylon went to stay with her, and this gave her real encouragement. She was also delighted about Kraemer's *Theology of the Laity* and sent copies to many friends.

In three handwritten letters which she sent me in 1960 she repeated with impressive consistency her one unchanging complaint: Why don't the churches take immediate action concerning Christian unity? Her last message to the World Council took the form of a word to the third Assembly in New Delhi in 1961 in which she expressed her joy that an open Holy Communion Service would be celebrated. She died in 1962. In a short radio address on the day of the funeral I said that through her life and her words she had asked us all one tremendous question – namely, whether we had the right sense of proportion. Was not the fact of God's action in Christ so overwhelming that everything else

had to make way for it and was not therefore all that separated Christians as
nothing compared with that which they had in common?

Since I served a world council of churches my main task was to get church
leaders to co-operate and to work for church unity. Today this is often called
somewhat sneeringly 'official' or 'institutional' ecumenism. But ecumenical
action 'from above' is just as much part of the ecumenical enterprise as ecumenism 'from below'. The best times are those in which there is an interplay between
the two types of action. Many of the pioneers of the ecumenical movement have
at one time concentrated their attention on the grass-roots and at other times on
the leadership of the churches.

So I have attended many church assemblies, synods, meetings of councils of
churches, pastoral conferences and ecclesiastical commemorations. The most
solemn of the solemn assemblies were those of the Church of Scotland during
which I was the guest of the Lord High Commissioner at Holyrood Palace in
Edinburgh and of the Church of Russia which received us in the incomparable
setting of the Troitsky Lavra at Sagorsk. There were deeply encouraging occasions when a new vision of their task was given to the churches, and there were
dull and merely formal gatherings. Sometimes I was treated as an intruder who
might introduce dangerous new ideas, and sometimes I was received as a
welcome guest who was expected to bring with him all the assembled wisdom and
experience of the church universal.

But I have never thought of my task as being exclusively concerned with the
leadership of the churches. The fourteen years spent in youth and student
movements had left their mark. So I was always glad to get opportunities to get
in direct contact with local congregations. I have preached in churches of
practically all confessions, including the Orthodox and the Roman Catholic, in
six continents. When I think of all these congregations I am first of all struck by
their incredible variety. There were dignified, sometimes too dignified, services,
but also services interrupted by hallelujahs or by the waving of handkerchiefs.
There were very large congregations in cathedrals and small groups in country
chapels. But even more impressive than the variety was the simple fact that all
these people, rich and poor, white and black and brown, Christians with a very
ancient tradition and Christians of the first or second generation, were looking
for the same thing – that is, a deeper and more dynamic encounter with Jesus
Christ. My task was therefore not in the first place to give them information
about the ecumenical movement or even to preach about church unity. It was
rather to give such a witness that they would discover themselves that this man
coming from another church, another country or continent, and they were
involved together in the same quest for deeper understanding of the gospel.
I found, therefore, that if I watched my illustrations which had to be adjusted to
the local situation, I could preach the same kind of sermon in practically all
churches. The conclusion is, of course, that the churches have far more in

common than they realize.

There were also many occasions for discussion with students and other young people or with laymen in an informal ecumenical setting. The World Student Christian Federation remained the place where one could get a glimpse of the shape of things to come. At the Ecumenical Institute at the Château de Bossey the students asked sharp and challenging questions about the life of the ecumenical movement. *Kirchentag* assemblies in Germany and similar gatherings in other countries mobilized vast crowds of laymen who were not concerned with the internal problems of the church, but with the relevance of Christianity for their life in a secularized society. I attended eight of the German *Kirchentag* assemblies and had to speak four times to the outdoor closing meetings. The most impressive of all was the one in 1951 in the Olympia stadium in Berlin with its more than two hundred thousand participants who came from the two very different worlds of East Germany and West Germany and experienced the deep joy of belonging together to one indestructible fellowship.

There were furthermore the moments when I had to speak to *ad hoc* audiences of people of all confessions and of no confession, who were completely unknown to me. Sermons on big or on small ships could lead to unexpected conversations. Marriages, baptisms and funerals were occasions when one could speak about the meaning of life and death to people who never entered a church building. And the many talks or sermons on radio and television had also to deal in the simplest possible language with the most central Christian truths.

So there were fortunately a good many opportunities to get out of the ecclesiastical world and to be reminded that the church, even in its ecumenical expression, is not the whole world. Travelling, especially in the old days when one had leisurely conversations with fellow-travellers on board ship or in a train compartment, meant that one could have unexpected human contacts. I think of the man with whom I spent most of my time on a liner from Europe to the United States. We talked about everything under the sun and I found him a most stimulating companion. We had not told each other to what professions we belonged, but on the last evening we could no longer suppress our curiosity about each other. So my companion said: 'I am a professional parachutist.' And I said: 'I am a clergyman.' We had at least in common that both of us had something to do with heaven.

There was a wonderful variety in the contacts which one could make during one's journeys. There were occasions for arguing with communist officials in Eastern European countries and there were opportunities, such as that offered by the 'Bilderberg' conference under the chairmanship of Prince Bernhard of the Netherlands, of meeting the captains of industry and Western statesmen. And in Buffalo (N.Y.) my brother Frans, who is a chemical engineer, and my sister-in-law Martha, who is a painter, liked to arrange dinners with their varied groups of friends – lawyers, businessmen and artists – who bombarded me with critical questions about my work and ideas in that straightforward way which is characteristic of the Americans. Or there were the many meetings with university students, the all too conservative students of the nineteen-fifties whom I wanted to stir up and the all too-radical students of the nineteen-sixties whom I wanted to calm down.

In the international community in Geneva one could meet men and women of the most varied background. I learned even to appreciate the use of cocktail parties, for it was often possible to take there the opportunity of expressing some specific concern to the representative of a government or an international organization or to get a piece of information that one could not get otherwise.

I enjoyed the way in which men of completely different professions were thrown together on the occasions when I received honorary doctorates. Yale University had the specialty that the names of the recipients were kept secret. So the dinner in the home of the president of the university on the night preceding commencement day began like a parlour game. One had not only to discover the names of the guests, but also the reason why they received the doctorate. The only fellow candidate I knew was Charles Malik of the Lebanon. The most original and unexpected contributions to the conversation came from Frank Lloyd Wright, the famous architect, who explained why skyscrapers should be built in the desert rather than in the cities.

But the most unusual mixture of people from all walks of life was the party given by *Time Magazine*, in 1963, on the occasion of its fortieth anniversary. Nearly three hundred of the men and women who had appeared on the cover of *Time* had accepted the invitation from editor-in-chief, Henry Luce, for a dinner in the vast ballroom of the Waldorf Astoria in New York. With wives, special guests and representatives of *Time*, there were sixteen hundred people. During the cocktail hour I found myself talking with Gina Lollobrigida and a moment later with Cardinal Spellman. Then I came across Paul Tillich who was a worried man because he was to address the motley crowd on 'The Human Condition'. How could you speak in such a way that you would be understood by statesmen, generals, baseball players, boxers, Hollywood stars, clerics, actors, journalists, scientists at one and the same time? When the dinner started all 'cover-guests' were individually introduced while their cover portraits were flashed on a screen. Everybody was trying to get a good look at his or her preferred celebrities. Vice-President Lyndon Johnson's most memorable remark in the course of a short speech was: 'As I have looked around the room tonight I have realized that many of us owe Henry Luce a very great debt for being the first publisher to select magazine cover models on a basis other than beauty.' When Tillich spoke and developed the theme that all perfection is ambiguous I saw a somewhat puzzled look on the face of the many participants who were not accustomed to listen to a philosophical discourse.

In 1956 when I had been general secretary of the World Council for fifteen years and when an inquiry came whether I would accept appointment as professor in the Faculty of Theology of the University of Utrecht, I asked the

Executive Committee whether the time had not come for a change in the general secretariat. But the committee decided unanimously to ask me to stay on. At New Delhi in 1961 I told the Central Committee that if they wanted to re-appoint me I would accept with the understanding that I would resign on reaching the age of 65, that is in 1965. It seemed to me that the job of the general secretary was so strenuous that it should not be held by a man beyond that age. Some did not agree. Thus some Orthodox church leaders told me that a general secretary of the World Council was like a Patriarch and that Patriarchs did not resign. But it seemed to me that there was more difference than similarity between these two positions.

At the meeting in Rochester in 1963, the Central Committee had to begin the process of selecting a new general secretary. There was no precedent to guide the committee. Franklin Clark Fry had worked out an ingenious plan to form a nomination committee consisting of the Chairman and Vice-Chairman of the Central Committee, of six members chosen by the Central Committee and four members chosen by the Executive Committee for the purpose of ensuring a proper confessional and geographical balance. But the Central Committee rejected this plan, mainly for reasons of economy and decided that the Executive Committee be empowered to nominate a general secretary. Practically nobody realized at that time that this could lead to considerable complications.

I did not of course attend the several closed sessions in which the Executive Committee sought to arrive at agreement concerning the name to be proposed to the Central Committee, but I was informed about the progress of their deliberations. In the summer of 1964 Franklin Clark Fry reported at an open meeting of the Executive Committee, at which many World Council staff members were present, that the committee had arrived at agreement and gave the name of the candidate whom they would recommend. He said that it had been the intention of the Executive Committee to report their nomination first to the Central Committee, but the circumstances had led to the decision to make an immediate announcement to the press.

At first it seemed that the problem had been solved. But before long there were clear indications that the nomination did not meet with general acceptance. Only now did the members of the Central Committee begin to realize that since they had asked the Executive Committee to make the nomination they had to face the choice between acceptance of the nomination and a conflict with the Executive Committee. The fact that they received the first information concerning the nomination through the press did not make the situation any easier.

The months between the meeting of the Executive Committee (July 1964) and the meeting of the Central Committee (January 1965) were an unhappy time for all concerned. I was in a strange position. It was clear that I should not express any preference concerning the choice of my successor. I told church leaders who asked me whom I would prefer for the general secretaryship that I was the only one in the council who did not have to make up his mind concerning the nomination. But I was still responsible for the wellbeing and cohesion of the World Council. My main concern was that the decision to be taken should be as nearly unanimous as possible. So I warned Fry and other Executive Committee members that according to my information there was a deep divergence of opinion among the members of the Central Committee and that this could have very grave consequences for the life of the Council. But the Executive Committee maintained its nomination. I did not attend the closed meetings in Enugu in which the matter was discussed. The outcome was that the Central Committee did not take action on the nomination of the Executive Committee and decided to set up a new nominations committee of eighteen members under the chairmanship of Bishop John Sadiq of India. The desire was expressed that no press release concerning the nomination would be given until the committee's report had been re-presented to the Central Committee. From this time onwards the nomination process took its normal course so that in February 1966 Eugene Carson Blake could be appointed as the new general secretary.

I have been criticized for my role in the last six months of 1964. I do not pretend that I made no mistakes. It was a situation in which it was impossible not to make any mistakes. For to have remained completely passive would also have been wrong. Fortunately the crisis did not do irreparable damage. Fry and I had for the first time in our many years together been on opposite sides, but our friendship was strong enough to stand the strain.

In his speech of acceptance of his election as general secretary Blake had said that it was his intention to preserve to the World Council the fullest possible continuance of my service. Later on he proposed that I should serve as consultant to the general secretary. I was grateful for this offer, for this seemed to me a very good solution of the problem of my relation to the council. It meant that I would have nothing to do with the administrative and organizational aspects of the World Council's life, but that I would stay in Geneva, have an office in the Ecumenical Centre and continue to remain in touch with ecumenical developments. After a period of trial and error the arrangement worked well. Blake and I had regular meetings to discuss current developments.

I would have found it very difficult to withdraw completely from the ecumenical scene. I had lived in the ecumenical atmosphere for forty years and found it hard to imagine life without it. At the Ecumenical Centre in Geneva one could meet almost every day visitors from different parts of the world or World Council secretaries returning from their journeys. And this was also the place where I could consult the records concerning the ecumenical developments of the last fifty years and write these memoirs.

And Geneva had become our home. We had been well received by the Genevese. The National Protestant Church of Geneva had given me my pastoral ordination. The University of Geneva had given me an honorary degree. In the delicate situation of the war years I had received much help from individual Genevese. Our children had become strongly attached to the city where they had been educated. And we had strong links of friendship with a number of Genevese families. This was largely due to the fact that in the nineteen-thirties, when Pierre Maury was living in Geneva, there had been formed a 'groupe Maury' consisting of seven couples who would meet regularly for a meal and for theological discussion. We were of the same generation and we had the same concern for the renewal of the church and for church unity. Maury was our *pastor pastorum*. In addition to Maury and me there were three professors of theology: Jaques Courvoisier, Henri d'Espine and Frantz Leenhardt, and two pastors: Max Dominicé and Jean de Saussure. In the early days we were so theologically minded that even on the occasion when we celebrated the Geneva *escalade* festival by appearing in fancy dress there was a theological lecture. It was not easy to listen to a learned discourse while facing one man dressed up as Calvin, another one as Mephistopheles and so on. The links created by the 'groupe Maury' had proved lasting and meant much to Jetty and to me.

The link with Geneva became even stronger when I was offered the *bourgeoisie d'honneur* of the Republic and Canton of Geneva. When Max Dominicé came to ask me whether I would accept this honour I said that I had never thought about this and was taken by surprise, but this seemed to be the kind of thing which one could only accept with gratitude. In April 1966 the Grand Conseil of Geneva adopted after a brief discussion with friendly speeches and without any opposition a law granting me honorary naturalization for the municipality of Chêne-Bougeries. I was glad to find that the proposal of the government had been so well received, but I was not quite prepared for the fact that the *bourgeoisie d'honneur* meant in this case a naturalization. I explained to the Geneva authorities that I had no intention of giving up my Dutch citizenship. They understood this very well. But on the Dutch side the situation was not so simple. In Dutch law citizenship is lost when a Dutchman acquires another nationality by his own will. Now I maintained that my role in this matter had been wholly passive and that the Genevese authorities had even agreed that I should not have to take an oath, but the Netherlands Embassy in Berne took the line that just by accepting the naturalization I would cease to be a Dutch citizen. This led to a voluminous correspondence between the Dutch consulate in Geneva, the Dutch embassy in Bern, the Ministries of Foreign Affairs and of Justice in The Hague and the Geneva government. I marvelled at the energy which some diplomats spent on this problem which did not seem to endanger the peace of the world! Fortunately the Dutch Minister of Foreign Affairs, Mr J. M. A. H. Luns, seeing that this storm in the juridical teapot was getting a little ridiculous, cut the Gordian knot and decided that since this naturalization would not take the form of a bilateral action and since I would play a purely passive role in it, I would not lose my Dutch citizenship. So in February 1967 Jetty and I could go to the city hall to receive the diploma which conferred on us all the rights inherent in the citizenship of Geneva. President Chavanne's speech showed great appreciation of the role of the World Council. I was glad to have an occasion to express my gratitude for the various forms of hospitality which we had found in Geneva. As to the problem of double citizenship I said that while you could not serve two masters you could love and respect two parents, especially when these two parents had a great deal in common.

I had never voted in my life. Now I had to learn to vote, and in Switzerland with its frequent referendums on all sorts of problems this meant doing a good deal of homework.

But I must go back to 1966. It was a year when new ground was broken as the World Conference on Church and Society in Geneva, ably prepared by Paul Abrecht, gave the World Council more precise goals in the realm of social action and international development. But it was for me also a year of looking at the twenty-eight years during which I had been general secretary. The Archbishop of Canterbury (Dr A. M. Ramsey) visited Geneva and we remembered that in the period before the Oxford Conference of 1937 he and I had been called 'the promising boys'. Farewell parties were given at the time of the Central Committee meeting in Geneva, and later in the year in Germany, Greece, Indonesia, the United States and Hongkong, which made me once more keenly aware of the privilege of having lived at the centre of a world-wide network of friends. But the truly unforgettable party was that given by the World Council staff which, through various types of representations, showed the lighter side of the ecumenical movement as only insiders can. I sang with the help of my daughter Anneke my last song. But the best moment came when Philippe Maury, the son of my friend Pierre, who had known me since his boyhood and was now director of the Department of Information, spoke on behalf of the staff. He said things which went straight to my heart.

So I had to begin a different kind of life. Jetty and I had of course often talked about the life we would like to live and the things we would like to do together after my retirement. We wanted to spend more time with our nine grandchildren. We had hoped that at last we would be able to discover what married life was like when it was not constantly interrupted by periods of separation. But this was not to be. During the last years Jetty's health had greatly deteriorated. In the year after my retirement she had to spend many months in hospital. She took it all in her calm, stoic way and became increasingly detached from the outside world. The end came in January 1968.

She had had a difficult life. Not only because of her health problems, but also because she had very many things on her mind and strong convictions in her heart which she wanted to express, but was often defeated in the struggle to express them. Her one overwhelming concern became that women did not get the chance of making their true contribution. In our civilization the norm of humanity was a male norm. It was not simply a question of giving women jobs or votes. The issue was whether we could learn again that when God created man in his own image he created them male and female. She wrote some eight or nine essays on the subject, each of which cost her much time and energy. The titles are significant: 'Eve, Where art thou?'[6]; 'Towards the funeral of man alone'; and 'Co-humanity and the Covenant'.[7] She convinced me that this was indeed one of the deepest unsolved problems of humanity and that was why I supported the setting up of a World Council Department on the Co-operation of Men and Women in Church and Society. Her problem was that her life was too introverted. My problem was that my life was too extroverted. This did not make things any easier. But it meant that we had something to give to each other. And I found it hard to go on without her.

At the fourth Assembly of the World Council which took place in Uppsala (Sweden) in 1968 I felt like an airplane pilot who travels for the first time in the cabin rather than in the cockpit. But there were great advantages in attending an assembly without having administrative responsibilities. I could at last spend time on renewing friendships with people from all over the world whose countries I had visited.

At the beginning of the meeting I had to give an address on 'The Mandate of the Ecumenical Movement'. My main point was that 'the ecumenical movement had entered into a period of reaping an astonishingly rich harvest, but that precisely at this moment the movement was more seriously called in question than ever before. And once again the basic issue was that of the relation between the church and the world.' Using a terminology which was not new, for Paul Tillich had often used it before, I tried to show that the vertical and horizontal dimensions of the Christian faith were inseparable and interdependent. The faith 'is man-centred because it is God-centred. We cannot speak of Christ as the man-for-others without speaking of him as the man who came from God and lived for God.'

It was a sign of the times that in the discussion about the vertical and horizontal aspects of the faith, not only in Uppsala but also after the Assembly, the most frequently quoted sentence from this address was: 'It must become clear that church members who deny in fact their responsibility for the needy in any part of the world are just as much guilty of heresy as those who deny this or that article of the faith.' If I had known beforehand that this sentence would become so popular, I would have added a complementary phrase such as: 'And church members who deny that God has reconciled men to himself in Christ are just as much guilty of heresy as those who refuse to be involved in the struggle for justice and freedom for all men and who do nothing to help their brethren in need.' For it seems to me that the health of the ecumenical movement depends on our readiness to stand with equal firmness for these two convictions at the same time.

The year 1968 was in a special sense the year of the revolt of youth. It was therefore natural that at Uppsala the voice of youth was heard far more clearly than at any previous assembly. I had been invited to speak to the youth delegates on the day before the assembly began. Since I included in my address some critical remarks about the lack of constructive ideas in the new youth movement I was suspect by many young people as being on the wrong side. When two days later in my address I asked the church delegates to take the youth protest seriously and said that when young people all over the world asked searching questions about the meaning of life, the churches should prick up their ears, some of the youth delegates declared that they had converted me. They forgot that my assembly address had been written weeks before the meeting. I had simply felt that in the given situation the emphasis in a speech to young people had to be different from that in a speech to representatives of the older generation.

Some of the interventions of youth, particularly in the daily 'Hot News', showed the weak sides of the younger generation. To fight paternalism coming from church leaders by paternalism coming from the young is not very effective. Talking down to the old is not much better than talking down to the young. But in the 'Club 1968', where assembly leaders had to appear before a crowd of young people and had to go through a regular examination with sharp and challenging questions, youth played its true role and there was real encounter and dialogue between the generations.

At Uppsala I was elected as Honorary President of the World Council of Churches. I found it difficult to think of myself as an elder statesman carrying the title which only John R. Mott, George Bell and J. H. Oldham had carried before me. But I was glad that in this way my relation to the council was further clarified. The remarkable thing about the Honorary Presidency in the World Council is that it is nowhere mentioned in the constitution or rules. So I took it that the Honorary President had no vote. But according to precedent he is expected to attend meetings of the Executive and Central Committees and to participate in the discussions.

I received more invitations to give addresses or to write articles than ever before, for many thought that I could not possibly refuse now that I had so much time at my disposal. But the advantage of my new situation was that I had much greater freedom to choose the ones which seemed to me the most worthwhile. Thus I accepted invitations to lectureships from Drew University, the Pacific School of Religion (Berkeley), the Canadian Council of Churches, the Council of Churches in Jaffna (Ceylon), the University of Capetown and the American University of Beirut. There were new openings. I enjoyed chairing the group which was to work out the new mandate for the Theological Education Fund with its programme of raising the level of theological education in Asia, Africa and Latin America. And I agreed to serve as a permanent consultant to the Presidium of the Conference of European Churches which is specially important as a platform on which the Churches of Eastern Europe and Western Europe enter into dialogue with each other. Rather to my surprise I was also asked to preside over the Alliance of Orders of St John. I had joined the order in Geneva because it brought together laymen who took their Christian faith seriously and because it maintained its ancient tradition of serving the suffering. I hoped that it would be possible to orientate the order as a whole towards concern for the

underdeveloped countries such as some branches of the order had already
shown. The first objective was to give common support to the Ophthalmological
Hospital in Jerusalem founded by the British Order of St John.

Visitors coming to the World Council in the time after my retirement and in
whose reception I was asked to share included Pope Paul VI, the Ecumenical
Patriarch Athenagoras and Catholicos Vazken of the Armenian Church.

I participated also in preparing the visit of Princess Beatrix and Prince Claus
of the Netherlands. This was a real working-visit during which they succeeded
in getting first-hand knowledge of the work of the principal international
organizations in Geneva. And this led to interesting discussions. I was impressed
by the depth of concern for the great human problems which both of them
showed.

Then there were the many students or scholars who came to Geneva to work
on historical or theological aspects of the ecumenical movement. The programme
became so crowded that I sometimes wondered whether the time had not come
to discover how one could retire from this kind of retirement.

As I now looked at the ecumenical scene I could not help realizing that the
ecumenical movement of 1970 was very different from the one I had known in
1930 or in 1950. First of all with regard to the *dramatis personae*. All the men of
the very first generation, to whom I had looked up as the true pioneers and with
whom I had collaborated closely, had gone: John R. Mott and J. H. Oldham,
Archbishop Germanos and Hamilcar Alivisatos, William Temple and George
Bell, William Adams Brown, Yngve Brilioth and Otto Dibelius. Marc Boegner
was the last of that generation of outstanding men to leave.

But so very many of the men and women who belonged to my own generation,
who had shared in the same struggles of the 1930s and 1940s and who were in a
special sense my companions, were no longer with us. I think of the theologians
who had influenced me or with whom I had been in constant conversation and
about whose opinions I had cared deeply: Karl Barth and Pierre Maury, Julius
Schniewind and Reinhold Niebuhr, Paul Tillich and Emil Brunner, Josef
Hromadka and Stephan Zankov had provided the frame of reference for my
theological thinking.

In matters of policy men and women such as Alphons Koechlin, William
Paton, Hendrik Kraemer, Eivind Berggrav and Sarah Chakko had been among
my most trusted counsellors. Even men who had started their ecumenical career
after the second world war and had made a decisive contribution at that time
such as Franklin Clark Fry, G. Bromley Oxnam, Z. K. Matthews and David
Moses had died. I felt even more deeply the loss of younger colleagues in whom
I had great confidence and who had become close friends: Leslie Cooke, whose
work as director of a far-flung operation of interchurch aid and relief was
inspired by his pastoral concern for people; D. T. Niles, charismatic evangelist
but also 'man of unity', who was always throwing new light on our problems or
on the best use to be made of individual persons; Philippe Maury, with his

insatiable *curiosité intellectuelle* and his catholic interest in all aspects of human life; Daisuke Kitagawa with his passion for racial justice and inter-cultural understanding.

And since other colleagues such as Robert Mackie, Reinold von Thadden, Roswell Barnes, Henry Van Dusen and Samuel McCrea Cavert were no longer participating in ecumenical meetings I sometimes felt like a pilgrim who had been part of a great company of pilgrims and who had lost nearly all his companions on the way; or perhaps like the sole survivor of a prehistoric species of creatures who had by some mistake escaped being put away in a palaeontological museum. This does not mean that I had no confidence in or contact with the new generation. But they represented precisely a new era which had on the basis of its own experiences worked out a new style of life. Was the ecumenical movement of 1970 then a real continuation of the movement as I had known it in its earlier days? Or was it in the process of becoming something quite different? That question is not so easily answered.

There had certainly been a change in the general climate. The first clear indication of this change came, as could be expected, from the World Student Christian Federation. The Federation had worked for years on a project called: 'The Life and Mission of the Church'. The underlying idea was that students should be made aware of the agreement which had arisen in the ecumenical movement about the task of the church. In 1960 a 'teaching conference' was held in Strasbourg to bring the project to its conclusion. But that conference became something very different from what the Federation leaders had hoped and expected. The addresses given by D. T. Niles, Lesslie Newbigin, Karl Barth and by me did not seem to give the students what they wanted. What had happened? David Edwards has put it this way: 'There seemed to be too much speaking about the life of the church; what students wanted was action in the world. And there seemed to be too much mission; what students wanted was a welcome to this world.'[8] Six years later at the World Conference on Church and Society in Geneva, and then again at the Assembly in Uppsala, it became clear that this new orientation had come to stay.

It is not easy to define the difference between the old and the new orientation. People who do not know their ecumenical history have said that the earlier ecumenical movement was introverted and the newer ecumenical movement is extroverted. But that is a distortion of the facts. Already in 1925 Nathan Søderblom made much of the Latin title which he had chosen for the Life and Work Conference, *communio in serviendo oecumenica*, that is ecumenical fellowship realized in common service to the world. In Oxford, in 1937, we had struggled with the problem of the right conception of the state and the nation. In Amsterdam, in 1948, we had worked out the concept of the responsible society. The world had not been absent in the life of the ecumenical movement.

But that is not to say that there was nothing new in the new orientation. The change was not in the fact that at last the churches were beginning to take the world seriously, but in the fact that they began to think in a different way about the relation between the church and the world. Robert McAfee Brown comes perhaps nearest to a definition of the new orientation when he speaks of a certain shifting of emphases and a reassignment of priorities in order that institutional Christianity may turn outward from institutional preoccupation and spend itself lavishly in the service of all men.[9]

It seems to me that this is not only a perfectly justifiable concern, but also an inevitable consequence of the discoveries which have been made in the history of the movement. When the World Council gives today such high priority to the issues of worldwide development, or when it takes very concrete steps in the fight against racism, it is certainly not denying the mandate which it has received. When we study the problems of church unity in the light of the unity of mankind we are not changing our course altogether, but seeking to bring together two dimensions which had always been there but which had not been sufficiently related to each other.

So I welcome the new orientation in principle. But that does not mean that I am happy about all that is being said or done in the name of the new orientation. I do not believe that taking the world seriously must mean that we conceive of the task of the church as simply answering the questions which the world asks and meeting the needs of which the world is aware. We have good reason to study the 'agenda of the world'. But in the last resort the agenda which God gives to the church (and which includes of course the affairs of the world) must have priority. Too often today the church is looked upon as if it were a sort of spiritual petrol-station. You decide first where you want to go and then you get the 'resources' (a typically impersonal expression) from the church pump. You are for development or emancipation, for revolution or for law and order, for this or that ideology or utopia, and the church must help you to get to your chosen destination. But if the Church is the church of Jesus Christ, it knows only one destination: The Kingdom of God. And all human goals must be critically analysed in the light of the information which we have received about the nature of that Kingdom and the road that leads towards it. The church must therefore ask: Which development, which emancipation, which revolution is in line with God's design? And what does our Lord say about the means of transforming our present established disorder? Whatever strength the ecumenical movement has had and still has, has come from the fact that it tried to raise these questions, which are finally more radical than any sociological analysis can be. We must not forget that at the heart of the definition of 'the Responsible Society', which has helped us to see our task in the world more clearly, there is the responsibility to God. All other responsibilities depend on that original one.

My hope is therefore that the result of the great and often chaotic debate about the relations of the church and the world which is going on today will not be that all we have learned in the last forty years will be swept aside, but rather that we will make full use of it, and elaborate its implications and correct its shortcomings in the light of the new tasks which are clearly given to us today. This is not a question of institutional continuity. The ecumenical structures which were worked out in the 1930s and 1940s are not sacrosanct. They must be constantly adapted to new tasks, new situations. But there is a deeper continuity. What has happened in the last forty of fifty years in and through the ecumenical movement can be interpreted in different ways. As in every other historical phenomenon different factors have contributed to its development. But those who have really lived inside the movement have become convinced that it is in the last analysis not 'a game which we play', but 'a game played upon us'.[10] It was not that we succeeded in gathering the churches and the Christians. It was that the churches and the Christians were being gathered. There was movement because there was the pressure from the Lord, to which we had only to respond. And because it is not really our movement but the movement of the Lord who unites his people, it will continue to move. There will be times when the ecumenical movement will be obviously successful and there will be times when it will seem to stagnate. There will be times when it will be popular and there will be times when only the truly convinced will continue to fight for it.

William Temple once said: 'Even if our cause was suffering defeat on every side, we should still serve it because that is God's call to us, and we should still know that through our loyal service he was accomplishing his purpose even though we could not see the evidence of this.'[11] In that sense we may confidently say about the ecumenical movement: 'But still it moves.'

NOTES

1. The expression used in the early Christian *Epistle to Diognetus* to describe the role of the Christians.

2. *Kirchliche Dogmatik* IV, 3, pp. 37–9.

3. After her abdication Queen Wilhelmina expressed the desire that she should no longer be called Queen, but Princess.

4. October 28th 1958.

5. Letter to the Central Committee in 1950.

6. In *The Student World*, Third quarter, 1936.

7. In *Theology Today*, April 1962, and in Dutch as a separate brochure.

8. In *The Ecumenical Advance. A history of the Ecumenical Movement 1948–1968*, page 400.

9. *The Ecumenical Revolution*, pp. 396–7.

10. Expressions which George Bernard Shaw used in a quite different connection in one of his plays.

11. In his sermon at the World Conference on Faith and Order, Edinburgh, 1937.

Index